Alexander Campbell Fraser

The Works of George Berkeley, D.D.

Alexander Campbell Fraser

The Works of George Berkeley, D.D.

ISBN/EAN: 9783741166396

Manufactured in Europe, USA, Canada, Australia, Japa

Cover: Foto ©Andreas Hilbeck / pixelio.de

Manufactured and distributed by brebook publishing software (www.brebook.com)

Alexander Campbell Fraser

The Works of George Berkeley, D.D.

THE WORKS

OF

GEORGE BERKELEY, D.D.

FORMERLY BISHOP OF CLOYNE.

COLLECTED AND EDITED
WITH PREFACES AND ANNOTATIONS

BY

ALEXANDER CAMPBELL FRASER, M.A.

PROFESSOR OF LOGIC AND METAPHYSICS IN THE
UNIVERSITY OF EDINBURGH.

IN THREE VOLUMES.

Vol. I.

Oxford
AT THE CLARENDON PRESS
M DCCC LXXI

PREFACE.

IT has often been remarked as singular that English literature should possess no complete edition of the works of Bishop Berkeley, and that no tolerable account of the life of one of the greatest philosophers of this nation should have been given to the world.

A few years since I was honoured by a request to undertake the present edition for the Clarendon Press. I have devoted to it some long summer vacations of the Scotch Universities. However imperfectly successful in the result, the work has been the occasion of pleasant hours to one whose own love for philosophy was first engaged by Berkeley in the morning of life, and who regards his writings as among the best in English literature, for a refined education of the heart and the intellect.

Berkeley has suffered more than perhaps any other great modern philosopher from misunderstanding. He lived through the most prosaic and least metaphysical age since the revival of letters: he was himself the greatest metaphysician in his own age. When reflection returned to the springs of thought and feeling, his philosophical language had in some measure lost the meaning which he intended, and no adequate attempt has since been made to recover his point of view, or to recognise the intellectual influence which, partly originating in him, has since been silently modifying all the deeper thought of the time in physics and in metaphysical philosophy. Is an unknowing and unknown something, called Matter, or is Intelligence the supreme reality; and are men the transient results of material organization, or are they immortal beings? This is Berkeley's implied question. His answer to it, although, in his own works, it has not been thought out by him into its primary principles, or sufficiently guarded in some parts, nevertheless marks the beginning of the second great period in modern thought, that in which we are living. The answer was virtually reversed in Hume, whose exclusive phenomenalism, reproduced in the Positivism of the nineteenth century, led to the Scotch conservative psychology, and to the great German speculation which Kant inaugurated.

It is as a spiritual philosopher, having warm and true sympathy in all human life, that Bishop Berkeley must be looked at, and not at all as a professional ecclesiastic. His writings and his life centre in speculative philosophy. But they radiate from it in various practical and fruitful directions; for his inclination was to what is concrete, at first in a more polemical, but afterwards in a meditative spirit. In their form, his works are numerous and occasional, not individually bulky or systematic.

Four editions of Berkeley's Collected Works have been already published. The first appeared in Dublin, in two quarto volumes, in 1784, more than thirty years after his death. The next was published in London, in three volumes, in 1820. A cheap edition, in one volume, followed in 1837. The last edition was a London one, in two volumes, in 1843. All of them omit important works which should have found a place, and the same works are omitted in all, as if by common consent. No attempt is made in any of them, except to a small extent in the last, to collate and revise the text, which is founded sometimes on one edition, and sometimes on another. The works are not arranged on any principle —chronological or philosophical.

In the preparation of the present edition I have had the following objects chiefly in view:—

(1) To revise the text of the works formerly published, and to present them in a satisfactory arrangement.

(2) To help the reader to reach Berkeley's own point of view in each work, by means of bibliographical and analytical prefaces, and occasional annotations or brief dissertations, in which the author might be compared with himself, and studied in his relations to the circumstances in which he wrote.

(3) To collect and publish any hitherto unpublished writings of Berkeley which might illustrate his opinions or character.

(4) To offer a comprehensive conception of his implied philosophy as a whole.

It was not easy to apply any satisfactory principle for the arrangement of the Works. On the whole it seemed well to divide them into three groups:—the Pure Philosophical; the Applied Philosophical; and the Miscellaneous, some even of the last containing a pretty distinct metaphysical ingredient.

I. THE PURE PHILOSOPHICAL WORKS.

Four small treatises present Berkeley's exposition of the Metaphysical Philosophy of his youth:—

1. *The Essay towards a New Theory of Vision* (1709).
2. *The Treatise concerning the Principles of Human Knowledge* (1710).

PREFACE.

3. *The Three Dialogues* (1713).
4. *The Theory of Vision, or Visual Language, vindicated and explained* (1733).

These form the first volume in the present edition. They contain his *reductio ad absurdum* of Abstract Matter, and his reasoned exposition of the merely phenomenal nature of the real material world, in opposition to scepticism, and especially to the materialistic denial that Active Intelligence is of the essence of things. The dependent, *sui generis*, existence of space and the sensible world, in which we nevertheless become aware of what is external to our own subjective personality, is with Berkeley a datum of intuitive experience; the independent or absolute existence of Matter is, on the contrary, an unintelligible hypothesis. He was the first in modern times to attack the root of what has been called Cosmothetic Idealism, and to lay the foundation, however indistinctly, of a reasoned Natural Realism—by discarding representative images in sense, and accepting instead what he believed to be the facts of consciousness. He maintains, accordingly, the certainty of sense perception, in opposition to ancient and modern sceptics, who dispute the possibility of any ascertainable agreement between our perceptions and reality; and, however defectively, in opposition also to a merely subjective Idealism, like Fichte's, which refers the orderly succession of sensible changes to the laws of the individual mind in which they are perceived.

The last of the four treatises in the first volume is a defence not only of the New Theory of Vision, but also, in a reserved way, of the Philosophy involved in that Theory, which was unfolded twenty years earlier in the *Principles* and *Dialogues*. It has hitherto been unaccountably omitted in all the collected editions.

II. THE APPLIED PHILOSOPHICAL WORKS.

In two other and larger works, Berkeley's Philosophy, in a popular form in the one, modified and carried forward in the other, is applied in the former to the defence of Christian Faith, and in the latter to recommend a supposed Medical Panacea for the relief of human suffering. They are:—

1. *Alciphron, or the Minute Philosopher* (1732).
2. *Siris: a Chain of Philosophical Reflections and Inquiries, &c.* (1744).

These two works form the second volume in this edition. The metaphysical importance of *Siris* has not been enough recognised. It is probably the profoundest English philosophical book of last century, and besides it gives Berkeley's philosophy in its latest form. In its mystical aphorisms about Life, one can, I think, trace germs of principles which supplement and correct extreme statements to which he was impelled in his youth by his enthusiasm against metaphysical abstractions. The speculative thought of Berkeley is only partially conceived by those who neglect the latter part of *Siris*.

III. THE MISCELLANEOUS WORKS.

All the other hitherto published works of Berkeley are for the most part short occasional tracts which seem best arranged when put nearly in chronological order. The third volume consists of these, under the vague designation of *Miscellaneous Works*, subdivided, however, as they are written in Latin or in English. The three Latin tracts—

1. *Arithmetica* (1707),
2. *Miscellanea Mathematica* (1707),
3. *De Motu* (1721),

are placed first. The *De Motu*, which relates to the

metaphysics of natural philosophy, might almost have been put in the first or in the second group, teaching as it does that all motion must be referred to intelligent activity as its cause, and that the space in which it occurs is relative to sense, and would pass away along with sensible things. But the language, and the way in which the subject is treated, seem to justify the place assigned to it.

The English Miscellaneous Works follow in the same volume, nearly chronologically:—

1. *Passive Obedience* (1712).
2. *Essays contributed to the Guardian* (1713). These Essays have hitherto been omitted in all the collected editions.
3. *Essay towards preventing the Ruin of Great Britain* (1720).
4. *A Proposal for the Better Supplying Churches in our Foreign Plantations, and for Converting the Savage Americans to Christianity, by a College* (1725).
5. *Verses on the Prospect of Planting Arts and Learning in America.* [*Date doubtful.*]
6. *A Sermon preached before the incorporated Society for the Propagation of the Gospel in Foreign Parts* (1732).
7. *The Analyst: or a Discourse addressed to an Infidel Mathematician* (1734).
8. *A Defence of Free-thinking in Mathematics: with an Appendix concerning Mr. Walton's Vindication of Sir Isaac Newton's Principle of Fluxions* (1735).
9. *Reasons for not replying to Mr. Walton's Full Answer* (1735).
10. *The Querist*—originally published in Three Parts, in 1735-36-37.

11. *A Discourse addressed to Magistrates and Men in Authority* (1736).
12. *A Letter to the Roman Catholics of the Diocese of Cloyne* (1745).
13. *A Word to the Wise* (1749).
14. *Maxims concerning Patriotism* (1750).
15. *Four Letters concerning Tar-water* (1744—47). One of these, addressed to Dr. Hales, was omitted in former collected editions.
16. *Farther Thoughts on Tar-water* (1752).

The English Miscellaneous Works, as appears from their titles, are chiefly on Moral, Social, and Economical questions; three are connected with Berkeley's American enterprise; three belong to the celebrated controversy with the mathematicians, and involve an important application of his metaphysical philosophy; others relate to tar-water, but only in its medical applications. All of them except the *Passive Obedience*, the *Essays in the Guardian*, the *Analyst* and relative tracts, and the *Letters concerning Tar-water*, were collected by Berkeley himself, and published in his *Miscellany*, a few months before his death.

The works thus arranged in the three volumes comprehend the writings of Berkeley which were published when he was alive. One other work, *The Memoirs of Signor Gaudentio di Lucca*, has occasionally been assigned to him, but, I think, on insufficient grounds, as I have elsewhere explained.

In an Appendix to the first volume, I have printed, with the various erasures and other changes, Berkeley's rough draft of the Introduction to the *Principles of Human Knowledge*, which is possessed in autograph by the Library of Trinity College, Dublin. The same Appendix also contains some other matter which illustrates the contents of the volume—especially the analogy of Collier's conception of the material world and Berkeley's.

The Appendix to the second volume describes the third edition of *Alciphron*, which I had not seen when that work was passing through the press.

Soon after the third volume was printed I was fortunate enough to find the Three Parts of the original edition of the *Querist*—sought for in vain by former editors of that remarkable tract. The large amount of additional matter contained in that edition is now given in an Appendix to the third volume. It may gratify those for whom the *Querist*, with its subtle yet practical social reforms, may have more interest than anything else that Berkeley has written.

A fourth, or supplementary volume, is biographical. As the reader chooses, it may be regarded as consisting either of *Prolegomena* or of *Addenda* to the other three. For a writer so full of warm human feeling as Berkeley, the best preliminary (or supplementary) dissertation to his Works, might, it seemed, be found in an account of his life, and of his philosophy regarded as the comprehensive unity which interprets his life. The events of the life have, however, been left in an obscurity which probably any effort that might now be made could only imperfectly remove. A Life of Berkeley, on any extended scale, was not part of the original plan of this edition. What has been in the end attempted has grown out of a gradual accumulation of materials, which continued research might perhaps increase, but which, even as they are, it seemed desirable to preserve.

The last chapter in the Life gives some critical account

of the implied Philosophy as a whole. It is necessary to unfold what is latent, as Berkeley presupposes important principles which he does not articulately express. His philosophical method, moreover, is throughout a peculiar sort of appeal, through reflection, to an assumed intuition of the constant omnipresence or omnipotence of Mind in the universe—an intuition apt to be dormant in the individual, so that his appeal sometimes has the appearance of reasoning in a circle. This chapter, under another arrangement, might have formed an Introduction to the Works.

More than a third of the Biographical Volume consists of writings of Berkeley hitherto unpublished, supplied by the valuable collection of Papers which Archdeacon Rose kindly placed at my disposal. This volume seems to be the proper place for writings which reflect so much light on Berkeley's character, and the growth of his opinions. That so much of his previously unpublished writing should be given to the world nearly a hundred and twenty years after his death is a remarkable circumstance, which gives an interest to this edition of his Works that no preceding one could possess.

The preface to the Biographical Volume gives a more particular account of its contents.

Much is still wanting to realize my own conception of what an edition of the Works of Bishop Berkeley ought to be. The prefaces and annotations have been written from time to time, as opportunity offered, and those in the first volume have been in print for two or three years. The annotations are in all cases by the Editor, except where they are expressly assigned to the 'AUTHOR.' Some of my comments in the earlier parts of the work are perhaps somewhat differently conceived and expressed in the supplementary volume; but perhaps there is no harm in the appearance, in a work done at intervals, of those modifications of thought and language which result from prolonged solitary reflection applied to a great thinker. It is unnecessary to add that the notes and discussions might have been indefinitely extended, and the work expanded far beyond the proposed size, if one had digressed into the many subjects of tempting intellectual interest associated especially with the philosophical writings. As it is, the edition is enlarged beyond the intention, although the references are confined chiefly to the latter part of the seventeenth century and to the eighteenth.

I am not without hope that this reappearance of Berkeley in the modern philosophical world, in these latter years of the nineteenth century, under the auspices of the great University with which death has associated him, may be the occasion of a candid consideration of this good philosopher's explanation of the meaning of human existence, and of a fresh impulse to philosophy, in Europe and America.

There are signs which encourage this hope, in a retrospect of the history of recent opinion and metaphysical literature in England.

The return to the deeper questions in metaphysics, inaugurated by Coleridge and Hamilton more than forty years since, in conjunction with the increased inclination in the interval to discuss first principles in theology, and in the physical sciences, including physiology, is more favourable to the entertainment of the thoughts which occupied so much of Berkeley's life, and perhaps to harmony between science and faith, than the state of things in almost any former period of the history of this country.

There are, besides, definite signs of an inclination to

reconsider Berkeley in particular, and to draw from him what may be available for amending our conception of the nature of the existence we are participating in among the phenomena of sense; or at least for assisting us before we finish our course to inquire what this sense-conscious life through which we are now passing really means. The ingenious and acute metaphysical works of the late Professor Ferrier may be referred to as an example, although they unfold a system which differs in some important respects from that of Berkeley, being constructed from the ontological, and not, like his, from the psychological point of view. With more form of demonstration, Ferrier leaves in the background the sense-symbolism, and intuition of efficient causality, which are essential to the externality and dualism of Berkeley —who, by the way, might as well be called a Sensationalist, or a Phenomenalist, or a Presentationist, as an Idealist, as far as his own use of the word *idea* goes. The strikingly candid speculations of the late Professor Grote of Cambridge, which contain some of the most interesting English contributions to the higher philosophy of this generation, have also a tendency to Berkeley's point of view. Dean Mansel's learned and closely reasoned works in philosophy, besides reviving metaphysical discussion in England, have occasionally approached the speculation of Berkeley, bringing valuable critical light. The assiduous zeal and subtlety of Mr. Collyns Simon, his book *On the Nature and Elements of the Material World*, and his various essays since have drawn attention to the subject, not only in these islands but also in Germany. Some chapters in Mr. J. S. Mill's *Examination of Sir W. Hamilton's Philosophy*, and passages in his other writings, show how much in the new conception of the sensible world is appreciated by a fair and able thinker of phenomenalist tendencies. Dr. J. H. Stirling, by directing reflection to fresh aspects of questions which Berkeley raised by implication, has prepared some for looking at the perennial philosophical problem with a fresh eye. Nor must Berkeley's own University be forgotten, where philosophy is now cultivated by men who are not unworthy of its fame, and who, either as expositors or as adverse critics, have not forgotten its greatest name in metaphysics.

I am inclined to believe that the present state of German speculation is not unfavourable to a more ample and appreciative consideration of Berkeley than he has hitherto received in the occasional allusions made by the philosophers and historians of philosophy of the chief speculative nation of Europe. Since the first volume of this edition was printed, an annotated translation into German of Berkeley's *Principles of Human Knowledge* has been supplied by Dr. Friedrich Ueberweg, the learned historian of philosophy, and Kant's successor in the Chair at Königsberg. This translation has, I understand, circulated widely in that country. It has been partly the occasion of recent discussions on Berkeley's Philosophy in some of the German periodicals.

Berkeley's remarkable relations to America, and the adoption of distinctive parts of his philosophy by two of his eminent American contemporaries, Samuel Johnson and Jonathan Edwards, should secure for him a hearing in that great country, whose advancement since he lived in it has almost realized the dream even of his benevolent imagination.

A. C. FRASER.

COLLEGE OF EDINBURGH,
February, 1871.

CONTENTS.

	PAGE
Editor's Preface to the Essay towards a New Theory of Vision	1
AN ESSAY TOWARDS A NEW THEORY OF VISION. First printed in 1709	25
Editor's Preface to the Treatise concerning the Principles of Human Knowledge	113
A TREATISE CONCERNING THE PRINCIPLES OF HUMAN KNOWLEDGE. [Part I.] Wherein the chief causes of Error and Difficulty in the Sciences, with the grounds of Scepticism, Atheism, and Irreligion, are inquired into. First printed in the year 1710	131
Editor's Preface to the Three Dialogues between Hylas and Philonous	239
THREE DIALOGUES BETWEEN HYLAS AND PHILONOUS. The design of which is plainly to demonstrate the reality and perfection of Human Knowledge, the Incorporeal nature of the Soul, and the Immediate Providence of a Deity, in opposition to Sceptics and Atheists. Also to open a method for rendering the Sciences more easy, useful, and compendious. First printed in the year 1713	255
Editor's Preface to The Theory of Vision, or Visual Language, vindicated and explained	361

CONTENTS.

THE THEORY OF VISION, OR VISUAL LANGUAGE, SHEWING THE IMMEDIATE PRESENCE AND PROVIDENCE OF A DEITY, VINDICATED AND EXPLAINED 369

A Letter from an Anonymous Writer to the Author of The Minute Philosopher 401

APPENDIX.

A. Berkeley's Rough Draft of the Introduction to the Principles of Human Knowledge 407

B. Arthur Collier 418

C. New Theory of Vision.—Experience of persons born blind . 444

EDITOR'S PREFACE

ERRATA.

Page 17, ll. 17, 18, *delete* 'who was tutor in Trinity College, Dublin, when Berkeley entered the University.'
Page 35, omitted on fly-leaf—'FIRST PRINTED IN 1709.'
Page 357, note 1, l. 15, *for* 'natural son' *read* 'grandson.'
Page 371, note 1, l. 1, *for* 'Dublin' *read* 'London.'
Page 446, l. 38, *for* 'Nunnely' *read* 'Nunneley.'

EDITOR'S PREFACE

TO THE

ESSAY TOWARDS A NEW THEORY OF VISION.

PREFACE.

BY THE EDITOR.

BERKELEY'S *Essay towards a New Theory of Vision* is the chronological and also a logical introduction to his metaphysical philosophy. It is virtually an inquiry into the nature and origin of our conception of Extension in Space, that distinctive characteristic of the material world. The *Essay* was the first fruits of Berkeley's philosophical studies at Dublin. It was also the first elaborate attempt to demonstrate that our apparently immediate visual perceptions of space, and of bodies existing in it apart from our organism, are actually suggestions induced by the constant association of visible ideas, and of certain organic sensations which accompany vision, with objects presented in our tactual experience.

The first edition of the *Essay* appeared early in 1709, when Berkeley was about twenty-five years of age. The second, with a few alterations, and an Appendix (not since reprinted), followed before the end of that year. Both were issued in Dublin, 'printed by Aaron Rhames, for Jeremy Pepyat, bookseller in Skinner Row.'

An edition was afterwards annexed to *Alciphron*, on its first appearance at Dublin and London, in March 1732. It was partly the criticism to which the theological application of the New Theory in the Fourth Dialogue of *Alciphron* gave rise that drew from Berkeley, early in the following year, his *Theory of Vision or Visual Language, shewing the immediate Presence and Providence of a Deity, vindicated and explained*. Both works reflect much light upon the *Essay*.

The edition of the *Essay* published in 1732 was the last in Berkeley's lifetime.

In the present edition the text has been corrected according to that of

1732, collated with the two preceding and with the posthumous ones. The Appendix is reprinted from the second edition.

The ascertainment by reflection of the contents and relations of purely visual consciousness is one of three problems professedly solved in Berkeley's metaphysical account of the material world. That visible objects are a system of arbitrary signs of tangible matter, is the conclusion of this *Essay*; that objects visible and tangible are a system of sensible signs of absent objects of sense, is the conclusion of the *Principles of Human Knowledge*, and especially of the *Dialogues of Hylas and Philonous*; and that this arbitrary system of signs, which cannot exist without a percipient, is a sensible expression of the Divine ideas, presence, and providence, is the conclusion common to all the three treatises. This last comprehensive conclusion is illustrated and applied in the *New Theory of Vision Vindicated*, and in Berkeley's other philosophical and theological works. We trace it in his old age throughout the contemplative and mystical philosophy of *Siris*.

A due appreciation of Berkeley's *New Theory of Vision*, and of its relative place in his metaphysics, thus requires a study not merely of this tentative and juvenile *Essay*, but also of its development and applications in his more matured works. This has been commonly forgotten, alike by the hostile critics and by the professed disciples of the Theory.

Various circumstances contribute to make this *Essay* more perplexing to the reader than perhaps any of Berkeley's other works.

Its occasion and design, and its relation to his conception of matter, are to some extent explained in the 43rd and 44th sections of the *Principles of Human Knowledge*. These sections are so far a key to the *Essay*. They inform us that in this earlier work Berkeley intentionally used language which seems to imply the absolute or independent existence of *tangible* objects,—it being 'beside his purpose' to 'examine and refute' that 'vulgar error' in 'a work on vision.' This reticence of his metaphysical conception of matter, in reasonings on vision which are fully explained only under that conception, is a chief occasion of the comparative obscurity of the *Essay*.

Another circumstance adds to our embarrassment. The earlier English writers in metaphysics were often careless in the employment of equivocal words. Even Berkeley was no exception. We are now accustomed to greater precision in the use of metaphysical language, and that language has itself undergone many changes. Some of the principal terms in the *Essay* are equivocal. It is enough to refer to the words *perception*, *sensation*, *sight*, *external*, and *distance*, with their conjugates. Others, for example *idea* and *touch*, have had their meaning modified, and it is difficult for the modern reader habitually to return to that with which they were associated in Berkeley's mind (cf. sect. 120).

The interchange of the terms 'outward,' 'outness,' 'externality,' 'without the mind,' and 'without the eye' is confusing, if we forget that Berkeley in this treatise adopts language which implies that mind is locally and literally diffused over our organism, and coextensive with it, so that being absent or at a distance from the organism is being absent or at a distance from mind. I have tried in the annotations to obviate some of these ambiguities.

The *Essay* abounds in repetition, while its logical structure, its train of thought, and even its leading generalization are not to be apprehended without a careful study and collation of passages. This, with the active exercise of thought, and exact use of words, which the nature of the subject requires, as Berkeley himself repeatedly reminds us, has enveloped the treatise in a cloud of misconceptions, which the author's subsequent *Vindication* has not removed.

I shall endeavour in what follows to present in an orderly way the principal propositions of the *Essay*, and to indicate the nature of the evidence by which they are sustained.

The reader must remember that the *Essay* is a professed appeal to pure consciousness. It is an analysis, immediately of what we are conscious in seeing, and by suggestion of what we are conscious in touch. It takes no observation of mere optical or physiological phenomena (cf. *Theory of Vision Vindicated*, sect. 43), in its exclusive attention to the facts of consciousness which underlie them; and it is only after what we are conscious of in seeing has been ascertained, that the result is incidentally, or now and then by way of verification, applied to solve some celebrated optical or physiological puzzle. The treatise is in short a professed account of the facts, the whole facts, and nothing but the facts of which we are visually conscious, as distinguished from pretended facts and metaphysical abstractions, which confused thought, an irregular exercise of imagination, or an abuse of words had substituted for them. It is a contribution to the psychological analysis of the fact of vision, and not a deduction from merely physical experiments in optics or the physiology of the eye.

The *Essay* contains some preliminary analyses, which gradually conduct to the constructive principle that properly constitutes the *New Theory*.

These preliminary inquiries enforce the *antithesis* of the two worlds of visible objects and tangible objects, as regards—

1. Distance, i. e. externality in space relatively to our organism;
2. Magnitude or size, i. e. occupancy of a larger or smaller quantity of space;
3. Situation, or position relatively to one another in space.

The constructive principle, or *New Theory* proper, is the explanation of the *synthesis* in which, notwithstanding this radical antithesis of their constituents, we are accustomed to blend in imagination what we see and what we touch, as common properties of 'the *same* thing.'*

From the beginning of the second section onwards, the *Essay* may be broadly divided into six Parts, devoted in succession to a proof of the six following theses, regarding the relation of Sight to Extension in its three dimensions :—

I. (Sect. 2–51.) Distance, or the fact of an interval between two points in the line of vision, in other words externality in space, in itself invisible, is, in all cases in which we appear to see it, only suggested to our imagination by certain visible phenomena and visual sensations, which are its arbitrary signs.

II. (Sect. 52–87.) Magnitude, or the external space that objects occupy, is absolutely invisible: all that we can see is merely a greater or less quantity of colour, and our apparently visual perceptions of real magnitude are interpretations of the tactual meaning of colours and other sensations in the visual organ.

III. (Sect. 88–120.) The Situation of objects, or their relation to one another in space, is invisible: all that we can see is variety in the relations of quantities of colour to one another, our supposed pure vision of actual locality being an interpretation of visual signs.

IV. (Sect. 121–146.) There is no sensible object common to sight and touch: space or extension, which has the best claim to this character, and which is nominally the object of both, is specifically as well as numerically different in each,—externality in space, or distance, being absolutely invisible, while size and situation, as visible, have nothing in common with size and situation as tangible.

V. (Sect. 147–148.) The explanation of the unity which we attribute

---

* In his two scientific expositions of his *New Theory of Vision* Berkeley reverses his order of procedure. In this *Essay* he ascends from the preliminary analyses of consciousness, which enforce the antithesis of the visual and tactual, to the summary generalisation or theory of their union; in the *Vindication* he descends synthetically from the *Theory* to those inferences regarding Situation, Magnitude, and Distance, which it involves. (See *Essay*, sect. 1; and cf. *Theory of Vision Vindicated*, &c., sect. 38.)

to sensible things, as complements of visible and tangible qualities of one and the same substance, is contained in the Theory that visible ideas and visual sensations, arbitrary signs in a Divine Language, are significant of distances, and of the real sizes and situations of distant things; while the constant association in nature of the two worlds of vision and touch, has so associated them in our thoughts, that visible and tangible extension are habitually regarded by us as specifically and even numerically one.

VI. (Sect. 149-160.) The proper object of geometry is the kind of Extension given in our tactual experience, and not the kind of Extension given in our visual experience; and neither real solids nor real planes can be seen—real Extension in all its phases being invisible, and colour in its modifications of quantity being the only proper object of sight, while colour, being a pure sensation, cannot exist extra-organically in space.

It is curious that the doctrine of the invisibility of distance is popularly regarded as Berkeley's *New Theory of Vision*. In reality this is the assumption with which the *Essay* sets out (sect. 2). The part of the treatise (sect. 2-51) which especially treats of Distance does not profess to prove its invisibility, but, taking this for granted, to show that near distances as well as the more remote are suggested in seeing by certain arbitrary signs. That the relation between the signs and distances signified is, whether the distance be remote or near, a purely arbitrary relation, discoverable only by experience, is the burden of sect. 2-40. The previously recognised arbitrary signs of 'considerably remote' distances—linear and aerial perspective—are mentioned (sect. 3). But distances less remote were then commonly supposed to be necessarily inferred, by a sort of visual geometry, and not to be merely suggested in imagination by experience. The determination of the true visual signs of *near* distances is the professed discovery of Berkeley regarding distance.

According to the *Essay* there are three sorts of arbitrary signs of near distances—

1. The peculiar organic sensation which accompanies the adjustment of the eye to what is presented to it (sect. 16-20);
2. The degree of confusion in the visible object (sect. 21-26);
3. The organic sensation of straining (sect. 27).

Berkeley endeavours so far to verify this, by applying the second sort of sign to explain an optical phenomenon which Dr. Barrow and others had given up as inexplicable (sect. 29-40).

This generalization of the arbitrary signs of distance, visible and organic, is followed (sect. 43) by a reference to the purely sensational nature of colour—the 'proper and immediate object of sight,' from which it is inferred that visible extension, as a quality of colour, must also be 'in the eye or rather in the mind.' We are thus led on, from the account given of the arbitrary signs of distances, to a proof that visible objects are not external to the animated organism, and that, inasmuch as they are sensations, they cannot exist without a mind. Berkeley's account of the manner in which distances are suggested in seeing, is his introduction to the doctrine that everything properly visible consists of, or is dependent on, the sensation of colour.

It is next argued (sect. 44) that this ideal world of visible objects bears no resemblance even to 'things placed at a distance' from us. Then the tangible nature of all things that are entitled to be called 'real' is enforced (sect. 45). Here, for the first time in the *Essay*, Touch and our tactual experience are mentioned. Tactual and locomotive experience is needed, we are virtually told, to infuse meaning into the term 'distance.' The notion cannot, it is alleged, be derived from seeing any more than from hearing (sect. 46). We can indeed both see and hear what suggests it, in consequence of our previous experience of the connexion of visible or audible signs with the tactual and locomotive meaning which they now signify. What we see is also apter, from its more frequent previous association, to suggest an ambient space, and objects existing at a distance in it, than audible objects are (sect. 47). Notwithstanding, it is as impossible to see and feel the *same* thing as it is to hear and feel the *same* thing. Visible objects and organic sensations—the arbitrary signs of distances, and of things placed at a distance—are, to all intents and purposes, a language; and they are one in which the signs are so blended with their significations that a life devoted to reflective analysis is not able fully to disentangle them (sect. 51).

Sections 43, 44, and 45 are in some respects the most important in the *Essay*. They represent visible extension as based upon sensation—the sensation of colour; they recognise, as real or external, only that extension which is derived from tactual and locomotive experience. If sensations, in their varieties of quality and quantity, are the only objects we see, it follows that the visible world cannot be 'without the mind.' The problem of the *Essay* is, to explain how sensations or ideas of colour, a consciousness of which constitutes vision, can inform us about tangible objects, which they do not in the least resemble, and with which they have no necessary connexion in thought. That certain visible ideas, and certain organic sensations which accompany vision (sect. 3, 16, 21, 27. 56,

&c.) *suggest* to us the real or tangible extensions with which they are arbitrarily connected in the system of nature, is the Berkeleian solution of this problem.

It is at this point, too, that the principal ambiguity of the *Essay* appears. It is argued, that visible objects and their accompanying organic sensations cannot exist 'without the mind,' and that they have no resemblance to what is external: at the same time it seems to be taken for granted by Berkeley that we are percipient of absolute externality in touch. We appear to be told that we cannot see, but that we can and do touch, a distant world that exists independently of our intelligence. The reader is ready to say that we are as much (or as little) conscious of this perception when we see as when we touch. This difficulty is relieved in the *Principles of Human Knowledge*, where the objects of sight and touch are put on the same level, and the possibility of the absolute or purely external existence of either is denied. The term 'external' may still be applied to our tactual and locomotive sensations or ideas, as contrasted with our visual; but that happens, according to Berkeley, not because of the ideal nature of what we see, and the absolute externality of what we touch, but only because our tactual and locomotive sensations are more steady and practically important, while 'externality' is a term appropriate to what is found to have these characteristics. In the developed philosophy of Berkeley, the tangible world itself, as well as its visible signs, consists of objects which cannot be independent of a mind; their *esse* is *percipi*. And, the distinction between organic and extra-organic existence is merged in the more general truth, that the human body and its organs, along with the entire extra-organic world, is itself dependent on mind. The organised body is contained in mind, and not mind in the organised body. Externality, in the deeper meaning of an absolute independence of all mind, is argued to be impossible, because contradictory; while 'externality,' either as significant of what is extra-organic, as contrasted with what is within our vital organism, or of what is tangible, as distinguished from what is visible, is simplified and rationalised. But Berkeley preferred, as he tells us, to insinuate his metaphysical system by degrees, and he has in consequence to some extent exposed his *Essay* to the charge of incoherence.

He seems in some passages (e.g. sect. 41) to take for granted that the visibility of distance in the line of sight would imply externality —i.e. independence of sensation—on the part of the objects we see, as if this independence could be determined at all by what we see or do not see. Even if distance, in the sense of extra-organic externality, could be seen, it would not follow that it was absolutely independent of mind: rather the contrary, on his own principles. That we are not conscious of seeing it only proves that an 'ambient space' is not an immediate object of sight—not that coloured extension, in its other and visible dimensions, is purely ideal*.

The way in which visual phenomena suggest extension in its third dimension, and objects as actually at a distance from the organ of vision, having been thus explained in the first part of the *Essay*, the second and third parts (sect. 52-120) profess to prove the invisibility of real extension in two other relations—magnitude and locality.

The proof consists of a reference to consciousness, for the purpose of purifying the meaning of the term 'real,' as applicable to sizes and situations; and an induction of the actual signs of real magnitude and situation. The only real sizes, shapes, and situations must, it is argued, be tangible ones, dependent on tactual and locomotive experience. The reason given for this is, that they only are steady, uniform, and practically connected with our physical comfort in this life of sense (sect. 55, 59). The signs (which are all arbitrary) of these tangible realities are partly visible, and partly muscular sensations in the organ of sight (sect. 56).

This theory of antithetical phenomena—visual and tactual—connected by arbitrary signs, is, in these two parts of the *Essay*, applied to solve two celebrated difficulties in optics—

1. The fact that the size of the horizontal moon is greater to the eye than that of the moon in its meridian (sect. 67-87). This problem of the visible appearance of the horizontal moon gives rise to some curious incidental discussions—in particular one regarding *minima visibilia*, or units of colour, pluralities of which constitute the various degrees of visible extension (sect. 79, &c.).

2. The physical fact that we see objects erect only on condition of the formation of inverted images of them on the retina (sect. 88-120). The explanation of this is sought for in a thorough-going application of the principle, that what we see and what we touch are extensions numerically different while nominally the same. In this part of the *Essay*

---

* The reasoning against the visibility of distance is not to be confounded with that against the absolute externality or non-ideal character of what we see. The proof of each thesis may be put thus—

1. The visibility of any distance implies the visibility of an interval between two visible points; but we are conscious of seeing only one point in the line of sight: therefore distance in the line of sight is invisible.

2. The absolute externality of what we see implies its independence of sensation; but seeing is simply being conscious of colours, which are sensations; therefore what we see is not independent of sensation—is not 'without the mind' or absolutely external.

the antithesis between the visible and the tangible world—the world of coloured extension and the world of resistant extension—is pushed to the utmost. The 'high and low' of the visible world is not the 'high and low' of the tangible world (sect. 91-106). In no case is there any resemblance between these two extensions; not even when the number of visible objects happens to coincide with the number of tangible objects of which they are signs, e.g. of visible and tangible fingers on the human hand. The mind constitutes its concrete units in an arbitrary way. At first we should not distinguish our feet as two, nor our fingers as five: we should not spontaneously recognise either a foot or a finger as one thing. A man born blind would not, on first seeing, parcel out phenomena as those do who have learned by experience what those phenomena are which may be most conveniently or most scientifically conjoined in thought, and afterwards spoken about as qualities of particular substances (sect. 107-110). On the whole, it is argued, that the famous difficulty about erect vision is one which illegitimately takes for granted a relation between the visible and tangible worlds can be shown, by analysis of our sense-consciousness, not to exist. The visible pictures on the retina no more resemble real things than what we see resembles what we touch. A purification of visual consciousness, by reflecting upon it, is assumed to be all that is required to remove the difficulty, and to unfold the true theory of vision—which however cannot become familiar to us without habitual thoughtfulness, and a precise use of the part of language which refers to seeing (sect. 111-120).

The fourth part of the *Essay* (sect. 121-145) seeks to prove not only the numerical but also the specific or generic difference of the objects of sight and touch. Its thesis is, that sight and touch have no sensible object, nor any abstract notion even, that is common to the two senses. Extension or space has the best claim to these characteristics. If its claim can be disposed of, the *a fortiori* argument may be applied to all other claimants. Now, coloured extension, which alone is visible, bears no resemblance to resistant extension, which alone is tangible.

And, if these concrete or sensible extensions have nothing in common, the dispute, it is maintained, is at an end. The one possible extension is a sensible extension (sect. 123). Extension in the abstract is incomprehensible and absurd, and cannot therefore be an object either of sight or touch, still less the common object of both (sect. 124-126). The only question is, whether the (so-called) extension we see is in any respect similar to the extension we touch. That they are absolutely heterogeneous has been proved, it is alleged, in the preceding parts of the *Essay*.

What remains is to marshal this scattered evidence, and to guard the foregoing conclusions against objections. This is attempted in sections 128-146.

The enunciation of the summary generalization, constructive principle, or *New Theory* proper (sect. 147, 148), forms what may be regarded as the fifth part of the *Essay*.

The last part of the *Essay* (sect. 149-160) relates to some deductions from the Theory which, with one exception, Berkeley declines to pursue. He restricts himself here to an inquiry as to the sort of extension with which geometry has to do—an investigation in harmony with the favourite mathematical studies of his youth. In concluding that tactual or real, and not visible or symbolical, extension is the only object reasoned about in geometry, he imagines the condition of Idomenians or unembodied spirits, endowed with only a visual sense-experience, and endeavours to determine what their conception of solid and plane extension should be (sect. 153, &c.). In arguing that planes of colour are as invisible as solids of colour (sect. 154-158), he opens the way to further refinements in the interpretation of our visual consciousness which have not escaped the attention of recent psychologists.

Whether we can see more than non-resembling, arbitrary signs of the real distances, sizes, shapes, and situations of things, is a question of fact. It may seem accordingly that experiments upon the visual and tactual consciousness of persons who are in circumstances to test the conclusions of the foregoing reflective analysis, is a suitable means for verifying its conclusions. Of this sort is the experience of persons who have been relieved from born blindness; the notion of extension and externality possessed by individuals originally destitute of the visual sense, who have not been so relieved; the experience (if it can be got) of those absolutely void of all tactual and locomotive experience, but endowed with visual; and even the phenomena of sight in infants of the human species, and in the lower animals.

Berkeley apparently made no observations of his own in this field. In various parts of the *Essay* (sect. 41, 42, 79, 92-99, 103, 106, 110, 128, 132-137), he infers, from the contrast of our visual and tactual consciousness, what the first experience of those rescued from born-blindness must be; he speculates about the experience of 'unbodied spirits,' able to see, but originally destitute of the sense of touch (sect. 153-159); and in the Appendix he refers, in corroboration of his theory, to a newly reported case of one born blind who had obtained sight. But he everywhere treats his Theory independently of these extremely delicate and difficult investigations. His testing facts were sought elsewhere. Nor is it difficult to understand his comparative indifference to empirical experiments. An appeal to consciousness on behalf of the principle, that we cannot see tangible objects, nor touch visible ones—with inductive evidence that our tendency to unite certain tangible and visible *qualities* in the same *substance* is a result of the constant association of the latter with the former—appeared to him to fulfil all the conditions of proof. Any apparently original fusion of tactual with visual experience was then dismissed as illusory. And indeed those physiologists and mental philosophers who have since tried to determine what vision in its purity is, by observation and experiment, in cases either of communicated sight, or of continued born-blindness, have illustrated the truth of Diderot's remark—"préparer et interroger un aveugle-né n'eût point été une occupation indigne des talens réunis de Newton, Des Cartes, Locke, et Leibnitz*."

Berkeley's *New Theory* has been quoted as an almost solitary example of a discovery in metaphysics. It has, on the whole, kept its ground, as the acknowledged modern theory of vision, amid the proverbial fluctuations of thought on such subjects. I venture to append to the preceding analysis of the *Essay* a few notices of the state in which it found philosophical opinion on the questions to which it relates, and of the change which it has inaugurated.

The subtle analysis which distinguishes *seeing* strictly so called from judgments about extended things, which are only suggested, after a sufficient tactual and locomotive experience, by what we see, appears to have been unknown to the ancient philosophers, who, it may be added, were ignorant of much now known with regard to the organic conditions of this sense. Aristotle, indeed, speaks of colour as the proper object of sight; but, in the passages of the *De Anima*† where he names properties peculiar to particular senses, he enumerates others, such as motion, rest, number, figure, and magnitude, which belong to all the senses in common. This

---

* In Diderot's *Lettre sur les aveugles, à l'usage de ceux qui voient*, where Berkeley, Molyneux, Condillac, and others are referred to. Cf. also Appendix, pp. 111, 112; and *Theory of Vision Vindicated*, sect. 71, with the note, in which some recorded experiments are alluded to.

† *De Anima*, II. 6, III. 1, &c. Aristotle assigns a pre-eminent intellectual value to the sense of sight. See, for instance, his *Metaphysics*, I. 1.

distinction of Proper and Common Sensibles appears at first to contradict Berkeley's doctrine of the absolute heterogeneity of the visible and the tangible. Aristotle, however, seems to question the perceptibility in mere sense of the Common Sensibles, and to regard them rather as produced by the activity of intelligence, in conjunction with sense.*

Some writers in Optics, in medieval times, and in the early period of modern philosophy, advanced beyond Aristotle, in explaining the relation of our matured notion of distance to what we are originally conscious of seeing, and in the fifteenth century it was discovered by Maurolyco that the rays of light from the object converge to a focus in the eye; but I have not been able to trace even the germ of the distinctive principles of the *New Theory* in any of these speculations.

Excepting some hints by Des Cartes, Malebranche was among the first dimly to anticipate Berkeley, in resolving our supposed power of seeing distances into an interpretation of arbitrary signs which we learn by experience gradually to understand; and also in founding his explanation upon consciousness. The most important part of Malebranche's account of vision is contained in his *Recherche de la Verité* (Liv. I. ch. 9), in one of those chapters in which he discusses the general fallaciousness of the senses, and in particular of sight, in its judgments about extension. He accounts for the inevitable uncertainty of what we take to be immediate visual perceptions of the distances of things, by an analysis of the manner in which these supposed perceptions are formed—in short, by assigning them not to sense proper but to the misinterpretation of our sense-experience in thought. He enumerates as signs of distance:— (1) The angle made by the rays of our eyes, and the change in the position of our eyes corresponding to the changes of this angle —which he illustrates, like Descartes and others, by the blind man and cross sticks; (2) the figure of the organ of vision, dependent on the tension of its muscles; (3) the size of the images painted at the bottom of the eye; (4) the power of the object upon the eye;

---

* Sir A. Grant (*Ethics of Aristotle*, vol. II. p. 172), remarks as to the doctrine that the Common Sensibles are apprehended concomitantly by the senses —' This is surely the true view; we see in the apprehension of number, figure, and the like, not an operation of sense, but the mind putting its own forms and categories, i. e. itself, on the external object. It would follow then that the senses cannot really be separated from the mind; the senses and the mind each contribute an element to every knowledge. Aristotle's doctrine of *αἴσθησις* also would go far, if carried out, to modify his doctrine of the simple and innate character of the senses, e. g. sight, &f. *Eth.* II. 1. 4), and would prevent its absolute collision with Berkeley's *Theory of Vision*.' —See Sir W. Hamilton, *Reid's Works*, pp. 828-830.

Mr. Stewart (*Collected Works*, vol. I. p. 341, note) quotes Aristotle's *Ethics* II. 1 as evidence that Berkeley's doctrine, 'with respect to the acquired perceptions of sight, was quite unknown to the best metaphysicians of antiquity.'

(5) the clearness and distinctness of the image formed in the eye; (6) the relation of the object to which the visual judgment refers to other intervening objects.

That the *Recherche* of Malebranche, published more than thirty years before the *Essay*, was familiar to Berkeley, and that this with other chapters was much under his eye, before the publication of his *New Theory*, is proved by internal evidence, and by his commonplace book. I am not able to discover signs of a similar connection between Berkeley and the chapter on the mystery of sensation, in Glanvill's *Scepsis Scientifica* (ch. 5), published some years before the *Recherche* of Malebranche, where Glanvill refers to 'a secret deduction,' through which—from motions, &c., of which we are immediately percipient—we 'spell out' figures, distances, magnitudes, and colours, which have no resemblance to them.

The nearest approach to the *New Theory* is to be found in a passage which first appeared in the fourth edition of Locke's *Essay*, published in 1694, to which Berkeley refers in his own *Essay* (sect. 132-35), and which, on account of its importance in the history of the Theory of Vision, and of our notion of Extension, I shall here transcribe at length:—

'We are further to consider concerning Perception that the ideas we receive by sensation are often, in grown people, altered by the judgment, without our taking notice of it. When we set before our eyes a round globe of any uniform colour, e. g. gold, alabaster, or jet, it is certain that the idea thereby imprinted in our mind is of a flat circle, variously shadowed, with several degrees of light and brightness coming to our eyes. But, we having by use been accustomed to perceive what kind of appearance convex bodies are wont to make in us, what alterations are made in the reflection of light by the difference in the sensible figures of bodies—the judgment presently, by an habitual custom, alters the appearances into their causes; so that, from that which is truly variety of shadow or colour, collecting the figure, it makes it pass for a mark of figure, and frames to itself the perception of a convex figure and an uniform colour, when the idea we receive from them is only a plane variously coloured, as is evident in painting.

'To which purpose I shall here insert a problem of that very ingenious and studious promoter of real knowledge, the learned and worthy Mr. Molyneux, which he was pleased to send me in a letter some months since, and it is this:—Suppose a man born blind, and now adult, and taught by his touch to distinguish between a cube and a sphere of the same metal, and nighly of the same bigness, so as to tell, when he felt the one and the other, which is the cube and which the sphere.

Suppose then the cube and the sphere placed on a table, and the blind man be made to see: quere, whether, by his sight, before he touched them, he could not distinguish and tell, which is the globe and which the cube? To which the acute and judicious proposer answers: 'Not.' For, though he has obtained the experience of how a globe, how a cube affects his touch; yet he has not obtained the experience that what affects his touch so and so, must affect his sight so and so; so that a protuberant angle in the cube, that pressed his hand unequally, shall appear to his eye as it does in the cube.—I agree with this thinking gentleman, whom I am proud to call my friend, in his answer to this his problem, and am of opinion that the blind man, at first sight, would not be able to say with certainty which was the globe and which the cube, whilst he only saw them; though he would unerringly name them by his touch, and certainly distinguish them by the difference in their figures felt.

'This I have set down, and leave with my reader, as an occasion for him to consider how much he may be beholden to experience, improvement, and acquired notions, where he thinks he had not the least use of, or help from them: and the rather because this observing gentleman further adds that, having, upon the occasion of my book, proposed this problem to divers very ingenious men, he hardly ever met with one that at first gave the answer to it which he thinks true, till by hearing his reasons they were convinced.

'But this is not I think usual in any of our ideas but those received by sight: because sight, the most comprehensive of the senses, conveying to our minds the ideas of light and colours, which are peculiar only to that sense; and also the far different ideas of space, figure, and motion, the several varieties of which change the appearance of its proper object, i. e. light and colours; we bring ourselves by use to judge of the one by the other. This, in many cases, by a settled habit, in things whereof we have frequent experience, is performed so constantly and so quick, that we take that for the perception of our sensation, which is an idea formed by our judgment; so that one, i. e. that of sensation, serves only to excite the other, and is scarce taken notice of itself; as a man who reads or hears with attention and understanding takes little notice of the characters or sounds, but of the ideas that are excited in him by them.

'Nor need we wonder that this is done with so little notice, if we consider how very quick the actions of the mind are performed; for, as itself is thought to take up no space, to have no extension, so its actions seem to require no time, but many of them seem to be crowded into an instant. I speak this in comparison of the actions of the body.... Secondly, we shall not be much surprised that this is done with us in so little notice, if we consider how the facility we get of doing things, by a custom of doing, makes them often pass in us without notice. Habits, especially such as are begun very early, come at last to produce actions in us which often escape our observation.... And therefore it is not so strange that our mind should often change the idea of its sensation into that of its judgment, and make the one serve only to excite the other, without our taking notice of it.' (*Essay concerning Human Understanding*, Book II. ch. 9, § 8.)

This remarkable passage anticipates by implication the conception of the synthetic operation of imagination and habit, upon the materials originally given in sense, which, under the name of 'suggestion,' is the constructive principle of the *New Theory*.

The following sentences, relative to the invisibility of distances, contained in the *Treatise of Dioptrics* (published in 1690) of Locke's friend and correspondent William Molyneux—who was tutor in Trinity College, Dublin, when Berkeley entered the University, and whose son was Berkeley's pupil—illustrate Locke's statements, while they may be compared with the opening sections of the following *Essay*:—

'In plain vision the estimate we make of the distance of objects (especially when so far removed that the interval between our two eyes bears no sensible proportion thereto, or when looked upon with one eye only) is rather the act of our judgment than of sense; and acquired by exercise, and a faculty of comparing, rather than natural. For, distance of itself is not to be perceived; for, 'tis a line (or a length) presented to our eye with its end toward us, which must therefore be only a point, and that is invisible. Wherefore distance is chiefly perceived by means of interjacent bodies, as by the earth, mountains, hills, fields, trees, houses, &c. Or by the estimate we make of the comparative magnitude of bodies, or of their faint colours, &c. These I say are the chief means of apprehending the distance of objects that are considerably remote. But as to nigh objects—to whose distance the interval of the eyes bears a sensible proportion—their distance is perceived by the turn of the eyes, or by the angle of the optic axes (*Gregorii Opt. Promot.* prop. 28). This was the opinion of the ancients, Alhazen, Vitellio, &c. And though the ingenious Jesuit Tacquet (*Opt. Lib. I.* prop. 2) disapprove thereof, and objects against it a new notion of Gassendus (of a man's seeing only with one eye at a time one and the same object), yet this notion of Gassendus being absolutely false (as I could demonstrate were it not beside my present purpose), it makes nothing against this opinion.

'Wherefore, distance being only a line and not of itself perceivable, if an object were conveyed to the eye by one single ray only, there were no other means of judging of its distance but by some of those hinted before. Therefore when we estimate the distance of nigh objects, either we take the help of both eyes, or else we consider the pupil of one eye as having breadth, and receiving a parcel of rays from each radiating point. And, according to the various inclinations of the rays from one point on the various parts of the pupil, we make our estimate of the distance of the object. And therefore (as is said before), by one single eye we can only judge of the distance of such objects to whose distance the breadth of the pupil has a sensible proportion. . . . For, it is observed before (prop. 29, sec. 2, see also *Gregorii Opt. Promot.* prop. 29) that for viewing objects remote and nigh, there are requisite various conformations of the eye—the rays from nigh objects that fall on the eye diverging more than those from more remote objects.' (*Treatise of Dioptrics*, Part I. prop. 31.)

The preceding passages indicate the state of opinion regarding the mental fact of vision about the time Berkeley's *Essay* appeared, especially among those with whose works he was familiar. I shall now refer to one or two illustrations of the change in scientific belief which his treatise produced.*

The *New Theory* has occasioned much interesting criticism since 1709. At first indeed it drew little attention. For twenty years after its publication the allusions to it were few. The account of Cheselden's famous experiment, published in 1728, in the *Philosophical Transactions*, which seemed to bring the Theory to the test of a palpable physical experiment, drew some scientific interest to Berkeley's reasonings. The state of theological controversy about the same time confirmed the tendency to discuss a doctrine which represented ordinary vision as the interpretation of divinely constituted signs.

Occasional discussions of some of the principles involved in the *New Theory* may be found in the *Gentleman's Magazine*, from 1732 till Berkeley's death in 1753. Some adverse criticism is also contained in Dr. Smith's *Optics*, published in 1738.

The essential parts of Berkeley's analysis are very well explained by Voltaire, in his *Elemens de la Philosophie de Newton*. The following passage from that work is here given on its own account, and also

---

* A work resembling Berkeley's in its title, but in little else, appeared more than twenty years before the *Essay*—the *Nova Visionis Theoria* of Dr. Briggs, published in 1685.

as a prominent recognition of the new doctrine in France, within thirty years from its first promulgation:—

'Il faut absolument conclure de tout ceci, que les distances, les grandeurs, les situations ne sont pas, à proprement parler, des choses visibles, c'est à dire, ne sont pas les objets propres et immédiats de la vue. L'objet propre et immédiat de la vue n'est autre chose que la lumière colorée: tout le reste, nous ne sentons qu'a la longue et par expérience. Nous apprenons à voir, precisement comme nous apprenons à parler et à lire. La difference est, que l'art de voir est plus facile, et que la nature est également à tous notre maitre.

'Les jugemens soudains, presque uniformes, que toutes nos âmes, à un certain age, portent des distances, des grandeurs, des situations, nous font penser, qu'il n'y à qu'à ouvrir les yeux, pour voir la manière dont nous les voyons. On se trompe; il est faut les secours des autres choses. Si les hommes n'avoient que le sens de la vue, ils n'auroient aucun moyen pour connaitre l'étendue en longueur, largeur et profondeur; et un pur esprit ne la connoitroit peut-etre, a moins que Dieu ne la lui révélât. Il est très difficile de separer dans notre entendement l'extension d'un objet d'avec les couleurs de cet objet. Nous ne voyons jamais rien que d'étendu, et de-là nous sommes toutes portés à croire, que nous voyons en esset l'étendue.' (*Élemens de la Philos. de Newton*, Second Partie, ch. 5.)

Condillac, in his *Essais sur l'Origine des Connaissances Humanes* (Part I. sect. 6), published in 1746, combats Berkeley's *New Theory*, and maintains that an extension exterior to the eye is discernible by sight, the eye being naturally capable of judging of figures, magnitudes, situations, and distances. His reasonings in support of this 'prejudice,' as he afterwards allowed it to be, may be found at length, in the section entitled 'De quelques jugemens qu'on a attribués à l'ame, sans fondement, ou solution d'un problème de métaphysique.' Here Locke, Molyneux, Berkeley, and Voltaire are criticised, and Cheselden's experiment is referred to. Condillac's subsequent recantation is contained in his *Traité des Sensations*, published in 1754, and in his *L'Art de Penser*. In the *Traité des Sensations* (Troisieme Partie, ch. 3, 4, 5, 6, 7, 8, &c.) the whole question is discussed at length, and Condillac vindicates what he allows must appear a marvellous paradox to the uninitiated—that we gradually learn to see, hear, smell, taste, and touch. He argues in particular that the eye cannot originally perceive an extension that is beyond itself, and that the notion of trinal space is due to what we experience in touch.

Voltaire and Condillac gave currency to the *New Theory* in France, and it soon became a commonplace with D'Alembert, Diderot, Buffon and other French philosophers. In Germany we have allusions to it in the Berlin Memoirs and elsewhere; but, although well known by name, if not in its distinctive principle and latent Idealism, it has not there obtained the consideration which its author's fully developed theory of matter has received. The Kantian account of Space, and of the origin of our mathematical notions, may have subsequently indisposed the German mind to the *a posteriori* reasoning of Berkeley's *Essay*.

Its influence is most apparent in British philosophy. The following passages in Hartley's *Observations on Man*, published in 1749, illustrate the extent to which some of the distinctive parts of Berkeley's doctrine were at that time received by an eminent English psychologist:—

'Distance is judged of by the quantity of motion, and figure by the relative quantity of distance. . . . And, as the sense of sight is much more extensive and expedite than feeling, we judge of tangible qualities chiefly by sight, which therefore may be considered, agreeably to Bishop Berkeley's remark, as a philosophical language for the ideas of feeling; being, for the most part, an adequate representative of them, and a language common to all mankind, and in which they all agree very nearly, after a moderate degree of experience.

'However, if the informations from touch and sight disagree at any time, we are always to depend upon touch, as that which, according to the usual ways of speaking upon these subjects, is the true representation of the essential properties, i. e. as the earnest and presage of what other tangible impressions the body under consideration will make upon our feeling in other circumstances; also what changes it will produce in other bodies; of which again we are to determine by our feeling, if the visual language should not happen to correspond to it exactly. And it is from this difference that we call the touch the reality, light the representative—also that a person born blind may foretell with certainty, from his present tangible impressions, what others would follow upon varying the circumstances; whereas, if we could suppose a person to be born without feeling, and to arrive at man's estate, he could not, from his present visible impressions, judge what others would follow upon varying the circumstances. Thus the picture of a knife, drawn so well as to deceive his eye, would not, when applied to another body, produce the same change of visible impressions as a real knife does, when it separates the parts of the body through which it passes. But the touch is not liable to these deceptions. As it is therefore the fundamental source of information in respect of the essential properties of matter, it may be considered as our first and principal key to the knowledge of the external world.' (Prop. 30.)

In other passages of Hartley's work (e.g. Prop. 58) the relation of our visual judgments of magnitude, figure, motion, distance, and position, to the doctrine of association is explained, and the associated circumstances by which these judgments are formed are enumerated in detail.

Dr. Porterfield of Edinburgh, in his *Treatise on the Eye, the Manner and Phenomena of Vision* (Edinburgh 1759), is an exception to the consent which the doctrine had then widely secured. He maintains, in opposition to Berkeley, that 'the judgments we form of objects being placed without the eye, in those perpendicular lines, or, which is nearly the same thing, the judgments we form of the situation and distance of visual objects, depend not on custom and experience, but on original, connate, and immutable law, to which our minds have been subjected from the time they were at first united to their bodies."[*]

Berkeley's Theory of Vision, in so far as it resolves our supposed visual perceptions of distance into an interpretation of suggestive signs, received the qualified approbation of Dr. Reid, in his *Inquiry into the Human Mind on the Principles of Common Sense* (1764). He criticises it in detail in successive chapters of the *Inquiry*, where the doctrine of arbitrary, natural signs, of which Berkeley's philosophy is the development, is accepted, and to some extent applied. With Reid it is divorced, however, from the Berkeleian metaphysics as a whole, although the Theory of Vision was the seminal principle of Berkeley's Theory of Matter.[†]

Berkeley's Theory of Matter was an object of professed hostility to Reid and his followers, while his Theory of Vision has obtained the almost unanimous consent of the Scotch metaphysicians. Adam Smith refers to it in his *Essays* (published in 1795) as 'one of the finest examples of philosophical analysis that is to be found either in our own or in any other language.' Mr. Stewart characterises it in his *Elements*, which had appeared three years before, as 'one of the most beautiful, and at the same time one of the most important theories of modern philosophy.' 'The solid additions,' he afterwards remarks in his *Dissertation*, 'made by Berkeley to the stock of human knowledge, were important and brilliant. Among these the first place is unquestionably due to his *New Theory of Vision*, a work abounding with ideas so different from those commonly received, and at the same time so profound and refined, that it was regarded by all but a few accustomed to deep

---

[*] See *Treatise on the Eye*, Vol. II, pp. 299, &c. Ch. vi. § 14, and *Essays on the Intellectual Powers*, II. Ch. 10 and 14.
[†] See Reid's *Inquiry*, Ch. v. §§ 3, 5, 6, 7.

metaphysical reflection, rather in the light of a philosophical romance than of a sober inquiry after truth. Such, however, has since been the progress and diffusion of this sort of knowledge, that the leading and most abstracted doctrines contained in it form now an essential part of every elementary treatise on optics, and are adopted by the most superficial smatterers in science as fundamental articles of their faith.' The *New Theory* is accepted by Dr. Thomas Brown, who proposes (*Lectures*, 29) to extend its reasonings to more refined conclusions. With regard to the perceptions of sight, Dr. John Young, in his *Lectures on Intellectual Philosophy* (p. 102), says that 'it has been universally admitted, at least since the days of Berkeley, that many of those which appear to us at present to be instantaneous and primitive, can yet be shewn to be acquired; that at least most of the perceptions of sight are founded on the previous information of touch;—that colour, considered as a mere sensation of the mind, can give us no conception originally of those qualities of bodies which produce it in us; and that primary vision gives us no notion of distance, nor of true relative magnitude, and, as I believe, no notion of magnitude at all. Most certainly, at least, it can give us no notion primarily of resistance, solidity, roughness and smoothness, in bodies; and yet these are among the chief elementary notions which we have of matter.' Sir James Mackintosh, in his *Dissertation*, characterises the *New Theory of Vision* as 'a great discovery in Mental Philosophy.' 'Nothing in the compass of inductive reasoning,' remarks Sir William Hamilton (Reid's *Works*, p. 182, note), 'appears more satisfactory than Berkeley's demonstration of the necessity and manner of our learning, by a slow process of observation and comparison alone, the connexion between the perceptions of vision and touch, and, in general, all that relates to the distance and real magnitude of external things.' 'With regard to the method by which we judge of distance, it was formerly,' he tells us in his *Lectures on Metaphysics* (XXVIII), 'supposed to depend upon an original law of the constitution, and to be independent of any knowledge gained through the medium of the external senses. This opinion was attacked by Berkeley in his *New Theory of Vision*, in which it appears most clearly demonstrated that our whole information on this subject is acquired by experience and association.'*

* While Sir W. Hamilton acknowledges the scientific validity of Berkeley's conclusions, as to the way we judge of distances in seeing, he curiously complains, in the same lecture, that 'the whole question is thrown into doubt by the analogy of the lower animals,' i.e. by their probable visual instinct of distances; and elsewhere (Reid's *Works*, p. 137, note) he seems to hesitate about Locke's Solution of Molyneux's Problem, at least in its application to Cheselden's case. Cf. Leibnitz, *Nouveaux Essais*, Liv. II. ch. 9.

It is worthy of remark that the *New Theory* has been generally accepted, so far as it was understood, alike by the followers of Hartley and by the associates and successors of Reid. Among British psychologists, it has recommended itself to metaphysical rationalists and sensationalists, to the advocates of innate principles, and to those who would explain, by the laws of mental association, what their rivals attribute to the absolute constitution of intelligence. This one doctrine, as Mr. J. S. Mill remarks, has been recognised and upheld with singular unanimity by the leaders of all schools of philosophical thought.* It may thus be fairly adduced as an example of an acknowledged discovery in metaphysics; while a careful study of its nature and evidence is among the best metaphysical exercises of the refined thought and exact use of words in which mental analysis is the only adequate education.

A. C. F.

---

* As almost solitary exceptions to this unusual uniformity of profession on a subtle question in psychology, I may refer to two works, which are valuable at least as much for the criticism they have occasioned as for their contents. In 1842 Mr. Samuel Bailey, of Sheffield, a candid and able inquirer, published a *Review of Berkeley's Theory of Vision*, designed to show the unsoundness of that celebrated Speculation. Mr. Bailey's book recalled attention, at the time of its appearance, to the basis in consciousness on which the theory rests. It was the subject of two interesting rejoinders—a well-weighed criticism, in the *Westminster Review*, by Mr. J. S. Mill, since republished in his *Dissertations*; and an ingenious Essay by the late Professor Ferrier, in *Blackwood's Magazine*, now republished in his *Philosophical Remains*. The controversy ended on that occasion with Mr. Bailey's *Letter to a Philosopher in reply to some recent attempts to vindicate Berkeley's Theory of Vision, and in further elucidation of its unsoundness*, and a reply to it by each of his critics. It was revived in 1864 by Mr. Abbott of Trinity College, Dublin, who produced his *Sight and Touch*, as 'an attempt to disprove the received (or Berkleian) Theory of Vision,' but he seems to have overlooked the nature of the Theory which he professes to disprove.

AN ESSAY

TOWARDS

A NEW THEORY OF VISION.

TO THE

RIGHT HON. SIR JOHN PERCIVALE, BART.[1],

ONE OF HER MAJESTY'S MOST HONOURABLE PRIVY COUNCIL
IN THE KINGDOM OF IRELAND.

Sir,

I could not, without doing violence to myself, forbear upon this occasion to give some public testimony of the great and well-grounded esteem I have conceived for you, ever since I had the honour and happiness of your acquaintance. The outward advantages of fortune, and the early honours with which you are adorned, together with the reputation you are known to have amongst the best and most considerable men, may well imprint veneration and esteem on the minds of those who behold you from a distance. But these are not the chief motives that inspire me with the respect I bear you. A nearer approach has given me the view of something in your person infinitely beyond the external ornaments of honour and estate. I mean, an intrinsic stock of virtue and good sense, a true concern for religion, and disinterested love of your country. Add to these an uncommon proficiency in the best and most useful parts of knowledge; together with (what in my mind is a perfection of the first rank) a surpassing goodness of nature. All which I have collected, not from the uncertain reports of fame, but from my own experience. Within these few months that I have the honour to be known unto you, the many delightful hours I have passed in your agreeable and improving conversation have afforded me the opportunity of discovering in you many excellent qualities, which at once fill me with admiration and esteem. That one at those years, and

---

[1] Afterwards (in 1733) Earl of Egmont. He succeeded to the Baronetcy in 1691, and, after sitting for several years in the Irish House of Commons, was in 1715 created Baron Percival, in the Irish peerage. In 1733 he obtained a charter to colonise the province of Georgia in North America. His name appears in the list of subscribers to Berkeley's Bermuda Scheme (1726). He died in 1748.

in those circumstances of wealth and greatness, should continue proof against the charms of luxury and those criminal pleasures so fashionable and predominant in the age we live in; that he should preserve a sweet and modest behaviour, free from that insolent and assuming air so familiar to those who are placed above the ordinary rank of men; that he should manage a great fortune with that prudence and inspection, and at the same time expend it with that generosity and nobleness of mind, as to shew himself equally remote from a sordid parsimony and a lavish inconsiderate profusion of the good things he is intrusted with—this, surely, were admirable and praiseworthy. But, that he should, moreover, by an impartial exercise of his reason, and constant perusal of the sacred Scriptures, endeavour to attain a right notion of the principles of natural and revealed religion; that he should with the concern of a true patriot have the interest of the public at heart, and omit no means of informing himself what may be prejudicial or advantageous to his country, in order to prevent the one and promote the other; in fine, that, by a constant application to the most severe and useful studies, by a strict observation of the rules of honour and virtue, by frequent and serious reflections on the mistaken measures of the world, and the true end and happiness of mankind, he should in all respects qualify himself bravely to run the race that is set before him, to deserve the character of great and good in this life, and be ever happy hereafter—this were amazing and almost incredible. Yet all this, and more than this, Sir, might I justly say of you, did either your modesty permit, or your character stand in need of it. I know it might deservedly be thought a vanity in me to imagine that anything coming from so obscure a hand as mine could add a lustre to your reputation. But, I am withal sensible how far I advance the interest of my own, by laying hold on this opportunity to make it known that I am admitted into some degree of intimacy with a person of your exquisite judgment. And, with that view, I have ventured to make you an address of this nature, which the goodness I have ever experienced in you inclines me to hope will meet with a favourable reception at your hands. Though I must own I have your pardon to ask, for touching on what may possibly be offensive to a virtue you are possessed of in a very distinguishing degree. Excuse me, Sir, if it was out of my power to mention the name of Sir John Percivale without paying some tribute to that extraordinary and surprising merit whereof I have so clear and affecting an idea, and which, I am sure, cannot be exposed in too full a light for the imitation of others. Of late, I have been agreeably employed in considering the most noble, pleasant, and comprehensive of all the

DEDICATION.

senses[1]. The fruit of that (labour shall I call it or) diversion is what I now present you with, in hopes it may give some entertainment to one who, in the midst of business and vulgar enjoyments, preserves a relish for the more refined pleasures of thought and reflexion. My thoughts concerning Vision have led me into some notions, so far out of the common road[2] that it had been improper to address them to one of a narrow and contracted genius. But, you, Sir, being master of a large and free understanding, raised above the power of those prejudices that enslave the far greater part of mankind, may deservedly be thought a proper patron for an attempt of this kind. Add to this, that you are no less disposed to forgive than qualified to discern whatever faults may occur in it. Nor do I think you defective in any one point necessary to form an exact judgment on the most abstract and difficult things, so much as in a just confidence of your own abilities. And, in this one instance, give me leave to say, you shew a manifest weakness of judgment. With relation to the following *Essay*, I shall only add that I beg your pardon for laying a trifle of that nature in your way, at a time when you are engaged in the important affairs of the nation, and desire you to think that I am, with all sincerity and respect,

SIR,

Your most faithful and most humble servant,

GEORGE BERKELEY.

---

[1] Similar terms are applied to this sense by writers with whom Berkeley was familiar. Thus Locke (*Essay* II. ix. 9) refers to sight as "the most comprehensive of all our senses." Des Cartes opens his *Dioptrique* by designating it as "le plus universel et le plus noble de nos sens;" and he alludes to it elsewhere (*Princip.* IV. 195) as "le plus subtil de tous les sens." Malebranche begins his analysis of sight (*Recherche* I. 6) by describing it as "le premier, le plus noble, et le plus etendu de tous les sens."—The high place assigned to this sense by Aristotle has been already alluded to. Its office as the chief organ through which objective reality is given to us is recognised by a multitude of psychologists and metaphysicians.

[2] On Berkeley's originality in his *Theory of Vision* see the Editor's Preface.

CONTENTS.

1. Design.
2. Distance of itself invisible.
3. Remote distance perceived rather by experience than by sense.
4. Near distance thought to be perceiv'd by the angle of the optic axes.
5. Difference between this and the former manner of perceiving distance.
6. Also by diverging rays.
7. This depends not on experience.
8. These the common accounts, but not satisfactory.
9. Some ideas perceived by the mediation of others.
10. No idea which is not itself perceived can be the means of perceiving another.
11. Distance perceived by means of some other idea.
12. Those lines and angles mentioned in optics are not themselves perceived.
13. Hence the mind does not perceive distance by lines and angles.
14. Also because they have no real existence.
15. And because they are insufficient to explain the phenomena.
16. The ideas that suggest distance are—*First*, the sensation arising from the turn of the eyes.
17. Betwixt which and distance there is no necessary connexion.
18. Scarce room for mistake in this matter.
19. No regard had to the angle of the optic axes.
20. Judgment of distance made with both eyes, the result of experience.
21. *Secondly*, confusedness of appearance.
22. This the occasion of those judgments attributed to diverging rays.
23. Objection answered.
24. What deceives the writers of optics in this matter.
25. The cause why one idea may suggest another.
26. This applied to confusion and distance.
27. *Thirdly*, the straining of the eye.
28. The occasions which suggest distance have in their own nature no relation to it.
29. A difficult case proposed by Dr. Barrow as repugnant to all the known theories.
30. This case contradicts a received principle in catoptrics.
31. It is shown to agree with the principles we have laid down.
32. This phenomenon illustrated.
33. It confirms the truth of the principle whereby it is explained.

CONTENTS.

34. Vision, when distinct and when confused.
35. The different effects of parallel, diverging, and converging rays.
36. How converging and diverging rays come to suggest the same distance.
37. A person extremely purblind would judge aright in the forementioned case.
38. Lines and angles why useful in optics.
39. The not understanding this a cause of mistake.
40. A query, proposed by Mr. Molyneux in his *Dioptrics*, considered.
41. One born blind would not at first have any idea of distance by sight.
42. This not agreeable to the common principles.
43. The proper objects of sight not without the mind, nor the images of anything without the mind.
44. This more fully explained.
45. In what sense we must be understood to see distance and external things.
46. Distance, and things placed at a distance, not otherwise perceived by the eye than by the ear.
47. The ideas of sight more apt to be confounded with the ideas of touch than those of hearing are.
48. How this comes to pass.
49. Strictly speaking, we never see and feel the same thing.
50. Objects of sight twofold—mediate and immediate.
51. These hard to separate in our thoughts.

52. The received accounts of our perceiving magnitude by sight, false.
53. Magnitude perceived as immediately as distance.
54. Two kinds of sensible extension, neither of which is infinitely divisible.
55. The tangible magnitude of an object steady, the visible not.
56. By what means tangible magnitude is perceived by sight.
57. This farther enlarged on.
58. No necessary connexion between confusion or faintness of appearance and small or great magnitude.
59. The tangible magnitude of an object more heeded than the visible, and why.
60. An instance of this.
61. Men do not measure by visible feet or inches.
62. No necessary connexion between visible and tangible extension.
63. Greater visible magnitude might signify lesser tangible magnitude.
64. The judgments we make of magnitude depend altogether on experience.
65. Distance and magnitude seen as shame or anger.
66. But we are prone to think otherwise, and why.
67. The moon seems greater in the horizon than in the meridian.
68. The cause of this phenomenon assigned.
69. The horizontal moon, why greater at one time than another.
70. The account we have given proved to be true.
71. And confirmed by the moon's appearing greater in a mist.
72. Objection answered.
73. The way wherein faintness suggests greater magnitude illustrated.

CONTENTS.

74. Appearance of the horizontal moon, why thought difficult to explain.
75. Attempts towards the solution of it made by several, but in vain.
76. The opinion of Dr. Wallis.
77. It is shewn to be unsatisfactory.
78. How lines and angles may be of use in computing apparent magnitudes.
79. One born blind, being made to see, what judgment he would make of magnitude.
80. The *minimum visibile* the same to all creatures.
81. Objection answered.
82. The eye at all times perceives the same number of visible points.
83. Two imperfections in the visive faculty.
84. Answering to which, we may conceive two perfections.
85. In neither of these two ways do microscopes improve the sight.
86. The case of microscopical eyes considered.
87. The sight admirably adapted to the ends of seeing.

88. Difficulty concerning erect vision.
89. The common way of explaining it.
90. The same shewn to be false.
91. Not distinguishing between ideas of sight and touch cause of mistake in this matter.
92. The case of one born blind proper to be considered.
93. Such a one might by touch attain to have ideas of upper and lower.
94. Which modes of situation he would attribute only to things tangible.
95. He would not at first sight think anything he saw, high or low, erect or inverted.
96. This illustrated by an example.
97. By what means he would come to denominate visible objects, 'high' or 'low,' &c.
98. Why he should think those objects highest which are painted on the lowest part of his eye, and *vice versa*.
99. How he would perceive by sight the situation of external objects.
100. Our propension to think the contrary no argument against what hath been said.
101. Objection.
102. Answer.
103. An object could not be known at first sight by the colour.
104. Nor by the magnitude thereof.
105. Nor by the figure.
106. In the first act of vision, no tangible thing would be suggested by sight.
107. Difficulty proposed concerning number.
108. Number of things visible would not, at first sight, suggest the like number of things tangible.
109. Number, the creature of the mind.
110. One born blind would not, at first sight, number visible things as others do.

CONTENTS.

111. The situation of any object determined with respect only to objects of the same sense.
112. No distance, great or small, between a visible and tangible thing.
113. The not observing this, cause of difficulty in erect vision.
114. Which otherwise includes nothing unaccountable.
115. What is meant by the pictures being inverted.
116. Cause of mistake in this matter.
117. Images in the eye not pictures of external objects.
118. In what sense they are pictures.
119. In this affair we must carefully distinguish between ideas of sight and touch.
120. Difficult to explain by words the true theory of vision.
121. The question, whether there is any idea common to sight and touch, stated.
122. Abstract extension inquired into.
123. It is incomprehensible.
124. Abstract extension not the object of geometry.
125. The general idea of a triangle considered.
126. Vacuum, or pure space, not common to sight and touch.
127. There is no idea, or kind of idea, common to both senses.
128. First argument in proof hereof.
129. Second argument.
130. Visible figure and extension not distinct ideas from colour.
131. Third argument.
132. Confirmation drawn from Mr. Molyneux's problem of a sphere and a cube, published by Mr. Locke.
133. Which is falsely solved, if the common supposition be true.
134. More might be said in proof of our tenet, but this suffices.
135. Farther reflection on the foregoing problem.
136. The same thing doth not affect both sight and touch.
137. The same idea of motion not common to sight and touch.
138. The way wherein we apprehend motion by sight easily collected from what hath been said.
139. *Ques.* How visible and tangible ideas came to have the same name, if not of the same kind?
140. This accounted for without supposing them of the same kind.
141. *Obj.* That a tangible square is liker to a visible square than to a visible circle.
142. *Ans.* That a visible square is fitter than a visible circle to represent a tangible square.
143. But it doth not hence follow that a visible square is like a tangible square.
144. Why we are more apt to confound visible with tangible ideas, than other signs with the things signified.
145. Several other reasons hereof assigned.

D

146. Reluctancy in rejecting any opinion no argument of its truth.
147. Proper objects of vision the Language of Nature.
148. In it there is much admirable and deserving our attention.
149. Question proposed concerning the object of geometry.
150. At first view we are apt to think visible extension the object of geometry.
151. Visible extension shewn not to be the object of geometry.
152. Words may as well be thought the object of geometry as visible extension.
153. It is proposed to inquire, what progress an intelligence that could see, but not feel, might make in geometry.
154. He cannot understand those parts which relate to solids, and their surfaces, and lines generated by their section.
155. Nor even the elements of plane geometry.
156. The proper objects of sight incapable of being managed as geometrical figures.
157. The opinion of those who hold plane figures to be the immediate objects of sight considered.
158. Planes no more the immediate objects of sight than solids.
159. Difficult to enter precisely into the thoughts of the above-mentioned intelligence.
160. The object of geometry, its not being sufficiently understood, cause of difficulty and useless labour in that science.

AN ESSAY

TOWARDS

A NEW THEORY OF VISION.

1. MY design is to shew the manner wherein we perceive by sight the distance, magnitude, and situation of objects. Also to consider the difference there is betwixt the ideas of sight and touch, and whether there be any idea common to both senses. [In treating of all which, it seems to me, the writers of optics have proceeded on wrong principles[1].]

2. It is, I think, agreed by all that distance of itself, and immediately, cannot be seen[2]. For distance[3] being a line directed endwise to the eye, it projects only one point in the fund of the eye—which point remains invariably the same, whether the distance be longer or shorter[4].

3. I find it also acknowledged that the estimate we make of the distance of objects considerably remote is rather an act of judgment grounded on experience than of sense. For example,

---

[1] This sentence is contained in the first and collected editions only.

[2] Sect. 2-51 explain the way in which we learn in seeing to judge of Distance, and of objects as existing at a distance from our organism, viz. by their association with what we see, and with certain organic sensations which accompany vision. Sect. 2 assumes, as already granted, the invisibility of distance in the line of sight. Cf. sect. 11 and 88—*First Dialogue between Hylas and Philonous*—*Alciphron*, IV. 8—*Theory of Vision Vindicated and Explained*, sect. 67-69.

[3] i. e. distance from the point of vision—distance in the line of sight—the third dimension of space. Visible distance is the visible space or interval between two points (see sect. 112). We can of course be sensibly con-

scious of it only when both its extreme points are seen.

[4] This section is erroneously adduced by some of Berkeley's critics, favourable and adverse, as if it were a summary of the evidence for his *New Theory*, instead of being, as it is, a mere reference to the scientific ground of the already received doctrine of the absolute invisibility of distance in the line of sight. See, for example, Bailey's *Review of Berkeley's Theory of Vision*, pp. 38-43, also his *Theory of Reasoning*, p. 179 and pp. 100-7—Mill's *Discussions*, vol. ii. p. 95—Abbott's *Sight and Touch*, p. 10, where this sentence is spoken of as "the sole positive argument advanced by Berkeley."

when I perceive a great number of intermediate objects, such as houses, fields, rivers, and the like, which I have experienced to take up a considerable space, I thence form a judgment or conclusion, that the object I see beyond them is at a great distance. Again, when an object appears faint and small which at a near distance I have experienced to make a vigorous and large appearance, I instantly conclude it to be far off [5].—And this, it is evident, is the result of experience; without which, from the faintness and littleness, I should not have inferred anything concerning the distance of objects.

4. But, when an object is placed at so near a distance as that the interval between the eyes bears any sensible proportion to it [6], the opinion of speculative men is, that the two optic axes (the fancy that we see only with one eye at once being exploded), concurring at the object, do there make an angle, by means of which, according as it is greater or lesser, the object is perceived to be nearer or farther off [7].

5. Betwixt which and the foregoing manner of estimating distance there is this remarkable difference:—that, whereas there was no apparent necessary connexion between small distance and a large and strong appearance, or between great distance and a little and faint appearance, there appears a very necessary connexion between an obtuse angle and near distance, and an acute angle and farther distance. It does not in the least depend upon experience, but may be evidently known by any one before he had experienced it, that the nearer the concurrence of the optic axes the greater the angle, and the remoter their concurrence is the lesser will be the angle comprehended by them.

6. There is another way, mentioned by optic writers, whereby they will have us judge of those distances in respect of which the breadth of the pupil hath any sensible bigness. And that is the greater or lesser divergency of the rays, which, issuing from the visible point, do fall on the pupil—that point being

---

[5] I. e. aerial and linear perspective are acknowledged signs of the more remote distances. But the question, in this and the thirty-six following sections, concerns the visibility of near distances only—a few yards in front of us. It was 'agreed by all' that beyond this limit distances are suggested by our experience of their arbitrary signs.

[6] Cf. this and the four following sections with the quotations in the Editor's Preface, from Molyneux's *Treatise of Dioptrics*.

[7] In the last edition we have this annotation: 'See what Des Cartes and others have written upon the subject.' Cf. Appendix, p. 109.

judged nearest which is seen by most diverging rays, and that remoter which is seen by less diverging rays; and so on, the apparent distance still increasing, as the divergency of the rays decreases, till at length it becomes infinite when the rays that fall on the pupil are to sense parallel. And after this manner it is said we perceive distance when we look only with one eye.

7. In this case also it is plain we are not beholden to experience: it being a certain, necessary truth that, the nearer the direct rays falling on the eye approach to a parallelism, the farther off is the point of their intersection, or the visible point from whence they flow.

8. Now, though the accounts here given of perceiving near distance by sight are received for true, and accordingly made use of in determining the apparent places of objects, they do nevertheless seem to me very unsatisfactory, and that for these following reasons[*]:—

9. [*First*[9],] It is evident that, when the mind perceives any idea, not immediately and of itself, it must be by the means of some other idea. Thus, for instance, the passions which are in the mind of another are of themselves to me invisible. I may nevertheless perceive them by sight, though not immediately, yet by means of the colours they produce in the countenance.' We often see shame or fear in the looks of a man, by perceiving the changes of his countenance to red or pale.

10. Moreover, it is evident that no idea which is not itself perceived can be to me the means of perceiving any other idea. If I do not perceive the redness or paleness of a man's face themselves, it is impossible I should perceive by them the passions which are in his mind.

11. Now, from sect. ii., it is plain that distance is in its own nature imperceptible, and yet it is perceived by sight[10]. It remains,

---

[*] In the first and collected editions this section stands thus: 'I have here set down the common current accounts that are given of our perceiving near distances by sight, which, though they are unquestionably received for true by mathematicians, and accordingly made use of by them in determining the apparent places of objects, do nevertheless,' &c.

[9] Omitted in the author's last edition.

[10] i.e. although immediately imperceptible, it is mediately perceived in seeing, through experience. Mark, here and elsewhere, the ambiguity of the term *perception*, which now signifies the act of being sensibly conscious, and again the inference—either instinctive or intelligent—of certain 'qualities' of the immediate objects of sense-consciousness, of which we are at the time inconscient; while elsewhere it is applied to the object instead of the act, and to imagination as well as to sense-consciousness. Cf. Locke's *Essay*, II. 9.

therefore, that it be brought into view by means of some other idea, that is itself immediately perceived in the act of vision.

12. But those lines and angles by means whereof some men[11] pretend to explain the perception[12] of distance, are themselves not at all perceived, nor are they in truth ever thought of by those unskilful in optics. I appeal to any one's experience, whether, upon sight of an object, he computes its distance by the bigness of the angle made by the meeting of the two optic axes? or whether he ever thinks of the greater or lesser divergency of the rays which arrive from any point to his pupil? nay, whether it be not perfectly impossible for him to perceive by sense the various angles wherewith the rays, according to their greater or lesser divergence, do fall on the eye[13]? Every one is himself the best judge of what he perceives, and what not. In vain shall any man[14] tell me, that I perceive certain lines and angles which introduce into my mind the various ideas of distance, so long as I myself am conscious of no such thing.

13. Since therefore those angles and lines are not themselves perceived by sight, it follows, from sect. x., that the mind does not by them judge of the distance of objects.

14. [*Secondly*[15],] The truth of this assertion will be yet farther evident to any one that considers those lines and angles have no real existence in nature, being only an hypothesis framed by the mathematicians, and by them introduced into optics that they might treat of that science in a geometrical way.

15. The [*third* and [16]] last reason I shall give for rejecting that doctrine is, that though we should grant the real existence of those optic angles, &c., and that it was possible for the mind to perceive them, yet these principles would not be found sufficient to explain the phenomena of distance, as shall be shewn hereafter.

16. Now, it being already shewn[17] that distance is suggested[18]

---

[11] 'Some men'—'mathematicians,' in first edition.

[12] I. e. the mediate perception.

[13] In the first and collected editions only.

[14] 'any man'—'all the mathematicians in the world,' in first edition.

[15] Omitted in the author's last edition.

[16] Omitted in the author's last edition.

[17] Sect. 9. From sect. 16 to sect. 27, we have Berkeley's arbitrary signs of near distances.

[18] Observe the first introduction by Berkeley of the term *suggestion*, used by him to express a leading conception in his *Theory of Vision*, and indeed in his whole metaphysical philosophy. It had been employed occasionally, among others, by Hobbes and Locke. There are three ways in which the objects we have an immediate perception of in sight may be supposed to occasion an imagination and belief of what we are not thus percipient: (1) by instinctive interpretation, or what Dr. Reid calls 'original suggestion' (*Inquiry*, Ch. VI. sect. 20-24); (2) through a cus-

to the mind, by the mediation of some other idea which is itself perceived in the act of seeing, it remains that we inquire what ideas or sensations there be that attend vision, unto which we may suppose the ideas of distance are connected, and by which they are introduced into the mind.—And, *first*, it is certain by experience, that when we look at a near object with both eyes, according as it approaches or recedes from us, we alter the disposition of our eyes, by lessening or widening the interval between the pupils. This disposition or turn of the eyes is attended with a sensation [19], which seems to me to be that which in this case brings the idea of greater or lesser distance into the mind.

17. Not that there is any natural or necessary connexion between the sensation we perceive by the turn of the eyes and greater or lesser distance. But—because the mind has, by constant experience, found the different sensations corresponding to the different dispositions of the eyes to be attended each with a different degree of distance in the object—there has grown an habitual or customary connexion between those two sorts of ideas; so that the mind no sooner perceives the sensation arising from the different turn it gives the eyes, in order to bring the pupils nearer or farther asunder, but it withal perceives the different idea of distance which was wont to be connected with that sensation. Just as, upon hearing a certain sound, the idea is immediately suggested to the understanding which custom had united with it.

18. Nor do I see how I can easily be mistaken in this matter. I know evidently that distance is not perceived of itself [20]—that, by consequence, it must be perceived by means of some other idea, which is immediately perceived, and varies with the different degrees of distance. I know also that the sensation arising from the turn of the eyes is of itself immediately perceived,

---

tomary association of ideas, gradually productive of the result, according to laws of imagination recognised since Aristotle; (3) by general reasoning from a recognised universal premiss. Berkeley's 'suggestion,' as afterwards Hume's 'custom,' corresponds to the second (cf. *Theory of Vision Vindicated*, sect. 42).—Mr. Bailey, misled apparently by the double meaning of the term 'perception,' charges Berkeley with holding that 'because the internal feeling has been found to be accompanied by the external one, it will, when experienced alone, not only suggest the external sensation, but absolutely be regarded as external itself;' and he justly adds that 'there is nothing in the whole operation of the human mind analogous to such a process.' (*Review*, p. 21.) See Mill's *Dissertations*, vol. II. pp. 92, 93.—Professor Ferrier's *Philosophical Remains*, vol. II. pp. 126-8, 163-4.

[19] Cf. *Theory of Vision Vindicated*, sect. 66, where it is added that this 'sensation' belongs properly to the sense of touch. Cf. also sect. 145 of *Essay*.

[20] Sect. 2.

and various degrees thereof are connected with different distances, which never fail to accompany them into my mind, when I view an object distinctly with both eyes whose distance is so small that in respect of it the interval between the eyes has any considerable magnitude.

19. I know it is a received opinion that, by altering the disposition of the eyes, the mind perceives whether the angle of the optic axes, or the lateral angles comprehended between the interval of the eyes or the optic axes, are made greater or lesser; and that, accordingly, by a kind of natural geometry, it judges the point of their intersection to be nearer or farther off. But that this is not true I am convinced by my own experience, since I am not conscious[21] that I make any such use of the perception I have by the turn of my eyes. And for me to make those judgments, and draw those conclusions from it, without knowing that I do so, seems altogether incomprehensible.

20. From all which it follows, that the judgment we make of the distance of an object viewed with both eyes is entirely the result of experience. If we had not constantly found certain sensations, arising from the various disposition of the eyes, attended with certain degrees of distance, we should never make those sudden judgments from them concerning the distance of objects; no more than we would pretend to judge of a man's thoughts by his pronouncing words we had never heard before.

21. *Secondly*, an object placed at a certain distance from the eye, to which the breadth of the pupil bears a considerable proportion, being made to approach, is seen more confusedly[22]. And the nearer it is brought the more confused appearance it makes. And, this being found constantly to be so, there arises in the mind an habitual connexion between the several degrees of confusion and distance; the greater confusion still implying the lesser distance, and the lesser confusion the greater distance of the object.

22. This confused appearance of the object doth therefore seem to be the medium whereby the mind judges of distance, in those cases wherein the most approved writers of optics will

---

[21] Here, as throughout the *Essay*, the appeal is to our experience in consciousness, and not to physiological phenomena in the organism of the eye.

[22] See sect. 35 for the difference between confused and faint vision. Cf. sect. 32-38 with this section. Also *Theory of Vision Vindicated*, sect. 68.

have it judge by the different divergency with which the rays flowing from the radiating point fall on the pupil[23]. No man, I believe, will pretend to see or feel those imaginary angles that the rays are supposed to form according to their various inclinations on his eye. But he cannot choose seeing whether the object appear more or less confused. It is therefore a manifest consequence from what has been demonstrated that, instead of the greater or lesser divergency of the rays, the mind makes use of the greater or lesser confusedness of the appearance, thereby to determine the apparent place of an object.

23. Nor doth it avail to say there is not any necessary connexion between confused vision and distance great or small. For I ask any man what necessary connexion he sees between the redness of a blush and shame? And yet no sooner shall he behold that colour to arise in the face of another but it brings into his mind the idea of that passion which hath been observed to accompany it.

24. What seems to have misled the writers of optics in this matter is, that they imagine men judge of distance as they do of a conclusion in mathematics; betwixt which and the premises it is indeed absolutely requisite there be an apparent, necessary connexion. But it is far otherwise in the sudden judgments men make of distance. We are not to think that brutes and children, or even grown reasonable men, whenever they perceive an object to approach or depart from them, do it by virtue of geometry and demonstration.

25. That one idea may suggest another to the mind, it will suffice that they have been observed to go together, without any demonstration of the necessity of their coexistence, or without so much as knowing what it is that makes them so to coexist. Of this there are innumerable instances, of which no one can be ignorant[24].

26. Thus, greater confusion having been constantly attended with nearer distance, no sooner is the former idea perceived but it suggests the latter to our thoughts. And, if it had been the ordinary course of nature that the farther off an object were placed the more confused it should appear, it is certain the

---

[23] See sect. 6.
[24] This and the following sections proceed on the recognition of association by previous contiguity, as a law of imagination.

very same perception that now makes us think an object approaches would then have made us to imagine it went farther off—that perception, abstracting from custom and experience, being equally fitted to produce the idea of great distance, or small distance, or no distance at all).

27. *Thirdly*, an object being placed at the distance above specified, and brought nearer to the eye, we may nevertheless prevent, at least for some time, the appearance's growing more confused, by straining the eye [25]. In which case that sensation supplies the place of confused vision, in aiding the mind to judge of the distance of the object; it being esteemed so much the nearer by how much the effort or straining of the eye in order to distinct vision is greater.

28. I have here [26] set down those sensations or ideas [27] that seem to be the constant and general occasions of introducing into the mind the different ideas of near distance. It is true, in most cases, that divers other circumstances contribute to frame our idea of distance, viz. the particular number, size, kind, &c. of the things seen. Concerning which, as well as all other the forementioned occasions which suggest distance, I shall only observe, they have none of them, in their own nature, any relation or connexion with it: nor is it possible they should ever signify the various degrees thereof, otherwise than as by experience they have been found to be connected with them.

29. I shall proceed upon these principles to account for a phenomenon which has hitherto strangely puzzled the writers of optics, and is so far from being accounted for by any of their theories of vision, that it is, by their own confession, plainly repugnant to them; and of consequence, if nothing else could be objected, were alone sufficient to bring their credit in question. The whole difficulty I shall lay before you in the words of the learned Doctor Barrow, with which he concludes his *Optic Lectures* [28].

---

[25] See Reid's *Inquiry*, Ch. VI. sect. 22.

[26] Sect. 16-27.—For the arbitrary signs of more remote distances, see sect. 3.

[27] i. e. muscular sensations in the organ, and degrees of confusion in the idea or object seen.—Berkeley's 'arbitrary' signs of distance, near and remote, are all either (*a*) states of the visual organ, or (*b*) states of the visible object.

[28] See Molyneux's *Treatise of Dioptrics*, Pt. I. prop. 31. sect. 9. in which Barrow's difficulty is stated. Cf. sect. 40 below.

'Hæc sunt, quæ circa partem opticæ præcipue mathematicam dicenda mihi suggessit meditatio. Circa reliquas (quæ φυσικώτεραι sunt, adeoque sæpiuscule pro certis principiis plausibiles conjecturas venditare necessum habent) nihil fere quicquam admodum verisimile succurrit, a pervulgatis (ab iis, inquam, quæ Keplerus, Scheinerus, Cartesius, et post illos alii tradiderunt) alienum aut diversum. Atqui tacere malo, quam toties oblatam crambem reponere. Proinde receptui cano; nec ita tamen ut prorsus discedam, anteaquam improbam quandam difficultatem (pro sinceritate quam et vobis et veritati debeo minime dissimulandam) in medium protulero, quæ doctrinæ nostræ, hactenus inculcatæ, se objicit adversam, ab ea saltem nullam admittit solutionem. Illa, breviter, talis est. Lenti vel speculo cavo EBF exponatur punctum visibile A, ita distans, ut radii ex A manantes ex inflectione versus axem AB cogantur. Sitque radiationis limes (seu puncti A imago, qualem supra passim statuimus) punctum Z. Inter hoc autem et inflectentis verticem B uspiam positus concipiatur oculus. Quæri jam potest, ubi loci debeat punctum A apparere? Retrorsum ad punctum Z videri non fert natura (cum omnis impressio sensum afficiens proveniat a partibus A) ac experientia reclamat. Nostris autem e placitis consequi videtur, ipsum ad partes anticas apparens, ab intervallo longissime dissito (quod et maximum sensibile quodvis intervallum quodammodo exsuperet), apparere. Cum enim quo radiis minus divergentibus attingitur objectum, eo (seclusis utique prænotionibus et præjudiciis) longius abesse sentiatur; et quod parallelos ad oculum radios projicit, remotissime positum æstimetur: exigere ratio videtur, ut quod convergentibus radiis apprehenditur, adhuc magis, si fieri posset, quoad apparentiam elongetur. Quin et circa casum hunc generatim inquiri possit, quidnam omnino sit, quod apparentem puncti A locum determinet, faciatque quod constanti ratione nunc propius, nunc remotius appareat? Cui itidem dubio nihil quicquam ex hactenus dictorum analogia responderi posse videtur, nisi debere punctum A perpetuo longissime semotum videri. Verum experientia secus

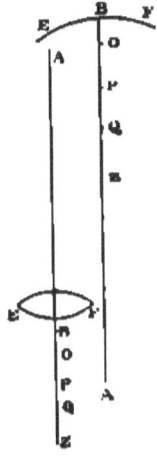

attestatur, illud pro diversa oculi inter puncta B, Z, positione
varie distans, nunquam fere (si unquam) longinquius ipso *A* libere
spectato, subinde vero multo propinquius adparere; quinimo, quo
oculum appellentes radii magis convergunt, eo speciem objecti
propius accedere. Nempe, si puncto B admoveatur oculus, suo
(ad lentem) fere nativo in loco conspicitur punctum *A* (vel æque
distans, ad speculum); ad O reductus oculus ejusce speciem appro-
pinquantem cernit; ad P adhuc vicinius ipsum existimat; ac ita
sensim, donec alicubi tandem, velut ad Q_, constituto oculo, objectum summe propinquum apparens, in meram confusionem in-
cipiat evanescere. Quæ sane cuncta rationibus atque decretis
nostris repugnare videntur, aut cum iis saltem parum amice con-
spirant. Neque nostram tantum sententiam pulsat hoc experi-
mentum, at ex æquo cæteras quas norim omnes: veterem imprimis
ac vulgatam, nostræ præ reliquis affinem, ita convellere videtur, ut
ejus vi coactus doctissimus A. Tacquetus isti principio (cui pene
soli totam inædificaverat *Catoptricam* suam) ceu infido ac incon-
stanti renunciarit, adeoque suam ipse doctrinam labefactarit? id
tamen, opinor, minime facturus, si rem totam inspexissit penitius,
atque difficultatis fundum attigissit. Apud me vero non ita pollet
hæc, nec eousque præpollebit ulla difficultas, ut ab iis quæ mani-
feste rationi consentanea video, discedam; præsertim quum, ut
hic acciuit, ejusmodi difficultas in singularis cujuspiam casus dis-
paritate fundetur. Nimirum in præsente casu peculiare quiddam,
naturæ subtilitati involutum, delitescit, ægre fortassis, nisi per-
fectius explorato videndi modo, detegendum. Circa quod nil,
fateor, hactenus excogitare potui, quod adblandiretur animo meo,
nedum plane satisfaceret. Vobis itaque nodum hunc, utinam
feliciore conatu, resolvendum committo.'

In English as follows:

'I have here delivered what my thoughts have suggested to me
concerning that part of optics which is more properly mathematical. As for the other parts of that science (which, being
rather physical, do consequently abound with plausible conjectures
instead of certain principles), there has in them scarce anything
occurred to my observation different from what has been already
said by Kepler, Scheinerus, Descartes, &c. And methinks I had

better say nothing at all than repeat that which has been so often said by others. I think it therefore high time to take my leave of this subject. But, before I quit it for good and all, the fair and ingenuous dealing that I owe both to you and to truth obliges me to acquaint you with a certain untoward difficulty, which seems directly opposite to the doctrine I have been hitherto inculcating, at least admits of no solution from it. In short it is this.

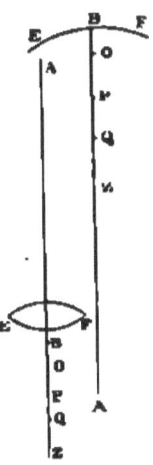

Before the double convex glass or concave speculum *EBF*, let the point *A* be placed at such a distance that the rays proceeding from *A*, after refraction or reflection, be brought to unite somewhere in the axis *AB*. And suppose the point of union (*i.e.* the image of the point *A*, as hath been already set forth) to be Z; between which and *B*, the vertex of the glass or speculum, conceive the eye to be anywhere placed. The question now is, where the point *A* ought to appear. Experience shews that it doth not appear behind at the point Z; and it were contrary to nature that it should; since all the impression which affects the sense comes from towards *A*. But, from our tenets it should seem to follow that it would appear before the eye at a vast distance off, so great as should in some sort surpass all sensible distance. For since, if we exclude all anticipations and prejudices, every object appears by so much the farther off by how much the rays it sends to the eye are less diverging; and that object is thought to be most remote from which parallel rays proceed unto the eye; reason would make one think that object should appear at yet a greater distance which is seen by converging rays. Moreover, it may in general be asked concerning this case, what it is that determines the apparent place of the point *A*, and maketh it to appear after a constant manner, sometimes nearer, at other times farther off? To which doubt I see nothing that can be answered agreeable to the principles we have laid down, except only that the point *A* ought always to appear extremely remote. But, on the contrary, we are assured by experience, that the point *A* appears variously distant, according to the different situations of the eye between the points *B* and *Z*. And that it doth almost never (if at all) seem farther off than it would if it were beheld by the naked eye; but, on the contrary, it doth sometimes appear much nearer. Nay, it is even certain that by how much the rays falling on the eye do more converge, by so much the nearer does the object seem to approach. For, the eye being placed close to the point *B*, the object *A* appears nearly in its own natural place, if the point *B* is taken in the glass, or at the same distance, if in the speculum. The eye being brought back to *O*, the object seems to draw near; and, being come to *P*, it beholds it still nearer: and so on by little and little, till at length the eye being placed somewhere, suppose at *Q*, the object appearing extremely near begins to vanish into mere confusion. All which doth seem repugnant to our principles; at least, not rightly to agree with them. Nor is our tenet alone struck at by this experiment, but likewise all others that ever came to my knowledge are every whit as much endangered by it. The ancient one especially (which is most commonly received, and comes nearest to mine) seems to be so effectually overthrown thereby that the most learned Tacquet has been forced to reject that principle, as false and uncertain, on which alone he had built almost his whole *Catoptrics*, and consequently, by taking away the foundation, hath himself pulled down the superstructure he had raised on it. Which, nevertheless, I do not believe he would have done, had he but considered the whole matter more thoroughly, and examined the difficulty to the bottom. But as for me, neither this nor any other difficulty shall have so great an influence on me, as to make me renounce that which I know to be manifestly agreeable to reason. Especially when, as it here falls out, the difficulty is founded in the peculiar nature of a certain odd and particular case. For, in the present case something peculiar lies hid, which, being involved in the subtilty of nature, will perhaps hardly be discovered till such time as the manner of vision is more perfectly made known. Concerning which, I must own I have hitherto been able to find out nothing that has the least show of probability, not to mention certainty. I shall therefore leave this knot to be untied by you, wishing you may have better success in it than I have had.'

30. The ancient and received principle, which Dr. Barrow

here mentions as the main foundation of Tacquet's [29] *Catoptrics*, is, that every 'visible point seen by reflection from a speculum shall appear placed at the intersection of the reflected ray and the perpendicular of incidence.' Which intersection in the present case happening to be behind the eye, it greatly shakes the authority of that principle whereon the aforementioned author proceeds throughout his whole *Catoptrics*, in determining the apparent place of objects seen by reflection from any kind of speculum.

31. Let us now see how this phenomenon agrees with our tenets [30]. The eye, the nearer it is placed to the point B in the above figures, the more distinct is the appearance of the object: but, as it recedes to O, the appearance grows more confused; and at P it sees the object yet more confused; and so on, till the eye, being brought back to Z, sees the object in the greatest confusion of all. Wherefore, by sect. 21, the object should seem to approach the eye gradually, as it recedes from the point B; that is, at O it should (in consequence of the principle I have laid down in the aforesaid section) seem nearer than it did at B, and at P nearer than at O, and at Q nearer than at P, and so on, till it quite vanishes at Z. Which is the very matter of fact, as any one that pleases may easily satisfy himself by experiment.

32. This case is much the same as if we should suppose an Englishman to meet a foreigner who used the same words with the English, but in a direct contrary signification. The Englishman would not fail to make a wrong judgment of the ideas annexed to those sounds, in the mind of him that used them. Just so in the present case, the object speaks (if I may so say) with words that the eye is well acquainted with, that is, confusions of appearance; but, whereas heretofore the greatest confusions were always wont to signify nearer distances, they have in this case a direct contrary signification, being connected with the greater distances. Whence it follows that the eye must unavoidably be mistaken, since it will take the confusions in the sense it has been used to, which is directly opposed to the true.

---

[29] Andreas Tacquet, a mathematician, born at Antwerp in 1611, and referred to by Molyneux as 'the ingenious Jesuit.' He published a number of mathematical treatises, most of which appeared after his death, in a collected form, at Antwerp in 1669.

[30] In what follows Berkeley would prove that the apparent contradictions, which puzzled the mathematicians, really arose from the occurrence, in connexion with certain distances, of certain arbitrary signs, which we thus learn to associate with them in imagination.

33. This phenomenon, as it entirely subverts the opinion of those who will have us judge of distance by lines and angles, on which supposition it is altogether inexplicable, so it seems to me no small confirmation of the truth of that principle whereby it is explained[a]. But, in order to a more full explication of this point, and to shew how far the hypothesis of the mind's judging by the various divergency of rays may be of use in determining the apparent place of an object, it will be necessary to premise some few things, which are already well known to those who have any skill in Dioptrics.

34. *First*, Any radiating point is then distinctly seen when the rays proceeding from it are, by the refractive power of the crystalline, accurately reunited in the retina or fund of the eye. But if they are reunited either before they arrive at the retina, or after they have passed it, then there is confused vision.

35. *Secondly*, Suppose, in the adjacent figures, NP represent

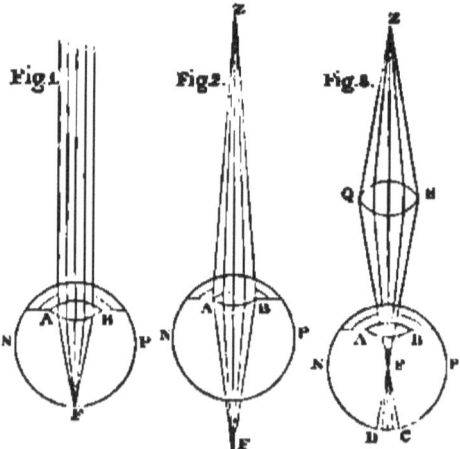

an eye duly framed, and retaining its natural figure. In fig. 1 the rays falling nearly parallel on the eye, are, by the crystalline AB,

---

[a] It is offered, in short, as a deductive verification of the theory that near distances are suggested by constant but arbitrary signs.

refracted, so as their focus, or point of union F, falls exactly on the retina. But, if the rays fall sensibly diverging on the eye, as in fig. 2, then their focus falls beyond the retina; or, if the rays are made to converge by the lens QS, before they come at the eye, as in fig. 3, their focus F will fall before the retina. In which two last cases it is evident, from the foregoing section, that the appearance of the point Z is confused. And, by how much the greater is the convergency or divergency of the rays falling on the pupil, by so much the farther will the point of their reunion be from the retina, either before or behind it, and consequently the point Z will appear by so much the more confused. And this, by the bye, may shew us the difference between confused and faint vision. Confused vision is, when the rays proceeding from each distinct point of the object are not accurately re-collected in one corresponding point on the retina, but take up some space thereon —so that rays from different points become mixed and confused together. This is opposed to a distinct vision, and attends near objects. Faint vision is when, by reason of the distance of the object, or grossness of the interjacent medium, few rays arrive from the object to the eye. This is opposed to vigorous or clear vision, and attends remote objects. But to return.

36. The eye, or (to speak truly) the mind, perceiving only the confusion itself, without ever considering the cause from which it proceeds, doth constantly annex the same degree of distance to the same degree of confusion. Whether that confusion be occasioned by converging or by diverging rays it matters not. Whence it follows that the eye, viewing the object Z through the glass QS (which by refraction causeth the rays ZQ, ZS, &c. to converge), should judge it to be at such a nearness, at which, if it were placed, it would radiate on the eye, with rays diverging to that degree as would produce the same confusion which is now produced by converging rays, *i.e.* would cover a portion of the retina equal to DC. (Vid. fig. 3, *sup*.) But then this must be understood (to use Dr. Barrow's phrase) 'seclusis prænotionibus et præjudiciis,' in case we abstract from all other circumstances of vision, such as the figure, size, faintness, &c. of the visible objects—all which do ordinarily concur to form our idea of distance, the mind having, by frequent experience, observed their several sorts or degrees to be connected with various distances.

37. It plainly follows from what has been said, that a person perfectly purblind (*i.e.* that could not see an object distinctly but when placed close to his eye) would not make the same wrong judgment that others do in the forementioned case. For, to him, greater confusions constantly suggesting greater distances, he must, as he recedes from the glass, and the object grows more confused, judge it to be at a farther distance, contrary to what they do who have had the perception of the objects growing more confused connected with the idea of approach.

38. Hence also it doth appear, there may be good use of computation, by lines and angles, in optics[a]; not that the mind judges of distance immediately by them, but because it judges by somewhat which is connected with them, and to the determination whereof they may be subservient. Thus, the mind judging of the distance of an object by the confusedness of its appearance, and this confusedness being greater or lesser to the naked eye according as the object is seen by rays more or less diverging, it follows that a man may make use of the divergency of the rays, in computing the apparent distance, though not for its own sake, yet on account of the confusion with which it is connected. But, so it is, the confusion itself is entirely neglected by mathematicians, as having no necessary relation with distance, such as the greater or lesser angles of divergency are conceived to have. And these (especially for that they fall under mathematical computation) are alone regarded, in determining the apparent places of objects, as though they were the sole and immediate cause of the judgments the mind makes of distance. Whereas, in truth, they should not at all be regarded in themselves, or any otherwise than as they are supposed to be the cause of confused vision.

39. The not considering of this has been a fundamental and perplexing oversight. For proof whereof, we need go no farther than the case before us. It having been observed that the most diverging rays brought into the mind the idea of nearest distance, and that still as the divergency decreased the distance increased, and it being thought the connexion between the various degrees of divergency and distance was immediate—this naturally leads one to conclude, from an ill-grounded analogy,

---

[a] Cf. sect. 78; also *Theory of Vision Vindicated*, sect. 31.

that converging rays shall make an object appear at an immense distance, and that, as the convergency increases, the distance (if it were possible) should do so likewise. That this was the cause of Dr. Barrow's mistake is evident from his own words which we have quoted. Whereas, had the learned Doctor observed that diverging and converging rays, how opposite soever they may seem, do nevertheless agree in producing the same effect, to wit, confusedness of vision, greater degrees whereof are produced indifferently, either as the divergency or convergency of the rays increaseth; and that it is by this effect, which is the same in both, that either the divergency or convergency is perceived by the eye—I say, had he but considered this, it is certain he would have made a quite contrary judgment, and rightly concluded that those rays which fall on the eye with greater degrees of convergency should make the object from whence they proceed appear by so much the nearer. But it is plain it was impossible for any man to attain to a right notion of this matter, so long as he had regard only to lines and angles, and did not apprehend the true nature of vision, and how far it was of mathematical consideration.

40. Before we dismiss this subject, it is fit we take notice of a query relating thereto, proposed by the ingenious Mr. Molyneux, in his *Treatise of Dioptrics* (par. i. prop. 31. sect. 9), where, speaking of the difficulty we have been explaining, he has these words: 'And so he (i.e. Dr. Barrow) leaves this difficulty to the solution of others, which I (after so great an example) shall do likewise; but with the resolution of the same admirable author, of not quitting the evident doctrine which we have before laid down, for determining the *locus objecti*, on account of being pressed by one difficulty, which seems inexplicable till a more intimate knowledge of the visive faculty be obtained by mortals. In the meantime I propose it to the consideration of the ingenious, whether the *locus apparens* of an object placed as in this ninth section be not as much before the eye as the distinct base is behind the eye?' To which query we may venture to answer in the negative. For, in the present case, the rule for determining the distance of the distinct base, or respective focus from the glass is this: *As the difference between the distance of the object and focus is to the focus or focal length, so the distance of the*

object from the glass is to the distance of the respective focus or distinct base from the glass. (Molyneux, *Dioptr.*, par. i. prop. 5.) Let us now suppose the object to be placed at the distance of the focal length, and one-half of the focal length from the glass, and the eye close to the glass. Hence it will follow, by the rule, that the distance of the distinct base behind the eye is double the true distance of the object before the eye. If, therefore, Mr. Molyneux's conjecture held good, it would follow that the eye should see the object twice as far off as it really is; and in other cases at three or four times its due distance, or more. But this manifestly contradicts experience, the object never appearing, at farthest, beyond its due distance. Whatever, therefore, is built on this supposition (vid. corol. i. prop. 57. ibid.) comes to the ground along with it.

41. From what hath been premised, it is a manifest consequence, that a man born blind, being made to see, would at first have no idea of distance by sight: the sun and stars, the remotest objects as well as the nearer, would all seem to be in his eye, or rather in his mind. The objects intromitted by sight would seem to him (as in truth they are) no other than a new set of thoughts or sensations, each whereof is as near to him as the perceptions of pain or pleasure, or the most inward passions of his soul. For, our judging objects perceived by sight to be at any distance, or without the mind, is (vid. sect. xxviii.) entirely the effect of experience, which one in those circumstances could not yet have attained to[10].

42. It is indeed otherwise upon the common supposition—that men judge of distance by the angle of the optic axes, just as one in the dark, or a blind man by the angle comprehended by two sticks, one whereof he held in each hand[11]. For, if this were true, it would follow that one blind from his birth, being made to see, should

---

[10] Berkeley in this section passes on from his proof of the 'suggestion' of all distances—i.e. intervals between two points in the line of sight, near or remote—by means of arbitrary signs, and approaches the more subtle question of externality or an objective independence of embodied mind. Cf. sect. 94, where he speaks of existence 'without mind' as existence 'in the ambient space;' sect. 112, where he denies that the relation of distance can hold between visible objects and tangible objects; and sect. 119, where he says the visible eye exists only in the mind. See also note in Hamilton's *Reid*, p. 177, on the distinction between a perception of externality or outness and a perception of distance through the eye.

[11] See Des Cartes, *Dioptrique*, VI—Malebranche, *Recherche*, liv. 1. ch. 9. 3—Reid's *Inquiry*, VI. 11.

stand in need of no new experience, in order to perceive distance by sight. But that this is false has, I think, been sufficiently demonstrated.

43. And perhaps, upon a strict inquiry, we shall not find that even those who from their birth have grown up in a continued habit of seeing are irrecoverably prejudiced on the other side, to wit, in thinking what they see to be at a distance from them. For, at this time it seems agreed on all hands, by those who have had any thoughts of that matter, that colours, which are the proper and immediate object of sight, are not without the mind.—But then, it will be said, by sight we have also the ideas of extension, and figure, and motion; all which may well be thought without and at some distance from the mind, though colour should not. In answer to this, I appeal to any man's experience, whether the visible extension of any object do not appear as near to him as the colour of that object; nay, whether they do not both seem to be in the very same place. Is not the extension we see coloured, and is it possible for us, so much as in thought, to separate and abstract colour from extension? Now, where the extension is, there surely is the figure, and there the motion too. I speak of those which are perceived by sight[35].

44. But for a fuller explication of this point, and to shew that the immediate objects of sight are not so much as the ideas or resemblances of things placed at a distance, it is requisite that we look nearer into the matter, and carefully observe what is meant in common discourse when one says, that which he sees is at a distance from him. Suppose, for example, that looking at the moon I should say it were fifty or sixty semidiameters of the earth distant from me. Let us see what moon this is spoken of. It is plain it cannot be the visible moon, or anything like the visible moon, or that which I see—which is only a round luminous plain, of about thirty visible points in diameter. For, in case I am carried from the place where I stand directly towards the moon, it is manifest the object varies still as I go on; and, by the time

---

[35] Berkeley here begins to found on the relation between extension and colour, and between visible and tangible extension, a proof of the invisibility of objects as distant, which gradually conducts to the main articles of the New Theory. From Aristotle downwards it had been assumed that colour is the object of which we are immediately conscious in seeing. Visible extension, visible figure, and visible motion are here assumed to be qualities of, or at least dependent on, the sensation or idea of colour.

that I am advanced fifty or sixty semidiameters of the earth, I shall be so far from being near a small, round, luminous flat that I shall perceive nothing like it—this object having long since disappeared, and, if I would recover it, it must be by going back to the earth from whence I set out [36]. Again, suppose I perceive by sight the faint and obscure idea of something, which I doubt whether it be a man, or a tree, or a tower, but judge it to be at the distance of about a mile. It is plain I cannot mean that what I see is a mile off, or that it is the image or likeness of anything which is a mile off; since that every step I take towards it the appearance alters, and from being obscure, small, and faint, grows clear, large, and vigorous. And when I come to the mile's end, that which I saw first is quite lost, neither do I find anything in the likeness of it [37].

45. In these and the like instances, the truth of the matter, I find, stands thus:—Having of a long time experienced certain ideas perceivable by touch [38]—as distance, tangible figure, and solidity—to have been connected with certain ideas of sight, I do, upon perceiving these ideas of sight, forthwith conclude what tangible ideas are, by the wonted ordinary course of nature, like to follow. Looking at an object, I perceive a certain visible figure and colour, with some degree of faintness and other circumstances, which, from what I have formerly observed, determine me to think that if I advance forward so many paces, miles, &c., I shall be affected

---

[36] In connexion with this and the following illustration, Berkeley virtually argues that we are not only unable to see near distance in the line of sight—it being in all cases suggested to us by arbitrary signs—but also, that we do not see a distant object in its real visible magnitude. His reasoning implies, in short, that *visibilia* are to be distinguished from their *majora* and *maxima visibilia*. But elsewhere he affirms that only tangible magnitude is entitled to be called 'real.' Cf. sect. 55, 59-61.

[37] 'What volumes of obscure disquisition (concerning the fallacy of the senses) might have been spared had this 44th section been given to the world in the days of Aristotle?'—Archer Butler. The sceptical objections to the trustworthiness of the senses, due to the Eleatics and others, and referred to by Descartes in his *Meditations*, and by Malebranche in the First Book of his *Recherche*, may have suggested the illustrations in this section. Cf. also Hume's *Essay On the Academical or Sceptical Philosophy*. The sceptical difficulty is founded on the assumption that the object visible at different distances is the same visible object: it is really different. Moreover, no one in the series of different, yet associated, visible objects bears any resemblance to its associated tangible object.

[38] This is Berkeley's first mention in the *Essay* of 'touch'—a term which with him includes not merely the organic sense of contact, but also the perception or sense-experience which he identifies with locomotion. From this point he begins to unfold the antithesis of visual and tactual phenomena, whose subsequent synthesis, by suggestion, it is the aim of the *New Theory* to describe. Cf. *Principles of Human Knowledge*, sect. 43—*Theory of Vision Vindicated*, sect. 22 and 23. Note here Berkeley's reticence of his more comprehensive Theory of Matter. Cf. *Principles*, sect. 44.

with such and such ideas of touch. So that, in truth and strictness of speech, I neither see distance itself, nor anything that I take to be at a distance. I say, neither distance nor things placed at a distance are themselves, or their ideas, truly perceived by sight. This I am persuaded of, as to what concerns myself. And I believe whoever will look narrowly into his own thoughts, and examine what he means by saying he sees this or that thing at a distance, will agree with me, that what he sees only suggests to his understanding that, after having passed a certain distance, to be measured by the motion of his body, which is perceivable by touch [39], he shall come to perceive such and such tangible ideas, which have been usually connected with such and such visible ideas. But, that one might be deceived by these suggestions of sense, and that there is no necessary connexion between visible and tangible ideas suggested by them, we need go no farther than the next looking-glass or picture to be convinced. Note that, when I speak of tangible ideas, I take the word idea for any the immediate object of sense, or understanding—in which large signification it is commonly used by the moderns [40].

46. From what we have shewn, it is a manifest consequence that the ideas of space, outness [41], and things placed at a distance are not, strictly speaking, the object of sight [42]; they are not otherwise perceived by the eye than by the ear. Sitting in my study I hear a coach drive along the street; I look through the casement

---

[39] This connexion of our notion of distance with locomotive experience points to a theory which ultimately resolves extension, apparently simultaneous, into some sort of continuous sense-experience or locomotive energy.—We cannot touch distances (in the limited application of 'touch') any more than we can see them. Moreover, in this analysis, under locomotion we must not forget the muscular movements of the visual organ itself.

[40] Locke (*Essay*, Introduction, § 8) takes *idea* as 'the term which serves best to stand for whatsoever is the object of the understanding when a man thinks.' In this large meaning, as significant of the object of consciousness—whether presented in sense or represented in imagination—the term was generally used, in the time of Locke and Berkeley. Berkeley indeed elsewhere objects to apply the term to the mere representations of fancy. 'If by *ideas* you mean fictions and fancies of the mind, then these are no ideas. If by *ideas* you mean immediate objects of the understanding, as sensible things.... then these things are ideas' (*Third Dialogue between Hylas and Philonous*). Oversight of this has made his theory of matter a riddle to many. But we here approach the great question of the true meaning of what he calls *ideas* in that theory, of which afterwards.

[41] The expressive term 'outness,' so favoured by Berkeley, is here first used.

[42] 'We get the idea of Space,' says Locke, 'both by our sight and touch' (*Essay*, II, 13, § 2). Locke did not contemplate Berkeley's proof of the absolute antithesis of visible and tangible space or extension, and the consequent ambiguity of the term extension, which sometimes signifies *released*, and at others *resistant* experience in sense.

and see it; I walk out and enter into it. Thus, common speech would
incline one to think I heard, saw, and touched the same thing,
to wit, the coach. It is nevertheless certain the ideas intromitted
by each sense are widely different, and distinct from each other;
but, having been observed constantly to go together, they are
spoken of as one and the same thing. By the variation of the
noise, I perceive the different distances of the coach, and know
that it approaches before I look out. Thus, by the ear I perceive
distance just after the same manner as I do by the eye.

47. I do not nevertheless say I hear distance, in like
manner as I say that I see it—the ideas perceived by hearing not
being so apt to be confounded with the ideas of touch as those of
sight are. So likewise a man is easily convinced that bodies and
external things are not properly the object of hearing, but only
sounds, by the mediation whereof the idea of this or that body, or
distance, is suggested to his thoughts. But then one is with more
difficulty brought to discern the difference there is betwixt the
ideas of sight and touch[13]: though it be certain, a man no more
sees and feels the same thing, than he hears and feels the same
thing.

48. One reason of which seems to be this. It is thought a
great absurdity to imagine that one and the same thing should
have any more than one extension and one figure. But, the extension and figure of a body being let into the mind two ways,
and that indifferently, either by sight or touch, it seems to follow
that we see the same extension and the same figure which we
feel.

49. But, if we take a close and accurate view of the matter,
it must be acknowledged that we never see and feel one and the
same object[14]. That which is seen is one thing, and that which is
felt is another. If the visible figure and extension be not the same
with the tangible figure and extension, we are not to infer that
one and the same thing has divers extensions. The true consequence is that the objects of sight and touch are two distinct
things[15]. It may perhaps require some thought rightly to conceive
this distinction. And the difficulty seems not a little increased,

---

[13] For an explanation of this difficulty, see sect. 144.

[14] 'Object'='thing,' in the earlier edition.

[15] This is the leading result in the analytical parts of the *Essay*.

because the combination of visible ideas hath constantly the same name as the combination of tangible ideas wherewith it is connected—which doth of necessity arise from the use and end of language [48].

50. In order, therefore, to treat accurately and unconfusedly of vision, we must bear in mind that there are two sorts of objects apprehended by the eye—the one primarily and immediately, the other secondarily and by intervention of the former. Those of the first sort neither are nor appear to be without the mind, or at any distance off [49]. They may, indeed, grow greater or smaller, more confused, or more clear, or more faint. But they do not, cannot approach, [or even seem to approach [50]] or recede from us. Whenever we say an object is at a distance, whenever we say it draws near, or goes farther off, we must always mean it of the latter sort, which properly belong to the touch [51], and are not so truly perceived as suggested by the eye, in like manner as thoughts by the ear.

51. No sooner do we hear the words of a familiar language pronounced in our ears but the ideas corresponding thereto present themselves to our minds: in the very same instant the sound and the meaning enter the understanding: so closely are they united that it is not in our power to keep out the one except we exclude the other also. We even act in all respects as if we heard the very thoughts themselves. So likewise the secondary objects, or those which are only suggested by sight, do often more strongly affect us, and are more regarded, than the proper objects of that sense; along with which they enter into the mind, and with which they have a far more strict connexion than ideas have with words [52]. Hence it is we find it so difficult to discriminate between the immediate and mediate objects of sight, and are so prone to attribute to the former what belongs only to the latter. They are, as it were, most closely twisted, blended,

---

[48] Cf. sect. 139-40.
[49] Here the question of externality to mind is again blended with that of the invisibility of distance in the line of sight from the point of vision.
[50] Omitted in author's last edition.
[51] i.e. tactual experience, in its wide meaning, which is assumed exclusively to constitute real objects or external things. But what are the assumed realities or *magnitudes* themselves? Are they too significant of an ulterior reality? This is the problem of the *Principles of Human Knowledge*. Note too that *visibilia* may suggest their own *minora* and *minima*, *majora* and *maxima*.
[52] In this section the conception of natural signs in a Visual Language, into which the *New Theory* ultimately resolves itself, makes its appearance. Cf. sect. 140, 147—*Principles*, sect. 44—*Dialogues of Hylas and Philonous — Alciphron*, IV. 8, 11—and *Theory of Vision Vindicated*, passim.

and incorporated together. And the prejudice is confirmed and
riveted in our thoughts by a long tract of time, by the use of language, and want of reflection. However, I doubt not but any
one that shall attentively consider what we have already said, and
shall say upon this subject before we have done (especially if he
pursue it in his own thoughts), may be able to deliver himself
from that prejudice. Sure I am, it is worth some attention to
whoever would understand the true nature of vision.

52. I have now done with distance, and proceed to shew how
it is that we perceive by sight the magnitude of objects[51]. It is
the opinion of some that we do it by angles, or by angles in conjunction with distance. But, neither angles nor distance being
perceivable by sight[52], and the things we see being in truth at no
distance from us[53], it follows that, as we have shewn lines and
angles not to be the medium the mind makes use of in apprehending the apparent place, so neither are they the medium
whereby it apprehends the apparent magnitude of objects.

53. It is well known that the same extension at a near distance shall subtend a greater angle, and at a farther distance a
lesser angle. And by this principle (we are told) the mind estimates the magnitude of an object[54], comparing the angle under
which it is seen with its distance, and thence inferring the magnitude thereof. What inclines men to this mistake (beside the
humour of making one see by geometry) is, that the same perceptions or ideas which suggest distance do also suggest magnitude.
But, if we examine it, we shall find they suggest the latter as
immediately as the former. I say, they do not first suggest distance and then leave it to the judgment to use that as a medium
whereby to collect the magnitude; but they have as close and
immediate a connexion with the magnitude as with the distance;
and suggest magnitude as independently of distance, as they do
distance independently of magnitude. All which will be evident
to whoever considers what has been already said and what
follows.

54. It has been shewn there are two sorts of objects appre-

---

[51] Sect. 52-87 treat of the invisibility of the real Magnitude of objects. Cf. *Theory of Vision Vindicated*, sect. 54-61.

[52] Sect. 2-15.

[53] See Molyneux's *Treatise on Dioptrics*, B. I. prop. 28.

[54] Sect. 41, &c.

hended by sight, each whereof has its distinct magnitude, or extension—the one, properly tangible, *i.e.* to be perceived and measured by touch, and not immediately falling under the sense of seeing; the other, properly and immediately visible, by mediation of which the former is brought in view. Each of these magnitudes are greater or lesser, according as they contain in them more or fewer points, they being made up of points or minimums. For, whatever may be said of extension in abstract[55], it is certain sensible extension is not infinitely divisible[56]. There is a *minimum tangibile*, and a *minimum visibile*, beyond which sense cannot perceive. This every one's experience will inform him.

55. The magnitude of the object which exists without the mind, and is at a distance, continues always invariably the same: but, the visible object still changing as you approach to or recede from the tangible object, it hath no fixed and determinate greatness. Whenever therefore we speak of the magnitude of any thing, for instance a tree or a house, we must mean the tangible magnitude; otherwise there can be nothing steady and free from ambiguity spoken of it [57]. Now, though the tangible and visible magnitude do in truth belong to two distinct objects[58], I shall nevertheless (especially since those objects are called by the same name, and are observed to coexist[59]), to avoid tediousness and singularity of speech, sometimes speak of them as belonging to one and the same thing.

56. Now, in order to discover by what means the magnitude of tangible objects is perceived by sight, I need only reflect on what passes in my own mind, and observe what those things be which introduce the ideas of greater or lesser into my thoughts when I look on any object. And these I find to be, *first*, the magnitude or extension of the visible object, which, being immediately perceived by sight, is connected with that other which is tangible and placed at a distance: *secondly*, the confusion or distinctness :

and *thirdly*, the vigorousness or faintness of the aforesaid visible appearance. *Cæteris paribus*, by how much the greater or lesser the visible object is, by so much the greater or lesser do I conclude the tangible object to be. But, be the idea immediately perceived by sight never so large, yet, if it be withal confused, I judge the magnitude of the thing to be but small. If it be distinct and clear, I judge it greater. And, if it be faint, I apprehend it to be yet greater. What is here meant by confusion and faintness has been explained in sect. 35.

57. Moreover, the judgments we make of greatness do, in like manner as those of distance, depend on the disposition of the eye; also on the figure, number, and situation[a] of intermediate objects, and other circumstances that have been observed to attend great or small tangible magnitudes. Thus, for instance, the very same quantity of visible extension which in the figure of a tower doth suggest the idea of great magnitude shall in the figure of a man suggest the idea of much smaller magnitude. That this is owing to the experience we have had of the usual bigness of a tower and a man, no one, I suppose, need be told.

58. It is also evident that confusion or faintness have no more a necessary connexion with little or great magnitude than they have with little or great distance. As they suggest the latter, so they suggest the former to our minds. And, by consequence, if it were not for experience, we should no more judge a faint or confused appearance to be connected with great or little magnitude than we should that it was connected with great or little distance.

59. Nor will it be found that great or small visible magnitude hath any necessary relation to great or small tangible magnitude—so that the one may certainly and infallibly be inferred from the other. But, before we come to the proof of this, it is fit we consider the difference there is betwixt the extension and figure which is the proper object of touch, and that other which is termed visible; and how the former is principally, though not immediately, taken notice of when we look at any object. This has been before mentioned[b], but we shall here inquire into the cause thereof. We regard the objects that environ us in proportion as

---

[a] 'Situation'—not in the earlier editions.   [b] Sect. 55.

they are adapted to benefit or injure our own bodies, and thereby produce in our minds the sensations of pleasure or pain. Now, bodies operating on our organs by an immediate application, and the hurt and advantage arising therefrom depending altogether on the tangible, and not at all on the visible, qualities of any object—this is a plain reason why those should be regarded by us much more than these. And for this end [chiefly[a]] the visive sense seems to have been bestowed on animals, to wit, that, by the perception of visible ideas (which in themselves are not capable of affecting or anywise altering the frame of their bodies), they may be able to foresee[b] (from the experience they have had what tangible ideas are connected with such and such visible ideas) the damage or benefit which is like to ensue upon the application of their own bodies to this or that body which is at a distance. Which foresight, how necessary it is to the preservation of an animal, every one's experience can inform him. Hence it is that, when we look at an object, the tangible figure and extension thereof are principally attended to; whilst there is small heed taken of the visible figure and magnitude, which, though more immediately perceived, do less sensibly affect us, and are not fitted to produce any alteration in our bodies.

60. That the matter of fact is true will be evident to any one who considers that a man placed at ten foot distance is thought as great as if he were placed at the distance only of five foot; which is true, not with relation to the visible, but tangible greatness of the object: the visible magnitude being far greater at one station than it is at the other.

61. Inches, feet, &c. are settled, stated lengths, whereby we measure objects and estimate their magnitude. We say, for example, an object appears to be six inches, or six foot long. Now, that this cannot be meant of visible inches, &c. is evident, because a visible inch is itself no constant determinate magnitude[c], and cannot therefore serve to mark out and determine the magnitude of any other thing. Take an inch marked upon a ruler; view it successively, at the distance of half a foot, a foot,

---

[a] Omitted in the author's last edition.
[b] i.e. what is called vision is virtually prevision. Cf. sect. 85.—See also Malebranche on the external senses, as given for the use and conservation of our bodies, and not for scientific and speculative knowledge. *Recherche*, liv. I. ch. 5, 6, 9, &c.
[c] Sect. 44.—See also sect. 55, and note.

a foot and a half, &c. from the eye: at each of which, and at all the intermediate distances, the inch shall have a different visible extension, *i.e.* there shall be more or fewer points discerned in it. Now, I ask which of all these various extensions is that stated determinate one that is agreed on for a common measure of other magnitudes? No reason can be assigned why we should pitch on one more than another. And, except there be some invariable determinate extension fixed on to be marked by the word inch, it is plain it can be used to little purpose; and to say a thing contains this or that number of inches shall imply no more than that it is extended, without bringing any particular idea of that extension into the mind. Farther, an inch and a foot, from different distances, shall both exhibit the same visible magnitude, and yet at the same time you shall say that one seems several times greater than the other. From all which it is manifest, that the judgments we make of the magnitude of objects by sight are altogether in reference to their tangible extension. Whenever we say an object is great or small, of this or that determinate measure, I say, it must be meant of the tangible and not the visible extension[a], which, though immediately perceived, is nevertheless little taken notice of.

62. Now, that there is no necessary connexion between these two distinct extensions is evident from hence—because our eyes might have been framed in such a manner as to be able to see nothing but what were less than the *minimum tangibile*. In which case it is not impossible we might have perceived all the immediate objects of sight the very same that we do now; but unto those visible appearances there would not be connected those different tangible magnitudes that are now. Which shews the judgments we make of the magnitude of things placed at a distance, from the various greatness of the immediate objects of sight, do not arise from any essential or necessary, but only a customary, tie which has been observed betwixt them.

63. Moreover, it is not only certain that any idea of sight might not have been connected with this or that idea of touch

---

[a] i. e. there are 'settled' *tangibilia*, but not 'settled' *visibilia*. Yet the sensible extension given in touch and locomotive experience is itself relative—an object being felt as larger or smaller according to the state of the organism.

we now observe to accompany it, but also that the greater visible magnitudes might have been connected with and introduced into our minds lesser tangible magnitudes, and the lesser visible magnitudes greater tangible magnitudes. Nay, that it actually is so, we have daily experience—that object which makes a strong and large appearance not seeming near so great as another the visible magnitude whereof is much less, but more faint, [66]and the appearance upper, or which is the same thing, painted lower on the retina, which faintness and situation suggest both greater magnitude and greater distance.

64. From which, and from sect. 57 and 58, it is manifest that, as we do not perceive the magnitude of objects immediately by sight, so neither do we perceive them by the mediation of anything which has a necessary connexion with them. Those ideas that now suggest unto us the various magnitudes of external objects before we touch them might possibly have suggested no such thing; or they might have signified them in a direct contrary manner, so that the very same ideas on the perception whereof we judge an object to be small might as well have served to make us conclude it great;—those ideas being in their own nature equally fitted to bring into our minds the idea of small or great, or no size at all, of outward objects[67], just as the words of any language are in their own nature indifferent to signify this or that thing, or nothing at all.

65. As we see distance so we see magnitude. And we see both in the same way that we see shame or anger in the looks of a man. Those passions are themselves invisible; they are nevertheless let in by the eye along with colours and alterations of countenance which are the immediate object of vision, and which signify them for no other reason than barely because they have been observed to accompany them. Without which experience we should no more have taken blushing for a sign of shame than of gladness.

66. We are nevertheless exceedingly prone to imagine those things which are perceived only by the mediation of others to be themselves the immediate objects of sight, or at least to have in

---

[a] What follows, to end of sect. 63, added in the author's last edition.

[b] 'outward objects,' i. e. objects of which we are percipient in—which are constituted by—our tactual and locomotive experience. See *Principles*, sect. 44.

their own nature a fitness to be suggested by them before ever
they had been experienced to coexist with them. From which
prejudice every one perhaps will not find it easy to emancipate
himself, by any the clearest convictions of reason. And there
are some grounds to think that, if there was one only invariable
and universal language in the world, and that men were born
with the faculty of speaking it, it would be the opinion of some,
that the ideas in other men's minds were properly perceived by
the ear, or had at least a necessary and inseparable tie with the
sounds that were affixed to them. All which seems to arise from
want of a due application of our discerning faculty, thereby to
discriminate between the ideas that are in our understandings,
and consider them apart from each other; which would preserve
us from confounding those that are different, and make us see
what ideas do, and what do not, include or imply this or that
other idea[a].

67. There is a celebrated phenomenon[b] the solution whereof
I shall attempt to give, by the principles that have been laid down,
in reference to the manner wherein we apprehend by sight the
magnitude of objects.—The apparent magnitude of the moon,
when placed in the horizon, is much greater than when it is in
the meridian, though the angle under which the diameter of the
moon is seen be not observed greater in the former case than in
the latter; and the horizontal moon doth not constantly appear
of the same bigness, but at some times seemeth far greater than
at others.

68. Now, in order to explain the reason of the moon's
appearing greater than ordinary in the horizon, it must be observed that the particles which compose our atmosphere do intercept the rays of light proceeding from any object to the eye; and,
by how much the greater is the portion of atmosphere interjacent
between the object and the eye, by so much the more are the rays

---

[a] Cf. sect. 144. Note, in this and the three preceding sections, the stress laid on the *arbitrariness* of the relation between the signs which suggest magnitudes or other modes of extension, and their significates—the fundamental fact of the *New Theory*, which thus resolves physical causality into a relation of signs to what they signify.

[b] In sect. 67-78, Berkeley attempts to verify the foregoing doctrine of the signs of size, by applying it to solve a phenomenon, the cause of which had been long debated among men of science—the visible magnitude of the moon and other heavenly bodies when in the horizon.

intercepted, and, by consequence, the appearance of the object rendered more faint—every object appearing more vigorous or more faint in proportion as it sendeth more or fewer rays into the eye. Now, between the eye and the moon when situated in the horizon there lies a far greater quantity of atmosphere than there does when the moon is in the meridian. Whence it comes to pass, that the appearance of the horizontal moon is fainter, and therefore, by sect. 56, it should be thought bigger in that situation than in the meridian, or in any other elevation above the horizon.

69. Farther, the air being variously impregnated, sometimes more and sometimes less, with vapours and exhalations fitted to retund and intercept the rays of light, it follows that the appearance of the horizontal moon hath not always an equal faintness, and, by consequence, that luminary, though in the very same situation, is at one time judged greater than at another.

70. That we have here given the true account of the phenomena of the horizontal moon, will, I suppose, be farther evident to any one from the following considerations:—*First*, it is plain, that which in this case suggests the idea of greater magnitude, must be something which is itself perceived; for, that which is unperceived cannot suggest to our perception any other thing[70]. *Secondly*, it must be something that does not constantly remain the same, but is subject to some change or variation; since the appearance of the horizontal moon varies, being at one time greater than at another. [*Thirdly*, it must not lie in the circumjacent or intermediate objects, such as mountains, houses, fields, &c.; because that when all those objects are excluded from sight the appearance is as great as ever[71].] And yet, *thirdly*[72], it cannot be the visible figure or magnitude; since that remains the same, or is rather lesser, by how much the moon is nearer to the horizon. It remains therefore, that the true cause is that affection or alteration of the visible appearance, which proceeds from the greater paucity of rays arriving at the eye, and which I term faintness; since this answers all the forementioned conditions, and I am not conscious of any other perception that does.

71. Add to this that in misty weather it is a common

---

[70] Cf. sect. 10.
[71] Omitted in the author's last edition. Cf. sect. 76, 77.—The explanation in question is attributed to Alhazen, and by Bacon to Ptolemy, while it is sanctioned by eminent scientific names before and since Berkeley.
[72] "Fourthly" in the second edition. Cf. what follows with sect. 74. Why 'lesser'?

observation, that the appearance of the horizontal moon is far larger than usual, which greatly conspires with and strengthens our opinion. Neither would it prove in the least irreconcilable with what we have said, if the horizontal moon should chance sometimes to seem enlarged beyond its usual extent, even in more serene weather. For, we must not only have regard to the mist which happens to be in the place where we stand; we ought also to take into our thoughts the whole sum of vapours and exhalations which lie betwixt the eye and the moon: all which cooperating to render the appearance of the moon more faint, and thereby increase its magnitude, it may chance to appear greater than it usually does even in the horizontal position, at a time when, though there be no extraordinary fog or haziness just in the place where we stand, yet the air between the eye and the moon, taken altogether, may be loaded with a greater quantity of interspersed vapours and exhalations than at other times[13].

72. It may be objected that, in consequence of our principles, the interposition of a body in some degree opaque, which may intercept a great part of the rays of light, should render the appearance of the moon in the meridian as large as when it is viewed in the horizon. To which I answer, it is not faintness anyhow applied that suggests greater magnitude; there being no necessary, but only an experimental connexion between those two things. It follows that the faintness which enlarges the appearance must be applied in such sort, and with such circumstances, as have been observed to attend the vision of great magnitudes. When from a distance we behold great objects, the particles of the intermediate air and vapours, which are themselves unperceivable, do interrupt the rays of light, and thereby render the appearance less strong and vivid. Now, faintness of appearance caused in this sort hath been experienced to coexist with great magnitude. But when it is caused by the interposition of an opaque sensible body, this circumstance alters the case; so that a faint appearance this way caused does not suggest greater magnitude, because it hath not been experienced to co-exist with it.

73. Faintness, as well as all other ideas or perceptions

---

[13] When Berkeley, some years afterwards, visited Italy, he remarked that distant objects appeared to him much nearer than they really were—a phenomenon which he attributed to the comparative purity of the southern air.

which suggest magnitude or distance, does it in the same way that words suggest the notions to which they are annexed. Now, it is known a word pronounced with certain circumstances, or in a certain context with other words, hath not always the same import and signification that it hath when pronounced in some other circumstances, or different context of words. The very same visible appearance as to faintness and all other respects, if placed on high, shall not suggest the same magnitude that it would if it were seen at an equal distance on a level with the eye. The reason whereof is, that we are rarely accustomed to view objects at a great height; our concerns lie among things situated rather before than above us; and accordingly our eyes are not placed on the top of our heads, but in such a position as is most convenient for us to see distant objects standing in our way. And, this situation of them being a circumstance which usually attends the vision of distant objects, we may from hence account for (what is commonly observed) an object's appearing of different magnitude, even with respect to its horizontal extension, on the top of a steeple, *e.g.* a hundred feet high, to one standing below, from what it would if placed at a hundred feet distance on a level with his eye. For, it hath been shewn that the judgment we make on the magnitude of a thing depends not on the visible appearance alone, but also on divers other circumstances, any one of which being omitted or varied may suffice to make some alteration in our judgment. Hence, the circumstance of viewing a distant object in such a situation as is usual, and suits with the ordinary posture of the head and eyes being omitted, and instead thereof a different situation of the object, which requires a different posture of the head, taking place—it is not to be wondered at if the magnitude be judged different. But it will be demanded, why a high object should constantly appear less than an equidistant low object of the same dimensions; for so it is observed to be. It may indeed be granted that the variation of some circumstances may vary the judgment made on the magnitude of high objects, which we are less used to look at; but it does not hence appear why they should be judged less rather than greater? I answer, that in case the magnitude of distant objects was suggested by the extent of their visible appearance alone, and thought proportional thereto, it is certain they would then be judged much less than now they seem to be. (Vid. sect. 79.) But, several circumstances concurring to form the judgment we make on the magnitude of distant objects, by means of which they appear far larger than others whose visible appearance hath an equal or even greater extension; it follows that upon the change or omission of any of those circumstances which are wont to attend the vision of distant objects, and so come to influence the judgments made on their magnitude, they shall proportionably appear less than otherwise they would. For, any of those things that caused an object to be thought greater than in proportion to its visible extension being either omitted, or applied without the usual circumstances, the judgment depends more entirely on the visible extension, and consequently the object must be judged less. Thus, in the present case the situation of the thing seen being different from what it usually is in those objects we have occasion to view, and whose magnitude we observe, it follows that the very same object being a hundred feet high, should seem less than if it was a hundred feet off, on (or nearly on) a level with the eye. What has been here set forth seems to me to have no small share in contributing to magnify the appearance of the horizontal moon, and deserves not to be passed over in the explication of it.

74. If we attentively consider the phenomenon before us, we shall find the not discerning between the mediate and immediate objects of sight to be the chief cause of the difficulty that occurs in the explication of it. The magnitude of the visible moon, or that which is the proper and immediate object of vision[74], is no greater when the moon is in the horizon than when it is in the meridian. How comes it, therefore, to seem greater in one situation than the other? What is it can put this cheat on the understanding? It has no other perception of the moon than what it gets by sight. And that which is seen is of the same extent—I say, the visible appearance hath the very same or rather a less magnitude, when the moon is viewed in the horizontal than when in the meridional position. And yet it is esteemed greater in the former than in the latter. Herein consists the difficulty, which doth vanish and admit of a most easy solution, if we consider that as the visible moon is not greater in the horizon than

---

[74] i.e. the pure sense-given intuition, apart from any synthetic operation of suggestion and thought.

in the meridian, so neither is it thought to be so. It hath been already shewn that, in any act of vision, the visible object absolutely, or in itself, is little taken notice of—the mind still carrying its view from that to some tangible ideas, which have been observed to be connected with it, and by that means come to be suggested by it. So that when a thing is said to appear great or small, or whatever estimate be made of the magnitude of any thing, this is meant not of the visible but of the tangible object. This duly considered, it will be no hard matter to reconcile the seeming contradiction there is, that the moon should appear of a different bigness, the visible magnitude thereof remaining still the same. For, by sect. 56, the very same visible extension, with a different faintness, shall suggest a different tangible extension. When therefore the horizontal moon is said to appear greater than the meridional moon, this must be understood, not of a greater visible extension, but of a greater tangible extension, which, by reason of the more than ordinary faintness of the visible appearance, is suggested to the mind along with it.

75. Many attempts have been made by learned men to account for this appearance[75]. Gassendus[76], Descartes[77], Hobbes[78], and several others have employed their thoughts on that subject; but how fruitless and unsatisfactory their endeavours have been is sufficiently shewn in the *Philosophical Transactions*[79] (Numb. 187, p. 314), where you may see their several opinions at large set forth and confuted, not without some surprise at the gross blunders that ingenious men have been forced into by endeavouring to reconcile this appearance with the ordinary principles of optics[80]. Since the writing of which there hath been published in the

---

[75] In Riccioli's *Almagest*, II. lib. X. sect. 6. quest. 14. we have an account of the many hypotheses then current to account for the apparent magnitude of the horizontal moon and other heavenly bodies.

[76] See Gassendi's 'Epistolae quatuor de apparente magnitudine solis humilis et sublimis,' —*Opera*, tom. III. pp. 420—477. Cf. Appendix to this *Essay*, p. 110.

[77] See *Dioptrique*, VI.

[78] *Opera Latina*, vol. I. p. 376, vol. II. pp. 26—61; *English Works*, vol. I. p. 462. (Molesworth's Edition.)

[79] The paper in the Transactions is by Molyneux.

[80] See Smith's *Optics*, pp. 64—67, and Remarks, pp. 48, &c. At p. 55 Berkeley's New Theory is referred to, and pronounced to be at variance with experience. Smith concludes by saying, that in 'the second (?) edition of Berkeley's *Essay*, and also in a Vindication and Explanation of it (called the *Visual Language*) very lately published, the author has made some additions to his solution of the said phenomenon, but seeing it still involves and depends on the principle of faintness, I may leave the rest of it to the reader's consideration.' This passage, which appeared in 1738, is one of the very few early references to Berkeley's *New Theory Vindicated*.

Transactions (Numb. 187, p. 323) another paper relating to the same affair, by the celebrated Dr. Wallis, wherein he attempts to account for that phenomenon, which, though it seems not to contain anything new, or different from what had been said before by others, I shall nevertheless consider in this place.

76. His opinion, in short, is this:—We judge not of the magnitude of an object by the optic angle alone, but by the optic angle in conjunction with the distance. Hence, though the angle remain the same, or even become less, yet, if withal the distance seem to have been increased, the object shall appear greater. Now, one way whereby we estimate the distance of anything is by the number and extent of the intermediate objects. When therefore the moon is seen in the horizon, the variety of fields, houses, &c., together with the large prospect of the wide extended land or sea that lies between the eye and the utmost limb of the horizon, suggest unto the mind the idea of greater distance, and consequently magnify the appearance. And this, according to Dr. Wallis, is the true account of the extraordinary largeness attributed by the mind to the horizontal moon, at a time when the angle subtended by its diameter is not one jot greater than it used to be.

77. With reference to this opinion, not to repeat what has been already said concerning distance[a], I shall only observe, *first*, that if the prospect of interjacent objects be that which suggests the idea of farther distance, and this idea of farther distance be the cause that brings into the mind the idea of greater magnitude, it should hence follow that if one looked at the horizontal moon from behind a wall, it would appear no bigger than ordinary. For, in that case, the wall interposing cuts off all that prospect of sea and land, &c. which might otherwise increase the apparent distance, and thereby the apparent magnitude of the moon. Nor will it suffice to say, the memory doth even then suggest all that extent of land, &c. which lies within the horizon—which suggestion occasions a sudden judgment of sense, that the moon is farther off and larger than usual. For, ask any man who from such a station beholding the horizontal moon shall think her greater than usual, whether he hath at that time in his mind any idea of the intermediate objects, or long tract of land that lies

[a] Sect. 3—51.

between his eye and the extreme edge of the horizon? and whether it be that idea which is the cause of his making the aforementioned judgment? He will, without doubt, reply in the negative, and declare the horizontal moon shall appear greater than the meridional, though he never thinks of all or any of those things that lie between him and it. [And as for the absurdity of any idea's introducing into the mind another, whilst itself is not perceived, this has already fallen under our observation, and is too evident to need any farther enlargement on it[a].] *Secondly*, it seems impossible, by this hypothesis, to account for the moon's appearing, in the very same situation, at one time greater than at another; which, nevertheless, has been shewn to be very agreeable to the principles we have laid down, and receives a most easy and natural explication from them.—[b] For the further clearing up of this point, it is to be observed, that what we immediately and properly see are only lights and colours in sundry situations and shades, and degrees of faintness and clearness, confusion and distinctness. All which visible objects are only in the mind; nor do they suggest aught external[c], whether distance or magnitude, otherwise than by habitual connexion, as words do things. We are also to remark, that beside the straining of the eyes, and beside the vivid and faint, the distinct and confused appearances (which, bearing some proportion to lines and angles, have been substituted instead of them in the foregoing part of this Treatise), there are other means which suggest both distance and magnitude—particularly the situation of visible points or objects, as upper or lower; the former suggesting a farther distance and greater magnitude, the latter a nearer distance and lesser magnitude—all which is an effect only of custom and experience, there being really nothing intermediate in the line of distance between the uppermost and the lowermost, which are both equidistant, or rather at no distance from the eye; as there is also nothing in upper or lower which by necessary connexion should suggest greater or lesser magnitude. Now, as these customary experimental means of suggesting distance do likewise suggest magnitude, so they suggest the one as immediately as the other. I say,

---

[a] This sentence omitted in the author's last edition.
[b] What follows to the end of this section is not contained in the two first editions.
[c] i. e. tangible.

they do not (vide sect. 53) first suggest distance, and then leave the mind from thence to infer or compute magnitude, but suggest magnitude as immediately and directly as they suggest distance.

78. This phenomenon of the horizontal moon is a clear instance of the insufficiency of lines and angles for explaining the way wherein the mind perceives and estimates the magnitude of outward objects. There is, nevertheless, a use of computation by them[15]—In order to determine the apparent magnitude of things, so far as they have a connexion with and are proportional to those other ideas or perceptions which are the true and immediate occasions that suggest to the mind the apparent magnitude of things. But this in general may, I think, be observed concerning mathematical computation in optics—that it can never[16] be very precise and exact[17], since the judgments we make of the magnitude of external things do often depend on several circumstances which are not proportional to or capable of being defined by lines and angles.

79. From what has been said, we may safely deduce this consequence, to wit, that a man born blind, and made to see, would, at first opening of his eyes, make a very different judgment of the magnitude of objects intromitted by them from what others do. He would not consider the ideas of sight with reference to, or as having any connexion with the ideas of touch. His view of them being entirely terminated within themselves, he can no otherwise judge them great or small than as they contain a greater or lesser number of visible points. Now, it being certain that any visible point can cover or exclude from view only one other visible point, it follows that whatever object intercepts the view of another hath an equal number of visible points with it; and, consequently, they shall both be thought by him to have the same magnitude. Hence, it is evident one in those circumstances would judge his thumb, with which he might hide a tower, or hinder its being seen, equal to that tower; or his hand, the interposition whereof might conceal the firmament from his view, equal to the firmament: how great an inequality soever there may, in our appre-

---

[15] Cf. sect. 38; and *Theory of Vision Vindicated*, sect. 31.
[16] "Never"—"hardly," in two first editions.
[17] Cf. Appendix, p. 110.—See Smith's *Optics*, B. I. ch. v., and *Remarks*, p. 56, in which he 'leaves it to be considered, whether the said phenomenon is not as clear an instance of the insufficiency of faintness' as of mathematical computation.

hensions, seem to be betwixt those two things, because of the customary and close connexion that has grown up in our minds between the objects of sight and touch, whereby the very different and distinct ideas of those two senses are so blended and confounded together as to be mistaken for one and the same thing—, out of which prejudice we cannot easily extricate ourselves.

80. For the better explaining the nature of vision, and setting the manner wherein we perceive magnitudes in a due light, I shall proceed to make some observations concerning matters relating thereto, whereof the want of reflection, and duly separating between tangible and visible ideas, is apt to create in us mistaken and confused notions. And, *first*, I shall observe, that the *minimum visibile* is exactly equal in all beings whatsoever that are endowed with the visive faculty[a]. No exquisite formation of the eye, no peculiar sharpness of sight, can make it less in one creature than in another; for, it not being distinguishable into parts, nor in anywise consisting of them, it must necessarily be the same to all. For, suppose it otherwise, and that the *minimum visibile* of a mite, for instance, be less than the *minimum visibile* of a man; the latter therefore may, by detraction of some part, be made equal to the former. It doth therefore consist of parts, which is inconsistent with the notion of a *minimum visibile* or point.

81. It will, perhaps, be objected, that the *minimum visibile* of a man doth really and in itself contain parts whereby it surpasses that of a mite, though they are not perceivable by the man. To which I answer, the *minimum visibile* having (in like manner as all other the proper and immediate objects of sight) been shewn not to have any existence without the mind of him who sees it, it follows there cannot be any part of it that is not actually per-

---

[a] A favourite doctrine with Berkeley, according to whose theory there can be no absolute visible (or tangible) magnitude, the *minimum* being that *perceivable*, and thus relative to the percipient. This section is thus criticised, in January, 1752, in a letter signed 'Anti-Berkeley,' in the *Gent. Mag.* (vol. XXII. p. 11): 'Upon what his lordship asserts with respect to the *minimum visibile*, I would observe that it is certain that there are infinite numbers of animals which are imperceptible to the naked eye, and cannot be perceived but by the help of a microscope; consequently there are animals whose whole bodies are far less than the *minimum visibile* of a man. Doubtless these animals have eyes, and, if their *minimum visibile* were equal to that of a man, it would follow that they cannot perceive anything but what is much larger than their whole body; and therefore their own bodies must be invisible to them, because we know they are so to men, whose *minimum visibile* is asserted by his lordship to be equal to theirs.' Cf. Appendix to *Essay*, p. 111.

ceived and therefore visible. Now, for any object to contain several distinct visible parts, and at the same time to be a *minimum visibile*, is a manifest contradiction.

82. Of these visible points we see at all times an equal number. It is every whit as great when our view is contracted and bounded by near objects as when it is extended to larger and remoter ones. For, it being impossible that one *minimum visibile* should obscure or keep out of sight more than one other, it is a plain consequence that, when my view is on all sides bounded by the walls of my study, I see just as many visible points as I could in case that, by the removal of the study-walls and all other obstructions, I had a full prospect of the circumjacent fields, mountains, sea, and open firmament. For, so long as I am shut up within the walls, by their interposition every point of the external objects is covered from my view. But, each point that is seen being able to cover or exclude from sight one only other corresponding point, it follows that, whilst my sight is confined to those narrow walls, I see as many points or *minima visibilia* as I should were those walls away, by looking on all the external objects whose prospect is intercepted by them. Whenever, therefore, we are said to have a greater prospect at one time than another, this must be understood with relation, not to the proper and immediate, but the secondary and mediate objects of vision—which, as hath been shewn, do properly belong to the touch.

83. The visive faculty, considered with reference to its immediate objects, may be found to labour of two defects. *First*, in respect of the extent or number of visible points that are at once perceivable by it, which is narrow and limited to a certain degree. It can take in at one view but a certain determinate number of *minima visibilia*, beyond which it cannot extend its prospect. *Secondly*, our sight is defective in that its view is not only narrow, but also for the most part confused. Of those things that we take in at one prospect, we can see but a few at once clearly and unconfusedly; and the more we fix our sight on any one object, by so much the darker and more indistinct shall the rest appear.

84. Corresponding to these two defects of sight, we may imagine as many perfections, to wit, 1st. That of comprehending in one view a greater number of visible points; 2dly. of being able to view them all equally and at once, with the utmost clearness

and distinction. That those perfections are not actually in some intelligences of a different order and capacity from ours, it is impossible for us to know[m].

85. In neither of those two ways do microscopes contribute to the improvement of sight. For, when we look through a microscope, we neither see more visible points, nor are the collateral points more distinct than when we look with the naked eye at objects placed at a due distance. A microscope brings us, as it were, into a new world. It presents us with a new scene of visible objects, quite different from what we behold with the naked eye. But herein consists the most remarkable difference, to wit, that whereas the objects perceived by the eye alone have a certain connexion with tangible objects, whereby we are taught to foresee what will ensue upon the approach or application of distant objects to the parts of our own body—which much conduceth to its preservation"[n]—there is not the like connexion between things tangible and those visible objects that are perceived by help of a fine microscope.

86. Hence, it is evident that, were our eyes turned into the nature of microscopes, we should not be much benefitted by the change. We should be deprived of the forementioned advantage we at present receive by the visive faculty, and have left us only the empty amusement of seeing, without any other benefit arising from it. But, in that case, it will perhaps be said, our sight would be endued with a far greater sharpness and penetration than it now hath. But I would fain know wherein consists that sharpness which is esteemed so great an excellency of sight. It is certain, from what we have already shewn[91], that the *minimum visibile* is never greater or lesser, but in all cases constantly the same. And, in the case of microscopical eyes, I see only this difference, to wit, that upon the ceasing of a certain observable connexion betwixt the divers perceptions of sight and touch, which before enabled us to regulate our actions by the eye, it would now be rendered utterly unserviceable to that purpose.

87. Upon the whole it seems that, if we consider the use and

---

[m] These two defects are common to every form of the intuitive consciousness of man. See Locke's *Essay*, II. 10, on the defects of memory. It is this defective power of intuition which calls for reasoning, to assist our finite consciousness—reasoning being, as Pascal says, the sign at once of our dignity and our degradation.

[n] Sect. 59.

[o] Sect. 80—81.

end of sight, together with the present state and circumstances of our being, we shall not find any great cause to complain of any defect or imperfection in it, or easily conceive how it could be mended. With such admirable wisdom is that faculty contrived, both for the pleasure and convenience of life.

88. Having finished what I intended to say concerning the distance and magnitude of objects, I come now to treat of the manner wherein the mind perceives by sight their situation[93]. Among the discoveries of the last age, it is reputed none of the least, that the manner of vision has been more clearly explained than ever it had been before. There is, at this day, no one ignorant that the pictures of external objects are painted on the retina or fund of the eye; that we can see nothing which is not so painted; and that, according as the picture is more distinct or confused, so also is the perception we have of the object[94]. But then, in this explication of vision, there occurs one mighty difficulty—The objects are painted in an inverted order on the bottom of the eye: the upper part of any object being painted on the lower part of the eye, and the lower part of the object on the upper part of the eye; and so also as to right and left. Since, therefore, the pictures are thus inverted, it is demanded how it comes to pass that we see the objects erect and in their natural posture?

89. In answer to this difficulty, we are told that the mind, perceiving an impulse of a ray of light on the upper part of the eye, considers this ray as coming in a direct line from the lower part of the object; and, in like manner, tracing the ray that strikes on the lower part of the eye, it is directed to the upper part of the object. Thus, in the adjacent figure, C, the lower point of the object ABC, is projected on c the upper part of the eye. So likewise, the highest point A is projected on a the lowest part of the eye; which makes the representation cba inverted. But the mind—considering the stroke that is made on c as coming in the straight line Cc from the lower end of

---

[93] Sect. 88—119 relate to the nature, invisibility, and arbitrary signs of Situation, including the celebrated paradox of erect vision, by means of inverted images on the retina. Cf. *Theory of Vision Vindicated*, Sect. 44—53.
[94] Cf. sect. 2, 114, 116, 118.

the object; and the stroke or impulse on *a*, as coming in the line *Aa* from the upper end of the object—is directed to make

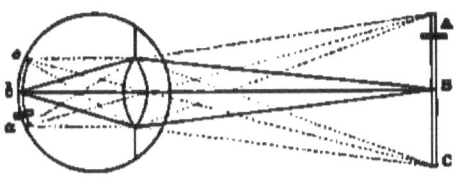

a right judgment of the situation of the object *ABC*, notwithstanding the picture of it be inverted. Moreover, this is illustrated by conceiving a blind man, who, holding in his hands two sticks that cross each other, doth with them touch the extremities of an object, placed in a perpendicular situation. It is certain this man will judge that to be the upper part of the object which he touches with the stick held in the undermost hand, and that to be the lower part of the object which he touches with the stick in his uppermost hand. This is the common explication of the erect appearance of objects, which is generally received and acquiesced in, being (as Mr. Molyneux tells us, *Diopt.* part ii. ch. vii. p. 289) 'allowed by all men as satisfactory.'

90. But this account to me does not seem in any degree true. Did I perceive[n] those impulses, decussations, and directions of the rays of light, in like manner as hath been set forth, then, indeed, it would not at first view be altogether void of probability. And there might be some pretence for the comparison of the blind man and his cross sticks. But the case is far otherwise. I know very well that I perceive no such thing. And, of consequence, I cannot thereby make an estimate of the situation of objects. Moreover, I appeal to any one's experience, whether he be conscious to himself that he thinks on the intersection made by the radius pencils, or pursues the impulses they give in right lines, whenever he perceives by sight the position of any object? To me it seems evident that crossing and tracing of the rays, &c. is never thought on by children, idiots, or, in truth, by any other, save only those who

[n] Sect. 10.

have applied themselves to the study of optics. And for the mind to judge of the situation of objects by those things without perceiving them, or to perceive them without knowing it[23], take which you please, it is perfectly beyond my comprehension. Add to this, that the explaining the manner of vision by the example of cross sticks, and hunting for the object along the axes of the radius pencils, doth suppose the proper objects of sight to be perceived at a distance from us, contrary to what hath been demonstrated[26]. [We may therefore venture to pronounce this opinion, concerning the way wherein the mind perceives the erect appearance of objects, to be of a piece with those other tenets of writers in optics, which in the foregoing parts of this treatise we have had occasion to examine and refute[27].]

91. It remains, therefore, that we look for some other explication of this difficulty. And I believe it not impossible to find one, provided we examine it to the bottom, and carefully distinguish between the ideas of sight and touch; which cannot be too oft inculcated in treating of vision[28]. But, more especially throughout the consideration of this affair, we ought to carry that distinction in our thoughts, for that from want of a right understanding thereof, the difficulty of explaining erect vision seems chiefly to arise.

92. In order to disentangle our minds from whatever prejudices we may entertain with relation to the subject in hand, nothing seems more apposite than the taking into our thoughts the case of one born blind, and afterwards, when grown up, made to see. And—though perhaps it may not be a task altogether easy and familiar to us, to divest ourselves entirely of the experiences received from sight, so as to be able to put our thoughts exactly in the posture of such a one's—we must, nevertheless, as far as possible, endeavour to frame true conceptions of what might reasonably be supposed to pass in his mind[29].

---

[25] Sect. 19.
[26] Sect. 2—51.
[27] Omitted in author's last edition.
[28] This is Berkeley's universal solvent of the psychological difficulties in optics and in sense-perception. The synthesis or construction in thought of the heterogeneous phenomena presented in the different senses is due, with him, to our tendency to associate their arbitrary but constant connexions—not to a mysterious percipient act, in which we are originally cognisant of the co-existence of sensible qualities in individual things.
[29] Cf. sect. 103, 106, 110, 139, &c. Berkeley treats this case hypothetically in the Essay, in defect of actual experiments, now so often referred to from Cheselden downwards. See however Appendix, p. 75; and Theory of Vision Vindicated, sect. 71.

93. It is certain that a man actually blind, and who had continued so from his birth, would, by the sense of feeling, attain to have ideas of upper and lower. By the motion of his hand, he might discern the situation of any tangible object placed within his reach. That part on which he felt himself supported, or towards which he perceived his body to gravitate, he would term 'lower,' and the contrary to this 'upper;' and accordingly denominate whatsoever objects he touched.

94. But then, whatever judgments he makes concerning the situation of objects are confined to those only that are perceivable by touch. All those things that are intangible, and of a spiritual nature—his thoughts and desires, his passions, and in general all the modifications of his soul—to these he would never apply the terms upper and lower, except only in a metaphorical sense. He may perhaps, by way of allusion, speak of high or low thoughts: but those terms, in their proper signification, would never be applied to anything that was not conceived to exist without the mind. For, a man born blind, and remaining in the same state, could mean nothing else by the words higher and lower than a greater or lesser distance from the earth—which distance he would measure by the motion or application of his hand, or some other part of his body. It is, therefore, evident that all those things which, in respect of each other, would by him be thought higher or lower, must be such as were conceived to exist without his mind, in the ambient space[100].

95. Whence it plainly follows, that such a one, if we suppose him made to see, would not at first sight think that anything he saw was high or low, erect or inverted. For, it hath been already demonstrated, in sect. 41, that he would not think the things he perceived by sight to be at any distance from him, or without his mind. The objects to which he had hitherto been used to apply the terms up and down, high and low, were such only as affected, or were some way perceived by his touch. But, the proper objects of vision make a new set of ideas, perfectly distinct and different from the former, and which can in no sort make themselves perceived by touch. There is, therefore, nothing at all that could induce him to think those terms applicable to them. Nor would he

---

[100] i. e. tangible things. Cf. *Principles*, sect. 44.

ever think it, till such time as he had observed their connexion with tangible objects, and the same prejudice[1] began to insinuate itself into his understanding, which, from their infancy, had grown up in the understandings of other men.

96. To set this matter in a clearer light, I shall make use of an example. Suppose the above-mentioned blind person, by his touch, perceives a man to stand erect. Let us inquire into the manner of this. By the application of his hand to the several parts of a human body, he had perceived different tangible ideas, which being collected into sundry complex ones have distinct names annexed to them. Thus, one combination of a certain tangible figure, bulk, and consistency of parts is called the head; another the hand; a third the foot, and so of the rest—all which complex ideas could, in his understanding, be made up only of ideas perceivable by touch. He had also, by his touch, obtained an idea of earth or ground, towards which he perceives the parts of his body to have a natural tendency. Now—by 'erect' nothing more being meant than that perpendicular position of a man wherein his feet are nearest to the earth—if the blind person, by moving his hand over the parts of the man who stands before him, do perceive the tangible ideas that compose the head to be farthest from, and those that compose the feet to be nearest to, that other combination of tangible ideas which he calls earth, he will denominate that man erect. But, if we suppose him on a sudden to receive his sight, and that he behold a man standing before him, it is evident, in that case, he would neither judge the man he sees to be erect nor inverted; for he, never having known those terms applied to any other save tangible things, or which existed in the space without him, and what he sees neither being tangible, nor perceived as existing without, he could not know that, in propriety of language, they were applicable to it.

97. Afterwards, when, upon turning his head or eyes[2] up and down to the right and left, he shall observe the visible objects to change, and shall also attain to know that they are called by the same names, and connected with the objects perceived by touch; then, indeed, he will come to speak of them and their situation in

---

[1] The 'prejudice,' to wit, which Berkeley sought, by his mental analysis of vision, to dissolve. Cf. *Theory of Vision Vindicated*, sect. 35.

[2] i.e. by locomotive experience in the organ.

the same terms that he has been used to apply to tangible things: and those that he perceives by turning up his eyes he will call upper, and those that by turning down his eyes he will call lower.

98. And this seems to me the true reason why he should think those objects uppermost that are painted on the lower part of his eye. For, by turning the eye up they shall be distinctly seen; as likewise they that are painted on the highest part of the eye shall be distinctly seen by turning the eye down, and are for that reason esteemed lowest. For, we have shewn that to the immediate objects of sight, considered in themselves, he would not attribute the terms high and low. It must therefore be on account of some circumstances which are observed to attend them. And these, it is plain, are the actions of turning the eye up and down, which suggest a very obvious reason why the mind should denominate the objects of sight accordingly high or low[a]. And, without this motion of the eye, this turning it up and down in order to discern different objects, doubtless 'erect,' 'inverse,' and other the like terms relating to the position of tangible objects, would never have been transferred, or in any degree apprehended to belong to the ideas of sight—the mere act of seeing including nothing in it to that purpose; whereas the different situations of the eye naturally direct the mind to make a suitable judgment of the situation of objects intromitted by it.

99. Farther, when he has by experience learned the connexion there is between the several ideas of sight and touch, he will be able, by the perception he has of the situation of visible things in respect of one another, to make a sudden and true estimate of the situation of outward, tangible things corresponding to them. And thus it is he shall perceive[1] by sight the situation of external[2] objects, which do not properly fall under that sense.

100. I know we are very prone to think that, if just made to see, we should judge of the situation of visible things as we do now. But, we are also as prone to think that, at first sight, we should in the same way apprehend the distance and magnitude of objects,

---

[a] This briefly is Berkeley's solution of 'the knot about inverted images.'

[1] i.e. mediately—visible objects, *per se*, having no place or situation at all. Pure vision and optics have nothing to do with 'high' and 'low,' 'great' and 'inverted,' in the real meaning of these terms.

[2] i.e. tangible.

as we do now; which hath been shewn to be a false and groundless persuasion. And, for the like reasons, the same censure may be passed on the positive assurance that most men, before they have thought sufficiently of the matter, might have of their being able to determine by the eye, at first view, whether objects were erect or inverse.

101. It will perhaps be objected to our opinion, that a man, for instance, being thought erect when his feet are next the earth, and inverted when his head is next the earth, it doth hence follow that, by the mere act of vision, without any experience or altering the situation of the eye, we should have determined whether he were erect or inverted. For both the earth itself, and the limbs of the man who stands thereon, being equally perceived by sight, one cannot choose seeing what part of the man is nearest the earth, and what part farthest from it, *i.e.* whether he be erect or inverted.

102. To which I answer, the ideas which constitute the tangible earth and man are entirely different from those which constitute the visible earth and man. Nor was it possible, by virtue of the visive faculty alone, without superadding any experience of touch, or altering the position of the eye, ever to have known, or so much as suspected, there had been any relation or connexion between them. Hence, a man at first view would not denominate anything he saw, 'earth,' or 'head,' or 'foot;' and consequently, he could not tell, by the mere act of vision, whether the head or feet were nearest the earth. Nor, indeed, would we have thereby any thought of earth or man, erect or inverse, at all—which will be made yet more evident, if we nicely observe, and make a particular comparison between, the ideas of both senses.

103. That which I see is only variety of light and colours. That which I feel is hard or soft, hot or cold, rough or smooth. What similitude, what connexion, have those ideas with these? Or, how is it possible that any one should see reason to give one and the same name* to combinations of ideas so very different, before he had experienced their co-existence? We do not find there is any necessary connexion betwixt this or that tangible quality, and any colour whatsoever. And we may sometimes per-

---

* e. g. 'extension,' which, according to Berkeley, is an equivocal term, common (in two quite different meanings) to *visibilia* and *tangibilia*. Cf. sect. 139, 140.

celve colours, where there is nothing to be felt. All which doth make it manifest that no man, at first receiving of his sight[1], would know there was any agreement between this or that particular object of his sight and any object of touch he had been already acquainted with. The colours therefore of the head would to him no more suggest the idea of head[a] than they would the idea of feet.

104. Farther, we have at large shewn (vid. sect. 63 and 64) there is no discoverable necessary connexion between any given visible magnitude and any one particular tangible magnitude; but that it is entirely the result of custom and experience, and depends on foreign and accidental circumstances, that we can, by the perception of visible extension, inform ourselves what may be the extension of any tangible object connected with it. Hence, it is certain, that neither the visible magnitude of head or foot would bring along with them into the mind, at first opening of the eyes, the respective tangible magnitudes of those parts.

105. By the foregoing section, it is plain the visible figure of any part of the body hath no necessary connexion with the tangible figure thereof, so as at first sight to suggest it to the mind. For, figure is the termination of magnitude. Whence it follows that no visible magnitude having in its own nature an aptness to suggest any one particular tangible magnitude, so neither can any visible figure be inseparably connected with its corresponding tangible figure, so as of itself, and in a way prior to experience, it might suggest it to the understanding. This will be farther evident, if we consider that what seems smooth and round to the touch may to sight, if viewed through a microscope, seem quite otherwise.

106. From all which, laid together and duly considered, we may clearly deduce this inference:—In the first act of vision, no idea entering by the eye would have a perceivable connexion with the ideas to which the names earth, man, head, foot, &c. were annexed in the understanding of a person blind from his birth; so as in any sort to introduce them into his mind, or make themselves be called by the same names, and reputed the same things with them, as afterwards they come to be.

107. There doth, nevertheless, remain one difficulty, which

---

[1] Cf. sect. 93, 1:6, 110, 128.   [a] i. e. real or tangible head.

to some may seem to press hard on our opinion, and deserve not
to be passed over. For, though it be granted that neither the colour,
size, nor figure of the visible feet have any necessary connexion
with the ideas that compose the tangible feet, so as to bring them
at first sight into my mind, or make me in danger of confounding
them, before I had been used to and for some time experienced
their connexion; yet thus much seems undeniable, namely, that the
number of the visible feet being the same with that of the tangible
feet, I may from hence, without any experience of sight, reasonably conclude that they represent or are connected with the feet
rather than the head. I say, it seems the idea of two visible feet
will sooner suggest to the mind the idea of two tangible feet than
of one head—so that the blind man, upon first reception of the
visive faculty, might know which were the feet or two, and which
the head or one.

108. In order to get clear of this seeming difficulty, we need
only observe that diversity of visible objects does not necessarily
infer diversity of tangible objects corresponding to them. A
picture painted with great variety of colours affects the touch in
one uniform manner; it is therefore evident that I do not, by any
necessary consecution, independent of experience, judge of the
number of things tangible from the number of things visible.
I should not therefore at first opening my eyes conclude that
because I see two I shall feel two. How, therefore, can I, before
experience teaches me, know that the visible legs, because two,
are connected with the tangible legs; or the visible head, because
one, is connected with the tangible head? The truth is, the things
I see are so very different and heterogeneous from the things I
feel that the perception of the one would never have suggested
the other to my thoughts, or enabled me to pass the least judgment
thereon, until I had experienced their connexion[a].

---

[a] Cf. sect. 140, 143. In *Gent. Mag.* (vol. XXII. p. 12), 'Anti-Berkeley' suggests the case of one born blind. 'This man' he adds, 'would, by being accustomed to feel one hand with the other, have perceived that the extremity of the hand was divided into fingers—that the extremities of these fingers were distinguished by certain hard, smooth surfaces, of a different texture from the rest of the fingers—and that each finger had certain joints or flexures. Now, if this man was restored to sight, and immediately viewed his hand before he touched it again, it is manifest that the divisions of the extremity of the hand into fingers would be visibly perceived. He would note too the small spaces at the extremity of each finger, which affected his sight differently from the rest of the fingers; upon moving his fingers he would see the joints. Though therefore, by means of this lately acquired sense of seeing, the object affected his mind in a new and different

109. But, for a fuller illustration of this matter, it ought to be considered, that number (however some may reckon it amongst the primary qualities[16]) is nothing fixed and settled, really existing in things themselves. It is entirely the creature of the mind, considering either a simple idea by itself, or any combination of simple ideas to which it gives one name, and so makes it pass for a unit. According as the mind variously combines its ideas, the unit varies; and as the unit, so the number, which is only a collection of units, doth also vary. We call a window one, a chimney one; and yet a house, in which there are many windows and many chimneys, has an equal right to be called one; and many houses go to the making of one city. In these and the like instances, it is evident the *unit* constantly relates to the particular draughts the mind makes of its ideas, to which it affixes names, and wherein it includes more or less, as best suits its own ends and purposes. Whatever therefore the mind considers as one, that is an unit. Every combination of ideas is considered as one thing by the mind, and in token thereof is marked by one name. Now, this naming and combining together of ideas is perfectly arbitrary, and done by the mind in such sort as experience shews it to be most convenient—without which our ideas had never been collected into such sundry distinct combinations as they now are.

110. Hence, it follows that a man born blind, and afterwards, when grown up, made to see, would not, in the first act of vision, parcel out the ideas of sight into the same distinct collections that others do who have experienced which do regularly co-exist and are proper to be bundled up together under one name. He would not, for example, make into one complex idea, and thereby esteem and unite all those particular ideas which constitute the visible head or foot. For, there can be no reason assigned why he should do so, barely upon his seeing a man stand upright before him. There crowd into his mind the ideas which compose the

---

manner from what it did before, yet, as by *touch* he had acquired the knowledge of these several divisions, marks, and distinctions of the hand, and, as the new object of *sight* appeared to be divided, marked, and distinguished in a similar manner, I think he would certainly conclude, *before he touched his hand*, that the thing which he now saw was the same which he had felt before and called his hand.'

[16] Locke, *Essay*, II. 8. 16. Aristotle regards number as one of the Communia Sensibles.—*De Anima*, II. 6, III. 1.

visible man, in company with all the other ideas of sight perceived at the same time. But, all these ideas offered at once to his view he would not distribute into sundry distinct combinations, till such time as, by observing the motion of the parts of the man and other experiences, he comes to know which are to be separated and which to be collected together[14].

111. From what hath been premised, it is plain the objects of sight and touch make, if I may so say, two sets of ideas, which are widely different from each other. To objects of either kind we indifferently attribute the terms high and low, right and left, and such like, denoting the position or situation of things; but then we must well observe that the position of any object is determined with respect only to objects of the same sense. We say any object of touch is high or low, according as it is more or less distant from the tangible earth: and in like manner we denominate any object of sight high or low, in proportion as it is more or less distant from the visible earth. But, to define the situation of visible things with relation to the distance they bear from any tangible thing, or *vice versa*, this were absurd and perfectly unintelligible. For all visible things are equally in the mind, and take up no part of the external space; and consequently are equidistant from any tangible thing which exists without the mind[15].

112. Or rather, to speak truly, the proper objects of sight are at no distance, neither near nor far from any tangible thing. For, if we inquire narrowly into the matter, we shall find that those things only are compared together in respect of distance which exist after the same manner, or appertain unto the same sense. For, by the distance between any two points, nothing more is meant than the number of intermediate points. If the given points are visible, the distance between them is marked out by the number of the interjacent visible points; if they are tangible, the distance between them is a line consisting of tangible points;

---

[14] 'If the visible appearance of two shillings had been found connected from the beginning with the tangible idea of one shilling, that appearance would as naturally and readily have signified the unity of the (real or tangible) object as it now signifies its duplicity.' Reid, *Inquiry*, VI. 11.

[15] Here again Berkeley's reticence of his developed theory of matter. Tangible things are meantime granted to be 'without the mind.' Cf. *Principles*, sect. 43, 44. 'Without the mind'—in contrast to what is visible, i.e. pure sensation or idea.

but, if they are one tangible and the other visible, the distance between them doth neither consist of points perceivable by sight nor by touch, *i.e.* it is utterly inconceivable[17]. This, perhaps, will not find an easy admission into all men's understanding. However, I should gladly be informed whether it be not true, by any one who will be at the pains to reflect a little, and apply it home to his thoughts.

113. The not observing what has been delivered in the two last sections, seems to have occasioned no small part of the difficulty that occurs in the business of direct appearances. The head, which is painted nearest the earth, seems to be farthest from it; and on the other hand, the feet, which are painted farthest from the earth, are thought nearest to it. Herein lies the difficulty, which vanishes if we express the thing more clearly and free from ambiguity, thus:—How comes it that, to the eye, the visible head, which is nearest the tangible earth, seems farthest from the earth; and the visible feet, which are farthest from the tangible earth, seem nearest the earth? The question being thus proposed, who sees not the difficulty is founded on a supposition that the eye or visive faculty, or rather the soul by means thereof, should judge of the situation of visible objects with reference to their distance from the tangible earth? Whereas, it is evident the tangible earth is not perceived by sight. And it hath been shewn, in the two last preceding sections, that the location of visible objects is determined only by the distance they bear from one another, and that it is nonsense to talk of distance, far or near, between a visible and tangible thing.

114. If we confine our thoughts to the proper objects of sight, the whole is plain and easy. The head is painted farthest from, and the feet nearest to, the visible earth; and so they appear to be. What is there strange or unaccountable in this? Let us suppose the pictures in the fund of the eye to be the immediate objects of sight[18]. The consequence is that things should appear in the same posture they are painted in; and is it not so? The head which is seen seems farthest from the earth which is seen; and the feet which are seen seem nearest to the earth which is seen. And just so they are painted.

[17] Cf. sect. 131.   [18] Sect. 2, 88, 116, 118.

115. But, say you, the picture of the man is inverted, and yet the appearance is erect. I ask, what mean you by the picture of the man, or, which is the same thing, the visible man's being inverted? You tell me it is inverted, because the heels are uppermost and the head undermost? Explain me this. You say that by the head's being undermost, you mean that it is nearest to the earth; and, by the heels being uppermost, that they are farthest from the earth. I ask again, what earth you mean? You cannot mean the earth that is painted on the eye or the visible earth— for the picture of the head is farthest from the picture of the earth, and the picture of the feet nearest to the picture of the earth; and accordingly the visible head is farthest from the visible earth, and the visible feet nearest to it. It remains, therefore, that you mean the tangible earth; and so determine the situation of visible things with respect to tangible things—contrary to what hath been demonstrated in sect. 111 and 112. The two distinct provinces of sight and touch should be considered apart, and as though their objects had no intercourse, no manner of relation to one another, in point of distance or position[19].

116. Farther, what greatly contributes to make us mistake in this matter is that, when we think of the pictures in the fund of the eye, we imagine ourselves looking on the fund of another's eye, or another looking on the fund of our own eye, and beholding the pictures painted thereon. Suppose two eyes, *A* and *B*. *A* from some distance looking on the pictures in *B* sees them inverted, and for that reason concludes they are inverted in *B*. But this is wrong. There are projected in little on the bottom of *A* the images of the pictures of, suppose, man, earth, &c., which are painted on *B*. And, besides these, the eye *B* itself, and the objects which environ it, together with another earth, are projected in a larger size on *A*. Now, by the eye *A* these larger images are deemed the true objects, and the lesser only pictures in miniature. And it is with respect to those greater images that it determines the situation of the smaller images; so that, comparing the little man with the great earth, *A* judges him inverted, or that the feet are farthest from and the head nearest to the great earth. Whereas,

---

[19] In short, we see only *quantities of colour*—the notions of real distance, size, shape, locality, up and down, right and left, &c., being gradually associated with these quantities, as we learn to connect what we see with our tactual and locomotive experience.

if *A* compare the little man with the little earth, then he will appear erect, *i.e.* his head shall seem farthest from and his feet nearest to the little earth. But we must consider that *B* does not see two earths as *A* does. It sees only what is represented by the little pictures in *A*, and consequently shall judge the man erect. For, in truth, the man in *B* is not inverted, for there the feet are next the earth; but it is the representation of it in *A* which is inverted, for there the head of the representation of the picture of the man in *B* is next the earth, and the feet farthest from the earth—meaning the earth which is without the representation of the pictures in *B*. For, if you take the little images of the pictures in *B*, and consider them by themselves, and with respect only to one another, they are all erect and in their natural posture.

117. Farther, there lies a mistake in our imagining that the pictures of external[16] objects are painted on the bottom of the eye. It has been shewn there is no resemblance between the ideas of sight and things tangible. It hath likewise been demonstrated[17], that the proper objects of sight do not exist without the mind. Whence it clearly follows that the pictures painted on the bottom of the eye are not the pictures of external[18] objects. Let any one consult his own thoughts, and then tell me, what affinity, what likeness, there is between that certain variety and disposition of colours which constitute the visible man, or picture of a man, and that other combination of far different ideas, sensible by touch, which compose the tangible man. But, if this be the case, how come they to be accounted pictures or images, since that supposes them to copy or represent some originals or other?

118. To which I answer—In the forementioned instance, the eye *A* takes the little images, included within the representation of the other eye *B*, to be pictures or copies, whereof the archetypes are not things existing without[19], but the larger pictures[20] projected on its own fund; and which by *A* are not thought pictures, but the originals or true things themselves. Though if we suppose a third eye *C*, from a due distance, to behold the fund of *A*, then indeed the things projected thereon shall, to *C*, seem pictures or images, in the same sense that those projected on *B* do to *A*.

119. Rightly to conceive the business in hand, we must carefully distinguish between the ideas of sight and touch, between the

[16] i. e. tangible. [17] Sect. 41—44. [18] i. e. tangible things. [19] i. e. visible.

visible and tangible eye; for certainly on the tangible eye nothing either is or seems to be painted. Again, the visible eye, as well as all other visible objects, hath been shewn to exist only in the mind [m]; which, perceiving its own ideas, and comparing them together, does call some pictures in respect to others. What hath been said, being rightly comprehended and laid together, does, I think, afford a full and genuine explication of the erect appearance of objects—which phenomenon, I must confess, I do not see how it can be explained by any theories of vision hitherto made public.

120. In treating of these things, the use of language is apt to occasion some obscurity and confusion, and create in us wrong ideas. For, language being accommodated to the common notions and prejudices of men, it is scarce possible to deliver the naked and precise truth, without great circumlocution, impropriety, and (to an unwary reader) seeming contradictions. I do, therefore, once for all, desire whoever shall think it worth his while to understand what I have written concerning vision, that he would not stick in this or that phrase or manner of expression, but candidly collect my meaning from the whole sum and tenor of my discourse, and, laying aside the words [n] as much as possible, consider the bare notions themselves, and then judge whether they are agreeable to truth and his own experience or no.

121. We have shewn the way wherein the mind, by mediation of visible ideas [o], doth perceive or apprehend the distance, magnitude, and situation of tangible objects [p]. I come now to inquire more particularly concerning the difference between the ideas of sight and touch which are called by the same names, and see whether there be any idea common to both senses [q]. From what we have at large set forth and demonstrated in the foregoing parts

---

[m] Cf. sect. 41—44. The 'eyes'—visible and tangible—are actually different objects.
[n] Cf. *Principles*, Introduction, sect. 2—25.
[o] 'Visible ideas'—including sensations muscular and locomotive, in the organ of vision. Sect. 16, 27, 57.
[p] I. e. objects which, in this *Essay*, are granted, for argument's sake, to be external to or independent of mind, having an absolute, as well as a merely ideal existence.
[q] i. e. to inquire whether there are, in this instance, any Common Sensibles, and, in particular, whether an *extension* of the same kind at least, if not numerically one, is presented in each. The theory of an *a priori* intuition of space, the common condition of tactual and visual experience, because implied in sense-experience as such, since so famous, through the Kantian criticism, and its effects on later metaphysical thought, is not here entertained by Berkeley. Cf. *Theory of Vision Vindicated*, sect. 15.

of this treatise, it is plain there is no one self-same numerical extension, perceived both by sight and touch; but that the particular figures and extensions perceived by sight, however they may be called by the same names, and reputed the same things with those perceived by touch, are nevertheless different, and have an existence very distinct and separate from them. So that the question is not now concerning the same numerical ideas, but whether there be any one and the same sort or species of ideas equally perceivable to both senses? or, in other words, whether extension, figure, and motion perceived by sight, are not specifically distinct from extension, figure, and motion perceived by touch?

122. But, before I come more particularly to discuss this matter, I find it proper to take into my thoughts extension in abstract[a]. For of this there is much talk; and I am apt to think that when men speak of extension as being an idea common to two senses, it is with a secret supposition that we can single out extension from all other tangible and visible qualities, and form thereof an abstract idea, which idea they will have common both to sight and touch. We are therefore to understand by extension in abstract, an idea[b] of extension—for instance, a line or surface entirely stripped of all other sensible qualities and circumstances that might determine it to any particular existence; it is neither black, nor white, nor red, nor hath it any colour at all, or any tangible quality whatsoever, and consequently it is of no finite determinate magnitude[c]; for that which bounds or distinguishes one extension from another is some quality or circumstance wherein they disagree.

123. Now, I do not find that I can perceive, imagine, or anywise frame in my mind such an abstract idea as is here spoken of. A line or surface which is neither black, nor white, nor blue, nor yellow, &c.; nor long, nor short, nor rough, nor smooth, nor square, nor round, &c. is perfectly incomprehensible. This I am sure of as to myself; how far the faculties of other men may reach they best can tell.

---

[a] In the following reasoning against the possibility of abstract, as distinguished from sensible (visible or tangible) extension, Berkeley urges his favourite objections to 'abstract ideas.' Cf. *Principles*, Introduction, sect. 6—10.—*Alciphron*, VII. 5—8.—*Theory of Vision Vindicated.—Defence of Free Thinking in Mathematics*, sect. 45—48.

[b] i. e. an intuition, either in sense or imagination.

[c] i. e. a supposed intuition, which per se cannot be individualized in any perceivable or imaginable object.

124. It is commonly said that the object of geometry is abstract extension. But geometry contemplates figures: now, figure is the termination of magnitude"; but we have shewn that extension in abstract hath no finite determinate magnitude; whence it clearly follows that it can have no figure, and consequently is not the object of geometry. It is indeed a tenet, as well of the modern as the ancient philosophers, that all general truths are concerning universal abstract ideas; without which, we are told, there could be no science, no demonstration of any general proposition in geometry. But it were no hard matter, did I think it necessary to my present purpose, to shew that propositions and demonstrations in geometry might be universal, though they who make them never think of abstract general ideas of triangles or circles.

125. After reiterated endeavours" to apprehend the general idea" of a triangle, I have found it altogether incomprehensible. And surely, if any one were able to let that idea into my mind, it must be the [deservedly admired"] author of the *Essay concerning Human Understanding*: he, who has so far distinguished himself from the generality of writers, by the clearness and significancy of what he says. Let us therefore see how this celebrated author" describes the general or [which is the same thing, the"] abstract idea of a triangle. 'It must be,' says he, 'neither oblique nor rectangle, neither equilateral, equicrural, nor scalenum; but all and none of these at once. In effect it is somewhat imperfect that cannot exist; an idea, wherein some parts of several different and inconsistent ideas are put together.' (*Essay on Human Understanding*, B. iv. ch. 7. s. 9.) This is the idea which he thinks needful for the enlargement of knowledge, which is the subject of mathematical demonstration, and without which we could never come to know any general proposition concerning triangles. [Sure I am, if this be the case, it is impossible for me to attain to know even the first elements of geometry: since I have not the faculty to frame in my mind such an idea as is here

described¹⁴.] That author acknowledges it doth 'require some pains and skill to form this general idea of a triangle.' (*Ibid.*) But, had he called to mind what he says in another place, to wit, 'that ideas of mixed modes wherein any inconsistent ideas are put together, cannot so much as exist in the mind, *i.e.* be conceived,' (vid. B. iii. ch. 10. s. 33, *ibid.*)—I say, had this occurred to his thoughts, it is not improbable he would have owned it above all the pains and skill he was master of, to form the above-mentioned idea of a triangle, which is made up of manifest staring contradictions. That a man [of such a clear understanding¹⁵], who thought so much and so well, and laid so great a stress on clear and determinate ideas, should nevertheless talk at this rate, seems very surprising. But the wonder will lessen, if it be considered that the source whence this opinion [of abstract figures and extension¹⁶] flows is the prolific womb which has brought forth innumerable errors and difficulties, in all parts of philosophy, and in all the sciences. But this matter, taken in its full extent, were a subject too vast and comprehensive to be insisted on in this place¹⁷. [I shall only observe that your metaphysicians and men of speculation seem to have faculties distinct from those of ordinary men, when they talk of general or abstracted triangles and circles, &c., and so peremptorily declare them to be the subject of all the eternal, immutable, universal truths in geometry¹⁸.] And so much for extension in abstract.

126. Some, perhaps, may think pure space, vacuum, or trine dimension, to be equally the object of sight and touch¹⁹. But, though we have a very great propension to think the ideas of outness and space to be the immediate object of sight, yet, if I mistake not, in the foregoing parts of this Essay, that hath been clearly demonstrated to be a mere delusion, arising from the quick and sudden suggestion of fancy, which so closely connects the idea of distance with those of sight, that we are apt to think it is itself a proper and immediate object of that sense, till reason corrects the mistake²⁰.

¹² Omitted in last edition.
¹³ Omitted in last edition.
¹⁴ Omitted in last edition.
¹⁵ See *Principles*, passim.
¹⁶ Omitted in last edition.
¹⁷ He probably has Locke in his eye.

¹⁹ On Berkeley's theory, space without bodies (i.e. intangible space) would not be extended, as not having parts: inasmuch as parts are assigned to it with relation to bodies, from which also the notion of distance is taken. Berkeley, moreover, does

127. It having been shewn that there are no abstract ideas of figure, and that it is impossible for us, by any precision of thought, to frame an idea of extension separate from all other visible and tangible qualities, which shall be common both to sight and touch—the question now remaining is[a], whether the particular extensions, figures, and motions perceived by sight, be of the same kind with the particular extensions, figures, and motions perceived by touch? In answer to which I shall venture to lay down the following proposition:—*The extension, figures, and motions perceived by sight are specifically distinct from the ideas of touch, called by the same names; nor is there any such thing as one idea, or kind of idea, common*[b] *to both senses*. This proposition may, without much difficulty, be collected from what hath been said in several places of this Essay. But, because it seems so remote from, and contrary to the received notions and settled opinion of mankind, I shall attempt to demonstrate it more particularly and at large by the following arguments:—

128. [*First*[c],] When, upon perception of an idea, I range it under this or that sort, it is because it is perceived after the same manner, or because it has a likeness or conformity with, or affects me in the same way as the ideas of the sort I rank it under. In short, it must not be entirely new, but have something in it old and already perceived by me. It must, I say, have so much, at least, in common with the ideas I have before known and named, as to make me give it the same name with them. But, it has been, if I mistake not, clearly made out[d] that a man born blind would not, at first reception of his sight, think the things he saw were of the same nature with the objects of touch, or had anything in common with them; but that they were a new set of ideas, perceived in a new manner, and entirely different from all he had ever perceived before. So that he would not call them by the same name, nor repute them to be of the same sort, with anything he had hitherto known. [And surely the judgment of such

---

not distinguish space from sensible extension. Cf. Reid's *Works*, p. 126, note—in which Sir W. Hamilton suggests that one may have an *a priori* conception of space, and also an *a posteriori* perception of matter as extended.

[b] Sect. 121. Cf. *Theory of Vision Vindicated*, sect. 15.

[c] i. e. there are no Common Sensibles; from which it follows that we can reason from the one sense to the other only by analogy, founded on the arbitrary but constant connexion of their respective phenomena. Cf. *Theory of Vision Vindicated*, sect. 27, 28.

[c] Omitted in last edition.

[d] Cf. sect. 93. 103. 106. 110.

an unprejudiced person is more to be relied on in this case than the sentiments of the generality of men; who, in this as in almost everything else, suffer themselves to be guided by custom, and the erroneous suggestions of prejudice, rather than reason and sedate reflection ⁿ.]

129. *Secondly*, Light and colours are allowed by all to constitute a sort or species entirely different from the ideas of touch; nor will any man, I presume, say they can make themselves perceived by that sense. But there is no other immediate object of sight besides light and colours ᵒ. It is therefore a direct consequence, that there is no idea common to both senses.

130. It is a prevailing opinion, even amongst those who have thought and writ most accurately concerning our ideas, and the ways whereby they enter into the understanding, that something more is perceived by sight than barely light and colours with their variations. [The excellent ᵖ] Mr. Locke termeth sight "the most comprehensive of all our senses, conveying to our minds the ideas of light and colours, which are peculiar only to that sense; and also the far different ideas of space, figure, and motion." (*Essay on Human Understanding*, B. iii. ch. 9. s. 9.) Space or distance ᵠ, we have shewn, is no otherwise the object of sight than of hearing. (Vid. sect. 46.) And, as for figure and extension, I leave it to any one that shall calmly attend to his own clear and distinct ideas to decide whether he has any idea intromitted immediately and properly by sight save only light and colours: or, whether it be possible for him to frame in his mind a distinct abstract idea of visible extension, or figure, exclusive of all colour; and, on the other hand, whether he can conceive colour without visible extension? For my own part, I must confess, I am not able to attain so great a nicety of abstraction. I know very well that, in a strict sense, I see nothing but light and colours, with their several shades and variations. He who beside these doth also perceive by sight ideas far different and distinct from them, hath that faculty in a degree more perfect and comprehensive than

---

ⁿ Omitted in last edition.

ᵒ Cf. sect. 43, 103, &c. A plurality of co-existent units or *minima* of colour constitutes Berkeley's visible extension; while a plurality of successively experienced *minima* of resistant points constitutes his locomotive extension. Whether we can perceive this visible extension without any experience of muscular movement in the eye he does not here say.

ᵖ Omitted in last edition.

ᵠ Here space = distance; and the notion of distance belongs with Berkeley originally to our tactual and locomotive experience.

I can pretend to. It must be owned, indeed, that, by the mediation of light and colours, other far different ideas are suggested to my mind. But so they are by hearing[u], which, beside sounds which are peculiar to that sense, doth, by their mediation, suggest not only space, figure, and motion, but also all other ideas whatsoever that can be signified by words.

131. *Thirdly*, It is, I think, an axiom universally received, that 'quantities of the same kind may be added together and make one entire sum.' Mathematicians add lines together; but they do not add a line to a solid, or conceive it as making one sum with a surface. These three kinds of quantity being thought incapable of any such mutual addition, and consequently of being compared together in the several ways of proportion, are by them for that reason esteemed entirely disparate and heterogeneous. Now let any one try in his thoughts to add a visible line or surface to a tangible line or surface, so as to conceive them making one continued sum or whole. He that can do this may think them homogeneous; but he that cannot must, by the foregoing axiom, think them heterogeneous. [I acknowledge myself to be of the latter sort[x].] A blue and a red line I can conceive added together into one sum and making one continued line; but, to make, in my thoughts, one continued line of a visible and tangible line added together, is, I find, a task far more difficult, and even insurmountable—and I leave it to the reflection and experience of every particular person to determine for himself.

132. A farther confirmation of our tenet may be drawn from the solution of Mr. Molyneux's problem, published by Mr. Locke in his *Essay*[y]: which I shall set down as it there lies, together with Mr. Locke's opinion of it :—' Suppose a man born blind, and now adult, and taught by his touch to distinguish between a cube and a sphere of the same metal, and nighly of the same bigness, so as to tell when he felt one and the other, which is the cube, and which the sphere. Suppose then the cube and sphere placed on a table, and the blind man made to see: Quære, Whether by his sight, before he touched them, he could now

---

[u] In second edition, 'But then, upon this score, I see no reason why the sight should be thought more comprehensive than the hearing, which.' &c.

[x] Omitted in last edition.

[y] See also Locke's 'Correspondence' with Molyneux, *Works*, vol. IX. p. 34.—Leibnitz, *Nouveaux Essais*, Liv. II. ch. 9, who, so far granting the fact, disputes the heterogeneity.—Smith's *Optics*.—*Remarks*, §§ 161—170.—Hamilton's Reid, p. 137, note, and *Lect. Metaph.* II. p. 176.

distinguish, and tell, which is the globe, which the cube. To which the acute and judicious proposer answers: Not. For, though he has obtained the experience of how a globe, how a cube affects his touch; yet he has not yet attained the experience, that what affects his touch so or so must affect his sight so or so: or that a protuberant angle in the cube, that pressed his hand unequally, shall appear to his eye as it doth in the cube. I agree with this thinking gentleman, whom I am proud to call my friend, in his answer to this his problem; and am of opinion that the blind man, at first sight, would not be able with certainty to say, which was the globe, which the cube, whilst he only saw them.' (*Essay on Human Understanding*, B. ii. ch. 9. s. 8.)

133. Now, if a square surface perceived by touch be of the same sort with a square surface perceived by sight, it is certain the blind man here mentioned might know a square surface as soon as he saw it. It is no more but introducing into his mind, by a new inlet, an idea he has been already well acquainted with. Since therefore he is supposed to have known by his touch that a cube is a body terminated by square surfaces; and that a sphere is not terminated by square surfaces—upon the supposition that a visible and tangible square differ only *in numero*, it follows that he might know, by the unerring mark of the square surfaces, which was the cube, and which not, while he only saw them. We must therefore allow, either that visible extension and figures are specifically distinct from tangible extension and figures, or else, that the solution of this problem, given by those two [very[a]] thoughtful and ingenious men, is wrong.

134. Much more might be laid together in proof of the proposition I have advanced. But, what has been said is, if I mistake not, sufficient to convince any one that shall yield a reasonable attention. And, as for those that will not be at the pains of a little thought, no multiplication of words will ever suffice to make them understand the truth, or rightly conceive my meaning[b].

135. I cannot let go the above-mentioned problem without some reflection on it. It hath been made evident that a man blind from his birth would not, at first sight, denominate anything he saw, by the names he had been used to appropriate to ideas of touch. (Vid. sect. 106.) Cube, sphere, table are words he has

[a] Omitted in last edition.   [b] Cf. *Theory of Vision Vindicated*, sect. 70.

known applied to things perceivable by touch, but to things perfectly intangible he never knew them applied. Those words, in their wonted application, always marked out to his mind bodies or solid things which were perceived by the resistance they gave. But there is no solidity, no resistance or protrusion, perceived by sight. In short, the ideas of sight are all new perceptions, to which there be no names annexed in his mind; he cannot therefore understand what is said to him concerning them. And, to ask of the two bodies he saw placed on the table, which was the sphere, which the cube, were to him a question downright bantering and unintelligible; nothing he sees being able to suggest to his thoughts the idea of body, distance, or, in general, of anything he had already known.

136. It is a mistake to think the same[54] thing affects both sight and touch. If the same angle or square which is the object of touch be also the object of vision, what should hinder the blind man, at first sight, from knowing it? For, though the manner wherein it affects the sight be different from that wherein it affected his touch, yet, there being, beside this manner or circumstance, which is new and unknown, the angle or figure, which is old and known, he cannot choose but discern it.

137. Visible figure and extension having been demonstrated to be of a nature entirely different and heterogeneous from tangible figure and extension, it remains that we inquire concerning motion. Now, that visible motion is not of the same sort with tangible motion seems to need no farther proof; it being an evident corollary from what we have shewn concerning the difference there is betwixt visible and tangible extension. But, for a more full and express proof hereof, we need only observe that one who had not yet experienced vision would not at first sight know motion[55]. Whence it clearly follows that motion perceivable by sight is of a sort distinct from motion perceivable by touch. The antecedent I prove thus—By touch he could not perceive any motion but what was up or down, to the right or left, nearer or farther from him; besides these, and their several varieties or complications, it is impossible he should have any idea of motion.

[54] Cf. sect. 47, 146, &c. Here 'same' includes 'similar.'
[55] i. e. visible and tangible motions being absolutely heterogeneous, and the former being only arbitrary signs of the latter, we should not, at first sight, be able to interpret the visible sign of tactual motion, i. e. of locomotion proper.

He would not therefore think anything to be motion, or give the name motion to any idea, which he could not range under some or other of those particular kinds thereof. But, from sect. 95, it is plain that, by the mere act of vision, he could not know motion upwards or downwards, to the right or left, or in any other possible direction. From which I conclude, he would not know motion at all at first sight. As for the idea of motion in abstract, I shall not waste paper about it, but leave it to my reader to make the best he can of it. To me it is perfectly unintelligible[56].

138. The consideration of motion may furnish a new field for inquiry[57]. But, since the manner wherein the mind apprehends by sight the motion of tangible objects, with the various degrees thereof, may be easily collected from what has been said concerning the manner wherein that sense doth suggest their various distances, magnitudes, and situations, I shall not enlarge any farther on this subject, but proceed to inquire what may be alleged, with greatest appearance of reason, against the proposition we have demonstrated to be true; for, where there is so much prejudice to be encountered, a bare and naked demonstration of the truth will scarce suffice. We must also satisfy the scruples that men may start in favour of their preconceived notions, shew whence the mistake arises, how it came to spread, and carefully disclose and root out those false persuasions that an early prejudice might have implanted in the mind.

139. *First*, therefore, it will be demanded how visible extension and figures come to be called by the same name with tangible extension and figures, if they are not of the same kind with them? It must be something more than humour or accident that could occasion a custom so constant and universal as this, which has obtained in all ages and nations of the world, and amongst all ranks of men, the learned as well as the illiterate.

140. To which I answer, we can no more argue a visible and tangible square to be of the same species, from their being called by the same name, than we can that a tangible square, and the monosyllable consisting of six letters whereby it is marked, are of the same species, because they are both called by the same name. It is customary to call written words, and the things they

---

[56] Cf. sect. 133—135.
[57] Cf. *Principles*, sect. 111—116: also *Analyst*, query 13. On Berkeley's system space is not conceivable without an experience of tactual or muscular locomotion.

signify, by the same name: for, words not being regarded in their own nature, or otherwise than as they are marks of things, it had been superfluous, and beside the design of language, to have given them names distinct from those of the things marked by them. The same reason holds here also. Visible figures are the marks of tangible figures; and, from sect. 59, it is plain that in themselves they are little regarded, or upon any other score than for their connexion with tangible figures, which by nature they are ordained to signify. And, because this language of nature[a] does not vary in different ages or nations, hence it is that in all times and places visible figures are called by the same names as the respective tangible figures suggested by them; and not because they are alike, or of the same sort with them.

141. But, say you, surely a tangible square is liker to a visible square than to a visible circle: it has four angles, and as many sides; so also has the visible square—but the visible circle has no such thing, being bounded by one uniform curve, without right lines or angles, which makes it unfit to represent the tangible square, but very fit to represent the tangible circle. Whence it clearly follows, that visible figures are patterns of, or of the same species with, the respective tangible figures represented by them; that they are like unto them, and of their own nature fitted to represent them, as being of the same sort; and that they are in no respect arbitrary signs, as words.

142. I answer, it must be acknowledged the visible square is fitter than the visible circle to represent the tangible square, but then it is not because it is liker, or more of a species with it; but, because the visible square contains in it several distinct parts, whereby to mark the several distinct corresponding parts of a tangible square, whereas the visible circle doth not. The square perceived by touch hath four distinct equal sides, so also hath it four distinct equal angles. It is therefore necessary that the visible figure which shall be most proper to mark it contain four distinct equal parts, corresponding to the four sides of the tangible square; as likewise four other distinct and equal parts, whereby to denote the four equal angles of the tangible square. And accordingly we see the visible figures contain in them distinct

---

[a] Here the term 'language of nature' makes its appearance, as applicable to visual signs of tangible realities.

visible parts, answering to the distinct tangible parts of the figures signified or suggested by them.

143. But, it will not hence follow that any visible figure is like unto or of the same species with its corresponding tangible figure—unless it be also shewn that not only the number, but also the kind of the parts be the same in both. To illustrate this, I observe that visible figures represent tangible figures much after the same manner that written words do sounds. Now, in this respect, words are not arbitrary; it not being indifferent what written word stands for any sound. But, it is requisite that each word contain in it as many distinct characters as there are variations in the sound it stands for. Thus, the single letter *a* is proper to mark one simple uniform sound; and the word *adultery* is accommodated to represent the sound annexed to it—in the formation whereof there being eight different collisions or modifications of the air by the organs of speech, each of which produces a difference of sound, it was fit the word representing it should consist of as many distinct characters, thereby to mark each particular difference or part of the whole sound. And yet nobody, I presume, will say the single letter *a*, or the word *adultery*, are alike unto or of the same species with the respective sounds by them represented. It is indeed arbitrary that, in general, letters of any language represent sounds at all; but, when that is once agreed, it is not arbitrary what combination of letters shall represent this or that particular sound. I leave this with the reader to pursue, and apply it in his own thoughts.

144. It must be confessed that we are not so apt to confound other signs with the things signified, or to think them of the same species, as we are visible and tangible ideas. But, a little consideration will shew us how this may well be, without our supposing them of a like nature. These signs are constant and universal; their connexion with tangible ideas has been learnt at our first entrance into the world; and ever since, almost every moment of our lives, it has been occurring to our thoughts, and fastening and striking deeper on our minds. When we observe that signs are variable, and of human institution; when we remember there was a time they were not connected in our minds with those things they now so readily suggest, but that their signification was learned by the slow steps of experience: this preserves us

from confounding them. But, when we find the same signs suggest the same things all over the world; when we know they are not of human institution, and cannot remember that we ever learned their signification, but think that at first sight they would have suggested to us the same things they do now: all this persuades us they are of the same species as the things respectively represented by them, and that it is by a natural resemblance they suggest them to our minds.

145. Add to this that whenever we make a nice survey of any object, successively directing the optic axis to each point thereof, there are certain lines and figures, described by the motion of the head or eye, which, being in truth perceived by feeling[59], do nevertheless so mix themselves, as it were, with the ideas of sight that we can scarce think but they appertain to that sense. Again, the ideas of sight enter into the mind several at once, more distinct and unmingled than is usual in the other senses beside the touch. Sounds, for example, perceived at the same instant, are apt to coalesce, if I may so say, into one sound: but we can perceive, at the same time, great variety of visible objects, very separate and distinct from each other. Now, tangible[60] extension being made up of several distinct coexistent parts, we may hence gather another reason that may dispose us to imagine a likeness or analogy between the immediate objects of sight and touch. But nothing, certainly, does more contribute to blend and confound them together, than the strict and close connexion[61] they have with each other. We cannot open our eyes but the ideas of distance, bodies, and tangible figures are suggested by them. So swift, and sudden, and unperceived is the transit from visible to tangible ideas that we can scarce forbear thinking them equally the immediate object of vision.

146. The prejudice[62] which is grounded on these, and whatever other causes may be assigned thereof, sticks so fast on our understandings, that it is impossible, without obstinate striving and labour of the mind, to get entirely clear of it. But then the reluctancy we find in rejecting any opinion can be no argument of its truth, to whoever considers what has been already shewn with regard to the prejudices we entertain concerning the distance,

---

[59] Cf. sect. 16, 27, 97.
[60] i. e. tangible in the strict meaning—excluding locomotive experience (?).
[61] i. e. as natural signs, associated with their thus implied meaning.
[62] Cf. *Theory of Vision Vindicated*, sect. 35.

magnitude, and situation of objects; prejudices so familiar to our minds, so confirmed and inveterate, as they will hardly give way to the clearest demonstration.

147. Upon the whole, I think we may fairly conclude[63] that the proper objects of vision constitute the universal language of nature, whereby we are instructed how to regulate our actions, in order to attain those things that are necessary to the preservation and well-being of our bodies, as also to avoid whatever may be hurtful and destructive of them. It is by their information that we are principally guided in all the transactions and concerns of life. And the manner wherein they signify and mark out unto us the objects which are at a distance is the same with that of languages and signs of human appointment; which do not suggest the things signified by any likeness or identity of nature, but only by an habitual connexion that experience has made us to observe between them[64].

148. Suppose one who had always continued blind be told by his guide that after he has advanced so many steps he shall come to the brink of a precipice, or be stopped by a wall; must not this to him seem very admirable and surprising? He cannot conceive how it is possible for mortals to frame such predictions as these, which to him would seem as strange and unaccountable as prophecy does to others. Even they who are blessed with the visive faculty may (though familiarity make it less observed) find therein sufficient cause of admiration. The wonderful art and

---

[63] Berkeley, in this section, enunciates the constructive principle of the Essay, with which he starts in his *Theory of Vision Vindicated*, where cf. sect. 38.—Reid and others have proposed objections to the arbitrary character of the relation between visible and tangible extension, founded on the rules of perspective and of the projection of the sphere.

[64] i.e. under the laws of reproductive imagination, or association of ideas. 'The "solution" of the phenomenon that we apprehend, by the ideas of sight, certain other ideas, which neither resemble them, nor cause them, nor are caused by them, nor have any necessary connexion with them,' comprehends, Berkeley tells us, (*Theory of Vision Vindicated*, sect. 42.) 'the whole Theory of Vision.'

'The imagination of every thinking person will supply him with instances to prove that the ideas received by any one of the senses do readily excite such other ideas, either of the same sense or of any other, as have habitually been associated with them. So that if, on this account, we are to suppose, with a late ingenious writer, that the ideas of sight constitute a Visual Language, because they readily suggest the corresponding ideas of touch, as the terms of a language excite the ideas answering to them, I see not but we may, for the same reason, allow of a tangible, audible, gustatory, and olfactory language, though doubtless the Visual Language will be abundantly more copious than the rest.' Smith's *Opticks.—Remarks*, p. 29.—And into this theory of physical causation and previsive interpretation, the philosophy of Berkeley ultimately resolves itself.

contrivance wherewith it is adjusted to those ends and purposes for which it was apparently designed; the vast extent, number, and variety of objects that are at once, with so much ease, and quickness, and pleasure, suggested by it—all these afford subject for much and pleasing speculation, and may, if anything, give us some glimmering analogous prænotion of things, that are placed beyond the certain discovery and comprehension of our present state[55].

149. I do not design to trouble myself much with drawing corollaries from the doctrine I have hitherto laid down. If it bears the test, others may, so far as they shall think convenient, employ their thoughts in extending it farther, and applying it to whatever purposes it may be subservient to. Only, I cannot forbear making some inquiry concerning the object of geometry, which the subject we have been upon does naturally lead one to. We have shewn there is no such idea as that of extension in abstract[56]; and that there are two kinds of sensible extension and figures, which are entirely distinct and heterogeneous from each other[57]. Now, it is natural to inquire which of these is the object of geometry[58].

150. Some things there are which, at first sight, incline one to think geometry conversant about visible extension. The constant use of the eyes, both in the practical and speculative parts of that science, doth very much induce us thereto. It would, without doubt, seem odd to a mathematician to go about to convince him the diagrams he saw upon paper were not the figures, or even the likeness of the figures, which make the subject of the demonstration,—the contrary being held an unquestionable truth, not only by mathematicians, but also by those who apply themselves more particularly to the study of logic; I mean who consider the nature of science, certainty, and demonstration; it being by them assigned as one reason of the extraordinary clearness and evidence of geometry, that in that science the reasonings are free from

---

[55] Cf. *Alciphron*, Dialogue IV, sect. 11—15.
[56] Sect. 122—125.
[57] Sect. 127—138.
[58] A large school of modern metaphysicians say that neither tangible nor visible extension is the object of geometry, but intelligible or *a priori* extension; and that space is rather a necessary concomitant, or implicate of our sense-experience, than, *per se*, an object of any sense. This theory, which is independent of the absolute heterogeneity of the extension given in sight and touch, is not entertained in the *Essay*. Cf. Kant's explanation of the origin of our mathematical knowledge, *Kritik der reinen Vernunft*, Elementarlehre, I.

those inconveniences which attend the use of arbitrary signs, the very ideas themselves being copied out, and exposed to view upon paper. But, by the bye, how well this agrees with what they likewise assert of abstract ideas being the object of geometrical demonstration I leave to be considered.

151. To come to a resolution in this point, we need only observe what has been said in sect. 59, 60, 61, where it is shewn that visible extensions in themselves are little regarded, and have no settled determinate greatness, and that men measure altogether by the application of tangible extension to tangible extension. All which makes it evident that visible extension and figures are not the object of geometry.

152. It is therefore plain that visible figures are of the same use in geometry that words are. And the one may as well be accounted the object of that science as the other; neither of them being any otherwise concerned therein than as they represent or suggest to the mind the particular tangible figures connected with them. There is, indeed, this difference betwixt the signification of tangible figures by visible figures, and of ideas by words—that whereas the latter is variable and uncertain, depending altogether on the arbitrary appointment of men, the former is fixed, and immutably the same in all times and places. A visible square, for instance, suggests to the mind the same tangible figure in Europe that it doth in America. Hence it is, that the voice of nature, which speaks to our eyes, is not liable to that misinterpretation and ambiguity that languages of human contrivance are unavoidably subject to[69]. From which may, in some measure, be derived that peculiar evidence and clearness of geometrical demonstrations.

153. Though what has been said may suffice to shew what ought to be determined with relation to the object of geometry, I shall, nevertheless, for the fuller illustration thereof, take into my thoughts the case of an intelligence or unbodied spirit, which is supposed to see perfectly well, *i.e.* to have a clear perception of the proper and immediate objects of sight, but to have no sense of touch[70]. Whether there be any such being in nature or no, is beside

---

[69] Cf. sect. 51—66, 144.

[70] This is a conjecture, not as to the possible notions of one born blind, but as to the notions of an 'unbodied' intelligence, capable only of the sense-experience of pure vision. See Reid's speculations on the 'Geometry of Visibles' and the Idomenians, *Inquiry*, VI. 9—as to which Priestley remarks, "I do not remember to have seen a more egregious piece of solemn trifling than

my purpose to inquire; it suffices, that the supposition contains no contradiction in it. Let us now examine what proficiency such a one may be able to make in geometry. Which speculation will lead us more clearly to see whether the ideas of sight can possibly be the object of that science.

154. *First*, then, it is certain the aforesaid intelligence could have no idea of a solid or quantity of three dimensions, which follows from its not having any idea of distance. We, indeed, are prone to think that we have by sight the ideas of space and solids; which arises from our imagining that we do, strictly speaking, see distance, and some parts of an object at a greater distance than others; which has been demonstrated to be the effect of the experience we have had what ideas of touch are connected with such and such ideas attending vision. But the intelligence here spoken of is supposed to have no experience of touch. He would not, therefore, judge as we do, nor have any idea of distance, outness, or profundity, nor consequently of space or body, either immediately or by suggestion. Whence it is plain he can have no notion of those parts of geometry which relate to the mensuration of solids, and their convex or concave surfaces, and contemplate the properties of lines generated by the section of a solid. The conceiving of any part whereof is beyond the reach of his faculties.

155. *Further*, he cannot comprehend the manner wherein geometers describe a right line or circle; the rule and compass, with their use, being things of which it is impossible he should have any notion. Nor is it an easier matter for him to conceive the placing of one plane or angle on another, in order to prove their equality; since that supposes some idea of distance, or external space. All which makes it evident our pure intelligence could never attain to know so much as the first elements of plain geometry. And perhaps, upon a nice inquiry, it will be found he cannot even have an idea of plain figures any more than he can of solids; since some idea of distance is necessary to form the idea of a geometrical plane, as will appear to whoever shall reflect a little on it.

the chapter which our author calls the 'Geometry of Visibles,' and his account of the 'Idomenians,' as he terms those imaginary beings who have no ideas of substance but from sight." Cf. Reid's allusion to this passage in his *Essays on the Intellectual Powers*, p. 182, Hamilton's Edition

156. All that is properly perceived by the visive faculty amounts to no more than colours with their variations, and different proportions of light and shade—but the perpetual mutability and fleetingness of those immediate objects of sight render them incapable of being managed after the manner of geometrical figures; nor is it in any degree useful that they should. It is true there be divers of them perceived at once; and more of some, and less of others: but accurately to compute their magnitude, and assign precise determinate proportions between things so variable and inconstant, if we suppose it possible to be done, must yet be a very trifling and insignificant labour.

157. I must confess, it seems to be the opinion of some very ingenious men that flat or plane figures are immediate objects of sight, though they acknowledge solids are not. And this opinion of theirs is grounded on what is observed in painting, wherein (say they) the ideas immediately imprinted in the mind are only of planes variously coloured, which, by a sudden act of the judgment, are changed into solids: but, with a little attention, we shall find the planes here mentioned as the immediate objects of sight are not visible but tangible planes. For, when we say that pictures are planes, we mean thereby that they appear to the touch smooth and uniform. But then this smoothness and uniformity, or, in other words, this planeness of the picture is not perceived immediately by vision; for it appeareth to the eye various and multiform.

158. From all which we may conclude that planes are no more the immediate object of sight than solids. What we strictly see are not solids, nor yet planes variously coloured—they are only diversity of colours. And some of these suggest to the mind solids, and others plane figures; just as they have been experienced to be connected with the one or the other: so that we see plains in the same way that we see solids—both being equally suggested by the immediate objects of sight, which accordingly are themselves denominated planes and solids. But, though they are called by the same names with the things marked by them, they are, nevertheless, of a nature entirely different, as hath been demonstrated[71].

[71] Cf. sect. 130, and *Theory of Vision Vindicated*, sect. 37. Does Berkeley, in this and the two preceding sections, mean to hint that the only proper object of sight is unextended colour, and that, apart from muscular movement in the eye and other locomotion, all *visibilia* are unextended points? This question has not

159. What has been said is, if I mistake not, sufficient to decide the question we proposed to examine, concerning the ability of a pure spirit, such as we have described, to know geometry. It is, indeed, no easy matter for us to enter precisely into the thoughts of such an intelligence; because we cannot, without great pains, cleverly separate and disentangle in our thoughts the proper objects of sight from those of touch which are connected with them. This, indeed, in a complete degree seems scarce possible to be performed; which will not seem strange to us, if we consider how hard it is for any one to hear the words of his native language, which is familiar to him, pronounced in his ears without understanding them. Though he endeavour to disunite the meaning from the sound, it will nevertheless intrude into his thoughts, and he shall find it extreme difficult, if not impossible, to put himself exactly in the posture of a foreigner that never learnt the language, so as to be affected barely with the sounds themselves, and not perceive the signification annexed to them.

160. By this time, I suppose, it is clear that neither abstract nor visible extension makes the object of geometry; the not discerning of which may, perhaps, have created some difficulty and useless labour in mathematics. [[71] Sure I am that somewhat relating thereto has occurred to my thoughts, which, though after the most anxious and repeated examination I am forced to think it true, doth, nevertheless, seem so far out of the common road of geometry, that I know not whether it may not be thought presumption if I should make it public in an age wherein that science hath received such mighty improvements by new methods; great part whereof, as well as of the ancient discoveries, may perhaps lose their reputation, and much of that ardour with which men study the abstruse and fine geometry be abated, if what to me, and those few to whom I have imparted it, seems evidently true, should really prove to be so.]

escaped more recent psychologists, including Stewart, Brown, and Mill, who hold that unextended colour is perceivable and imaginable. See also Professor Bain's *Senses and Intellect*, p. 376.

[71] The following sentence is not contained in the last edition, in which the first sentence of sect. 160 is the concluding one of sect. 159, and of the *Essay*.

AN APPENDIX.

[*This Appendix, which first appeared in the second, is omitted in the last and in all the collected editions.*]

THE censures which, I am informed, have been made on the foregoing Essay inclined me to think I had not been clear and express enough in some points; and, to prevent being misunderstood for the future, I was willing to make any necessary alterations or additions in what I had written. But that was impracticable, the present edition having been almost finished before I received this information. Wherefore, I think it proper to consider in this place the principal objections that are come to my notice.

In the *first* place, it is objected, that in the beginning of the Essay I argue either against all use of lines and angles in optics, and then what I say is false; or against those writers only who will have it that we can perceive by sense the optic axes, angles, &c., and then it is insignificant, this being an absurdity which no one ever held. To which I answer that I argue only against those who are of opinion that we perceive the distance of objects by lines and angles, or, as they term it, by a kind of innate geometry. And, to shew that this is not fighting with my own shadow, I shall here set down a passage from the celebrated Descartes[73]:—

'Distantiam præterea discimus, per mutuam quandam conspirationem oculorum. Ut enim cæcus noster duo bacilla tenens, *A E* et *C E*, de quorum longitudine incertus, solumque intervallum manuum *A* et *C*, cum magnitudine angulorum *A C E*, et *C A E* exploratum habens, inde, ut ex Geometria quadam omnibus innata, scire potest ubi sit punctum *E*. Sic quum nostri oculi *R S T* et

---

[73] This passage is contained in the *Dioptrics* of Des Cartes, VI. 13; see also VI. 11.

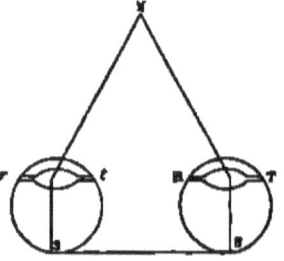

r s t ambo, vertuntur ad *X*, magnitudo lineæ *S s*, et angulorum *X S s* et *X s S*, certos nos reddunt ubi sit punctum *X*. Et idem opera alterutrius possumus indagare, loco illum movendo, ut si versus *X* illum semper dirigentes, primo sistamus in puncto *S*, et statim post in puncto *s*, hoc sufficiet ut magnitudo lineæ *S s*, et duorum angulorum *X S s* et *X s S* nostræ imaginationi simul occurrant, et distantiam puncti *X* nos edoceant: idque per actionem mentis, quæ licet simplex judicium esse videatur, ratiocinationem tamen quandam involutam habet, similem illi, qua Geometræ per duas stationes diversas, loca inaccessa dimetiuntur.'

I might amass together citations from several authors to the same purpose, but, this being so clear in the point, and from an author of so great note, I shall not trouble the reader with any more. What I have said on this head was not for the sake of finding fault with other men; but, because I judged it necessary to demonstrate in the first place that we neither see distance immediately, nor yet perceive it by the mediation of anything that hath (as lines and angles) a necessary connexion with it. For on the demonstration of this point[n] the whole theory depends.

Secondly, it is objected, that the explication I give of the appearance of the horizontal moon (which may also be applied to the sun) is the same that Gassendus had given before. I answer, there is, indeed, mention made of the grossness of the atmosphere in both, but then the methods wherein it is applied to solve the phenomenon are widely different, as will be evident to whoever shall compare what I have said on this subject with the following words of Gassendus:—

'Hinc dici posse videtur: solem humilem oculo spectatum ideo apparere majorem, quam dum altius egreditur, quia dum vicinus est horizonti prolixa est series vaporum, atque adeo corpus-

---

[n] I. e. the arbitrariness, as far as our thought is concerned, of the apparently constant relation between the proper objects of sight and certain visual sensations, on the one hand, and the distances perceived, through their means, on the other.

An Appendix.

culorum quæ solis radios ita retundunt, ut oculus minus conniveat, et pupilla quasi umbrefacta longe magis amplificetur, quam dum sole multum elato rari vapores intercipiuntur, solque ipse ita splendescit, ut pupilla in ipsum spectans contractissima efficiatur. Nempe ex hoc esse videtur, cur visibilis species ex sole procedens, et per pupillam amplificatam intromissa in retinam, ampliorem in illa sedem occupet, majoremque proinde creet solis apparentiam, quam dum per contractam pupillam eodem intromissa contendit.' Vid. *Epist.* 1. *De Apparente Magnitudine Solis Humilis et Sublimis*, p. 6. This solution of Gassendus proceeds on a false principle, to wit, that the pupil's being enlarged augments the species or image on the fund of the eye.

Thirdly, against what is said in Sect. 80, it is objected, that the same thing which is so small as scarce to be discerned by a man, may appear like a mountain to some small insect; from which it follows that the *minimum visibile* is not equal in respect of all creatures[73]. I answer, if this objection be sounded to the bottom, it will be found to mean no more than that the same particle of matter which is marked to a man by one *minimum visibile*, exhibits to an insect a great number of *minima visibilia*. But this does not prove that one *minimum visibile* of the insect is not equal to one *minimum visibile* of the man. The not distinguishing between the mediate and immediate objects of sight is, I suspect, a cause of misapprehension in this matter.

Some other misinterpretations and difficulties have been made, but, in the points they refer to, I have endeavoured to be so very plain, that I know not how to express myself more clearly. All I shall add is that, if they who are pleased to criticise on my Essay would but read the whole over with some attention, they might be the better able to comprehend my meaning, and consequently to judge of my mistakes.

⁎⁎⁎ I am informed that, soon after the first edition of this treatise, a man somewhere near London was made to see, who had been born blind and continued so for about twenty years[74]. Such

---

[73] Cf. sect. 80—83.
[74] The reference here seems to be to the case described in the *Tatler* (No. 55) of August 16, 1709, which contains an account of a young man, William Jones, born blind, who, at the age of twenty, on the 29th of June preceding, had received sight by a surgical operation. See also a narrative of

a one may be supposed a proper judge to decide how far some tenets laid down in several places of the foregoing Essay are agreeable to truth; and if any curious person hath the opportunity of making proper interrogatories to him thereon, I should gladly see my notions either amended or confirmed by experience [77].

this case, entitled *A full and true account of a miraculous cure of a Young Man in Newington, who was born blind, and was in five minutes brought to perfect sight by* Mr. *Roger Grant*, *oculist*. London 1709.

[77] Cf. *New Theory of Vision Vindicated*, sect. 71, with the relative note.

EDITOR'S PREFACE

TO THE

TREATISE CONCERNING THE PRINCIPLES OF HUMAN KNOWLEDGE.

EDITOR'S PREFACE

TO THE

TREATISE CONCERNING THE PRINCIPLES OF HUMAN KNOWLEDGE.

BERKELEY'S *Treatise concerning the Principles of Human Knowledge* is the most systematically reasoned exposition of his peculiar philosophy which his works contain.

Like the *New Theory of Vision*, its pioneer, it was composed at Trinity College, Dublin. The first edition, 'printed by Aaron Rhames, for Jeremy Pepyat,' appeared in Dublin in 1710. The next, which contains some additions and other changes, was published in London in 1734, 'printed by Jacob Tonson,' the *Three Dialogues between Hylas and Philonous* being conjoined with it in the same volume. This edition was the last in the author's lifetime. The variations in these are carefully marked in the present edition.

An edition of the *Principles* appeared in London in 1776, more than twenty years after Berkeley's death, 'with *Remarks* on each section, in which his doctrines are carefully examined, and shewn to be repugnant to facts, his principles incompatible with the constitution of human nature, and the reason and fitness of things.' To this edition, likewise, the *Dialogues between Hylas and Philonous* are appended, followed by 'A Philosophical Discourse on the Nature of Human Being, containing a defence of Mr. Locke's Principles, and some remarks on Dr. Beattie's *Essay on Truth*,' by the author of the *Remarks*.

To the edition of 1776 the following 'Advertisement' is prefixed:—

'Bishop Berkeley's *Principles of Human Knowledge*, and his *Dialogues between Hylas and Philonous* on the same subject, being out of print, and both being much inquired for, the Editor thought a new edition of them, with an Answer thereto, might not be unacceptable to the public. The tenets maintained in the *Dialogues* are precisely the same with those in the *Principles*, and the arguments are the same, though put into a different form; but it was thought quite unnecessary to make any Reply to them, as the *Remarks* on the former are equally applicable to the latter.

'How far the author of the *Remarks* is right in believing they contain a full refutation of the doctrines of the Bishop must be left to the judgment of the candid reader; he has, however, the satisfaction of knowing the rectitude of his intentions, and the pleasing hopes he entertains that his endeavours may be attended with some success in the cause of truths of the greatest importance.'

The *Remarks* are printed on the right-hand page of the 1776 edition, in sections corresponding in number and length to those of the *Principles*. Their acuteness and conclusiveness, however, is by no means proportioned to their bulk: many of the glaring and ludicrous misrepresentations of which Berkeley's philosophy has been the subject are here gathered and served up.

Although this Treatise is the fullest explanation of Substance and Power, the two central conceptions of Berkeley's philosophy, that he has given, it bears the marks of an unfinished work. It is expressly designated 'Part I,' and in the Preface to the *Dialogues between Hylas and Philonous* the author promises a Second Part, which never appeared. Passages in the work itself, as well as allusions in Berkeley's Commonplace Book, suggest that only a portion of what is required to complete his conception is here executed. In referring Dr. Samuel Johnson, of New York, many years after their publication, to this and his two other early metaphysical essays, Berkeley thus describes their character:—
'I had no inclination to trouble the world with large volumes. What I have done was rather with the view of giving hints to thinking men, who have leisure and curiosity to go to the bottom of things, and pursue them in their own minds. Two or three times reading these small tracts, and making what is read the occasion of thinking, would, I believe, render the whole familiar and easy to the mind, and take off that shocking appearance which hath often been observed to attend speculative truths.'

The contents and language of the *Principles of Human Knowledge* prove that Berkeley had been a careful student of Locke's *Essay*, published twenty years previously, and dedicated, like the *Principles*, to the Earl of Pembroke. This was to be expected, for the *Essay*, partly through the influence of William Molyneux, the friend and correspondent of Locke, had become an authority in Trinity College in Berkeley's undergraduate days. The *Principles* are proposed as a refutation of leading doctrines in the *Essay*. The term 'Idea' is as characteristic of the former as of the latter; in both it stands for the *immediate object of consciousness*—alike in external and internal intuition—in memory, imagination, and generalisation. With both, the only objective universe of which we are directly aware consists of the 'ideas' that we are conscious of, and by both this is assumed as a self-evident truth. Both appeal exclusively to this experience as their final test. Locke's classification of ideas as simple and complex, with some of his divisions and sub-divisions in each class, re-appear, sometimes in altered phraseology, in the *Principles*. Berkeley's whole theory of Substance and Cause, Matter and Mind, Space and Time, is a bold and subtle modification of Locke's theory of 'ideas.' A distinguishing feature in Berkeley is, that he recognises signs of independent reality in one order of Locke's 'ideas'—those given in the senses, and is thus able to dispense with the reasonings in the Fourth Book of the *Essay* on behalf of a real material world. Then, the meaning of the word 'Substance,' which perplexes Locke, is resolved by Berkeley into the concrete and familiar meaning of the word 'I' (*ego*)—the permanent syntheses of ideas perceivable in sense being, according to him, *substances* only in a secondary meaning of that term. 'Cause' or 'Power' he finds exclusively in voluntary activity. Finite 'Space' is with him experience in unresisted organic movement, which is capable of being symbolised in the visual consciousness of coexisting colours. Finite 'Time' is the apprehension of changes in our ideas, length of time being measured by the number of changes. 'Infinite Space' and 'Infinite Time,' because inapprehensible by intelligence, are dismissed from philosophy, as terms void of meaning, or which involve contradictions.

Next to Locke, the influence of Malebranche is apparent in the following Treatise; but Berkeley is not so much at home in the 'Divine vision' of the French metaphysician as among the 'ideas' of the English philosopher. The mysticism of the *Réchérche de la Vérité* was repelled by the transparent clearness of Berkeley's thought. The slender hold that is retained by Malebranche of external substance, as well as the theory of merely occasional causation of matter, common to him and Des Cartes, naturally attracted Berkeley, however, to the Cartesian school, then dominant in France, and reproduced in its mystical form in England by Mr. Norris.

The Platonism which pervades Malebranche perhaps tended to encourage the Platonic thought and varied learning that appear in Berkeley's own later writings; but Locke, Malebranche, and Des Cartes are almost the only philosophers directly or indirectly recognised in the *Principles of Human Knowledge*. In fact, this juvenile Treatise moves, as it seems on the surface, towards the opposite pole from Platonism and a Platonic idealism; for, Berkeley by 'ideas' means phenomena and sensible things, not supersensible realities and Divine Reason of Ontology.

The 'Introduction' to the *Principles* proclaims war with Universals, and more immediately war with Locke. Its remedy for the disorders of philosophy is the expulsion of *abstract ideas*—which, as understood by Berkeley, involve a contradiction; and the restriction of philosophers to the intelligible, concrete objects of which mind can be conscious. The metaphysician is here required to resolve the meaning of such terms as Matter, Substance, Space, and Time into ideas, relations of ideas, and mind which is the one necessary condition on which all ideas and their relations depend; and he is promised that, as the consequence of this, the real world, hitherto obscured by abstractions, will become intelligible. All ideas—in other words, all phenomena or objects of which we can be conscious—must, it is argued, be concrete and particular. It is relations among objects of which we can be conscious, and not pretended abstractions, that can be signified by universal terms. Abstract Matter, abstract Substance, abstract Space, abstract Time—that is Matter, Substance, Space, and Time which are supposed to be what cannot be resolved into particular ideas, and relations among such ideas—are thus in the sequel proved to be absolutely unintelligible. Berkeley's reformed doctrine of abstraction, and of the office of language, virtually banishes them all. With him, 'abstract ideas' are absurdities, resulting from an unlawful analysis, which attempts to penetrate beneath perception or conscious experience —that essence or ground of existence; and the lesson of the 'Introduction' is virtually, that objective existence must consist exclusively of what is particular and concrete. The only lawful kind of abstraction is, that through which we have what Berkeley calls *notions* of *relations* among ideas, as distinguished from ideas themselves. And, as *names* are required to constitute notions, this introductory polemic against abstract ideas, or pretended analyses of the original synthesis of knowledge and existence in perception, takes the form of what is called Nominalism*.

The first two of the 156 sections which compose the *Principles of Human Knowledge* contain a classification of the objects of which we are conscious, and a recognition of Mind as the one condition common to them all.

When we reflect upon our knowledge, we find (sect. 1) that its *ideas* or *immediate objects* are—(a) the phenomena presented to us in or through our different organs of external sense; (b) those of which we are conscious in our internal thoughts, feelings, desires, and volitions; and (c) representations (or misrepresentations) of both of these in memory and imagination. Of these three sorts of ideas, the sensible ones are found in experience to be associated together independently of the will of the percipient, in objective groups, forming what are commonly called 'sensible things,' or (in the popular meaning of substance) material substances†. And all, whether called phenomena, or objects, or ideas; whether presented in external senses, or feelings and operations confined to the individual who is conscious of them, or merely imaginary objects—inasmuch as they are all objects of consciousness—imply (sect. 2) a *subject*, *mind*, *self*, or *ego*, that perceives them, remembers them, and judges of their relations. On mind they must all depend, so far at least as they are actual objects of consciousness, that is to say, so far as they are *ideas*.

What is immediately given to us in experience thus consists of Mind or Spirit, in the state of being conscious of ideas or objects that

---

* The relation between the Phenomenalism (apt at first to be confounded with the assertion of Protagoras) and Nominalist Idealism of Berkeley's early metaphysical writings, on the one hand, and the Platonic Realism and Idealism of his *Siris*, on the other, is one of the most important, and yet hitherto least considered, aspects of his philosophy. In *Siris* (e.g. sect. 335, &c.) he distinguishes the Platonic Ideas (a) from the 'inert, inactive objects' or phenomena of which we are conscious, in our presentative and representative experience (i.e. his own 'ideas'); and also (b) from 'abstract ideas, in the modern sense.' Plato's Ideas are characterised by Berkeley as 'the most real beings, intellectual and unchangeable; and therefore more real than the fleeting, transient objects of sense, which, wanting stability, cannot be subjects of science, much less of intellectual knowledge.'

† According to Berkeley, we are immediately percipient in sense only of *simple ideas*; our so-called perception of sensible *things* (i.e. combinations of simple ideas) is in a great degree mediate—involving a representative, along with a purely presentative, perception. When we see what we recognise to be an apple, but without touching, tasting, or smelling it, we have already learned by custom to combine its qualities; and we have learned also to represent in idea its other than visible qualities, on occasion of the purely visual state of being conscious of the colour, which alone is visible.

belong to one or other of the three classes already mentioned. *Spirits* and *ideas* constitute Berkeley's Dualism. (The exact definition of this duality has been one of the difficulties in his philosophy.)

The lawful aims of human intelligence accordingly seem to be:—

1. The observation of particular ideas, i.e. objects or phenomena.
2. The scientific determination of the relations of particular ideas to one another.
3. The philosophical recognition of their common relation of dependence on Mind; and the study of Mind, as manifested in various orders of intelligent beings.

But, according to the old 'Principles' of metaphysicians, this is not philosophy at all. Philosophy has to do with what is real, absolute, or substantial—with Matter or Substance, and other abstractions, which are assumed to be independent of, i.e. external to, the perceptions of every mind.

The design of the sections which follow the two first is, to state and defend new universal or philosophical Principles, for the regulation of the understanding in its attempts to conceive and reason about the universe. They are proposed instead of the old ones which assumed that *real things* must be abstract entities, independent of Mind. The sections in which they are explained, defended, and applied, may be arranged in three Divisions, thus:—

I. (Sect. 3—33.) Here the new Principles of philosophical knowledge are stated, illustrated, supported by facts and abstract reasoning, and contrasted with the old Principles to which Berkeley attributes the confusion and scepticism involved in all previous attempts. They are virtually three in number—one negative and two affirmative, viz.—

1. The negation of Matter, in the philosophical meaning, or rather no-meaning, of the word; i. e. as signifying an unperceiving and unperceived substance and cause.
2. The affirmation, as Substance proper, of what is signified by the terms mind, spirit, soul, or self—in short, by 'I' (*ego*); and, as Cause proper, of what we are conscious in voluntary effort—a reasonable will.
3. The affirmation of *matter*, in the only intelligible meaning of that term, viz. as consisting of the ideas, objects, or perceptions of sense—which appear, disappear, and re-appear, independently of the will of the mind that is conscious of them, in uniform order of co-existence and succession, so that their changes may be foreseen, and which are the medium of intercourse between one mind and

another; of *material substances*, or groups of co-existing sense-perceptions, united in conscious experience independently of our will, and commonly called 'sensible things;' and of *material causes*, or uniform antecedents in the permanent and rational order of sensible changes.

In short, the universe in which we find ourselves is a universe that consists, in the last analysis, of *mind conscious of ideas or phenomena*. The ideas of *sense* appear in an order which, because independent of our individual will, may be called *external* to each of us; and which, being uniform, is capable of being interpreted; while it affords, through its meaning or reasonableness, exercise and development to reason, and, as a whole, perpetually illustrates the universal supremacy of Divine Mind. Abstract or unperceived Matter, and abstract or unconscious Mind, are banished from philosophy and from the universe; particular ideas or objects, perceived or imagined, and dependent for their existence on conscious minds, capable of interpreting their relations, are alone recognised as real, by the new Principles. What we have, or can have, to do with in the universe, must, accordingly, consist of the conscious experience of conscious agents, in the indefinite varieties of that experience which each may manifest. Unexperienced abstractions are negation or absurdity, to be exploded under the name of 'abstract ideas.' They can neither be believed in nor conceived.

II. (Sect. 34—84.) A series of supposed Objections to the foregoing Principles of the philosophical knowledge of the world and man are stated and refuted in succession in these sections.

III. (Sect. 85—156.) The logical Consequences of the new Principles, in their application to our knowledge of (a) the *ideas* or objective things, and (b) the *minds* or subjective things that constitute the universe, are here unfolded. A restoration of belief, and a simplification and purification of the sciences, by the exclusion of unmeaning abstract questions, are represented as among their chief advantages.

Let us now look at the grounds, in faith, reasoning, and experience, on which Berkeley rests these new Principles, in the thirty-one sections which form the First Division of his work. The discussion may be said to take its rise from a question which is virtually proposed in section 3. The objects of conscious experience—in a word our ideas—were alleged, in section 1, to be (a) sense-given or external phenomena, (b) internal phenomena, (c) phenomena which may be representative or misrepresentative of both these. The question proposed, by implication, in section 3 is this:—

Are any of these phenomena *not ideas merely*, but also things that exist *absolutely*—that is to say, independently of their ideal character, and in complete abstraction from a conscious mind; or, if the very phenomena of which we are immediately percipient be not themselves thus independent of being perceived, do all, or any of them, represent something that does exist absolutely? In short, are we can we be, either directly or indirectly, cognisant of aught existing unintelligibly or without a Mind?

Now, the objects or phenomena of which we are conscious in the senses, i. e. our *sense*-ideas or perceptions, are, it is assumed, the only ones about which this question can be raised. Hence the problem of this Division of the Treatise is—to find whether the phenomena presented in the five senses, are either *themselves* in substance external, or *represent* things that are in substance external—meaning by 'external,' without (i. e. unperceived and unconceived by) a mind, foreign to all conscious experience.

That the ideas or phenomena actually presented to us in the five senses cannot *themselves* be qualities of what is external, in this meaning of the term 'external,' is affirmed (sect. 3) to be 'intuitively evident.' An object is called an *idea* because it is present in a conscious experience. Now, we have no sensible proof that it continues to exist when it is not thus present; and every sensible thing includes qualities which, by the consent of all who think, are dependent on a sentient organization.

But, although our very sense-given ideas themselves cannot exist substantially, when divested of their ideal or immediately objective character, and put out of all relation to a conscious mind, may they not, it is asked (sect. 8), *represent* what exists in an unthinking substance? This supposition, it is answered, is a mere unproved supposition, and it even involves a contradiction. Those supposed solid, extended, and coloured *originals* or *archetypes* of our sense-ideas are themselves perceived, or they are not. If they are perceived, they are *ipso facto* ideas; for, an idea is simply that which, whatever else it may be, is the immediate object of a conscious mind. On the other hand, if they are not themselves, and cannot be, contained in a conscious experience, they cannot resemble what is so contained. 'An idea can be like nothing but an idea.' A quantity of conscious experience can be like nothing but another quantity of conscious experience. This conclusion cannot be evaded, it is argued (sect. 9), by Locke's favourite discrimination of the qualities of this unperceiving and unperceived Matter into primary and secondary: so that if solid, extended, coloured substances exist *per se*, or absolutely, it is impossible that we should come to know this; and, if they do not thus exist, we should have exactly the same reason for believing in their absolute existence that we now have (sect. 20).

The very supposition, however, of the existence of anything out of conscious experience involves, Berkeley further argues, a contradiction in terms (sect. 23). We may, indeed, imagine trees in a park, or books in our study, with no one at hand to perceive them, and maintain their existence in a *presentative* experience. But, are we not ourselves, in the very act of thus imagining them, keeping them in existence in our *representative* experience? Thus, when we do our utmost, by imagination, to conceive bodies existing externally or absolutely, we are, in the very act of doing so, making them ideas—not of sense, indeed, but of imagination. The supposition itself of their unideal existence makes them ideas; inasmuch as it makes them imaginary objects, dependent on an imagining mind.

On the whole, to say that sensible objects either themselves are, or themselves represent substances that exist independent of Mind, is to say what involves a contradiction in terms, or it is to use words which mean nothing. It is to speak unintelligibly, in short, according to the general conclusion of this part of the Treatise.

In thus banishing Absolute Material Substance, Berkeley does not allow that he has banished Substance—a substantiating or uniting principle, in which phenomena have their ground and meaning. He substitutes an intelligible, because intelligent, substantiating principle, of which we are conscious, for an unintelligible and contradictory one, of which we neither are nor can be conscious. Here Berkeley's thought becomes obscure. I think it may be worked out in this way:—Absolute Material Substance is, he says, an empty abstraction of metaphysicians, and every real substance must be either perceived or percipient; for we cannot go below experience or consciousness. Now, every percept or phenomenon perceived implies a percipient, and every percipient implies a percept. Are substances, then (i.e. the ultimate ground of phenomena), percepts, or are they percipient minds? When we compare these, we find that the deepest and truest ground of things lies in the latter, and not in the former; in a mind, and not in percepts or phenomena which depend upon a mind. We are aware in memory of the mysterious identity of the former, and to this *personal identity* there is no counterpart in the perpetual changes of the perceived or objective world. The *substances* of the universe are thus properly the minds or persons that exist in it. There is, strictly speaking, 'no other Substance than *Spirit*, or that which perceives' (sect. 7).

It is next argued (sect. 25—27), that voluntary mental activity is the only Causation in the universe—that all Power, as well as all Substance, is essentially mental. To satisfy ourselves that changes among phenomena are only the passive effects of spiritual agency, it is maintained that we have only to observe them. As the essence of all phenomena has been proved to consist in perception of them, it follows that they cannot contain anything of which the percipient is incognisant. Now, power or activity is not exhibited by any. Sensible (or other) phenomena, therefore, cannot be the cause of our being conscious. Nor can they cause the changes which occur among themselves: phenomena are related to each other as signs and significates, not as causes and effects.

But, while the universe of ideas or phenomena is void of causality, power (implied in the changes of the objects of consciousness) must exist. As it cannot be attributed to ideas, it must belong to that on which they depend. Now, Berkeley has already concluded that what they depend on must be conscious Mind, Self, or Ego. To conscious Mind, Self, or Ego, accordingly, he refers all the changes in existence. Minds not only substantiate phenomena; they cause changes.

But there is a plurality of powers at work among ideas. Each one of us finds, on trial, that his personal power over the phenomena of which he is conscious varies (sect. 28—33). We can make and unmake at pleasure the objects of *imagination;* the ideas of the *senses* are independent in a much greater degree of the mind to which they are present. When in broad daylight we open our eyes, it is not in our power to choose whether we shall see or not, or to determine what particular objects shall present themselves to our view. In our sense-experience we find ourselves confronted by the signs of a larger reason and a firmer will than are exhibited in the arbitrary constructions of our own imagination; we encounter the Supreme Power signified by the steady natural laws of sense-given phenomena. In and through our senses, we awaken to the discovery, that our individual conscious life is, in the sense-given part of it, a portion of the Universal System, which is evolved in a manner so orderly and constant that we can, by interpreting what we perceive, foresee the future, and regulate our lives. What we perceive places us habitually in relation to Supreme or Essential Intelligence expressed in the laws of nature; and to other minds, like our own, who share with us this experience of the senses, and who, through its means, can (we find) convey to us, and we to them, indications of our respective experiences. The ideas which are given to us in the Senses are thus distinguished from all our other ideas. Their arrangements of co-existence and succession are not merely the arbitrary results of our own imaginative activity; they are independent of, or external to, our will. They thus reveal to us the only contemporaneous External World of which we have any proof, or of which we can even conceive the possibility—a world in other minds. Ideas of this sort (if, indeed, one should call *them* 'ideas' at all) may emphatically be distinguished from all other ideas, as *real* ones; and their established combinations are what men commonly call 'real things.'

These sections (28—33) are among the most important in the Treatise. They express Berkeley's reasons for distinguishing groups of real or sense ideas—which, irrelative to anything beyond, can neither be representative nor misrepresentative—from ideas in an individual imagination. All truth and all error belong to the latter, not to the former. Physical truth is the true interpretation of real or sense ideas. Physical error is the misinterpretation of *these* ideas. But sense-ideas themselves, which may be thus interpreted or misinterpreted, represent nothing—except, indeed, the Divine meaning of which their laws are signs, and of which human science is the imperfect interpretation. They can have no archetypes behind them, existing in an unconscious substance. Imagination is the only representative faculty. *A representative sense-perception is an absurdity*[*]. The ideas of sense are what they are, and we cannot go deeper. If they were themselves representations of other ideas, then these others would become the real ideas, and those so called would be relegated to imagination. And Absolute Matter is not their archetype, which, as it cannot be perceived in sense, can as little be suggested by custom and association, inferred by abstract reasoning, or believed in by the common faith or reason of men. . The world of material things is thus substantially syntheses of phenomena in conscious minds, and Intelligence is the essence of the universe.

Such in spirit are Berkeley's new Principles, with the grounds in reason and experience to which he refers them. What I have called

[*] Illustrations of this statement, and a comparison of Berkeley's presentative perception with that of the Scotch psychologists, will be given afterwards.

the Second Division of the Treatise (sect. 34—84) is devoted to the statement and refutation of supposed Objections to the Principles.

The objections and answers may be briefly presented as follows:—

First objection. (Sect. 34—40.) The preceding Principles banish from existence all that is real and substantial, and substitute a universe of mere ideas or chimeras.

Answer. This objection is a play upon the popular meaning of the word 'idea.' That word may be used to signify objects of sense—in respect of their necessary dependence upon mind; and not merely fancies and chimeras, the 'ideas' of popular language, creatures of individual minds, which may, and often do, misrepresent the real ideas of the natural system that is independent of our will, while dependent on Divine Mind and Will. An idea, in the language of this system, is simply that of which we are conscious.

Second objection. (Sect. 41.) The preceding Principles abolish the distinction between Perception and Imagination—between imagining one's self burnt and actually being burnt.

Answer. Real fire differs from the mere thought or fancy of it, as real pain does from the mere thought or fancy of pain; and yet no one supposes that real any more than imaginary pain can exist unperceived, or in an unperceiving substance.

Third objection. (Sect. 42—44.) We see sensible things actually existing at a distance from us. Now, whatever is thus seen at a distance is surely seen as external, which contradicts the foregoing Principles.

Answer. Distance, or outness, is absolutely invisible. It is a conception which is suggested gradually, by our experience of the connection between colours (which alone we see) and visual sensations that accompany seeing, on the one hand, and certain varieties of tactual and locomotive experience, on the other—as was proved in the *Essay towards a New Theory of Vision*, in which the mere ideality of the *visible* world is demonstrated*.

Fourth objection. (Sect. 45—48.) It follows from the new Principles, that real things, i.e. combinations of real or sense ideas, must be at every moment annihilated and created anew.

Answer. On the contrary, it is quite consistent with the new Principles that a sensible thing may actually exist, in the sense-experience of other minds, during the intervals of perception by an individual

---

* Moreover, even if the outness or distance of things were visible, it would not follow that either they or their distance exist unperceived. On the contrary, the very hypothesis implies that they are perceived visually.

mind; for the Principles do not affirm their substantial and causal dependence on this, that, or the other mind, but on Mind. They imply, indeed, a constant creation or presentation in finite minds; but the conception of the universe in a state of constant creation was familiar to the Schoolmen and other Theists, and enables us impressively to realise Divine Providence.

Fifth objection. (Sect. 49.) If extension and the other primary qualities of matter can exist only *in mind*, it follows that extension is an attribute of mind—that mind is extended.

Answer. Extension and other sensible qualities exist *in mind* not as modes or attributes, which is unintelligible, but as *ideas*, or objects of which Mind is percipient; and this is absolutely inconsistent with the supposition that mind itself is extended or solid*.

Sixth objection. (Sect. 50.) The Newtonian and other discoveries in natural philosophy proceed on an assumption of external Matter, and are thus inconsistent with the new Principles.

Answer. On the contrary, external Matter—if 'external' means what exists in absolute independence of Mind—is useless in natural philosophy, which is conversant exclusively with particular ideas, phenomena, or concrete things, and not with mere abstractions.

Seventh objection. (Sect. 51.) It is absurd, because at variance with the universal use of language, to exclude power or causation from Matter, and to attribute every sensible phenomenon to Mind, as the foregoing Principles do.

Answer. While we may continue to speak as the unreflecting multitude do, we should learn to think with the reflecting or philosophical. We may still speak of physical causes, even when, as philosophers, we have recognised that all true efficiency is in mind, and that the material world is only a system of sensible symbols regulated by mind.

Eighth objection. (Sect. 54, 55.) The Common Sense or universal belief of men is inconsistent with the exclusively ideal character of real or external things.

Answer. This is doubtful, when we consider that, in their natural confusion of thought, ordinary men do not comprehend the metaphysical

---

* It is also to be remembered that sensible things may exist 'in mind,' without being *mine*—meaning by 'mine' the creatures of my will. Mind and they are connected, but not as cause and effect. Properly speaking, that only is mine in which my will exerts itself. But, in another view, my involuntary states of feeling and imagination are mine, because their existence depends on my individual consciousness of them; and even sensible things are *mine*, because, though present in many minds in common, they are, for me, dependent on my mind.

meaning of their own assumptions; and it seems a small objection, when we recollect the prejudices, dignified as Common Sense, which have successively surrendered to philosophy.

Ninth objection. (Sect. 56, 57.) Any Principle that is inconsistent with the common belief in the existence of an external world must be rejected.

Answer. The fact that we are conscious of not being ourselves the cause of changes in our *sense*-ideas, which we gradually learn by experience to foresee, sufficiently accounts for the common belief in externality, and is what men really mean by the word.

Tenth objection. (Sect. 58, 59.) The foregoing Principles concerning Matter and Mind are inconsistent with various established truths in mathematics and natural philosophy.

Answer. The laws of motion, and the other truths here referred to, may be all conceived and expressed in perfect consistency with the new Principles about the substantiality and causality of Minds, and the absence of all proper substance and causation in Matter.

Eleventh objection. (Sect. 60—66.) If, according to the foregoing Principles, the material world is merely the series of phenomenal or ideal effects of which we are conscious in our senses, the elaborate contrivances which it contains are useless.

Answer. These elaborate contrivances, while unnecessary as causes, are relatively necessary as signs: they express to *us* the occasional presence of other finite minds, the constant presence and power of Supreme Mind, and the Divine Ideas of which the objective universe is the symbol.

Twelfth objection. (Sect. 67—79.) Although the impossibility of an Absolute Material Substance that is active, solid, and extended may be a demonstrable Principle, this does not prove the impossibility of one that is *inactive,* and *neither solid nor extended,* which may be the occasion of our sense-ideas, or which at any rate may exist.

Answer. This supposition is unintelligible: the words in which it is expressed cannot convey any meaning.

Thirteenth objection. (Sect. 80, 81.) Notwithstanding the foregoing Principles, Matter may be *an unknown somewhat,* neither substance nor accident, cause nor effect, spirit nor idea; and all the reasonings against the notion of Matter, conceived as something positive, fail, when this purely negative notion is maintained.

Answer. This is to use the word 'Matter' as people use the word 'nothing:' the supposed abstract existence cannot be distinguished from nothing.

Fourteenth objection. (Sect. 82—84.) Although we cannot, in opposition to the new Principles, infer by reasoning the independent or absolute existence of Matter, according to any possible conception, either positive or negative, of what Matter is; and although we may be unable even to understand what the word means, yet, Holy Scripture is sufficient to convince every Christian of the existence of an external material world—as an object of faith.

Answer. The absolute or independent existence of a material world is nowhere affirmed in Scripture, which employs language in its popular and practical meaning.

In what I have called the Third Division of the Treatise (sect. 85—156), the new Principles, thus guarded against objections, are applied to invigorate belief, which was suffering from the paralysis of metaphysical Scepticism. They are also employed to purify and simplify the sciences which relate to the *ideal world of the senses*—the Physical Sciences; and those which relate to *spirits*, by whom ideas are sustained, and their changes determined—the science of Minds, and Theology. It may be thus subdivided:—

I. (Sect. 85—134.) Application of the new Principles, concerning Matter, Mind, Substance, and Cause, to our knowledge of the objective and physical world of *ideas*—

1. To the refutation of Scepticism, as to the existence of sensible things (sect. 85—91); and of God (sect. 92—96);
2. To the liberation of Thought from the bondage of unmeaning abstractions (sect. 97—100);
3. To the purification of Natural Philosophy, by correcting paradoxical conceptions of Time, Space, and Motion (sect. 101—116);
4. And of Mathematics, through criticism of our notions of Number and Extension, and by the abolition of the contradictions involved in the common doctrine of Infinites (sect. 117—134).

II. (Sect. 135—156.) Application of the new Principles to our *notions* of Mind or Spirit—

1. To explain and sustain our faith in our natural Immortality (sect. 137—144);
2. To explain and vindicate the belief which each man has in the existence of other men (sect. 145);
3. To vindicate belief in the existence of Supreme Mind (sect. 146—156).

It was only by degrees that this scheme of Berkeley's philosophy attracted the attention due to so original and ingenious a mode of conceiving the Universe. A fragment of metaphysics, by a young and almost unknown author, published at a distance from the centre of English intellectual life, was apt to be overlooked. In connection with the *Essay on Vision*, however, it drew enough of regard to carry its author with *éclat* on his first visit to London, three years after the publication of the *Principles*. He then published the immortal *Dialogues between Hylas and Philonous*, in which the absurdity of Absolute Matter is illustrated, and the doctrine defended against objections, in a manner meant to recommend to popular acceptance what, on the first statement, seemed an unpopular paradox.

A. C. F.

A TREATISE

CONCERNING

THE PRINCIPLES OF HUMAN KNOWLEDGE.

[¹ PART I.]

WHEREIN THE CHIEF CAUSES OF ERROR AND DIFFICULTY IN THE SCIENCES, WITH THE GROUNDS OF SCEPTICISM, ATHEISM, AND IRRELIGION, ARE INQUIRED INTO.

First Printed in the Year 1710.

---

[1] Omitted on the title-page, but retained in the body of the work in the second or 1734 edition.

TO THE RIGHT HONOURABLE

THOMAS, EARL OF PEMBROKE[1], &c.,

KNIGHT OF THE MOST NOBLE ORDER OF THE GARTER, AND ONE OF THE LORDS OF HER MAJESTY'S MOST HONOURABLE PRIVY COUNCIL.

My Lord,

You will perhaps wonder that an obscure person, who has not the honour to be known to your lordship, should presume to address you in this manner. But that a man who has written something with a design to promote Useful Knowledge and Religion in the world should make choice of your lordship for his patron, will not be thought strange by any one that is not altogether unacquainted with the present state of the church and learning, and consequently ignorant how great an ornament and support you are to both. Yet, nothing could have induced me to make you this present of my poor endeavours, were I not encouraged by that candour and native goodness which is so bright a part in your lordship's character. I might add, my lord, that the extraordinary favour and bounty you have been pleased to shew towards our Society[2] gave me hopes you would not be unwilling to countenance the studies of one of its members. These considerations determined me to lay this treatise at your lordship's feet, and the rather because I was ambitious to have it known that I am with the truest and most profound respect, on account of that learning and virtue which the world so justly admires in your lordship,

My Lord,

Your lordship's most humble

and most devoted servant,

GEORGE BERKELEY.

---

[1] Thomas Herbert, eighth Earl of Pembroke and fifth Earl of Montgomery, the friend of Locke—who dedicated his *Essay* to him, as a work 'having some little correspondence with some parts of that nobler and vast system of the sciences your lordship has made so new, exact, and instructive a draft of'—and representative of a family renowned in English political and literary history. He was born in 1656; was a nobleman of Christ Church, Oxford, in 1673; succeeded to his titles in 1683; was sworn of the Privy Council in 1689; and was made a Knight of the Garter in 1700. He filled some of the highest offices in the state, in the reigns of William and Mary, and of Anne. He was Lord Lieutenant of Ireland in 1707, having previously been one of the Commissioners by whom the union between England and Scotland was negotiated. He died in January 1733.

[2] Trinity College, Dublin.

THE PREFACE.

What I here make public has, after a long and scrupulous inquiry[1], seemed to me evidently true and not unuseful to be known—particularly to those who are tainted with Scepticism, or want a demonstration of the existence and immateriality of God, or the natural immortality of the soul. Whether it be so or no I am content the reader should impartially examine; since I do not think myself any farther concerned for the success of what I have written than as it is agreeable to truth. But, to the end this may not suffer, I make it my request that the reader suspend his judgment till he has once at least read the whole through with that degree of attention and thought which the subject-matter shall seem to deserve. For, as there are some passages that, taken by themselves, are very liable (nor could it be remedied) to gross misinterpretation, and to be charged with most absurd consequences, which, nevertheless, upon an entire perusal will appear not to follow from them; so likewise, though the whole should be read over, yet, if this be done transiently, it is very probable my sense may be mistaken; but to a thinking reader, I flatter myself it will be throughout clear and obvious. As for the characters of novelty and singularity[2] which some of the following notions may seem to bear, it is, I hope, needless to make any apology on that account. He must surely be either very weak, or very little acquainted with the sciences, who shall reject a truth that is capable of demonstration[3], for no other reason but because it is newly known[4], and contrary to the prejudices of mankind. Thus much I thought fit to premise, in order to prevent, if possible, the hasty censures of a sort of men who are too apt to condemn an opinion before they rightly comprehend it[5].

---

[1] In his Common-place Book Berkeley seems to refer his speculations to his boyhood. The theory of the sensible world propounded in the following Treatise was obviously conceived by him before the publication of the *New Theory of Vision*, which was a first instalment of it.

[2] Cf. Locke, in the 'Epistle Dedicatory' of his *Essay*. As regards the 'novelty' of the chief principles of the following treatise, viz. the *negation of Abstract Entities* (absolute or unperceived Matter, absolute Space, absolute Time, absolute Substance, and absolute Cause); and the *affirmation of Mind*, as the Synthesis, Substance, and Cause of all ideas or objects—the best preceding philosophy, ancient and modern, was a dim anticipation of it.

[3] Cf. sect. 6, 22, 24, &c., in illustration of the demonstrative character of Berkeley's distinctive doctrine.

[4] Berkeley's one request to his reader, here and throughout his writings, is, to take pains to understand his meaning. This especially requires us to avoid confounding his *sense-ideas* with mere fancies or chimeras—arbitrary creations of the individual mind. The history of this doctrine has been a history of its misinterpretation.

INTRODUCTION.

1. Philosophy being nothing else but the study of wisdom and truth[1], it may with reason be expected that those who have spent most time and pains in it should enjoy a greater calm and serenity of mind, a greater clearness and evidence of knowledge, and be less disturbed with doubts and difficulties than other men. Yet so it is, we see the illiterate bulk of mankind, that walk the high-road of plain common sense, and are governed by the dictates of nature, for the most part easy and undisturbed. To them nothing that is familiar appears unaccountable or difficult to comprehend. They complain not of any want of evidence in their senses, and are out of all danger of becoming Sceptics. But no sooner do we depart from sense and instinct to follow the light of a superior principle—to reason, meditate, and reflect on the nature of things, but a thousand scruples spring up in our minds concerning those things which before we seemed fully to comprehend. Prejudices and errors of sense do from all parts discover themselves to our view; and, endeavouring to correct these by reason, we are insensibly drawn into uncouth paradoxes, difficulties, and inconsistencies, which multiply and grow upon us as we advance in speculation, till at length, having wandered through many intricate mazes, we find ourselves just where we were, or, which is worse, sit down in a forlorn Scepticism[2].

2. The cause of this is thought to be the obscurity of things, or the natural weakness and imperfection of our understandings. It

---

[1] 'Philosophy, which is nothing but the true knowledge of things.' Locke.
[2] The purpose of these early essays of Berkeley was to reconcile philosophy with common sense, by employing demonstration to make common sense reveal itself truly. Cf. the closing sentences in the *Third Dialogue between Hylas and Philonous*.

is said, 'the faculties we have are few, and those designed by nature for the support and pleasure of life, and not to penetrate into the inward essence and constitution of things. Besides, the mind of man being finite, when it treats of things which partake of infinity, it is not to be wondered at if it run into absurdities and contradictions, out of which it is impossible it should ever extricate itself, it being of the nature of infinite not to be comprehended by that which is finite[a].'

3. But, perhaps, we may be too partial to ourselves in placing the fault originally in our faculties, and not rather in the wrong use we make of them. It is a hard thing to suppose that right deductions from true principles should ever end in consequences which cannot be maintained or made consistent. We should believe that God has dealt more bountifully with the sons of men than to give them a strong desire for that knowledge which he had placed quite out of their reach. This were not agreeable to the wonted indulgent methods of Providence, which, whatever appetites it may have implanted in the creatures, doth usually furnish them with such means as, if rightly made use of, will not fail to satisfy them. Upon the whole, I am inclined to think that the far greater part, if not all, of those difficulties which have hitherto amused philosophers, and blocked up the way to knowledge, are entirely owing to ourselves—that we have first raised a dust and then complain we cannot see.

4. My purpose therefore is, to try if I can discover what those Principles are[b] which have introduced all that doubtfulness and uncertainty, those absurdities and contradictions, into the several sects of philosophy; insomuch that the wisest men have thought our ignorance incurable, conceiving it to arise from the natural dulness and limitation of our faculties[a]. And surely it is a work well deserving our pains to make a strict inquiry concerning the First Principles of Human Knowledge, to sift and examine them on all sides, especially since there may be some grounds to suspect

---

[a] Cf. Locke's *Essay*, Introduction, sect. 4—7; B. II. ch. 23, § 12, &c. Locke (who is here in Berkeley's eye) attributes the perplexities of philosophy to our narrow faculties, which are meant, he maintains, to regulate our lives, and not to explain the mysteries of Being. See also Des Cartes, *Principia*, I. 26, 27, &c.; Malebranche, *Recherche*, III. 2.

[b] The assumption that Matter, Space, Time, Substance, Cause, may and do exist as abstract entities, i.e. unperceived and unconceived by a mind, is, with Berkeley, the fundamental false principle, to which is due the alleged confusion and inconsistency of philosophy, and the consequent inclination to philosophical and religious scepticism.

Introduction. 139

that those lets and difficulties, which stay and embarrass the mind in its search after truth, do not spring from any darkness and intricacy in the objects, or natural defect in the understanding, so much as from false Principles which have been insisted on, and might have been avoided.

5. How difficult and discouraging soever this attempt may seem, when I consider what a number of very great and extraordinary men have gone before me in the like designs[3], yet I am not without some hopes—upon the consideration that the largest views are not always the clearest, and that he who is short-sighted will be obliged to draw the object nearer, and may, perhaps, by a close and narrow survey, discern that which had escaped far better eyes.

6. In order to prepare the mind of the reader for the easier conceiving what follows, it is proper to premise somewhat, by way of Introduction, concerning the nature and abuse of Language. But the unravelling this matter leads me in some measure to anticipate my design, by taking notice of what seems to have had a chief part in rendering speculation intricate and perplexed, and to have occasioned innumerable errors and difficulties in almost all parts of knowledge. And that is the opinion that the mind hath a power of framing *abstract ideas* or notions of things[4]. He who is not a perfect stranger to the writings and disputes of philosophers must needs acknowledge that no small part of them are spent about abstract ideas. These are in a more

---

[3] A work previously undertaken under the same designation, by Des Cartes in his *Principia*, and, in fact if not in name, by Locke in his *Essay*.

[4] Here 'abstract idea' and 'notion' are used convertibly. Cf. sect. 143. Cf. with what follows against abstract ideas in the remainder of the Introduction, sect. 97—100, 118—132, 143; *New Theory of Vision*, sect. 121—125; *Alciphron*, Dial. vii. 5—7; *Defence of Free Thinking in Mathematics*, sect. 45—48; *Siris*, sect. 323, 335, &c., where he distinguishes the Platonic Ideas from the 'ideas' and Nominalism of his own early philosophy.

In the following sections Berkeley has Locke chiefly in view. He appears here as the second great modern defender of Nominalism, and is so referred to by Hume, *Treatise of Human Nature*, B. I. part I, ch. 7. Hobbes was the first. Berkeley's reasonings, in the sections which follow, have become commonplace in later discussions of the question. What are we cognisant of when we use the common terms on which human science depends? According to Berkeley, it is not an idea, inasmuch as all ideas (i.e. presentative and representative objects) must either be particular or else involve contradictory characters; it is, he concludes, a relation among ideas that we know when we employ general terms. Yet, many who have accepted his reasonings against abstract ideas have not discerned their connexion with his abolition of abstract Matter and Space.

especial manner thought to be the object of those sciences which go by the name of Logic and Metaphysics, and of all that which passes under the notion of the most abstracted and sublime learning, in all which one shall scarce find any question handled in such a manner as does not suppose their existence in the mind, and that it is well acquainted with them.

7. It is agreed on all hands that the qualities or modes of things do never really exist each of them apart by itself, and separated from all others, but are mixed, as it were, and blended together, several in the same object. But, we are told, the mind being able to consider each quality singly, or abstracted from those other qualities with which it is united, does by that means frame to itself abstract ideas. For example, there is perceived by sight an object extended, coloured, and moved: this mixed or compound idea the mind resolving into its simple, constituent parts, and viewing each by itself, exclusive of the rest, does frame the abstract ideas of extension, colour, and motion. Not that it is possible for colour or motion to exist without extension; but only that the mind can frame to itself by *abstraction* the idea of colour exclusive of extension, and of motion exclusive of both colour and extension.

8. Again, the mind having observed that in the particular extensions perceived by sense there is something common and alike in all, and some other things peculiar, as this or that figure or magnitude, which distinguish them one from another; it considers apart or singles out by itself that which is common, making thereof a most abstract idea of extension, which is neither line, surface, nor solid, nor has any figure or magnitude, but is an idea entirely prescinded from all these. So likewise the mind, by leaving out of the particular colours perceived by sense that which distinguishes them one from another, and retaining that only which is common to all, makes an idea of colour in abstract which is neither red, nor blue, nor white, nor any other determinate colour. And, in like manner, by considering motion abstractedly not only from the body moved, but likewise from the figure it describes, and all particular directions and velocities, the abstract idea of motion is framed; which equally corresponds to all particular motions whatsoever that may be perceived by sense.

Introduction. 141

9. And as the mind frames to itself abstract ideas of qualities or modes, so does it, by the same precision or mental separation, attain abstract ideas of the more compounded beings[1] which include several coexistent qualities. For example, the mind having observed that Peter, James, and John resemble each other in certain common agreements of shape and other qualities, leaves out of the complex or compounded idea it has of Peter, James and any other particular man, that which is peculiar to each, retaining only what is common to all, and so makes an abstract idea wherein all the particulars equally partake—abstracting entirely from and cutting off all those circumstances and differences which might determine it to any particular existence. And after this manner it is said we come by the abstract idea of man, or, if you please, humanity, or human nature; wherein it is true there is included colour, because there is no man but has some colour, but then it can be neither white, nor black, nor any particular colour, because there is no one particular colour wherein all men partake. So likewise there is included stature, but then it is neither tall stature, nor low stature, nor yet middle stature, but something abstracted from all these. And so of the rest. Moreover, there being a great variety of other creatures that partake in some parts, but not all, of the complex idea of man, the mind, leaving out those parts which are peculiar to men, and retaining those only which are common to all the living creatures, frames the idea of *animal*, which abstracts not only from all particular men, but also all birds, beasts, fishes, and insects. The constituent parts of the abstract idea of animal are body, life, sense, and spontaneous motion. By *body* is meant body without any particular shape or figure, there being no one shape or figure common to all animals, without covering, either of hair, or feathers, or scales, &c., nor yet naked: hair, feathers, scales, and nakedness being the distinguishing properties of particular animals, and for that reason left out of the *abstract idea*. Upon the same account the spontaneous motion must be neither walking, nor flying, nor creeping; it is nevertheless a motion, but what that motion is it is not easy to conceive.

10. Whether others have this wonderful faculty of abstracting

---

[1] Cf. sect. 1 of the *Principles*.

their ideas⁸, they best can tell: for myself, [⁹ I dare be confident I have it not.] I find indeed I have indeed a faculty of imagining, or representing to myself, the ideas of those particular things I have perceived, and of variously compounding and dividing them. I can imagine a man with two heads, or the upper parts of a man joined to the body of a horse. I can consider the hand, the eye, the nose, each by itself abstracted or separated from the rest of the body. But then whatever hand or eye I imagine, it must have some particular shape and colour. Likewise the idea of man that I frame to myself must be either of a white, or a black, or a tawny, a straight, or a crooked, a tall, or a low, or a middle-sized man. I cannot by any effort of thought conceive the abstract idea above described. And it is equally impossible for me to form the abstract idea of motion distinct from the body moving, and which is neither swift nor slow, curvilinear nor rectilinear; and the like may be said of all other abstract general ideas whatsoever. To be plain, I own myself able to abstract in one sense, as when I consider some particular parts or qualities separated from others, with which, though they are united in some object, yet it is possible they may really exist without them. But I deny that I can abstract from one another, or conceive separately, those qualities which it is impossible should exist so separated; or that I can frame a general notion, by abstracting from particulars in the manner aforesaid—which last are the two proper acceptations of *abstraction*. And there is ground to think most men will acknowledge themselves to be in my case. The generality of men which are simple and illiterate never pretend to *abstract notions*[10]. It is said they are difficult and not to be attained without pains and study; we may therefore reasonably conclude that, if such there be, they are confined only to the learned.

11. I proceed to examine what can be alleged in defence of the doctrine of abstraction[11], and try if I can discover what it is that inclines the men of speculation to embrace an opinion so remote

from common sense as that seems to be. There has been a late [[1]excellent] and deservedly esteemed philosopher who, no doubt, has given it very much countenance, by seeming to think the having abstract general ideas is what puts the widest difference in point of understanding betwixt man and beast. 'The having of general ideas,' saith he, 'is that which puts a perfect distinction betwixt man and brutes, and is an excellency which the faculties of brutes do by no means attain unto. For, it is evident we observe no foot-steps in them of making use of general signs for universal ideas; from which we have reason to imagine that they have not the faculty of abstracting, or making general ideas, since they have no use of words or any other general signs.' And a little after, 'Therefore, I think, we may suppose that it is in this that the species of brutes are discriminated from men, and it is that proper difference wherein they are wholly separated, and which at last widens to so wide a distance. For, if they have any ideas at all, and are not bare machines (as some would have them), we cannot deny them to have some reason. It seems as evident to me that they do, some of them, in certain instances reason as that they have sense; but it is only in particular ideas, just as they receive them from their senses. They are the best of them tied up within those narrow bounds, and have not (as I think) the faculty to enlarge them by any kind of abstraction.'—*Essay on Human Understanding*, B. II. ch. 11. § 10 and 11. I readily agree with this learned author, that the faculties of brutes can by no means attain to abstraction. But then if this be made the distinguishing property of that sort of animals, I fear a great many of those that pass for men must be reckoned into their number. The reason that is here assigned why we have no grounds to think brutes have abstract general ideas is, that we observe in them no use of words or any other general signs; which is built on this supposition—that the making use of words implies the having general ideas. From which it follows that men who use language are able to abstract or generalize their ideas. That this is the sense and arguing of the author will further appear by his answering the question he in another place puts: 'Since all things that exist are only particulars,

objects or ideas, e.g. 'Existence,' after abstraction of all the phenomena in which it manifests itself to us; or 'Matter,' after abstraction of all the phenomena which appear to the senses—perception or intelligence being abstracted, in short.

[1] Omitted in second edition.

how come we by general terms?' His answer is: 'Words become general by being made the signs of general ideas.'—*Essay on Human Understanding*, B. III. cb. 3. § 6. But it seems that a word[13] becomes general by being made the sign, not of an abstract general idea, but of several particular ideas, any one of which it indifferently suggests to the mind[14]. For example, when it is said 'the change of motion is proportional to the impressed force,' or that 'whatever has extension is divisible,' these propositions are to be understood of motion and extension in general; and nevertheless it will not follow that they suggest to my thoughts an idea of motion without a body moved, or any determinate direction and velocity, or that I must conceive an abstract general idea of extension, which is neither line, surface, nor solid, neither great nor small, black, white, nor red, nor of any other determinate colour. It is only implied that whatever particular motion I consider, whether it be swift or slow, perpendicular, horizontal, or oblique, or in whatever object, the axiom concerning it holds equally true. As does the other of every particular extension, it matters not whether line, surface, or solid, whether of this or that magnitude or figure.

12. By observing how ideas become general, we may the better judge how words are made so. And here it is to be noted that I do not deny absolutely there are general ideas, but only that there are any *abstract* general ideas[15]; for, in the passages we have quoted wherein there is mention of general ideas, it is always supposed that they are formed by abstraction, after the manner set forth in sections 8 and 9. Now, if we will annex a meaning to our words, and speak only of what we can conceive, I believe we shall acknowledge that an idea which, considered in itself, is particular,

[13] 'To this I cannot assent, being of opinion that a word,' &c.—in first edition.

[14] Though we cannot have the logical extent and content of our concepts intuitively exhibited to us, either in a percept or in an image, it is to be noted that we may have resembling signs of conceptual relations, as well as verbal or non-resembling signs. We think by means of specimen-objects, in which our concepts are exemplified; as well as by means of arbitrary verbal symbols—in short, after the analogy of geometry, as well as after the analogy of algebra. Cf. the following section.

[15] Berkeley distinguishes between (a) seeing or thinking, e. g. about length without any reference to breadth, which he allows; and (b) having an idea or intuition of length without breadth, which he denies the possibility of. Length and breadth combined make only one *idea*, or sensuous presentation or representation. All ideas, whether in sense or imaginary, must be particular. We rise above them only in a less or more extensive apprehension of their *relations*,—not by the apprehension of *ideas* different in kind, because abstract, and which were supposed to be the object-matter of metaphysics.

becomes general by being made to represent or stand for all other particular ideas of the same sort. To make this plain by an example, suppose a geometrician is demonstrating the method of cutting a line in two equal parts. He draws, for instance, a black line of an inch in length: this, which in itself is a particular line, is nevertheless with regard to its signification general, since, as it is there used, it represents all particular lines whatsoever; so that what is demonstrated of it is demonstrated of all lines, or, in other words, of a line in general. And, as *that particular line* becomes general by being made a sign, so the *name* 'line,' which taken absolutely is particular, by being a sign is made general. And as the former owes its generality not to its being the sign of an abstract or general line, but of all particular right lines that may possibly exist, so the latter must be thought to derive its generality from the same cause, namely, the various particular lines which it indifferently denotes.

13. To give the reader a yet clearer view of the nature of abstract ideas, and the uses they are thought necessary to, I shall add one more passage out of the *Essay on Human Understanding*, which is as follows: "*Abstract ideas* are not so obvious or easy to children or the yet unexercised mind as particular ones. If they seem so to grown men it is only because by constant and familiar use they are made so. For, when we nicely reflect upon them, we shall find that general ideas are fictions and contrivances of the mind, that carry difficulty with them, and do not so easily offer themselves as we are apt to imagine. For example, does it not require some pains and skill to form the general idea of a triangle (which is yet none of the most abstract, comprehensive, and difficult); for it must be neither oblique nor rectangle, neither equilateral, equicrural, nor scalenon, but all and none of these at once? In effect, it is something imperfect that cannot exist, an idea wherein some parts of several different and inconsistent ideas are put together. It is true the mind in this imperfect state has need of such ideas, and makes all the haste to them it can, for the conveniency of communication and enlargement of knowledge, to both which it is naturally very much inclined. But yet one has reason to suspect such ideas are marks of our imperfection. At least this is enough to shew that the most abstract and general ideas are not those that the mind is first and most easily

acquainted with, nor such as its earliest knowledge is conversant about."—B. iv. ch. 7. § 9. If any man has the faculty of framing in his mind such an idea of a triangle as is here described, it is in vain to pretend to dispute him out of it, nor would I go about it. All I desire is that the reader would fully and certainly inform himself whether he has such an idea or no. And this, methinks, can be no hard task for any one to perform. What more easy than for any one to look a little into his own thoughts, and there try whether he has, or can attain to have, an idea that shall correspond with the description that is here given of the general idea of a triangle—which is neither oblique nor rectangle, equilateral, equicrural nor scalenon, but all these and none of these at once"?

14. Much is here said of the difficulty that abstract ideas carry with them, and the pains and skill requisite to the forming them. And it is on all hands agreed that there is need of great toil and labour of the mind, to emancipate our thoughts from particular objects, and raise them to those sublime speculations that are conversant about abstract ideas. From all which the natural consequence should seem to be, that so difficult a thing as the forming abstract ideas was not necessary for *communication*, which is so easy and familiar to all sorts of men. But, we are told, if they seem obvious and easy to grown men, it is only because by constant and familiar use they are made so. Now, I would fain know at what time it is men are employed in surmounting that difficulty, and furnishing themselves with those necessary helps for discourse. It cannot be when they are grown up, for then it seems they are not conscious of any such painstaking; it remains therefore to be the business of their childhood. And surely the great and multiplied labour of framing abstract notions[17] will be found a hard task for that tender age. Is it not a hard thing to imagine that a couple of children cannot prate together of their sugar-plums and rattles and the rest of their little trinkets, till they have first tacked together numberless inconsistencies, and so framed in their minds abstract general ideas, and annexed them to every common name they make use of?

15. Nor do I think them a whit more needful for the *enlarge-*

---

[16] Cf. *Alciphron*, Dial. VII. 7.
[17] In Berkeley's language, we have notions but no ideas of substance proper (i. e. Mind), or of relations among particular phenomena. Sensible objects, passive states of mind, and representations (or misrepresentations) of these in imagination, are alone *ideas*. Cf. sect. 142; also *Siris*, sect. 308.

ment of knowledge than for communication. It is, I know, a point much insisted on, that all knowledge and demonstration are about universal notions [13], to which I fully agree: but then it does not appear to me that those notions [14] are formed by abstraction in the manner premised—*universality*, so far as I can comprehend, not consisting in the absolute, positive nature or conception of anything, but in the relation it bears to the particulars signified or represented by it; by virtue whereof it is that things, names, or notions [15], being in their own nature *particular*, are rendered *universal* [16]. Thus, when I demonstrate any proposition concerning triangles, it is to be supposed that I have in view the universal idea of a triangle; which ought not to be understood as if I could frame an idea of a triangle which was neither equilateral, nor scalenon, nor equicrural; but only that the particular triangle I consider, whether of this or that sort it matters not, doth equally stand for and represent all rectilinear triangles whatsoever, and is in that sense *universal*. All which seems very plain and not to include any difficulty in it.

16. But here it will be demanded, how we can know any proposition to be true of all particular triangles, except we have first seen it demonstrated of the abstract idea of a triangle which equally agrees to all? For, because a property may be demonstrated to agree to some one particular triangle, it will not thence follow that it equally belongs to any other triangle, which in all respects is not the same with it. For example, having demonstrated that the three angles of an isosceles rectangular triangle are equal to two right ones, I cannot therefore conclude this affection agrees to all other triangles which have neither a right angle nor two equal sides. It seems therefore that, to be certain this proposition is universally true, we must either make a particular demonstration for every particular triangle, which is impossible, or once for all demonstrate it of the abstract idea of a triangle, in which all the particulars do indifferently partake and by which they are all equally represented. To which I answer, that, though the idea

---

[13] See note 17 on preceding page.
[14] i.e. 'things' and 'notions' which are resembling, and 'names' which are non-resembling signs, are in themselves *particular*, as every immediate object of which we are conscious must be. They are universalized in the act of thinking their relations—the apprehension of relations being the essence of thought. Note that 'notions' are here said to be particular; which they are, in so far as they must be capable of being individualised or exemplified in individual experiences. Notion seems here to be used for relative image.

I have in view whilst I make the demonstration be, for instance, that of an isosceles rectangular triangle whose sides are of a determinate length, I may nevertheless be certain it extends to all other rectilinear triangles, of what sort or bigness soever. And that because neither the right angle, nor the equality, nor determinate length of the sides are at all concerned in the demonstration. It is true the diagram I have in view includes all these particulars, but then there is not the least mention made of them in the proof of the proposition. It is not said the three angles are equal to two right ones, because one of them is a right angle, or because the sides comprehending it are of the same length. Which sufficiently shews that the right angle might have been oblique, and the sides unequal, and for all that the demonstration have held good. And for this reason it is that I conclude that to be true of any obliquangular or scalenon which I had demonstrated of a particular right-angled equicrural triangle, and not because I demonstrated the proposition of the abstract idea of a triangle. [*And here it must be acknowledged that a man may consider a figure merely as triangular, without attending to the particular qualities of the angles, or relations of the sides. So far he may abstract; but this will never prove that he can frame an abstract, general, inconsistent idea of a triangle. In like manner we may consider Peter so far forth as man, or so far forth as animal, without framing the forementioned abstract idea, either of man or of animal, inasmuch as all that is perceived is not considered.]

17. It were an endless as well as an useless thing to trace the Schoolmen, those great masters of abstraction, through all the manifold inextricable labyrinths of error and dispute which their doctrine of abstract natures and notions seems to have led them into. What bickerings and controversies, and what a learned dust have been raised about those matters, and what mighty advantage has been from thence derived to mankind, are things at this day too clearly known to need being insisted on. And it had been well if the ill effects of that doctrine were confined to those only who make the most avowed profession of it. When men consider the great pains, industry, and parts that have for so many ages been laid out on the cultivation and advancement of the sciences, and that notwithstanding all this the far greater part of

---

* What follows, to the end of this section, was added in the 1734 edition.

them remain full of darkness and uncertainty, and disputes that are like never to have an end, and even those that are thought to be supported by the most clear and cogent demonstrations contain in them paradoxes which are perfectly irreconcilable to the understandings of men, and that, taking all together, a very small portion of them does supply any real benefit to mankind, otherwise than by being an innocent diversion and amusement."[1]—I say, the consideration of all this is apt to throw them into a despondency and perfect contempt of all study. But this may perhaps cease upon a view of the false principles that have obtained in the world, amongst all which there is none, methinks, hath a more wide and extended sway over the thoughts of speculative men than this[2] of *abstract* general ideas.

18. I come now to consider the *source* of this prevailing notion, and that seems to me to be language. And surely nothing of less extent than reason itself could have been the source of an opinion so universally received. The truth of this appears as from other reasons so also from the plain confession of the ablest patrons of abstract ideas, who acknowledge that they are made in order to naming; from which it is a clear consequence that if there had been no such thing as speech or universal signs [3] there never had been any thought of abstraction. See B. iii. ch. 6. § 39, and elsewhere of the *Essay on Human Understanding*. Let us examine the manner wherein words have contributed to the origin of that mistake.—First then, it is thought that every name has, or ought to have, one only precise and settled signification, which inclines men to think there are certain abstract, determinate ideas that constitute the true and only immediate signification of each general name; and that it is by the mediation of these abstract ideas that a general name comes to signify any particular thing. Whereas, in truth, there is no such thing as one precise and definite signification [4] annexed to any general name, they all signifying indifferently a great number of particular ideas. All which does

---

[1] So Bacon in the *Novum Organum*.
[2] Cf. Introduction, sect. 1—'this that we have been endeavouring to overthrow'—in first edition.
[3] This should include resembling as well as non-resembling signs—relative images as well as verbal symbols. But no particular image can represent in the phantasy the *content* and *extent* of a notion, which imply the recognition by the mind of a relation among a plurality of particular objects.
[4] This must be understood of the denotation of names.

evidently follow from what has been already said, and will clearly appear to any one by a little reflexion. To this it will be objected that every name that has a definition is thereby restrained to one certain signification. For example, a triangle is defined to be 'a plain surface comprehended by three right lines,' by which that name is limited to denote one certain idea and no other. To which I answer, that in the definition it is not said whether the surface be great or small, black or white, nor whether the sides are long or short, equal or unequal, nor with what angles they are inclined to each other; in all which there may be great variety, and consequently there is no one settled idea[25] which limits the signification of the word triangle. It is one thing for to keep a name constantly to the same definition, and another to make it stand everywhere for the same idea[25]; the one is necessary[26], the other useless and impracticable.

19. But, to give a farther account how words came to produce the doctrine of abstract ideas, it must be observed that it is a received opinion that language has no other end but the communicating our ideas, and that every significant name stands for an idea. This being so, and it being withal certain that names which yet are not thought altogether insignificant do not always mark out particular conceivable ideas, it is straightway concluded that they stand for abstract notions. That there are many names in use amongst speculative men which do not always suggest to others determinate, particular ideas, or in truth anything at all, is what nobody will deny. And a little attention will discover that it is not necessary (even in the strictest reasonings) significant names which stand for ideas should, every time they are used, excite in the understanding the ideas they are made to stand for—in reading and discoursing, names being for the most part used as letters are in Algebra, in which, though a particular quantity be marked by each letter, yet to proceed right it is not requisite that in every step each letter suggest to your thoughts that particular quantity it was appointed to stand for[27].

20. Besides, the communicating of ideas marked by words is

---

[24] i.e. presentative or representative intuition.

[25] A definition determines the ideas or particular objects to which the name is applicable, but the notion signified by the name cannot be individualised in an abstract object.

[26] See Leibnitz on Symbolical Knowledge (*Opera Philosophica*, pp. 79-80, Erdmann), and Stewart on 'Abstraction,' in his *Elements*, vol. I. ch. 4, § 1. Names are constructive in their office, as ministers of thought. Cf. *Principles*, sect. 1.

not the chief and only end of language, as is commonly supposed. There are other ends, as the raising of some passion, the exciting to or deterring from an action, the putting the mind in some particular disposition—to which the former [18] is in many cases barely subservient, and sometimes entirely omitted, when these can be obtained without it, as I think does not unfrequently happen in the familiar use of language. I entreat the reader to reflect with himself, and see if it does not often happen, either in hearing or reading a discourse, that the passions of fear, love, hatred, admiration, and disdain, and the like, arise immediately in his mind upon the perception of certain words, without any ideas [19] coming between. At first, indeed, the words might have occasioned ideas [19] that were fitting to produce those emotions; but, if I mistake not, it will be found that, when language is once grown familiar, the hearing of the sounds or sight of the characters is oft immediately attended with those passions which at first were wont to be produced by the intervention of ideas [19] that are now quite omitted. May we not, for example, be affected with the promise of a *good thing*, though we have not an idea of what it is? Or is not the being threatened with danger sufficient to excite a dread, though we think not of any particular evil likely to befal us, nor yet frame to ourselves an idea of danger in abstract? If any one shall join ever so little reflection of his own to what has been said, I believe that it will evidently appear to him that general names are often used in the propriety of language without the speakers designing them for marks of ideas [19] in his own, which he would have them raise in the mind of the hearer. Even proper names themselves do not seem always spoken with a design to bring into our view the ideas [19] of those individuals that are supposed to be marked by them. For example, when a schoolman tells me 'Aristotle hath said it,' all I conceive he means by it is to dispose me to embrace his opinion with the deference and submission which custom has annexed to that name. And this effect is often so instantly produced in the minds of those who are accustomed to resign their judgment to authority of that philosopher, as it is impossible any idea either of his person, writings, or reputation should go before. [[20] So close

---

[18] i.e. the communication of ideas—in other words, the excitement of particular images in the fancy, which verbal language often supersedes to a great extent.

[19] 'ideas,' i.e. images of particular objects to which the words are applicable.
[20] This sentence is omitted in the second edition.

and immediate a connexion may custom establish betwixt the very word Aristotle and the motions of assent and reverence in the minds of some men.] Innumerable examples of this kind may be given, but why should I insist on those things which every one's experience will, I doubt not, plentifully suggest unto him?

21. We have, I think, shewn the impossibility of Abstract Ideas. We have considered what has been said for them by their ablest patrons; and endeavoured to shew they are of no use for those ends to which they are thought necessary. And lastly, we have traced them to the source from whence they flow, which appears evidently to be language.—It cannot be denied that words are of excellent use, in that by their means all that stock of knowledge which has been purchased by the joint labours of inquisitive men in all ages and nations may be drawn into the view and made the possession of one single person. But most parts of knowledge have been [³¹so] strangely perplexed and darkened by the abuse of words, and general ways of speech wherein they are delivered, [³¹that it may almost be made a question whether language has contributed more to the hindrance or advancement of the sciences]. Since therefore words are so apt to impose on the understanding, [³¹I am resolved in my inquiries to make as little use of them as possibly I can]: whatever ideas I consider, I shall endeavour to take them bare and naked into my view, keeping out of my thoughts, so far as I am able, those names which long and constant use hath so strictly united with them; from which I may expect to derive the following advantages:—

22. *First*, I shall be sure to get clear of all controversies purely verbal—the springing up of which weeds in almost all the sciences has been a main hindrance to the growth of true and sound knowledge. *Secondly*, this seems to be a sure way to extricate myself out of that fine and subtle net of *abstract ideas* which has so miserably perplexed and entangled the minds of men; and that with this peculiar circumstance, that by how much the finer and more curious was the wit of any man, by so much the deeper was he likely to be ensnared and faster held therein. *Thirdly*, so long as I confine my thoughts to my own ideas⁷⁹ divested of words, I

---

³¹ Omitted in second edition.
⁷⁹ 'My own ideas,' i.e. the particular objects of which I am presentatively or representatively conscious.

do not see how I can easily be mistaken. The objects I consider, I clearly and adequately know. I cannot be deceived in thinking I have an idea which I have not. It is not possible for me to imagine that any of my own ideas are alike or unlike that are not truly so. To discern the agreements or disagreements there are between my ideas, to see what ideas are included in any compound idea and what not, there is nothing more requisite than an attentive perception of what passes in my own understanding.

23. But the attainment of all these advantages does presuppose an entire deliverance from the deception of words, which I dare hardly promise myself; so difficult a thing it is to dissolve an union so early begun, and confirmed by so long a habit as that betwixt words and ideas. Which difficulty seems to have been very much increased by the doctrine of *abstraction*. For, so long as men thought abstract ideas were annexed to their words, it does not seem strange that they should use words for ideas—it being found an impracticable thing to lay aside the word, and retain the *abstract* idea in the mind, which in itself was perfectly inconceivable. This seems to me the principal cause why those[33] who have so emphatically recommended to others the laying aside all use of words in their meditations, and contemplating their bare ideas, have yet failed to perform it themselves. Of late many have been very sensible of the absurd opinions and insignificant disputes which grow out of the abuse of words. And, in order to remedy these evils, they[33] advise well, that we attend to the ideas signified, and draw off our attention from the words which signify them. But, how good soever this advice may be they have given others, it is plain they could not have a due regard to it themselves, so long as they thought the only immediate use of words was to signify ideas, and that the immediate signification of every general name was a determinate abstract idea.

24. But, these being known to be mistakes, a man may with greater ease prevent his being imposed on by words. He that knows he has no other than *particular* ideas, will not puzzle himself in vain to find out and conceive the *abstract* idea annexed to any name. And he that knows names do not always stand for

---

[33] He probably refers to Locke.

ideas"⁴ will spare himself the labour of looking for ideas where there are none to be had. It were, therefore, to be wished that every one would use his utmost endeavours to obtain a clear view of the ideas he would consider, separating from them all that dress and incumbrance of words which so much contribute to blind the judgment and divide the attention. In vain do we extend our view into the heavens and pry into the entrails of the earth, in vain do we consult the writings of learned men and trace the dark footsteps of antiquity — we need only draw the curtain of words, to behold the fairest tree of knowledge, whose fruit is excellent, and within the reach of our hand.

25. Unless we take care to clear the First Principles of Knowledge from the embarras and delusion of words, we may make infinite reasonings upon them to no purpose; we may draw consequences from consequences, and be never the wiser. The farther we go, we shall only lose ourselves the more irrecoverably, and be the deeper entangled in difficulties and mistakes. Whoever therefore designs to read the following sheets, I entreat him that he would make my words the occasion of his own thinking, and endeavour to attain the same train of thoughts in reading that I had in writing them. By this means it will be easy for him to discover the truth or falsity of what I say. He will be out of all danger of being deceived by my words, and I do not see how he can be led into an error by considering his own naked, undisguised ideas.

---

²⁴ Inasmuch as they may stand for relations of ideas, whether in sense or imagination: and for a Mind or Self, as distinguished from any of its particular ideas. Cf. sect. 142. In the state which Leibnitz calls 'symbolical consciousness' we can use words without realising their meaning.

OF THE

PRINCIPLES

OF

HUMAN KNOWLEDGE.

PART I.

1. IT is evident to any one who takes a survey of the *objects*[1] of human knowledge, that they are either ideas actually imprinted on the senses; or else such as are perceived by attending to the passions and operations of the mind; or lastly, ideas formed by help of memory and imagination—either compounding, dividing, or barely representing those originally perceived in the aforesaid ways. By sight I have the ideas of light and colours, with their several degrees and variations. By touch I perceive hard and soft, heat and cold, motion and resistance, and of all these more and less either as to quantity or degree. Smelling furnishes me with odours; the palate with tastes; and hearing conveys sounds to the mind in all their variety of tone and composition. And as several of these are observed to accompany each other,

---

[1] This threefold division of the *objects* or *phenomena* of which we are conscious—viz. (a) *Sense-ideas* or *presentations*; (b) the ideas of the 'passions and operations' of mind, by some called *internal presentations*; (c) *representations*, which may be more or less elaborated—nearly corresponds to Locke's simple ideas of sense and reflection, and his complex ideas. The two first are Hume's 'impressions,' and the last his 'ideas.' But Berkeley raises a question which Locke did not conceive, viz. Do any of the three classes of objects or ideas of which we are conscious exist independently of a conscious mind; or, if not, do any represent or suggest what exists thus absolutely? Are they, or at any rate do they stand for, 'things in themselves' —substances from which all perception or consciousness may be abstracted? Can we, in short, find in perception, by any analysis, Mind and Matter existing in a *mutually independent* duality? This Treatise is an answer to this question. Cf. sect. 86, 89.

156   *Of the Principles*   PART I.

they come to be marked by one name, and so to be reputed as one thing[1]. Thus, for example, a certain colour, taste, smell, figure and consistence having been observed to go together, are accounted one distinct thing, signified by the name *apple*; other collections of ideas constitute a stone, a tree, a book, and the like sensible things—which as they are pleasing or disagreeable excite the passions of love, hatred, joy, grief, and so forth.

2. But, besides all that endless variety of ideas or objects of knowledge, there is likewise something[2] which knows or perceives them, and exercises divers operations, as willing, imagining, remembering, about them. This perceiving, active being is what I call *mind*, *spirit*, *soul*, or *myself*. By which words I do not denote any one of my ideas, but a thing entirely distinct from them, wherein they exist, or, which is the same thing, whereby they are perceived—for the existence of an idea consists in being perceived[3].

3. That neither our thoughts, nor passions, nor ideas formed by the imagination, exist without the mind[4], is what everybody will allow. And to me it is no less evident that the various sensations or ideas imprinted on the sense, however blended or combined together (that is, whatever objects[5] they compose), cannot exist otherwise than in a mind[6] perceiving them.—I think an intuitive

---

[1] This is the synthetic or constructive function of names, according to Berkeley. He here and elsewhere distinguishes between sensible things properly so called, and the *simple ideas* or objects of sense, of which 'things' are composed. Cf. sect. 33. 38.

[2] This 'something' is the Ego or conscious subject, which the object-world implies, through which it is unified and becomes intelligible, and by which it is causally regulated. But Berkeley does not affirm of the Ego, any more than of the world of ideas, that it exists *absolutely*, i.e. independently of being conscious—that the *percipient* is independent of ideas, any more than that these last are independent of a percipient.—For Berkeley's meaning of Self, as distinguished from his ideas, cf. sect. 7, where he speaks of the Self or Ego as the only 'substance;' and sect. 27, 135—140. Though he affirms, in this section and elsewhere, that Self and his ideas are 'entirely distinct' from one another, he denies that they are distinct *substances*. The Du-

alism of Berkeley—*spirits* and *ideas*—does not *underlie* perception, but is, so to speak, co-extensive with it. It is resolvable into the distinction between the Ego, as *personal* or *identical*, and the phenomena of which each Ego is conscious, in sense or otherwise, as *changing*—with whatever is implied in this, which, however, he does not try to analyse.

[3] i.e. by a percipient—but not necessarily by *me*. Cf. sect. 48. An idea must now be, or have been, or hereafter become, part of the experience of a mind, in order to its present, past, or future actual existence. Cf. sect. 6.

[4] 'without the mind,' i.e. unperceived and unimagined.

[5] Here 'objects' = sensible things. This is the popular meaning of the term object, as distinguished from its more extensive or philosophical meaning. Cf. *Theory of Vision Vindicated*, sect. 9—11.

[6] 'in a mind,' i.e. as phenomena of which a mind is conscious. The main pro-

knowledge may be obtained of this by any one that shall attend to what is meant by the term *exist* when applied to sensible things. The table I write on I say exists, that is, I see and feel it; and if I were out of my study I should say it existed—meaning thereby that if I was in my study I might perceive it, or that some other spirit actually does perceive it [8]. There was an odour, that is, it was smelt; there was a sound, that is, it was heard; a colour or figure, and it was perceived by sight or touch. This is all that I can understand by these and the like expressions. For as to what is said of the absolute existence of unthinking things without any relation to their being perceived; that is to me perfectly unintelligible. Their *esse* is *percipi*, nor is it possible they should have any existence out of the minds or thinking things which perceive them.

4. [9] It is indeed an opinion [10] strangely prevailing amongst men, that houses, mountains, rivers, and in a word all sensible objects, have an existence, natural or real, distinct from their being perceived by the understanding. But, with how great an assurance and acquiescence soever this principle may be entertained in the world, yet whoever shall find in his heart to call it in question may, if I mistake not, perceive it to involve a manifest contradiction. For, what are the forementioned objects but the things we perceive by sense? and what do we perceive besides our own ideas or sensations? and is it not plainly repugnant that any one of these, or any combination of them, should exist unperceived [11]?

---

blem of the book is, To determine whether those objects or ideas which constitute what are commonly called real or sensible things are independent of a conscious mind, in a way that thoughts and passions and fancies are not—whether, in short, the presented world of the senses is non-egoistic, in another manner than the presented world of our own feelings, or than the representative world of imagination; and, if so, what that manner may be. What should we mean when we say that sense-ideas—in other words, objects of sense—are 'external?' Is it that they exist independently of a percipient mind; or merely of my mind, they being my medium of intercourse with other minds, and of other minds with me? Berkeley's solution, here given by anticipation, is that sense-ideas, like all other objects of consciousness, cannot exist actually, otherwise than in a mind perceiving them (i.e. as objects immediately present to an intelligence). He afterwards enumerates marks by which real or sensible are distinguishable from merely imaginary objects. See sect. 29—33.

[8] This is part of Berkeley's interpretation of our belief in the distinct and permanent existence of sensible things. It is a belief that they are conditionally presentable in sense—' permanent possibilities of sensation,' as Mr. J. S. Mill would say. See *Examination of Hamilton's Philosophy*, pp. 220-33, third edition.

[9] Sect. 4—24 contain Berkeley's proof of his doctrine, contained in sect. 3, about sensible ideas and things.

[10] He does not seem to say that this opinion can be held intelligently by those to whom he here attributes it. Cf. sect. 54, 56.

[11] That all the objects of which we are actually percipient are ideas or sensations

5. If we throughly examine this tenet it will, perhaps, be found at bottom to depend on the doctrine of *abstract ideas*. For can there be a nicer strain of abstraction than to distinguish the existence of sensible objects from their being perceived, so as to conceive them existing unperceived? Light and colours, heat and cold, extension and figures—in a word the things we see and feel—what are they but so many sensations, notions[10], ideas, or impressions on the sense? and is it possible to separate, even in thought, any of these from perception? For my part, I might as easily divide a thing from itself. I may, indeed, divide in my thoughts, or conceive apart from each other, those things which, perhaps, I never perceived by sense so divided. Thus, I imagine the trunk of a human body without the limbs, or conceive the smell of a rose without thinking on the rose itself. So far, I will not deny, I can abstract—if that may properly be called *abstraction* which extends only to the conceiving separately such objects as it is possible may really exist or be actually perceived asunder. But my conceiving or imagining power does not extend beyond the possibility of real existence or perception. Hence, as it is impossible for me to see or feel anything without an actual sensation of that thing, so is it impossible for me to conceive in my thoughts any sensible thing or object distinct[12] from the sensation or perception of it. [[11]In truth, the object and the sensation are the same thing[13], and cannot therefore be abstracted from each other.]

6. Some truths there are so near and obvious to the mind that a man need only open his eyes to see them. Such I take this important one to be, viz. that all the choir of heaven and furniture

of the earth, in a word all those bodies which compose the mighty frame of the world, have not any subsistence without a mind, that their *being* is to be perceived or known; that consequently so long as they are not actually perceived by me, or do not exist in my mind or that of any other created spirit, they must either have no existence at all, or else subsist in the mind of some Eternal Spirit —it being perfectly unintelligible, and involving all the absurdity of abstraction, to attribute to any single part of them an existence independent of a spirit. [[16] To be convinced of which, the reader need only reflect, and try to separate in his own thoughts the *being* of a sensible thing from its *being perceived*.]

7. From what has been said it is evident there is not any other Substance than *Spirit*, or that which perceives[17]. But, for the fuller demonstration of this point, let it be considered the sensible qualities are colour, figure, motion, smell, taste, &c., *i.e.* the ideas perceived by sense. Now, for an idea to exist in an unperceiving thing is a manifest contradiction, for to have an idea is all one as to perceive; that therefore wherein colour, figure, &c. exist must perceive them; hence it is clear there can be no unthinking substance or *substratum* of those ideas.

8. But, say you, though the ideas themselves do not exist without the mind[18], yet there may be things like them, whereof they are copies or resemblances, which things exist without the mind in an unthinking substance[19]. I answer, an idea can be like nothing but an idea; a colour or figure can be like nothing but another colour or figure. If we look but never so little into our thoughts, we shall find it impossible for us to conceive a likeness except only between our ideas. Again, I ask whether those supposed originals or external things, of which our ideas are the pictures or

---

[16] In the first edition, instead of this sentence, we have the following: 'To make this appear with all the light and evidence of an Axiom, it seems sufficient if I can but awaken the reflexion of the reader, that he may take an impartial view of his own meaning, and turn his thoughts upon the subject itself, free and disengaged from all embarras of words and prepossession in favour of received mistakes.'

[17] Berkeley thus holds a *duality* of 'things' (viz. spirits and ideas), and a *unity* of 'substance.' Moreover, he does not say that this 'substance' may exist unparticipated of any ideas, whilst ideas or objects necessarily depend on being perceived. On the contrary he goes on to say that 'there can be no *unthinking* substance or substratum' of ideas. And elsewhere he argues that a mind must be always conscious. Cf. sect. 98, and also sect. 139, where he appears to hold that the very existence of a spirit or substance consists in perceiving ideas or being conscious— that its *esse* is *percipere*.

[18] As Sir W. Hamilton (e.g. Reid's *Works*, pp. 883 &c.) seems to say the immediate objects or ideas of sense do.

[19] As some who hold a representative perception say.

representations, be themselves perceivable or no? If they are, then they are ideas and we have gained our point; but if you say they are not, I appeal to any one whether it be sense to assert a colour is like something which is invisible; hard or soft, like something which is intangible; and so of the rest.

9. Some there are who make a distinction betwixt *primary* and *secondary* qualities[20]. By the former they mean extension, figure, motion, rest, solidity or impenetrability, and number; by the latter they denote all other sensible qualities, as colours, sounds, tastes, and so forth. The ideas we have of these they acknowledge not to be the resemblances of anything existing without the mind, or unperceived, but they will have our ideas of the primary qualities to be patterns or images of things which exist without the mind, in an unthinking substance which they call Matter. By Matter, therefore, we are to understand an inert, senseless substance, in which extension, figure, and motion do actually subsist. But it is evident, from what we have already shewn, that extension, figure, and motion are only ideas existing in the mind, and that an idea can be like nothing but another idea, and that consequently neither they nor their archetypes can exist in an unperceiving substance. Hence, it is plain that the very notion of what is called *Matter* or *corporeal substance*, involves a contradiction in it. [[21]Insomuch that I should not think it necessary to spend more time in exposing its absurdity. But, because the tenet of the existence of Matter seems to have taken so deep a root in the minds of philosophers, and draws after it so many ill consequences, I choose rather to be thought prolix and tedious than omit anything that might conduce to the full discovery and extirpation of that prejudice.]

10. They who assert that figure, motion, and the rest of the primary or original[21] qualities do exist without the mind in unthinking substances, do at the same time acknowledge that colours, sounds, heat, cold, and suchlike secondary qualities, do not — which they tell us are sensations existing in the mind alone, that depend on and are occasioned by the different

---

[20] Here again he refers to Locke, whose notion of material substance is charged with being self-contradictory. See *Essay*, B. II. ch. 8.

[21] What follows to the end of the section is omitted in the second edition.

[22] Sometimes called *objective* qualities—which are supposed to exist without a mind or unperceived, and in an unperceiving substance. Cf. *First Dialogue between Hylas and Philonous*, pp. 279, &c.

size, texture, and motion of the minute particles of matter[20]. This they take for an undoubted truth, which they can demonstrate beyond all exception. Now, if it be certain that those original qualities are inseparably united with the other sensible qualities, and not, even in thought, capable of being abstracted from them, it plainly follows that they exist only in the mind. But I desire any one to reflect and try whether he can, by any abstraction of thought, conceive the extension and motion of a body without all other sensible qualities. For my own part, I see evidently that it is not in my power to frame an Idea of a body extended and moving, but I must withal give it some colour or other sensible quality which is acknowledged to exist only in the mind. In short, extension, figure, and motion, abstracted from all other qualities, are inconceivable. Where therefore the other sensible qualities are, there must these be also, to wit, in the mind and nowhere else?[21].

11. Again, *great* and *small*, *swift* and *slow*, are allowed to exist nowhere without the mind, being entirely relative, and changing as the frame or position of the organs of sense varies. The extension therefore which exists without the mind is neither great nor small, the motion neither swift nor slow, that is, they are nothing at all. But, say you, they are extension in general, and motion in general: thus we see how much the tenet of extended moveable substances existing without the mind[25] depends on that strange doctrine of *abstract ideas*. And here I cannot but remark how nearly the vague and indeterminate description of Matter or corporeal substance, which the modern philosophers are run into by their own principles, resembles that antiquated and so much ridiculed notion of *materia prima*, to be met with in Aristotle and his followers. Without extension solidity cannot be conceived; since therefore it has been shewn that extension[26] exists not in an unthinking substance, the same must also be true of solidity.

---

[20] Cf. sect. 10. See Locke's *Essay*, B. II. ch. 8, § 18; ch. 13, § 11; B. IV. ch. 3. § 14—16.

[21] 'in the mind, and nowhere else'—i.e. perceived or conceived, and in no other manner. Cf. *Third Dialogue between Hylas and Philonous* p. 346.

[25] 'without the mind' = without a mind, or in an absolute negation of all intelligence, Divine or finite.

[26] Extension is thus the fundamental characteristic of the material world. Both geometrical and physical solidity, as well as motion, are said to imply extension. But Berkeley's analysis rather resolves extension into a locomotive experience in sense, which visual sensations of colour may symbolize.

12. That number is entirely the creature of the mind[17], even though the other qualities be allowed to exist without, will be evident to whoever considers that the same thing bears a different denomination of number as the mind views it with different respects. Thus, the same extension is one, or three, or thirty-six, according as the mind considers it with reference to a yard, a foot, or an inch. Number is so visibly relative, and dependent on men's understanding, that it is strange to think how any one should give it an absolute existence without the mind. We say one book, one page, one line, &c.; all these are equally units, though some contain several of the others. And in each instance, it is plain, the unit relates to some particular combination of ideas arbitrarily put together by the mind[28].

13. Unity I know some[29] will have to be a simple or uncompounded idea, accompanying all other ideas into the mind. That I have any such idea answering the word *unity* I do not find; and if I had, methinks I could not miss finding it: on the contrary, it should be the most familiar to my understanding, since it is said to accompany all other ideas, and to be perceived by all the ways of sensation and reflexion. To say no more, it is an *abstract idea*.

14. I shall farther add, that, after the same manner as modern philosophers prove[30] certain sensible qualities to have no existence in Matter, or without the mind, the same thing may be likewise proved of all other sensible qualities whatsoever. Thus, for instance, it is said that heat and cold are affections only of the mind, and not at all patterns of real beings, existing in the corporeal substances which excite them, for that the same body which appears cold to one hand seems warm to another. Now, why may we not as well argue that figure and extension are not patterns or resemblances of qualities existing in Matter, because to the same eye at different stations, or eyes of a different texture

---

[17] 'the creature of the mind,' i.e. dependent on being conceived by a mind. Cf. *Siris*, sect. 288. This dependence is here illustrated by the relation of *number* to the point of view of the individual mind; as the dependence of the other primary qualities was illustrated by their relation to the organisation of the percipient. In this, the preceding, and the following sections, Berkeley argues the inconsistency of the *absoluteness* attributed to the primary qualities, with their acknowledged dependence on our organisation, and on our intellectual point of view.

[28] Cf. *New Theory of Vision*, sect. 107—110.

[29] e.g. Locke, *Essay*, b. II, ch. 7, § 7; ch. 16, § 1.

[30] 'certain sensible qualities'—'colours, tastes, &c.'—In first edition.

at the same station, they appear various, and cannot therefore be the images of anything settled and determinate without the mind? Again, it is proved that sweetness is not really in the sapid thing, because the thing remaining unaltered the sweetness is changed into bitter, as in case of a fever or otherwise vitiated palate. Is it not as reasonable to say that motion is not without the mind, since if the succession of ideas in the mind become swifter the motion, it is acknowledged, shall appear slower without[1] any alteration in any external object.

15. In short, let any one consider those arguments which are thought manifestly to prove that colours and tastes exist only in the mind, and he shall find they may with equal force be brought to prove the same thing of extension, figure, and motion[2]. Though it must be confessed this method of arguing does not so much prove that there is no extension or colour in an outward object[3], as that we do not know by sense which is the true extension or colour of the object. But the arguments foregoing plainly shew it to be impossible that any colour or extension at all, or other sensible quality whatsoever, should exist in an unthinking subject without the mind, or in truth, that there should be any such thing as an outward object.

16. But let us examine a little the received opinion.—It is said extension is a mode or accident of Matter, and that Matter is the *substratum* that supports it. Now I desire that you would explain to me what is meant by Matter's *supporting* extension. Say you, I have no idea of Matter and therefore cannot explain it. I answer, though you have no positive, yet, if you have any meaning at all, you must at least have a relative idea of Matter; though you know not what it is, yet you must be supposed to know what relation it bears to accidents, and what is meant by its supporting them. It is evident 'support' cannot here be taken in its usual or literal sense —as when we say that pillars support a building; in what sense therefore must it be taken? [[4]For my part, I am not able to discover any sense at all that can be applicable to it.]

---

[1] 'without any alteration in any external object'—'without any external alteration' —in first edition.

[2] Cf. *First Dialogue between Hylas and Philonous*, pp. 178—185.

[3] 'an outward object,' i.e. an object abstracted from all intelligence—an *absolute* object, which is alleged to be a contradiction, all objectivity implying relation to an intelligence, and the qualities in question relation to an *embodied* intelligence, with its organic variation.

[4] This sentence is omitted in the second edition.

17. If we inquire into what the most accurate philosophers declare themselves to mean by *material substance*, we shall find them acknowledge they have no other meaning annexed to those sounds but the idea of Being in general, together with the relative notion of its supporting accidents. The general idea of Being appeareth to me the most abstract and incomprehensible of all other; and as for its supporting accidents, this, as we have just now observed, cannot be understood in the common sense of those words; it must therefore be taken in some other sense, but what that is they do not explain. So that when I consider the two parts or branches which make the signification of the words *material substance*, I am convinced there is no distinct meaning annexed to them. But why should we trouble ourselves any farther, in discussing this material *substratum* or support of figure and motion, and other sensible qualities? Does it not suppose they have an existence without the mind? And is not this a direct repugnancy, and altogether inconceivable?

18. But, though it were possible that solid, figured, moveable substances may exist without the mind, corresponding to the ideas we have of bodies, yet how is it possible for us to know this? Either we must know it by sense or by reason[35].—As for our senses, by them we have the knowledge only of our sensations, ideas, or those things that are immediately perceived by sense, call them what you will: but they do not inform us that things exist without the mind, or unperceived, like to those which are perceived. This the materialists themselves acknowledge.—It remains therefore that if we have any knowledge at all of external things, it must be by reason, inferring their existence from what is immediately perceived by sense. But ([36] I do not see) what reason can induce us to believe the existence of bodies without the mind, from what we perceive, since the very patrons of Matter themselves do not pretend there is any necessary connexion betwixt them and our ideas? I say it is granted on all hands (and what happens in dreams, frensies, and the like, puts it beyond dispute) that it is possible we might be affected with all the ideas we have now,

---

[35] 'reason,' i.e. reasoning, or inference from our immediate sense-experience—our sensations or ideas of sense. It is argued, in this and the next section, that the absolute existence of Matter cannot be proved, either by the senses, or by reasoning from our sense-perceptions.

[36] Omitted in the second edition, and the sentence converted into a question.

though there were no bodies existing without resembling them[27]. Hence, it is evident the supposition of external bodies[28] is not necessary for the producing our ideas; since it is granted they are produced sometimes, and might possibly be produced always in the same order, we see them in at present, without their concurrence.

19. But, though we might possibly have all our sensations without them, yet perhaps it may be thought easier to conceive and explain the manner of their production, by supposing external bodies in their likeness rather than otherwise; and so it might be at least probable there are such things as bodies that excite their ideas in our minds. But neither can this be said; for, though we give the materialists their external bodies, they by their own confession are never the nearer knowing how our ideas are produced; since they own themselves unable to comprehend in what manner body can act upon spirit, or how it is possible it should imprint any idea in the mind[39]. Hence it is evident the production[40] of ideas or sensations in our minds, can be no reason why we should suppose Matter or corporeal substances[41], since that is acknowledged to remain equally inexplicable with or without this supposition. If therefore it were possible for bodies to exist without the mind, yet to hold they do so, must needs be a very precarious opinion; since it is to suppose, without any reason at all, that God has created innumerable beings that are entirely useless, and serve to no manner of purpose.

20. In short, if there were external bodies[42], it is impossible we should ever come to know it; and if there were not, we might have the very same reasons to think there were that we have now. Suppose—what no one can deny possible—an intelligence without the help of external bodies[43], to be affected with the same train of

---

[27] But the ideas or objects of which we are cognizant in dreams, &c. differ in important characteristics from the ideas or objects of which we are conscious in sense. Cf. sect. 29—33. The former are not in harmony with what may be called the universal and well-ordered dream of real life.

[28] 'external bodies,' i. e. bodies that exist absolutely or unperceived—independently of any sense-experience.

[29] i. e. they cannot shew how the unintelligible or contradictory hypothesis of Absolute Matter accounts for our having the sense-experience we have had, are conscious of having, or expect to have; or which we suppose other conscious minds to be having, to have had, or to be about to have.

[30] 'the production,' &c., i. e. the fact that we and others actually have sense-perceptions.

[31] 'Matter,' in an intelligible meaning of the term, he not only allows to exist, but maintains its existence to be intuitively evident.

[32] i. e. bodies existing without being perceived or conceived by any knowing substance.

sensations or ideas that you are, imprinted in the same order and with like vividness in his mind[43]. I ask whether that intelligence hath not all the reason to believe the existence of corporeal substances, represented by his ideas, and exciting them in his mind, that you can possibly have for believing the same thing? Of this there can be no question—which one consideration were enough to make any reasonable person suspect the strength of whatever arguments he may think himself to have, for the existence of bodies without the mind.

21. Were it necessary to add any farther proof against the existence of Matter[44], after what has been said, I could instance several of those errors and difficulties (not to mention Impieties) which have sprung from that tenet. It has occasioned numberless controversies and disputes in philosophy, and not a few of far greater moment in religion. But I shall not enter into the detail of them in this place, as well because I think arguments *a posteriori* are unnecessary for confirming what has been, if I mistake not, sufficiently demonstrated *a priori*, as because I shall hereafter find occasion to speak somewhat of them[45].

22. I am afraid I have given cause to think I am needlessly prolix in handling this subject. For, to what purpose is it to dilate on that which may be demonstrated with the utmost evidence in a line or two, to any one that is capable of the least reflection? It is but looking into your own thoughts, and so trying whether you can conceive it possible for a sound, or figure, or motion, or colour to exist without the mind or unperceived. This easy trial[46] may perhaps make you see that what you contend for is a downright contradiction. Insomuch that I am content to put the whole upon this issue :—If you can but conceive it possible for one extended moveable substance, or, in general, for any one idea, or anything like an idea, to exist otherwise than in a mind perceiving it[47], I shall readily give up the cause. And, as for all that compages of external bodies you contend for, I shall grant you its existence,

---

[43] i.e. to have all our sense-experience.
[44] i.e. absolute or uncognised Matter—not interpretable sense-perceptions, the existence of which last Berkeley assumes.
[45] Cf. sect. 85—156.
[46] The appeal here and elsewhere is to reflection—directly upon our own experience and indirectly upon that of others.
[47] i.e. otherwise than as an idea—perceived or conceived—a presented or represented object.

though you cannot either give me any reason why you believe it exists, or assign any use to it when it is supposed to exist. I say, the bare possibility of your opinions being true shall pass for an argument that it is so.

23. But, say you, surely there is nothing easier than for me to imagine trees, for instance, in a park, or books existing in a closet, and nobody by to perceive them. I answer, you may so, there is no difficulty in it; but what is all this, I beseech you, more than framing in your mind certain ideas which you call books and trees, and at the same time omitting to frame the idea of any one that may perceive them? But do not you yourself perceive or think of them all the while [18]? This therefore is nothing to the purpose: it only shews you have the power of imagining or forming ideas in your mind; but it does not shew that you can conceive it possible the objects of your thought may exist without the mind. To make out this, it is necessary that you conceive them existing unconceived or unthought of, which is a manifest repugnancy. When we do our utmost to conceive the existence of external bodies [19], we are all the while only contemplating our own ideas [20]. But the mind taking no notice of itself, is deluded to think it can and does conceive bodies existing unthought of or without the mind, though at the same time they are apprehended by or exist in itself [21]. A little attention will discover to any one the truth and evidence of what is here said, and make it unnecessary to insist on any other proofs against the existence of *material substance*.

24. [[22]Could men but forbear to amuse themselves with words, we should, I believe, soon come to an agreement in this point.] It is very obvious, upon the least inquiry into our own thoughts, to know whether it be possible for us to understand what is meant by the *absolute existence of sensible objects in themselves, or*

---

[18] There seems to be a confusion of existence in *sense* with existence in *imagination*, in this section. To exist as an object in fancy is indeed to exist, but not as part of the universal system of sensible order; and it is the apparently interrupted existence of *this* system, on his doctrine, that Berkeley has to reconcile with the common belief, on which we all act.

[19] 'to conceive the existence of external bodies,' i.e. to conceive bodies that are neither perceived nor conceived—that are not ideas or objects at all, but which exist absolutely. To suppose what we conceive to be thus unconceived, when we are actually conceiving it, is, it is argued, to suppose a contradiction in terms. Such Being is absolutely unapproachable by intelligence.

[20] 'Ideas'—i. e. ideas of imagination, not of sense.

[21] A delusion which is at the root of those objections to metaphysics which overlook the subjective phase of all physics.

[22] This sentence is omitted in the second edition.

without the mind[34]. To me it is evident those words mark out either a direct contradiction, or else nothing at all. And to convince others of this, I know no readier or fairer way than to entreat they would calmly attend to their own thoughts; and if by this attention the emptiness or repugnancy of those expressions does appear, surely nothing more is requisite for their conviction. It is on this therefore that I insist, to wit, that the absolute existence of unthinking things are words without a meaning, or which include a contradiction. This is what I repeat and inculcate, and earnestly recommend to the attentive thoughts of the reader.

25. All our ideas, sensations, notions[34], or the things which we perceive, by whatsoever names they may be distinguished, are visibly inactive—there is nothing of power or agency included in them. So that one idea or object of thought cannot produce or make any alteration in another[35]. To be satisfied of the truth of this, there is nothing else requisite but a bare observation of our ideas. For, since they and every part of them exist only in the mind, it follows that there is nothing in them but what is perceived: but whoever shall attend to his ideas, whether of sense or reflection, will not perceive in them any power or activity; there is, therefore, no such thing contained in them. A little attention will discover to us that the very being of an idea implies passiveness and inertness in it, insomuch that it is impossible for an idea to do anything, or, strictly speaking, to be the cause of anything: neither can it be the resemblance or pattern of any active being, as is evident from sect. 8. Whence it plainly follows that extension, figure, and motion cannot be the cause of our sensations. To say, therefore, that these are the effects of powers resulting from the configuration, number, motion, and size of corpuscles, must certainly be false.

---

[34] 'The absolute existence of sensible objects, i.e. in themselves or without a mind,' is the principle which Berkeley argues against as either meaningless or contradictory—not the existence of a material world or sensible order, regulated independently of our individual will, and to which our actions must conform if we are to avoid pain and secure pleasure.

[34] Here again 'notion' applied to ideas or inactive things.

[35] In this and the next section, Berkeley argues that there can be no power or causality proper, in the world of ideas or objects, uniformities of co-existence and succession alone being either immediately or mediately perceivable—the doctrine of Hume, Brown, Comte, and Mr. Mill.

26. We perceive a continual succession of ideas, some are anew excited, others are changed or totally disappear. There is therefore some cause[16] of these ideas, whereon they depend[17], and which produces and changes them. That this cause cannot be any quality or idea or combination of ideas, is clear from the preceding section. It must therefore be a substance[18]; but it has been shewn that there is no corporeal or material substance: it remains therefore that the cause of ideas is an incorporeal active substance or Spirit.

27. A Spirit is one simple, undivided, active being—as it perceives ideas it is called the *understanding*, and as it produces or otherwise operates about them it is called the *will*. Hence there can be no *idea* formed of a soul or spirit; for all ideas whatever, being passive and inert, (vid. sect. 25,) they cannot represent unto us, by way of image or likeness, that which acts. A little attention will make it plain to any one that to have an idea which shall be like that active principle of motion and change of ideas is absolutely impossible. Such is the nature of *spirit*, or that which acts, that it cannot be of itself perceived, but only by the effects which it produceth[19]. If any man shall doubt of the truth of what is here delivered, let him but reflect and try if he can frame the idea of any power or active being; and whether he has ideas of two principal powers, marked by the names *will* and *understanding*, distinct from each other as well as from a third idea of Substance or Being in general, with a relative notion of its supporting or being the subject of the aforesaid powers—which is signified by the name *soul* or *spirit*. This is what some hold; but, so far as I can see, the words *will*, [*understanding, mind,*] *soul, spirit*, do not stand for different ideas, or, in truth, for any idea at all, but for something which is

---

[16] Berkeley here assumes as granted the metaphysical and synthetical principle of causality—that every phenomenal change implies a cause—which cause, he goes on to shew, cannot be itself phenomenal.

[17] 'depend'—not for their very *existence*, which, according to Berkeley, depends upon their being perceived, but for the *changing forms* in which they exist relatively to one another.

[18] He here connects the metaphysical and synthetical principles of Cause and Substance—finding them united and realised in actively conscious Mind.

[19] In other words, it cannot be an object of perception, though its effects can. We are conscious of it as percipient only, not as perceived. Does this consciousness of being percipient imply consciousness of active will? For Berkeley's treatment of the objection that *mental substances* and *causes* are as unmeaning or contradictory as *material substances* or *causes*, see *Third Dialogue between Hylas and Philonous*, pp. 317–329.

[b] Omitted in second edition.

very different from ideas, and which, being an agent, cannot be like unto, or represented by, any idea whatsoever. [⁶¹Though it must be owned at the same time that we have some *notion* of soul, spirit, and the operations of the mind⁶²; such as willing, loving, hating—inasmuch as we know or understand the meaning of these words.]

28. I find I can excite ideas⁶³ in my mind at pleasure, and vary and shift the scene as oft as I think fit. It is no more than willing, and straightway this or that idea arises in my fancy; and by the same power it is obliterated and makes way for another. This making and unmaking of ideas doth very properly denominate the mind active. Thus much is certain and grounded on experience: but when we talk of unthinking agents, or of exciting ideas exclusive of volition, we only amuse ourselves with words⁶⁴.

29. But, whatever power I may have over my own thoughts, I find the ideas actually perceived by Sense have not a like dependence on my will⁶⁵. When in broad daylight I open my eyes, it is not in my power to choose whether I shall see or no, or to determine what particular objects shall present themselves to my view; and so likewise as to the hearing and other senses, the ideas imprinted on them are not creatures of my will. There is therefore some *other* Will or Spirit that produces them.

30. The ideas of Sense are more strong, lively, and distinct than those of the imagination⁶⁶; they have likewise a steadiness, order, and coherence, and are not excited at random, as those

---

⁶¹ This sentence is not contained in the first edition.

⁶² In sect. 1 he speaks of '*ideas* perceived by attending to the operations of the mind.'

⁶³ '*ideas*,' i.e. of imagination.

⁶⁴ With Berkeley the object-world of ideas is partly distinguished from Self by its essential passivity. Every object is caused; nothing except a Self or Ego causes. Cause or power is with him of the essence of our notion of mind, to which we necessarily attribute power or activity—thus distinguishing our Self from the changing ideas of which we are conscious. Except figuratively, we never attribute action to ideas or objects. Cf. *Siris*, sect. 249, 250, 291—295.

⁶⁵ In this and the four following sections, Berkeley mentions marks by which sense-phenomena are found in experience to be distinguished from all the other ideas of which we are cognisant, and in consequence of which they are termed 'real,' 'external,' or properly 'objective;' while other phenomena (those of feeling and imagination) are called subjective or individual. The changes in the ideas or phenomena presented in the senses are found to be part of Universal External Order—*natural*, inasmuch as it is independent of the will of the sense-percipient—the interpretation of which enables us to foresee (sect. 31) more or less of our future sense-experience; thus determining our pleasures and pains, and also informing us of the existence of other conscious minds.

⁶⁶ This mark—the superior strength, liveliness, and distinctness of our sense-ideas—was afterwards noted by Hume. See *Inquiry concerning Human Understanding*, sect. II.

which are the effects of human wills often are, but in a regular train or series—the admirable connexion whereof sufficiently testifies the wisdom and benevolence of its Author. Now the set rules or established methods wherein the Mind we depend on excites in us the ideas of sense, are called the *laws of nature*; and these we learn by experience, which teaches us that such and such ideas are attended with such and such other ideas, in the ordinary course of things.

31. This gives us a sort of foresight which enables us to regulate our actions for the benefit of life. And without this we should be eternally at a loss; we could not know how to act anything that might procure us the least pleasure, or remove the least pain of sense. That food nourishes, sleep refreshes, and fire warms us; that to sow in the seed-time is the way to reap in the harvest; and in general that to obtain such or such ends, such or such means are conducive—all this we know, not by discovering any necessary[7] connexion between our ideas, but only by the observation of the settled laws of nature, without which we should be all in uncertainty and confusion, and a grown man no more know how to manage himself in the affairs of life than an infant just born.

32. And yet this consistent uniform working, which so evidently displays the goodness and wisdom of that Governing Spirit whose Will constitutes the laws of nature, is so far from leading our thoughts to Him, that it rather sends them wandering after second causes. For, when we perceive certain ideas of Sense constantly followed by other ideas, and we know this is not of our own doing, we forthwith attribute power and agency to the ideas themselves, and make one the cause of another, than which nothing can be more absurd and unintelligible. Thus, for example, having observed that when we perceive by sight a certain round luminous figure we at the same time perceive by touch the idea or sensation called heat, we do from thence conclude the sun to be the cause of heat. And in like manner perceiving the motion and collision of bodies to be attended with sound, we are inclined to think the latter the effect of the former[8].

---

[7] Berkeley insists throughout his writings on the arbitrary character of the laws of nature in general, and of those by which the phenomena of vision symbolize those of touch in particular.

[8] So Schiller, in *Don Carlos*, Act III, where he represents the scrutinies as failing to see the God who veils Himself in everlasting laws. Berkeley, like Hume, Brown, Comte, Mill, &c., eliminates all power or

33. The ideas imprinted on the Senses by the Author of nature are called *real things*: and those excited in the imagination being less regular, vivid, and constant, are more properly[69] termed *ideas*, or *images of things*, which they copy and represent. But then our sensations, be they never so vivid and distinct, are nevertheless ideas, that is, they exist in the mind, or are perceived by it, as truly as the ideas of its own framing. The ideas of Sense are allowed to have more reality in them, that is, to be more strong, orderly, and coherent than the creatures of the mind; but this is no argument that they exist without the mind. They are also less dependent on the spirit, or thinking substance which perceives them, in that they are excited by the will of another and more powerful spirit; yet still they are *ideas*, and certainly no idea, whether faint or strong, can exist otherwise than in a mind perceiving it.[70]

34. Before we proceed any farther it is necessary we spend some time in answering objections[71] which may probably be made against the principles we have hitherto laid down. In doing of which, if I seem too prolix to those of quick apprehensions, I desire I may be excused, since all men do not equally apprehend things of this nature, and I am willing to be understood by every one.

First, then, it will be objected that by the foregoing principles all

---

causality from the material world; but, unlike them, he recognises power or causality, properly so called, in conscious mind—in the Ego—distinguished from the ideas of which it is immediately cognisant as contemporaneous and successive. 'Physical causation,' or constant order in the co-existence and succession of phenomena, accordingly, is not causation proper, but the effect of it.

[69] In popular language 'idea' is applied exclusively to the representations and misrepresentations of fancy or thought, and not, as with Berkeley, to the 'real things' present in the senses. See Leibnitz, *De modo distinguendi Phænomena Realia ab Imaginariis*.

[70] In the thirty-one preceding sections, two relations should be carefully distinguished—that of conscious mind to the *sense-ideas* of which it is conscious, and which depend upon conscious mind for their very existence; and that of mind to the changes of such ideas or phenomena. The former relation—that of percipient and percept—is not the relation of cause and effect at all, but is *sui generis*. The latter and correlative relation, also involved in our consciousness, is alone causal, and is our only proper example of causality—the orderly relations of phenomena to one another being only results of causal energy —of intending volition—and not power or causality itself. Note also that while Berkeley regards all phenomena as dependent on an intelligence and a will, he regards the changes in *sense-phenomena* as emphatically independent, for all practical purposes, of the *will* of the finite sense-percipient.

[71] Sect. 34—84 contain Berkeley's answers to supposed objections to the foregoing principles, concerning the true meaning of the terms 'Matter' and 'Mind,' 'Substance' and 'Cause;' and to his distinction between the presented realities of the material or sensible world, and the chimeras of imagination.

that is real and substantial in nature is banished out of the world, and instead thereof a chimerical scheme of *ideas* takes place. All things that exist exist only in the mind, that is, they are purely notional. What therefore becomes of the sun, moon, and stars? What must we think of houses, rivers, mountains, trees, stones; nay, even of our own bodies? Are all these but so many chimeras and illusions on the fancy? To all which, and whatever else of the same sort may be objected, I answer, that by the principles premised we are not deprived of any one thing in nature. Whatever we see, feel, hear, or any wise conceive or understand, remains as secure as ever, and is as real as ever. There is a *rerum natura*, and the distinction between realities and chimeras retains its full force. This is evident from sect. 29, 30, and 33, where we have shewn what is meant by *real things*, in opposition to *chimeras* or ideas of our own framing; but then they both equally exist in the mind, and in that sense[72] are alike *ideas*.

35. I do not argue against the existence of any one thing that we can apprehend either by sense or reflection. That the things I see with my eyes and touch with my hands do exist, really exist, I make not the least question. The only thing whose existence we deny is that which *philosophers* call Matter or corporeal substance. And in doing of this there is no damage done to the rest of mankind, who, I dare say, will never miss it. The Atheist indeed will want the colour of an empty name to support his impiety; and the Philosophers may possibly find they have lost a great handle for trifling and disputation. [73 But that is all the harm that I can see done.]

36. If any man thinks this detracts from the existence or reality of things, he is very far from understanding what hath been premised in the plainest terms I could think of. Take here an abstract of what has been said:—There are spiritual substances, minds, or human souls, which will or excite[74] ideas in themselves at pleasure; but these[74] are faint, weak, and unsteady in respect of others they perceive by sense—which, being impressed upon

---

[72] To be an 'idea' is, with Berkeley, to be the object of a conscious intelligence. But he does not define precisely the relation of ideas to minds conscious of them. 'Existence in the mind' is existence in this relation. His problem (which he determines in the negative) is, the possibility of the existence of sense-ideas—objects of sense-experience—out of this relation.

[73] Omitted in second edition.

[74] I.e. of imagination. Cf. sect. 18—30.

them according to certain rules or laws of nature, speak themselves the effects of a mind more powerful and wise than human spirits[75]. These latter are said to have more *reality* in them than the former;—by which is meant that they are more affecting, orderly, and distinct, and that they are not fictions of the mind perceiving them[76]. And in this sense the sun that I see by day is the real sun, and that which I imagine by night is the idea of the former. In the sense here given of *reality*, it is evident that every vegetable, star, mineral, and in general each part of the mundane system, is as much a *real being* by our principles as by any other. Whether others mean anything by the term *reality* different from what I do, I entreat them to look into their own thoughts and see[77].

37. It will be urged that thus much at least is true, to wit, that we take away all corporeal substances. To this my answer is, that if the word *substance* be taken in the vulgar sense—for a combination of sensible qualities, such as extension, solidity, weight, and the like—this we cannot be accused of taking away[78]: but if it be taken in a philosophic sense—for the support of accidents or qualities without the mind[78]—then indeed I acknowledge that we take it away, if one may be said to take away that which never had any existence, not even in the imagination.

38. But after all, say you, it sounds very harsh to say we eat and drink ideas, and are clothed with ideas. I acknowledge it does so—the word *idea* not being used in common discourse to signify the several combinations of sensible qualities which are called *things*; and it is certain that any expression which varies from the familiar use of language will seem harsh and ridiculous. But this doth not concern the truth of the proposition, which in other words is no more than to say, we are fed and clothed with those things which we perceive immediately by our senses[79]. The hardness or softness, the colour, taste, warmth, figure, or suchlike

---

[75] Cf. sect. 29.
[76] Cf. sect. 33. 'Not fictions,' i.e. they are presentative, and therefore cannot be misrepresentative in their character.
[77] The metaphysic of Berkeley is an endeavour to convert the word 'real' from being the symbol of an unintelligible abstraction into that of the conscious experience of a mind.

[78] With Berkeley *substances* are either (a) conscious minds, which are substances proper, or (b) the divinely conceived and constituted groups of sense-phenomena called 'sensible things,' which are substances conventionally.
[79] And which, because perceived, are ideas —an idea being with Berkeley a *perceived* or *imagined object*.

qualities, which combined together [20] constitute the several sorts of victuals and apparel, have been shewn to exist only in the mind that perceives them; and this is all that is meant by calling them *ideas*; which word if it was as ordinarily used as *thing*, would sound no harsher nor more ridiculous than it. I am not for disputing about the propriety, but the truth of the expression. If therefore you agree with me that we eat and drink and are clad with the immediate objects of sense, which cannot exist unperceived or without the mind, I shall readily grant it is more proper or conformable to custom that they should be called things rather than ideas.

39. If it be demanded why I make use of the word *idea*, and do not rather in compliance with custom call them *things*, I answer, I do it for two reasons:—first, because the term *thing*, in contradistinction to *idea*, is generally supposed to denote somewhat existing without the mind; secondly, because *thing* hath a more comprehensive signification than *idea*, including spirit or thinking things as well as ideas. Since therefore the objects of sense exist only in the mind, and are withal thoughtless and inactive, I chose to mark them by the word *idea*, which implies those properties [21].

40. But, say what we can, some one perhaps may be apt to reply, he will still believe his senses, and never suffer any arguments, how plausible soever, to prevail over the certainty of them. Be it so; assert the evidence of sense as high as you please, we are willing to do the same. That what I see, hear, and feel doth exist, that is to say, is perceived by me, I no more doubt than I do of my own being. But I do not see how the testimony of sense can be alleged as a proof for the existence of anything which is not perceived by sense [22]. We are not for having any man turn sceptic

---

[20] 'combined together,' i. e. as 'sensible things,' according to the natural laws of the contemporaneity and succession of ideas or phenomena. Cf. sect. 33.

[21] Berkeley's philosophy is a system of Intelligible Realism or Dualism, rather than of Idealism in the popular meaning of *idea*—for, he uses the word idea merely to mark the fact that he recognises the existence of objective things only so far as they are perceived and passive objects of a conscious mind; and he does not, as the term Idealism suggests, regard 'sensible things' as created or constructed by the voluntary activity of the individual mind in which they appear. They are perceived, but neither created nor regulated, by the finite percipient, and are thus *external* in the only practical meaning of that term.

[22] The existence of Matter, out of the relation of percept and percipient, cannot, without a contradiction, be said to be sensibly perceived. Therefore, our sense-perceptions, at any rate, do not justify us in affirming more about their immediate objects than that they are ideas or objects of which

and disbelieve his senses; on the contrary, we give them all the stress and assurance imaginable; nor are there any principles more opposite to Scepticism than those we have laid down, as shall be hereafter clearly shewn[a].

41. *Secondly*, it will be objected that there is a great difference betwixt real fire for instance, and the idea of fire, betwixt dreaming or imagining oneself burnt, and actually being so: if you suspect it to be only the idea of fire which you see, do but put your hand into it and you will be convinced with a witness. This and the like may be urged in opposition to our tenets. To all which the answer is evident from what hath been already said [64]; and I shall only add in this place, that if real fire be very different from the idea of fire, so also is the real pain that it occasions very different from the idea of the same pain, and yet nobody will pretend that real pain either is, or can possibly be, in an unperceiving thing, or without the mind, any more than its idea[65].

42. *Thirdly*, it will be objected that we see things actually without or at a distance from us, and which consequently do not exist in the mind; it being absurd that those things which are seen at the distance of several miles should be as near to us as our own thoughts[66]. In answer to this, I desire it may be considered that in a dream we do oft perceive things as existing at a great distance off, and yet for all that, those things are acknowledged to have their existence only in the mind.

43. But, for the fuller clearing of this point, it may be worth while to consider how it is that we perceive distance and things placed at a distance by sight. For, that we should in truth see external space, and bodies actually existing in it, some nearer,

others farther off, seems to carry with it some opposition to what hath been said of their existing nowhere without the mind. The consideration of this difficulty it was that gave birth to my *Essay towards a New Theory of Vision*, which was published not long since [87]—wherein it is shewn that distance or outness is neither immediately of itself perceived by sight [88], nor yet apprehended or judged of by lines and angles, or anything that hath a necessary connexion with it [89]; but that it is only suggested to our thoughts by certain visible ideas and sensations attending vision, which in their own nature have no manner of similitude or relation either with distance or things placed at a distance [90]; but, by a connexion taught us by experience, they come to signify and suggest them to us, after the same manner that words of any language suggest the ideas they are made to stand for [91]; insomuch that a man born blind and afterwards made to see, would not, at first sight, think the things he saw to be without his mind, or at any distance from him. See sect. 41 of the forementioned treatise.

44. The ideas of sight and touch make two species entirely distinct and heterogeneous [92]. The former are marks and prognostics of the latter. That the proper objects of sight neither exist without the mind, nor are the images of external things, was shewn even in that treatise [93]. Though throughout the same the contrary be supposed true of tangible objects—not that to suppose that vulgar error was necessary for establishing the notion therein laid down, but because it was beside my purpose to examine and refute it in a discourse concerning *Vision*. So that in strict truth the ideas of sight [94], when we apprehend by them distance and things placed at a distance, do not suggest or mark out to us things actually existing at a distance, but only admonish us what ideas of touch [95] will be imprinted in our minds at such and such distances of time, and in consequence of such or such actions. It is, I say, evident from what has been said in the foregoing parts of this Treatise, and in sect. 147 and elsewhere of the Essay concerning Vision, that

---

[87] See the Editor's preface to the *Essay*.
[88] *Essay*, sect. 2.
[89] *Ibid.* sect. 11—15.
[90] *Ibid.* sect. 16—28.
[91] *Ibid.* sect. 51.
[92] *Ibid.* sect. 47—49, 121—141.
[93] *Ibid.* sect. 43.
[94] i. e. what we are conscious of in seeing.

[95] i. e. tactual sensations. Touch is here taken in its wider meaning, and includes our muscular and locomotive experience, which with Berkeley is involved in the conception of distance. Cf. Mr. Mill's *Examination of Sir W. Hamilton's Philosophy*, chap. 13, in third edition.

visible ideas are the Language whereby the Governing Spirit on whom we depend informs us what tangible ideas he is about to imprint upon us, in case we excite this or that motion in our own bodies. But for a fuller information in this point I refer to the Essay itself.

45. *Fourthly*, it will be objected that from the foregoing principles it follows things are every moment annihilated and created anew[96]. The objects of sense exist only when they are perceived; the trees therefore are in the garden, or the chairs in the parlour, no longer than while there is somebody by to perceive them. Upon shutting my eyes all the furniture in the room is reduced to nothing, and barely upon opening them it is again created. In answer to all which, I refer the reader to what has been said in sect. 3, 4, &c., and desire he will consider whether he means anything by the actual existence[97] of an idea distinct from its being perceived. For my part, after the nicest inquiry I could make, I am not able to discover that anything else is meant by those words; and I once more entreat the reader to sound his own thoughts, and not suffer himself to be imposed on by words. If he can conceive it possible either for his ideas or their archetypes to exist without being perceived, then I give up the cause; but if he cannot, he will acknowledge it is unreasonable for him to stand up in defence of he knows not what, and pretend to charge on me as an absurdity the not assenting to those propositions which at bottom have no meaning in them.

46. It will not be amiss to observe how far the received principles of philosophy are themselves chargeable with those pretended absurdities. It is thought strangely absurd that upon closing my eyelids all the visible objects around me should be reduced to nothing; and yet is not this what philosophers commonly ac-

---

[96] To define the condition of sensible things *during the intervals of our perception of them*, consistently with the belief of all sane persons regarding the material world, is a challenge which has been often addressed to the advocates of an Intelligible Realism. According to Berkeley, there are no intervals in the existence—either actual, i. e. as perceived, or potential, i. e. as perceivable—of sensible things. They are permanently perceivable, under the laws of nature, though not perpetually perceived by this, that, or the other finite percipient. In other words, they always exist actually in the Divine Conception, and potentially, in relation to finite minds. In the Divine Will, the evolutions of external nature being the constant expression of that Will.—As to creation, cf. *Siris*, sect. 338—338, &c.

[97] Berkeley allows to unperceived bodies a potential or conditional, though not an actual, existence relatively to us. When we say a body exists *potentially*, we mean that if, in the light, we open our eyes, and look towards it, we shall see it, and that if we place our hand where it is we shall feel it.

knowledge, when they agree on all hands that light and colours, which alone are the proper and immediate objects of sight, are mere sensations that exist no longer than they are perceived? Again, it may to some perhaps seem very incredible that things should be every moment creating, yet this very notion is commonly taught in the schools. For the Schoolmen, though they acknowledge the existence of Matter[98], and that the whole mundane fabric is framed out of it, are nevertheless of opinion that it cannot subsist without the divine conservation, which by them is expounded to be a continual creation[99].

47. Farther, a little thought will discover to us that though we allow the existence of Matter or corporeal substance, yet it will unavoidably follow, from the principles which are now generally admitted, that the particular bodies, of what kind soever, do none of them exist whilst they are not perceived. For, it is evident from sect. 11 and the following sections, that the Matter philosophers contend for is an incomprehensible somewhat, which hath none of those particular qualities whereby the bodies falling under our senses are distinguished one from another. But, to make this more plain, it must be remarked that the infinite divisibility of Matter is now universally allowed, at least by the most approved and considerable philosophers, who on the received principles demonstrate it beyond all exception. Hence, it follows there is an infinite number of parts in each particle of Matter which are not perceived by sense[100]. The reason therefore that any particular body seems to be of a finite magnitude, or exhibits only a finite number of parts

---

[98] 'Matter,' i.e. material substance or Matter existing *per se*.

[99] 'Those who have contended for a material world have yet acknowledged that *natura naturans* (to use the language of the Schoolmen) is God, and that the Divine conservation of things is equipollent to and in fact the same thing with a continued repeated creation; in a word, that conservation and creation differ only as the *terminus a quo*. These are the common opinions of Schoolmen; and Durandus, who held the world to be a machine, like a clock made up and put in motion by God, but afterwards continued to go of itself, was therein particular, and had few followers. The very poets teach a doctrine not unlike the Schools — *mens agitat molem* (Vergil, Æneid, VI). The Stoics and Platonists are everywhere full of the same notion. I am not therefore singular in this point itself, so much as in my way of proving it.' (Berkeley's Letter to Dr. Samuel Johnson of New York.) Cf. *Alciphron*, Dial. IV. sect. 14; *Vindication of New Theory of Vision*, sect. 8, 17, &c.; *Siris, passim*, but especially in the latter part. See also *Correspondence between Clarke and Leibniz*. Jonathan Edwards, in his book on *Original Sin*, and elsewhere, maintains the continual creation of all existing persons as well as things, and employs it in defence of his theology. In several of his writings Edwards approaches the peculiar doctrines of Berkeley regarding the material world. It is worthy of note that when Berkeley was in Rhode Island, Edwards was settled in Massachusetts.

[100] Cf. sect. 123—132.

to sense, is, not because it contains no more, since in itself it contains an infinite number of parts, but because the sense is not acute enough to discern them. In proportion therefore as the sense is rendered more acute, it perceives a greater number of parts in the object, that is, the object appears greater, and its figure varies, those parts in its extremities which were before unperceivable appearing now to bound it in very different lines and angles from those perceived by an obtuser sense. And at length, after various changes of size and shape, when the sense becomes infinitely acute the body shall seem infinite. During all which there is no alteration in the body, but only in the sense. Each body therefore, considered in itself, is infinitely extended, and consequently void of all shape and figure. From which it follows that, though we should grant the existence of Matter to be never so certain, yet it is withal as certain, the materialists themselves are by their own principles forced to acknowledge, that neither the particular bodies perceived by sense, nor anything like them, exists without the mind. Matter, I say, and each particle thereof, is according to them infinite and shapeless, and it is the mind that frames all that variety of bodies which compose the visible world, any one whereof does not exist longer than it is perceived.

48. But, after all, if we consider it, the objection proposed in sect. 45 will not be found reasonably charged on the principles we have premised, so as in truth to make any objection at all against our notions. For, though we hold indeed the objects of sense to be nothing else but ideas which cannot exist unperceived; yet we may not hence conclude they have no existence except only while they are perceived by us, since there may be some other spirit that perceives them though we do not. Wherever bodies are said to have no existence without the mind, I would not be understood to mean this or that particular mind, but all minds whatsoever[1]. It does not therefore follow from the foregoing principles that bodies are annihilated and created every moment, or exist not at all during the intervals between our perception of them.

49. *Fifthly*, it may perhaps be objected that if extension and figure exist only in the mind, it follows that the mind is extended and figured; since extension is a mode or attribute which (to

---

[1] Cf. sect. 2, 3, &c., and the *Second and Third Dialogues of Hylas and Philonous*.

speak with the schools) is predicated of the subject in which it exists. I answer, those qualities are in the mind only as they are perceived by it—that is, not by way of *mode* or *attribute*, but only by way of *idea*[1]; and it no more follows the soul or mind is extended, because extension exists in it alone, than it does that it is red or blue, because those colours are on all hands acknowledged to exist in it, and nowhere else[2]. As to what philosophers say of subject and mode, that seems very groundless and unintelligible. For instance, in this proposition 'a die is hard, extended, and square,' they will have it that the word *die* denotes a subject or substance, distinct from the hardness, extension, and figure which are predicated of it, and in which they exist. This I cannot comprehend: to me a die seems to be nothing distinct from those things which are termed its modes or accidents. And, to say a die is hard, extended, and square is not to attribute those qualities to a subject distinct from and supporting them, but only an explication of the meaning of the word *die*.

50. *Sixthly*, you will say there have been a great many things explained by matter and motion; take away these and you destroy the whole corpuscular philosophy, and undermine those mechanical

principles which have been applied with so much success to account for the phenomena. In short, whatever advances have been made, either by ancient or modern philosophers, in the study of nature do all proceed on the supposition that corporeal substance or Matter doth really exist. To this I answer that there is not any one phenomenon explained on that supposition which may not as well be explained without it, as might easily be made appear by an induction of particulars. To explain the phenomena, is all one as to shew why, upon such and such occasions, we are affected with such and such ideas. But how Matter should operate on a Spirit, or produce any idea in it [1], is what no philosopher will pretend to explain; it is therefore evident there can be no use of Matter in natural philosophy. Besides, they who attempt to account for things do it not by corporeal substance, but by figure, motion, and other qualities, which are in truth no more than mere ideas, and therefore cannot be the cause of anything, as hath been already shewn. See sect. 25.

51. *Seventhly*, it will upon this be demanded whether it does not seem absurd to take away natural causes, and ascribe everything to the immediate operation of Spirits? We must no longer say upon these principles that fire heats, or water cools, but that a Spirit heats, and so forth. Would not a man be deservedly laughed at, who should talk after this manner? I answer, he would so; in such things we ought to 'think with the learned, and speak with the vulgar.' They who to demonstration are convinced of the truth of the Copernican system do nevertheless say 'the sun rises,' 'the sun sets,' or 'comes to the meridian;' and if they affected a contrary style in common talk it would without doubt appear very ridiculous. A little reflection on what is here said will make it manifest that the common use of language would receive no manner of alteration or disturbance from the admission of our tenets.

52. In the ordinary affairs of life, any phrases may be retained, so long as they excite in us proper sentiments, or dispositions to

---

[1] Philosophers have treated the relation of Matter to Mind in perception as one of cause and effect—the result, according to Berkeley, of illegitimate analysis or abstraction, which creates a fictitious duality of substance. By his new principles, philosophy is based on a recognition of the fact that perception is neither the cause nor the effect of its objects, but in a relation to it that is *sui generis* and ultimate. Cf. Prof. Ferrier on 'perception' and 'matter,' in his *Institutes of Metaphysics*, Prop. IV., and *Remains*, Vol. II. pp. 151—188, 407—409.

act in such a manner as is necessary for our well-being, how false soever they may be if taken in a strict and speculative sense. Nay, this is unavoidable, since, propriety being regulated by custom, language is suited to the received opinions, which are not always the truest. Hence it is impossible—even in the most rigid, philosophic reasonings—so far to alter the bent and genius of the tongue we speak, as never to give a handle for cavillers to pretend difficulties and inconsistencies. But, a fair and ingenuous reader will collect the sense from the scope and tenor and connexion of a discourse, making allowances for those inaccurate modes of speech which use has made inevitable.

53. As to the opinion that there are no Corporeal Causes, this has been heretofore maintained by some of the Schoolmen, as it is of late by others among the modern philosophers, who though they allow Matter to exist, yet will have God alone to be the immediate efficient cause of all things[5]. These men saw that amongst all the objects of sense there was none which had any power or activity included in it; and that by consequence this was likewise true of whatever bodies they supposed to exist without the mind, like unto the immediate objects of sense[6]. But then, that they should suppose an innumerable multitude of created beings, which they acknowledge are not capable of producing any one effect in nature, and which therefore are made to no manner of purpose, since God might have done everything as well without them—this I say, though we should allow it possible, must yet be a very unaccountable and extravagant supposition[7].

54. In the *eighth* place, the universal concurrent assent of mankind[8] may be thought by some an invincible argument in behalf of Matter, or the existence of external things. Must we

---

[5] We refer to Des Cartes, and especially Geulinx, Malebranche, &c., who, while they argued for material substance, denied the causality of sensible things. With them, as with Berkeley, there are no causes in the material or phenomenal world—only effects, which are evolved in a constant order, contemporaneous and successive, and thus express the meaning of the Supreme Power. See Malebranche, *Entretiens*, VI., VII.

[6] I.e. of their hypothetical material world, existing unperceived.

[7] On the principle, 'Entia non sunt multiplicanda praeter necessitatem.'

[8] Commonly called the argument from Common Sense, and illustrated in the writings of Reid and other Scotch psychologists. That the unreflecting part of mankind should hold an unintelligible, or at least confused, Realism is not to be wondered at, when we recollect that it is the very office of philosophy to interpret the sensible reality, which they and philosophers acknowledge in common to be 'external,' *in some meaning of the term*.

suppose the whole world to be mistaken? And if so, what cause can be assigned of so widespread and predominant an error?—I answer, first, that, upon a narrow inquiry, it will not perhaps be found so many as is imagined do really believe the existence of Matter or things without the mind. Strictly speaking, to believe that which involves a contradiction, or has no meaning in it [9], is impossible; and whether the foregoing expressions are not of that sort, I refer it to the impartial examination of the reader. In one sense, indeed, men may be said to believe that Matter exists, that is, they act as if the immediate cause of their sensations, which affects them every moment, and is so nearly present to them, were some senseless unthinking being. But, that they should clearly apprehend any meaning marked by those words, and form thereof a settled speculative opinion, is what I am not able to conceive. This is not the only instance wherein men impose upon themselves, by imagining they believe those propositions which they have often heard, though at bottom they have no meaning in them.

55. But secondly, though we should grant a notion to be never so universally and stedfastly adhered to, yet this is but a weak argument of its truth to whoever considers what a vast number of prejudices and false opinions are everywhere embraced with the utmost tenaciousness, by the unreflecting (which are the far greater) part of mankind. There was a time when the antipodes and motion of the earth were looked upon as monstrous absurdities even by men of learning: and if it be considered what a small proportion they bear to the rest of mankind, we shall find that at this day those notions have gained but a very inconsiderable footing in the world.

56. But it is demanded that we assign a cause of this prejudice, and account for its obtaining in the world. To this I answer, that men knowing they perceived several ideas [10], whereof they themselves were not the authors—as not being excited from within nor depending on the operation of their wills—this made them maintain those ideas [10] or objects of perception had an existence independent of and without the mind, without ever dreaming that

---

[9] Sect. 4, 9, 15, 17, 22, 24.
[10] I.e. sense-ideas.—Though his own sense-ideas or objects are independent of the will of the finite percipient, it does not follow that they are independent of his perception. Cf. sect. 29—33.

a contradiction was involved in those words. But, philosophers having plainly seen that the immediate objects of perception do not exist without the mind, they in some degree corrected the mistake of the vulgar[11]; but at the same time run into another which seems no less absurd, to wit, that there are certain objects really existing without the mind, or having a subsistence distinct from being perceived, of which our ideas are only images or resemblances, imprinted by those objects[12] on the mind. And this notion of the philosophers owes its origin to the same cause with the former, namely, their being conscious that they were not the authors of their own sensations, which they evidently knew were imprinted from without, and which therefore must have some cause distinct from the minds on which they are imprinted.

57. But why they should suppose the ideas of sense to be excited in us by things in their likeness, and not rather have recourse to *Spirit* which alone can act, may be accounted for, first, because they were not aware of the repugnancy there is, as well in supposing things like unto our ideas existing without, as in attributing to them power or activity. Secondly, because the Supreme Spirit which excites those ideas in our minds, is not marked out and limited to our view by any particular finite collection of sensible ideas, as human agents are by their size, complexion, limbs, and motions. And thirdly, because His operations are regular and uniform. Whenever the course of nature is interrupted by a miracle, men are ready to own the presence of a superior agent. But, when we see things go on in the ordinary course they do not excite in us any reflection; their order and concatenation, though it be an argument of the greatest wisdom, power, and goodness in their creator, is yet so constant and familiar to us that we do not think them the immediate effects of a *Free Spirit*; especially since inconsistency and mutability in acting, though it be an imperfection, is looked on as a mark of *freedom*[13].

---

[11] By recognising that what we are immediately percipient of must be *ideal*, or at least that it is only known by us in sense as ideal—as a sense-percept.

[12] i.e. by the unperceived or absolute objects which, on this hypothesis of a representative sense-perception, were assumed to exist *behind* the properly perceived objects or ideas, and to be (according to some) the cause of their appearance in our consciousness. Cf. *Third Dialogue between Hylas and Philonous*, p. 359.

[13] Hence the difficulty men have in recognising that the Divine Ideas and Will, and the Laws of Nature, are coincident. But in fact the scientific discovery of Laws in nature, instead of narrowing, extends the sphere of intelligible Divine agency.

58. *Tenthly*, it will be objected that the notions we advance are inconsistent with several sound truths in philosophy and mathematics. For example, the motion of the earth is now universally admitted by astronomers as a truth grounded on the clearest and most convincing reasons. But, on the foregoing principles, there can be no such thing. For, motion being only an idea, it follows that if it be not perceived it exists not: but the motion of the earth is not perceived by sense. I answer, that tenet, if rightly understood, will be found to agree with the principles we have premised; for, the question whether the earth moves or no amounts in reality to no more that this, to wit, whether we have reason to conclude, from what has been observed by astronomers, that if we were placed in such and such circumstances, and such or such a position and distance both from the earth and sun, we should perceive the former to move among the choir of the planets, and appearing in all respects like one of them; and this, by the established rules of nature which we have no reason to mistrust, is reasonably collected from the phenomena.

59. We may, from the experience we have had of the train and succession of ideas[14] in our minds, often make, I will not say uncertain conjectures, but sure and well-grounded predictions concerning the ideas[14] we shall be affected with pursuant to a great train of actions, and be enabled to pass a right judgment of what would have appeared to us, in case we were placed in circumstances very different from those we are in at present. Herein consists the knowledge of nature, which may preserve its use and certainty very consistently with what hath been said. It will be easy to apply this to whatever objections of the like sort may be drawn from the magnitude of the stars, or any other discoveries in astronomy or nature.

60. In the *eleventh* place, it will be demanded to what purpose serves that curious organization of plants, and the animal mechanism in the parts of animals; might not vegetables grow, and shoot forth leaves and blossoms, and animals perform all their

---

[14] 'Ideas,' i.e. sense-ideas or sensations. This 'experience' consists of the established association of sensations or *percepta* in the order of external nature, not mere 'association of ideas'—in the popular meaning of the word idea.

motions as well without as with all that variety of internal parts so elegantly contrived and put together; which, being ideas, have nothing powerful or operative in them, nor have any necessary [15] connexion with the effects ascribed to them? If it be a Spirit that immediately produces every effect by a *fiat* or act of his will, we must think all that is fine and artificial in the works, whether of man or nature, to be made in vain. By this doctrine, though an artist has made the spring and wheels, and every movement of a watch, and adjusted them in such a manner as he knew would produce the motions he designed, yet he must think all this done to no purpose, and that it is an Intelligence which directs the index, and points to the hour of the day. If so, why may not the Intelligence do it, without his being at the pains of making the movements and putting them together? Why does not an empty case serve as well as another? And how comes it to pass that whenever there is any fault in the going of a watch, there is some corresponding disorder to be found in the movements, which being mended by a skilful hand all is right again? The like may be said of all the clockwork of nature, great part whereof is so wonderfully fine and subtle as scarce to be discerned by the best microscope. In short, it will be asked, how, upon our principles, any tolerable account can be given, or any final cause assigned of an innumerable multitude of bodies and machines, framed with the most exquisite art, which in the common philosophy have very apposite uses assigned them, and serve to explain abundance of phenomena?

61. To all which I answer, first, that though there were some difficulties relating to the administration of Providence, and the uses by it assigned to the several parts of nature, which I could not solve by the foregoing principles, yet this objection could be of small weight against the truth and certainty of those things which may be proved *a priori*, with the utmost evidence and rigour of demonstration [16]. Secondly, but neither are the received principles free from the like difficulties; for, it may still be demanded to what end God should take those roundabout methods of effecting

---

[15] Cf. sect. 25, and also various passages in Berkeley's writings in which he insists upon the *arbitrariness* of the so-called causal relations among sensible things, and the consequent sense-symbolism of Nature. It is thus that he speaks of a *language* of Vision. Cf. *Theory of Vision Vindicated*, passim.

[16] Cf. sect. 3, 4, 22—24.

things by instruments and machines, which no one can deny might have been effected by the mere command of His will without all that apparatus; nay, if we narrowly consider it, we shall find the objection may be retorted with greater force on those who hold the existence of those machines without the mind; for it has been made evident that solidity, bulk, figure, motion, and the like have no *activity* or *efficacy* in them, so as to be capable of producing any one effect in nature. See sect. 25. Whoever therefore supposes them [17] to exist (allowing the supposition possible) when they are not perceived does it manifestly to no purpose; since the only use that is assigned to them [17], as they exist unperceived, is that they produce those perceivable effects which in truth cannot be ascribed to anything but Spirit.

62. But, to come nigher the difficulty, it must be observed that though the fabrication of all those parts and organs be not absolutely necessary to the producing any effect, yet it is necessary to the producing of things in a constant regular way according to the laws of nature. There are certain general laws that run through the whole chain of natural effects: these are learned by the observation and study of nature, and are by men applied as well to the framing artificial things for the use and ornament of life as to the explaining the various phenomena—which explication consists only in shewing the conformity any particular phenomenon hath to the general laws of nature, or, which is the same thing, in discovering the *uniformity* there is in the production of natural effects; as will be evident to whoever shall attend to the several instances wherein philosophers pretend to account for appearances. That there is a great and conspicuous use in these regular constant methods of working observed by the Supreme Agent hath been shewn in sect. 31. And it is no less visible that a particular size, figure, motion, and disposition of parts are necessary, though not absolutely to the producing any effect, yet to the producing it according to the standing mechanical laws of nature. Thus, for instance, it cannot be denied that God, or the Intelligence that sustains and rules the ordinary course of things, might if He were minded to produce a miracle, cause all the motions on

---

[17] 'them,' i.e. the solid and extended objects, which are supposed to exist unperceived and unpercipient—as distinguished from the Intelligent Cause to whom Berkeley attributes the orderly appearance, disappearance, and reappearance of ideas or objects in the senses.

the dial-plate of a watch, though nobody had ever made the movements and put them in it: but yet, if He will act agreeably to the rules of mechanism, by Him for wise ends established and maintained in the creation, it is necessary that those actions of the watchmaker, whereby he makes the movements and rightly adjusts them, precede the production of the aforesaid motions; as also that any disorder in them be attended with the perception of some corresponding disorder in the movements, which being once corrected all is right again.

63. It may indeed on some occasions be necessary that the Author of nature display His overruling power in producing some appearance out of the ordinary series of things [18]. Such exceptions from the general rules of nature are proper to surprise and awe men into an acknowledgment of the Divine Being; but then they are to be used but seldom, otherwise there is a plain reason why they should fail of that effect. Besides, God seems to choose the convincing our reason of His attributes by the works of nature, which discover so much harmony and contrivance in their make, and are such plain indications of wisdom and beneficence in their Author, rather than to astonish us into a belief of His Being by anomalous and surprising events.

64. To set this matter in a yet clearer light, I shall observe that what has been objected in sect. 60 amounts in reality to no more than this:—Ideas are not anyhow and at random produced, there being a certain order and connexion between them, like to that of cause and effect: there are also several combinations of them made in a very regular and artificial manner, which seem like so many instruments in the hand of nature that, being hid as it were behind the scenes, have a secret operation in producing those appearances which are seen on the theatre of the world, being themselves discernible only to the curious eye of the philosopher. But, since one idea cannot be the cause of another, to what purpose is that connexion? And, since those instruments, being barely *inefficacious perceptions* [19] in the mind, are not subservient to the production of natural effects, it is demanded why they are made; or, in other words, what reason can be assigned

---

[18] So far as that series has been interpreted by us. The nature and moral office of miraculous or supernatural events, in a system of Universal Providence, is here touched upon.

[19] Cf. sect. 25.

why God should make us, upon a close inspection into His works, behold so great variety of ideas so artfully laid together, and so much according to rule; it not being [20 credible] that He would be at the expense (if one may so speak) of all that art and regularity to no purpose.

65. To all which my answer is, first, that the connexion of ideas does not imply the relation of *cause* and *effect*, but only of a mark or *sign* with the thing *signified*. The fire which I see is not the cause of the pain I suffer upon my approaching it, but the mark that forewarns me of it. In like manner the noise that I hear is not the effect of this or that motion or collision of the ambient bodies, but the sign thereof[21]. Secondly, the reason why ideas are formed into machines, that is, artificial and regular combinations, is the same with that for combining letters into words[22]. That a few original ideas may be made to signify a great number of effects and actions, it is necessary they be variously combined together. And, to the end their use be permanent and universal, these combinations must be made by *rule*, and with *wise contrivance*. By this means abundance of information is conveyed unto us, concerning what we are to expect from such and such actions, and what methods are proper to be taken for the exciting such and such ideas—which in effect is all that I conceive to be distinctly meant when it is said[23] that, by discerning the figure, texture, and mechanism of the inward parts of bodies, whether natural or artificial, we may attain to know the several uses and properties depending thereon, or the nature of the thing.

66. Hence, it is evident that those things which, under the notion of a cause co-operating or concurring to the production of effects, are altogether inexplicable, and run us into great

---

[20] 'imaginable'—in first edition.

[21] According to Berkeley, Minds, Spirits, Persons are the only proper causes; and it is only by an abuse of language that the term 'cause' is applied to the ideas or objects which are invariable antecedents of other ideas or objects—the prior form of their objective or phenomenal existence. He contrasts so-called Physical with Spiritual Causation—the latter being implied in our conception of mind; the former consisting in the observable relations of phenomena, in which causation proper is unperceived, and therefore non-existent. Physical Science is the interpretation of natural signs, and is only confused (Berkeley would say) by reference to an unconscious agency which is inconceivable.

[22] Berkeley, in meeting this objection, thus reverts to his favourite theory of a Universal Natural Symbolism as the true character of the sensible world. See next section, which describes the orderly co-existences and sequences of nature as not causally necessary, but arbitrarily constructed—in order to be a means of social intercourse, and for the use of man in his contemplation of the Supreme Mind.

[23] See Locke's *Essay*, B. IV. ch. 3. § 25—28, &c.

absurdities, may be very naturally explained, and have a proper and obvious use assigned to them, when they are considered only as marks or signs for our information. And it is the searching after and endeavouring to understand this Language (if I may so call it) of the Author of nature, that ought to be the employment of the natural philosopher; and not the pretending to explain things by corporeal causes, which doctrine seems to have too much estranged the minds of men from that active principle, that supreme and wise Spirit 'in whom we live, move, and have our being.'

67. In the *twelfth* place, it may perhaps be objected that—though it be clear from what has been said that there can be no such thing as an inert, senseless, extended, solid, figured, moveable substance existing without the mind, such as philosophers describe Matter—yet, if any man shall leave out of his idea of *matter* the positive ideas of extension, figure, solidity and motion, and say that he means only by that word an inert, senseless substance, that exists without the mind or unperceived, which is the occasion of our ideas, or at the presence whereof God is pleased to excite ideas in us—it doth not appear but that Matter taken in this sense may possibly exist. In answer to which I say, first, that it seems no less absurd to suppose a substance without accidents, than it is to suppose accidents without a substance [24]. But secondly, though we should grant this unknown substance may possibly exist, yet where can it be supposed to be? That it exists not in the mind [25] is agreed; and that it exists not in place is no less certain—since all place or extension exists only in the mind [26], as hath been already proved. It remains therefore that it exists nowhere at all.

68. Let us examine a little the description that is here given us of *matter*. It neither acts, nor perceives, nor is perceived; for this is all that is meant by saying it is an inert, senseless, unknown substance; which is a definition entirely made up of negatives, excepting only the relative notion of its standing under

---

[24] With Berkeley, *material substance* is merely the complement of simple ideas or phenomena which *arbitrarily* constitute a particular thing. (Cf. sect. 37.) The Divine Will is, with him, the cause of phenomena being thus constituted, combined, or substantiated. His substance-proper, i.e. mind, is necessary, because an object-perceived necessarily implies a percipient.

[25] I.e. that it is not perceived.

[26] I.e. 'place' exists only as perceived or conceived by an intelligence—sense-perception being its real, and conception its imagined existence. Mind is thus, with Berkeley, the *place* of locality and of space. Cf. *Siris*, sect. 185, &c.

or supporting. But then it must be observed that it supports nothing at all, and how nearly this comes to the description of a *nonentity* I desire may be considered. But, say you, it is the *unknown occasion* [18], at the presence of which ideas are excited in us by the will of God. Now, I would fain know how anything can be present to us, which is neither perceivable by sense nor reflection, nor capable of producing any idea in our minds, nor is at all extended, nor hath any form, nor exists in any place. The words 'to be present,' when thus applied, must needs be taken in some abstract and strange meaning, and which I am not able to comprehend.

69. Again, let us examine what is meant by *occasion*. So far as I can gather from the common use of language, that word signifies either the agent which produces any effect, or else something that is observed to accompany or go before it in the ordinary course of things. But, when it is applied to Matter as above described, it can be taken in neither of those senses; for Matter is said to be passive and inert, and so cannot be an agent or efficient cause. It is also unperceivable, as being devoid of all sensible qualities, and so cannot be the occasion of our perceptions in the latter sense—as when the burning my finger is said to be the occasion of the pain that attends it. What therefore can be meant by calling matter an *occasion*? This term is either used in no sense at all, or else in some very distant from its received signification.

70. You will perhaps say that Matter, though it be not perceived by us, is nevertheless perceived by God, to whom it is the occasion of exciting ideas in our minds [19]. For, say you, since we observe our sensations to be imprinted in an orderly and constant manner, it is but reasonable to suppose there are certain constant and regular occasions of their being produced. That is to say, that there are certain permanent and distinct parcels of Matter, corresponding to our ideas, which, though they do not excite them in our minds, or anywise immediately affect us, as being altogether passive and unperceivable to us, they are nevertheless to God, by whom they are perceived [20], as it were so many occasions to remind

---

[18] He refers to the Cartesian theory of occasional causes.
[19] So Geulinx and Malebranche.
[20] As known by the Divine intelligence, they are accordingly ideas. And, if this means merely that the sensible system is the expression of Divine Ideas, which are its ultimate archetype—that the Ideas of God

Him when and what ideas to imprint on our minds—that so things may go on in a constant uniform manner.

71. In answer to this, I observe that, as the notion of Matter is here stated, the question is no longer concerning the existence of a thing distinct from *Spirit* and *idea*, from perceiving and being perceived; but whether there are not certain ideas of I know not what sort, in the mind of God, which are so many marks or notes that direct Him how to produce sensations in our minds in a constant and regular method—much after the same manner as a musician is directed by the notes of music to produce that harmonious train and composition of sound which is called a tune, though they who hear the music do not perceive the notes, and may be entirely ignorant of them. But, this notion of Matter (which after all is the only intelligible one that I can pick from what is said of unknown occasions) seems too extravagant to deserve a confutation. Besides, it is in effect no objection against what we have advanced, viz. that there is no senseless unperceived substance.

72. If we follow the light of reason, we shall, from the constant uniform method of our sensations, collect the goodness and wisdom of the Spirit who excites them in our minds; but this is all that I can see reasonably concluded from thence. To me, I say, it is evident that the being of a Spirit infinitely wise, good, and powerful is abundantly sufficient to explain all the appearances of nature [x]. But, as for *inert, senseless Matter*, nothing that I perceive has any the least connexion with it, or leads to the thoughts of it. And I would fain see any one explain any the meanest phenomenon in nature by it, or shew any manner of reason, though in the lowest rank of probability, that he can have for its existence, or even make any tolerable sense or meaning of that supposition. For, as to its being an occasion, we have, I think, evidently shewn that with regard to us it is no occasion. It remains therefore that it must be, if at all, the occasion to God of exciting ideas in us; and what this amounts to we have just now seen.

---

are symbolised in our senses, to be interpreted or misinterpreted by human minds, as reason in man is applied or misapplied—this theory allies itself with the Platonic. It is partly worked out in *Siris*.

[x] 'It seems to me,' says Hume, 'that this theory of the universal energy and operation of the Supreme Being is too bold ever to carry conviction with it to a mind sufficiently apprised of the weakness of human reason, and the narrow limits to which it is confined in all its operations.' *Inquiry concerning Human Understanding*, sect. VII. p. L.

73. It is worth while to reflect a little on the motives which induced men to suppose the existence of *material substance*; that so having observed the gradual ceasing and expiration of those motives or reasons, we may proportionably withdraw the assent that was grounded on them. First, therefore, it was thought that colour, figure, motion, and the rest of the sensible qualities or accidents, did really exist without the mind; and for this reason it seemed needful to suppose some unthinking *substratum* or substance wherein they did exist—since they could not be conceived to exist by themselves[31]. Afterwards, in process of time, men being convinced that colours, sounds, and the rest of the sensible, secondary qualities had no existence without the mind, they stripped this *substratum* or material substance of those qualities[32], leaving only the primary ones, figure, motion, and suchlike, which they still conceived to exist without the mind, and consequently to stand in need of a material support. But, it having be shewn that none even of these can possibly exist otherwise than in a Spirit or Mind which perceives them, it follows that we have no longer any reason to suppose the being of Matter[33]; nay, that it is utterly impossible there should be any such thing, so long as that word is taken to denote an *unthinking substratum* of qualities or accidents wherein they exist without the mind.

74. But—though it be allowed by the materialists themselves that Matter was thought of only for the sake of supporting accidents, and, the reason entirely ceasing[34], one might expect the mind should naturally, and without any reluctance at all, quit the belief of what was solely grounded thereon—yet the prejudice is riveted so deeply in our thoughts, that we can scarce tell how to part with it, and are therefore inclined, since the *thing* itself is indefensible, at least to retain the *name*, which we apply to I know not what abstracted and indefinite notions of being, or occasion, though without any show of reason, at least so far as I can see. For, what is there on our part, or what do we perceive, amongst all the ideas, sensations, notions which are imprinted on our minds,

---

[31] Is the assumption of the need for substance of some sort, percipient if not corporeal, regarded by Berkeley as a truth of the absolute or common reason?

[32] e.g. Des Cartes, Malebranche, Locke, &c.

[33] That is, if we mean by Matter, something existing unperceived and unperceiving. But 'matter,' in another and intelligible meaning of the word, according to Berkeley, may and does exist.

[34] Seeing that sensible phenomena are sufficiently 'supported' by mind.

either by sense or reflection, from whence may be inferred the existence of an inert, thoughtless, unperceived occasion? and, on the other hand, on the part of an All-sufficient Spirit, what can there be that should make us believe or even suspect He is directed by an inert occasion[35] to excite ideas in our minds?

75. It is a very extraordinary instance of the force of prejudice, and much to be lamented, that the mind of man retains so great a fondness, against all the evidence of reason, for a stupid thoughtless *somewhat*, by the interposition whereof it would as it were screen itself from the Providence of God, and remove it farther off from the affairs of the world. But, though we do the utmost we can to secure the belief of Matter, though, when reason forsakes us, we endeavour to support our opinion on the bare possibility of the thing, and though we indulge ourselves in the full scope of an imagination not regulated by reason to make out that poor possibility, yet the upshot of all is—that there are certain *unknown Ideas* in the mind of God; for this, if anything, is all that I conceive to be meant by *creation* with regard to God. And this at the bottom is no longer contending for the thing, but for the name.

76. Whether therefore there are such Ideas in the mind of God, and whether they may be called by the name *Matter*, I shall not dispute [36]. But, if you stick to the notion of an unthinking substance or support of extension, motion, and other sensible qualities, then to me it is most evidently impossible there should be any such thing; since it is a plain repugnancy that those qualities should exist in or be supported by an unperceiving substance [37].

77. But, say you, though it be granted that there is no thoughtless support of extension and the other qualities or accidents which we perceive, yet there may perhaps be some inert, unperceiving substance or *substratum* of some other qualities, as incomprehensible to us as colours are to a man born blind, because we have not a

---

[35] unless that 'occasion' is only another term for His own Ideas?

[36] Berkeley's philosophy seems to imply the existence of Divine Ideas, which receive expression in the laws of nature, and of which human science is the imperfect interpretation. In this view, the assertion of the existence of Matter, material substance, or occasion is simply an assertion that the phenomenal universe into which we are born is a reasonable or interpretable universe; and that it would be actually interpreted, if our conceptions were harmonized with the Divine or Absolute Conception which it expresses. The Divine Thought would thus be Absolute Truth or Being. Cf. *Siris* passim.

[37] Cf. sect. 3–24.

sense adapted to them. But, if we had a new sense, we should possibly no more doubt of their existence than a blind man made to see does of the existence of light and colours.—I answer, first, if what you mean by the word *Matter* be only the unknown support of unknown qualities, it is no matter whether there is such a thing or no, since it no way concerns us; and I do not see the advantage there is in disputing about what we know not *what*, and we know not *why*.

78. But, secondly, if we had a new sense it could only furnish us with new ideas or sensations; and then we should have the same reason against their existing in an unperceiving substance that has been already offered with relation to figure, motion, colour, and the like. Qualities, as hath been shewn, are nothing else but *sensations* or *ideas*, which exist only in a *mind* perceiving them; and this is true not only of the ideas we are acquainted with at present, but likewise of all possible ideas whatsoever.

79. But, you will insist, what if I have no reason to believe the existence of Matter? what if I cannot assign any use to it or explain anything by it, or even conceive what is meant by that word? yet still it is no contradiction to say that Matter exists, and that this Matter is in general a *substance*, or *occasion of ideas*; though indeed to go about to unfold the meaning or adhere to any particular explication of those words may be attended with great difficulties. I answer, when words are used without a meaning, you may put them together as you please without danger of running into a contradiction. You may say, for example, that twice two is equal to seven, so long as you declare you do not take the words of that proposition in their usual acceptation but for marks of you know not what. And, by the same reason, you may say there is an inert thoughtless substance without accidents which is the occasion of our ideas. And we shall understand just as much by one proposition as the other.

80. In the *last* place, you will say, what if we give up the cause of material Substance, and stand to it that Matter is an unknown *somewhat*—neither substance nor accident, spirit nor idea, inert, thoughtless, indivisible, immoveable, unextended, existing in no place? For, say you, whatever may be urged against *substance* or *occasion*, or any other positive or relative notion of Matter, hath

no place at all, so long as this *negative* definition of Matter is adhered to. I answer, you may, if so it shall seem good, use the word 'Matter' in the same sense as other men use 'nothing,' and so make those terms convertible in your style. For, after all, this is what appears to me to be the result of that definition—the parts whereof when I consider with attention, either collectively or separate from each other, I do not find that there is any kind of effect or impression made on my mind different from what is excited by the term *nothing*.

81. You will reply, perhaps, that in the foresaid definition is included what doth sufficiently distinguish it from nothing—the positive abstract idea of *quiddity*, *entity*, or *existence*. I own, indeed, that those who pretend to the faculty of framing abstract general ideas do talk as if they had such an idea, which is, say they, the most abstract and general notion of all; that is, to me, the most incomprehensible of all others. That there are a great variety of spirits of different orders and capacities, whose faculties both in number and extent are far exceeding those the Author of my being has bestowed on me, I see no reason to deny. And for me to pretend to determine by my own few, stinted, narrow inlets of perception, what ideas the inexhaustible power of the Supreme Spirit may imprint upon them were certainly the utmost folly and presumption—since there may be, for aught that I know, innumerable sorts of ideas or sensations, as different from one another, and from all that I have perceived, as colours are from sounds [36]. But, how ready soever I may be to acknowledge the scantiness of my comprehension with regard to the endless variety of spirits and ideas that may possibly exist, yet for any one to pretend to a notion of Entity or Existence, *abstracted* from *spirit* and *idea*, from perceived and being perceived, is, I suspect, a downright repugnancy and trifling with words.—It remains that we consider the objections which may possibly be made on the part of Religion.

82. Some there are who think that, though the arguments for the real existence of bodies which are drawn from Reason be allowed not to amount to demonstration, yet the Holy Scriptures are so

---

[36] Matter and physical science is relative, inasmuch as we may suppose an indefinite number of additional senses, affording corresponding varieties of sense-experience, of course at present inconceivable by man. Or, we may suppose an intelligence destitute of all sense-perceptions, and having ideas or objects of another sort altogether.

clear in the point, as will sufficiently convince every good Christian that bodies do really exist, and are something more than mere ideas; there being in Holy Writ innumerable facts related which evidently suppose the reality of timber and stone, mountains and rivers, and cities, and human bodies[39]. To which I answer that no sort of writings whatever, sacred or profane, which use those and the like words in the vulgar acceptation, or so as to have a meaning in them, are in danger of having their truth called in question by our doctrine. That all those things do really exist, that there are bodies, even corporeal substances, when taken in the vulgar sense, has been shewn to be agreeable to our principles: and the difference betwixt *things* and *ideas*, *realities* and *chimeras*, has been distinctly explained. See sect. 29, 30, 33, 36, &c. And I do not think that either what philosophers call *Matter*, or the existence of objects without the mind[40], is anywhere mentioned in Scripture.

83. Again, whether there be or be not external things[41], it is agreed on all hands that the proper use of words is the marking our conceptions, or things only as they are known and perceived by us; whence it plainly follows that in the tenets we have laid down there is nothing inconsistent with the right use and significancy of language, and that discourse, of what kind soever, so far as it is intelligible, remains undisturbed. But all this seems so very manifest, from what has been largely set forth in the premises, that it is needless to insist any farther on it.

84. But, it will be urged that miracles do, at least, lose much of their stress and import by our principles. What must we think of Moses' rod? was it not *really* turned into a serpent, or was there only a change of *ideas* in the minds of the spectators? And, can it be supposed that our Saviour did no more at the marriage-feast in Cana than impose on the sight, and smell, and taste of the guests, so as to create in them the appearance or idea only of wine? The same may be said of all other miracles; which, in

---

[39] Holy Scripture, and the assumed possibility of its existence, added to our natural tendency to believe, are the grounds on which Malebranche and Norris infer the existence of a material world. Berkeley's material world needs no proof—unless of its permanent orderliness, which he rests on suggestion and custom. His aim is not to prove that the material world exists, but to explain what we should mean when we say that it exists.

[40] i.e. existing uncognised by any intelligence—finite or Divine.

[41] 'external things,' i.e. things existing absolutely, or out of all relation to any cognitive agent.

consequence of the foregoing principles, must be looked upon only as so many cheats, or illusions of fancy.—To this I reply, that the rod was changed into a real serpent, and the water into real wine. That this does not in the least contradict what I have elsewhere said will be evident from sect. 34 and 35. But this business of *real* and *imaginary* has been already so plainly and fully explained, and so often referred to, and the difficulties about it are so easily answered from what has gone before, that it were an affront to the reader's understanding to resume the explication of it in its place. I shall only observe that if at table all who were present should see, and smell, and taste, and drink wine, and find the effects of it, with me there could be no doubt of its reality⁴²; —so that at bottom the scruple concerning real miracles has no place at all on ours, but only on the received principles, and consequently makes rather for than against what has been said.

85. Having done with the Objections, which I endeavoured to propose in the clearest light, and gave them all the force and weight I could, we proceed in the next place to take a view of our tenets in their Consequences⁴³. Some of these appear at first sight— as that several difficult and obscure questions, on which abundance of speculation has been thrown away, are entirely banished from philosophy. 'Whether corporeal substance can think,' 'whether Matter be infinitely divisible,' and 'how it operates on spirit'—these and the like inquiries have given infinite amusement to philosophers in all ages; but, depending on the existence of Matter, they have no longer any place on our principles. Many other advantages there are, as well with regard to religion as the sciences, which it is easy for any one to deduce from what has been premised; but this will appear more plainly in the sequel.

86. From the principles we have laid down it follows human knowledge may naturally be reduced to two heads—that of IDEAS and that of SPIRITS. Of each of these I shall treat in order.

⁴² The simultaneous consciousness of, or participation in, the 'same' sense-ideas, by different persons, as distinguished from the purely individual or personal consciousness of imaginary objects and emotions, is here referred to as a test of the *reality* of the former.

⁴³ They are unfolded in the remaining sections of the Treatise, sect. 85—156: those which apply to ideas and sensible things in sect. 86—134; what belongs to spirits, or subjective substances and powers, in the remainder of the Treatise.

And *first* as to ideas or unthinking things. Our knowledge of these has been very much obscured and confounded, and we have been led into very dangerous errors, by supposing a two-fold existence of the objects of sense [44]—the one *intelligible* or in the mind, the other *real* and without the mind; whereby unthinking things are thought to have a natural subsistence of their own distinct from being perceived by spirits. This, which, if I mistake not, hath been shewn to be a most groundless and absurd notion, is the very root of Scepticism [45]; for, so long as men thought that real things subsisted without the mind, and that their knowledge was only so far forth *real* as it was conformable to *real things*, it follows they could not be certain that they had any real knowledge at all. For how can it be known that the things which are perceived are conformable to those which are not perceived, or exist without the mind?

87. Colour, figure, motion, extension, and the like, considered only as so many *sensations* in the mind, are perfectly known, there being nothing in them which is not perceived. But, if they are looked on as notes or images, referred to *things* or *archetypes* existing without the mind, then are we involved all in scepticism. We see only the appearances, and not the real qualities of things. What may be the extension, figure, or motion of anything really and absolutely, or in itself, it is impossible for us to know, but only the proportion or relation they bear to our senses. Things remaining the same, our ideas vary, and which of them, or even whether any of them at all, represent the true quality really existing in the thing, it is out of our reach to determine. So that, for aught we know, all we see, hear, and feel, may be only phantom and vain chimera, and not at all agree with the real things existing in *rerum natura*. All this sceptical cant follows from our supposing a difference between *things* and *ideas*, and that the former have a subsistence without the mind or unperceived. It were easy to dilate on this subject, and shew how the arguments urged by sceptics in all ages depend on the supposition

---

[44] Berkeley's 'principles' abolish this representative idea in perception, and recognise as the real object only what we are sensibly conscious of—not any uncognised archetype.

[45] So Hume, Reid, and Hamilton, who see in the hypothesis of a representative perception, implying 'a twofold existence of the objects of sense,' the germ of scepticism. Berkeley claims that under his interpretation of what reality, externality, and existence mean, an intuitive knowledge of the real existence of sensible things is given to us.

of external objects. [⁴⁶ But this is too obvious to need being insisted on.]

88. So long as we attribute a real existence to unthinking things, distinct from their being perceived, it is not only impossible for us to know with evidence the nature of any real unthinking being, but even that it exists. Hence it is that we see philosophers distrust their senses, and doubt of the existence of heaven and earth, of everything they see or feel, even of their own bodies. And, after all their labouring and struggle of thought, they are forced to own we cannot attain to any self-evident or demonstrative knowledge of the existence of sensible things⁴⁷. But, all this doubtfulness, which so bewilders and confounds the mind and makes philosophy ridiculous in the eyes of the world, vanishes if we annex a meaning to our words, and not amuse ourselves with the terms 'absolute,' 'external,' 'exist,' &c.—signifying we know not what. For my part, I can as well doubt of my own being as of the being of those things which I actually perceive by sense; it being a manifest contradiction that any sensible object should be immediately perceived by sight or touch, and at the same time have no existence in nature, since the very *existence* of an unthinking being consists in *being perceived*⁴⁸.

89. Nothing seems of more importance towards erecting a firm system of sound and real knowledge, which may be proof against the assaults of Scepticism, than to lay the beginning in a distinct explication of what is meant by *thing, reality, existence*; for in vain shall we dispute concerning the real existence of things, or pretend to any knowledge thereof, so long as we have not fixed the meaning of those words⁴⁹. *Thing* or *Being* is the most

---

⁴⁶ This sentence is omitted in the second edition.

⁴⁷ This is admitted by Des Cartes, Malebranche, and Locke.

⁴⁸ On Berkeley's own principles, there is no contradiction in the non-existence in *rerum* of these 'qualities' of a material substance which we are not at the moment sensibly percipient of—which we merely infer we should be percipient of on certain conditions, e.g. the smell, &c. of an orange whilst we are only looking at it. Their non-existence in imagination, when they are suggested by what we are sensibly conscious of, is indeed, on his principles, contradictory.

⁴⁹ The chief end of the Berkeleian philosophy is to reach an *intelligible* conception of Being, Existence, or Thing. (favourite terms with philosophers); which, according to Berkeley, are not, as Locke would have it, simple ideas, but general names. Being or Existence, as explained by Berkeley, may be viewed either in relation to its permanent or to its variable element. In the former aspect it is the spiritual substance or self; in the latter, when manifested in the sense-given co-existences of simple ideas of objects, it is what we call material or sensible existence. Spirits and also synthesis of sense-given objects may be called 'things.' With Berkeley the word 'thing' stands, not for

general name of all; it comprehends under it two kinds entirely distinct and heterogeneous, and which have nothing common but the name, viz. *spirits* and *ideas*. The former are active, indivisible, [⁴⁹incorruptible] substances: the latter are inert, fleeting, [⁵⁰perishable passions,] or dependent beings, which subsist not by themselves⁵¹, but are supported by, or exist in minds or spiritual substances. [⁵² We comprehend our own existence by inward feeling or reflection, and that of other spirits by reason⁵³. We may be said to have some knowledge or notion of our own minds, of spirits and active beings, whereof in a strict sense we have not ideas⁵⁴. In like manner, we know and have a notion of relations⁵⁵ between things or ideas—which relations are distinct from the ideas or things related, inasmuch as the latter may be perceived by us without our perceiving the former. To me it seems that *ideas*, *spirits*, and *relations* are all in their respective kinds the object of human knowledge and⁵⁶ subject of discourse; and that the term *idea* would be improperly extended to signify everything we know or have any notion of.]

90. Ideas imprinted on the senses are real things, or do really exist⁵⁷; this we do not deny, but we deny they can subsist without the minds which perceive them, or that they are resemblances of any archetypes existing without the mind⁵⁸; since the very being of a sensation or idea consists in being perceived, and an idea can be like nothing but an idea. Again, the things perceived by sense may be termed *external*, with regard to their origin—in that they are not generated from within by the mind itself, but imprinted by a Spirit distinct from that which perceives them. Sensible objects may likewise be said to be 'without the mind' in

---

an *archetype* of the associated groups of phenomena of which a mind is percipient, but either for the groups themselves, or for the minds cognizant of them, and who cause the changes which they manifest.

⁵⁰ Omitted in second edition.

⁵¹ But whilst ideas or objects depend on being perceived, do not spirits depend on ideas in order to be percipient?

⁵² What follows to the end of this section was added in the second edition.

⁵³ 'reason,' i.e. reasoning or inference, from the changes in the sense-ideas or phenomena of which we are conscious.

⁵⁴ Cf. sect. 139—141.

⁵⁵ 'Notion' is thus applied by Berkeley to our knowledge of minds, and to our knowledge of *relations among ideas*.

⁵⁶ 'and'—or (?),—unless 'object' is used in a vague meaning, including more than idea. Cf. sect. 1; also *New Theory of Vision Vindicated*, sect. 11, 12; *Siris*, sect. 297, 308.

⁵⁷ Cf. sect. 33, for the meaning of the term 'real.'

⁵⁸ i.e. without or unperceived by any mind, human or Divine; which is quite consistent with their being 'external' to a finite percipient, i.e. independent of his will, and determined by the conceptions of a higher mind than his—consistent also with the existence of archetypal ideas in the Divine Mind.

another sense, namely when they exist in some other mind; thus, when I shut my eyes, the things I saw may still exist, but it must be in another mind[59].

91. It were a mistake to think that what is here said derogates in the least from the reality of things. It is acknowledged, on the received principles, that extension, motion, and in a word all sensible qualities, have need of a support, as not being able to subsist by themselves. But the objects perceived by sense are allowed to be nothing but combinations of those qualities, and consequently cannot subsist by themselves[60]. Thus far it is agreed on all hands. So that in denying the things perceived by sense an existence independent of a substance or support wherein they may exist, we detract nothing from the received opinion of their *reality*, and are guilty of no innovation in that respect. All the difference is that, according to us, the unthinking beings perceived by sense have no existence distinct from being perceived, and cannot therefore exist in any other substance than those unextended indivisible substances or *spirits* which act and think and perceive them; whereas philosophers vulgarly hold the sensible qualities do exist in an inert, extended, unperceiving substance which they call *Matter*—to which they attribute a natural subsistence, exterior to all thinking beings, or distinct from being perceived by any mind whatsoever, even the eternal mind of the Creator, wherein they suppose only ideas of the corporeal substances[61] created by Him: if indeed they allow them to be at all created[62].

92. For, as we have shewn the doctrine of Matter or corporeal substance to have been the main pillar and support of Scepticism,

---

[a] Berkeley here explains what he regards as the legitimate meanings of the term *externality*. Men cannot act, cannot live, without assuming an external world—in some conception of the term 'external.' It is the business of the philosopher to say what that conception ought to be. Berkeley here acknowledges (a) an externality in our own possible experience, past and future, as determined by natural laws, which are independent of the *will* of the percipient; and (b) an externality to our own conscious experience, in the contemporaneous, as well as in the past or future, experience of other minds, finite or Divine.

[b] i.e. they are not properly substances, though Berkeley sometimes speaks of them as such. Cf. sect. 37.

[c] 'ideas of the corporeal substances'—whereas Berkeley might say real ideas which are themselves our world of sensible things.

[d] On the scheme of intelligible Realism, 'creation' of matter is the production, in finite minds, of sense-objects or ideas, which are, as it were, letters of the alphabet, in a language which God employs for the expression of His Ideas, and of which human science is the partial interpretation. Cf. *Siris*, sect. 326.

so likewise upon the same foundation have been raised all the impious schemes of Atheism and Irreligion. Nay, so great a difficulty has it been thought to conceive Matter produced out of nothing, that the most celebrated among the ancient philosophers, even of those who maintained the being of a God, have thought Matter[1] to be uncreated and coeternal with Him. How great a friend *material substance* has been to Atheists in all ages were needless to relate. All their monstrous systems have so visible and necessary a dependence on it that, when this corner-stone is once removed, the whole fabric cannot choose but fall to the ground, insomuch that it is no longer worth while to bestow a particular consideration on the absurdities of every wretched sect of Atheists.

93. That impious and profane persons should readily fall in with those systems which favour their inclinations, by deriding immaterial substance, and supposing the soul to be divisible and subject to corruption as the body; which exclude all freedom, intelligence, and design from the formation of things, and instead thereof make a self-existent, stupid, unthinking substance the root and origin of all beings; that they should hearken to those who deny a Providence, or inspection of a Superior Mind over the affairs of the world, attributing the whole series of events either to blind chance or fatal necessity arising from the impulse of one body on another—all this is very natural. And, on the other hand, when men of better principles observe the enemies of religion lay so great a stress on *unthinking Matter*, and all of them use so much industry and artifice to reduce everything to it, methinks they should rejoice to see them deprived of their grand support, and driven from that only fortress, without which your Epicureans, Hobbists, and the like, have not even the shadow of a pretence, but become the most cheap and easy triumph in the world.

94. The existence of Matter, or bodies unperceived, has not only been the main support of Atheists and Fatalists, but on the same principle doth Idolatry likewise in all its various forms depend. Did men but consider that the sun, moon, and stars, and every

---

[1] 'Matter,' i.e. an unperceiving and unperceived Substance and Cause—to which Atheists attribute our personal existence and that of the universe in which we find ourselves. Such Matter once allowed, what proof that it is not Supreme or Absolute Being?

other object of the senses, are only so many sensations in their minds, which have no other existence but barely being perceived, doubtless they would never fall down and worship their own *ideas*—but rather address their homage to that Eternal Invisible Mind which produces and sustains all things.

95. The same absurd principle, by mingling itself with the articles of our faith, has occasioned no small difficulties to Christians. For example, about the Resurrection, how many scruples and objections have been raised by Socinians and others? But do not the most plausible of them depend on the supposition that a body is denominated the *same*, with regard not to the form or that which is perceived by sense[64], but the material substance, which remains the same under several forms? Take away this *material substance*—about the identity whereof all the dispute is—and mean by *body* what every plain ordinary person means by that word, to wit, that which is immediately seen and felt, which is only a combination of sensible qualities or ideas, and then their most unanswerable objections come to nothing.

96. Matter[65] being once expelled out of nature drags with it so many sceptical and impious notions, such an incredible number of disputes and puzzling questions, which have been thorns in the sides of divines as well as philosophers, and made so much fruitless work for mankind, that if the arguments we have produced against it are not found equal to demonstration (as to me they evidently seem), yet I am sure all friends to knowledge, peace, and religion have reason to wish they were.

97. Beside the external[66] existence of the objects of perception, another great source of errors and difficulties with regard to ideal knowledge is the doctrine of *abstract ideas*, such as it hath been set forth in the Introduction. The plainest things in the world, those we are most intimately acquainted with and perfectly know, when they are considered in an abstract way, appear strangely difficult and incomprehensible. Time, place, and motion, taken in particular or concrete, are what everybody knows; but, having

---

[64] Of which Berkeley does not predicate a numerical identity. Cf. *Third Dialogue between Hylas and Philonous*, pp. 343–348.

[65] 'matter,' i.e. absolute Matter, unknowing, and unknown by any intelligence.

[66] 'external,' i.e. in the philosophical, but not in Berkeley's meaning of externality. Cf. sect. 90, note.

passed through the hands of a metaphysician, they become too abstract and fine to be apprehended by men of ordinary sense. Bid your servant meet you at such a *time* in such a *place*, and he shall never stay to deliberate on the meaning of those words; in conceiving that particular time and place, or the motion by which he is to get thither, he finds not the least difficulty. But if *time* be taken exclusive of all those particular actions and ideas that diversify the day, merely for the continuation of existence or duration in abstract, then it will perhaps gravel even a philosopher to comprehend it.

98. For my own part, whenever I attempt to frame a simple idea of *time*, abstracted from the succession of ideas in my mind, which flows uniformly and is participated by all beings, I am lost and embrangled in inextricable difficulties. I have no notion of it at all, only I hear others say it is infinitely divisible, and speak of it in such a manner as leads me to harbour odd thoughts of my existence [67];—since that doctrine lays one under an absolute necessity of thinking, either that he passes away innumerable ages without a thought, or else that he is annihilated every moment of his life, both which seem equally absurd. Time therefore being nothing, abstracted from the succession of ideas in our minds, it follows that the duration of any finite spirit must be estimated by the number of ideas or actions succeeding each other in that same spirit or mind. Hence, it is a plain consequence that the soul always thinks; and in truth whoever shall go about to divide in his thoughts, or abstract the *existence* of a spirit from its *cogitation*, will, I believe, find it no easy task [68].

99. So likewise when we attempt to abstract extension and motion from all other qualities, and consider them by themselves, we presently lose sight of them, and run into great extravagances. [[69]Hence spring those odd paradoxes, that the 'fire is not hot,' nor 'the wall white,' &c., or that heat and colour are in the objects nothing but figure and motion.] All which depend on a twofold

---

[67] i. e. of what Mind, Self, the Ego means, of its relation to time, and what personal identity consists in. Berkeley sometimes seems to imply that the existence of the Ego is independent of time or succession, in an eternal present (an *I am*), amid the changes of phenomena of which it is conscious.

[68] As the *esse* of sense-ideas or sensible objects is *percipi*, according to Berkeley, so the *esse* of minds or persons is *percipere*. The existence of a Mind thus depends on consciousness, and the sensible existence of Matter depends on a sense-percipient.

[69] This sentence is omitted in the second edition.

abstraction; first, it is supposed that extension, for example, may be abstracted from all other sensible qualities; and secondly, that the entity of extension may be abstracted from its being perceived. But, whoever shall reflect, and take care to understand what he says, will, if I mistake not, acknowledge that all sensible qualities are alike *sensations* and alike *real*; that where the extension is, there is the colour too, *i.e.* in his mind[70], and that their archetypes can exist only in some other *mind*[71]; and that the objects of sense[72] are nothing but those sensations combined, blended, or (if one may so speak) concreted together; none of all which can be supposed to exist unperceived. [[73] And that consequently the wall is as truly white as it is extended, and in the same sense.]

100. What it is for a man to be happy, or an object good, every one may think he knows. But to frame an abstract idea of happiness, prescinded from all particular pleasure, or of goodness from everything that is good, this is what few can pretend to. So likewise a man may be just and virtuous without having precise ideas of justice and virtue. The opinion that those and the like words stand for general notions, abstracted from all particular persons and actions, seems to have rendered morality very difficult, and the study thereof of small use to mankind. And in effect one may make a great progress in school-ethics without ever being the wiser or better man for it, or knowing how to behave himself in the affairs of life more to the advantage of himself or his neighbours than he did before. This hint may suffice to let any one see the doctrine of *abstraction* has not a little contributed towards spoiling the most useful parts of knowledge.

101. The two great provinces of speculative science conversant about ideas received from sense, are Natural Philosophy and Mathematics; with regard to each of these I shall make some observations.—And first I shall say somewhat of Natural Philosophy. On this subject it is that the sceptics triumph. All that stock of arguments they produce to depreciate our faculties and make mankind appear ignorant and low, are drawn principally from this head, namely, that we are under an invincible blindness as to the

---

[70] Cf. *New Theory of Vision*, sect. 43, &c.
[71] i.e. as Ideas, sensible or intelligible—human or Divine.
[72] 'objects of sense,' i.e. sensible or external things. Cf. sect. 1, on the meaning of *thing*, as distinct from object-proper or simple idea.
[73] This sentence is omitted in the second edition.

true and *real* nature of things. This they exaggerate, and love to enlarge on. We are miserably bantered, say they, by our senses, and amused only with the outside and show of things. The real essence [74], the internal qualities and constitution of every the meanest object, is hid from our view; something there is in every drop of water, every grain of sand, which it is beyond the power of human understanding to fathom or comprehend. But, it is evident from what has been shewn that all this complaint is groundless, and that we are influenced by false principles to that degree as to mistrust our senses, and think we know nothing of those things which we perfectly comprehend.

102. One great inducement to our pronouncing ourselves ignorant of the nature of things is the current opinion that everything includes within itself the cause of its properties; or that there is in each object an inward essence which is the source whence its discernible qualities flow, and whereon they depend. Some have pretended to account for appearances by occult qualities, but of late they are mostly resolved into mechanical causes, to wit, the figure, motion, weight, and suchlike qualities, of insensible particles [75]; whereas, in truth, there is no other agent or efficient cause than *spirit*, it being evident that motion, as well as all other *ideas*, is perfectly inert. See sect. 25. Hence, to endeavour to explain the production of colours or sounds, by figure, motion, magnitude and the like, must needs be labour in vain. And accordingly we see the attempts of that kind are not at all satisfactory. Which may be said in general of those instances wherein one idea or quality is assigned for the cause of another. I need not say how many hypotheses and speculations are left out, and how much the study of nature is abridged by this doctrine [76].

103. The great mechanical principle now in vogue is *attraction*. That a stone falls to the earth, or the sea swells towards the moon,

---

[74] With Berkeley, the nominal or logical essence is the real essence of things, in as far as things are in sense what they are conceived to be. But this is quite consistent with the fact that we may and do misinterpret the sensible symbols which constitute our material universe; and thus our conceptions of their meaning are often misconceptions—so that their logical or nominal essence becomes different from their real essence.

[75] e.g. Locke's *Essay*, IV. 3.

[76] Berkeleyism is so far a Spiritual Positivism, which eliminates all causation from the objective world, concentrates it in Mind, and seeks among phenomena or ideas only for the laws of their constant co-existence and succession. But the modern Positivists deny that we may thus infer the ultimate causality of Mind, holding that the ultimate cause or power is incognisable—that the universe is a 'singular effect.'

may to some appear sufficiently explained thereby. But how are we enlightened by being told this is done by attraction? Is it that that word signifies the manner of the tendency, and that it is by the mutual drawing of bodies instead of their being impelled or protruded towards each other? But, nothing is determined of the manner or action, and it may as truly (for aught we know) be termed 'impulse,' or 'protrusion,' as 'attraction.' Again, the parts of steel we see cohere firmly together, and this also is accounted for by attraction; but, in this as in the other instances, I do not perceive that anything is signified besides the effect itself; for as to the manner of the action whereby it is produced, or the cause which produces it, these are not so much as aimed at.

104. Indeed, if we take a view of the several phenomena, and compare them together, we may observe some likeness and conformity between them. For example, in the falling of a stone to the ground, in the rising of the sea towards the moon, in cohesion, crystallization, &c., there is something alike, namely, an union or mutual approach of bodies. So that any one of these or the like phenomena may not seem strange or surprising to a man who has nicely observed and compared the effects of nature. For that only is thought so which is uncommon, or a thing by itself, and out of the ordinary course of our observation. That bodies should tend towards the centre of the earth is not thought strange, because it is what we perceive every moment of our lives. But, that they should have a like gravitation towards the centre of the moon may seem odd and unaccountable to most men, because it is discerned only in the tides. But a philosopher, whose thoughts take in a larger compass of nature, having observed a certain similitude of appearances, as well in the heavens as the earth, that argue innumerable bodies to have a mutual tendency towards each other, which he denotes by the general name 'attraction,' whatever can be reduced to that he thinks justly accounted for. Thus he explains the tides by the attraction of the terraqueous globe towards the moon, which to him does not appear odd or anomalous, but only a particular example of a general rule or law of nature.

105. If therefore we consider the difference there is betwixt natural philosophers and other men, with regard to their knowledge of the phenomena, we shall find it consists not in an exacter knowledge of the efficient cause that produces them—for that can

be no other than the *will of a spirit*—but only in a greater largeness of comprehension, whereby analogies, harmonies, and agreements are discovered in the works of nature, and the particular effects explained, that is, reduced to general rules, see sect. 62, which rules, grounded on the analogy and uniformness observed in the production of natural effects, are most agreeable and sought after by the mind; for that they extend our prospect beyond what is present and near to us, and enable us to make very probable conjectures touching things that may have happened at very great distances of time and place, as well as to predict things to come; which sort of endeavour towards omniscience is much affected by the mind.

106. But we should proceed warily in such things, for we are apt to lay too great a stress on analogies, and, to the prejudice of truth, humour that eagerness of the mind whereby it is carried to extend its knowledge into general theorems. For example, in the business of gravitation or mutual attraction, because it appears in many instances, some are straightway for pronouncing it *universal*; and that to attract and be attracted by every other body is an essential quality inherent in all bodies whatsoever. Whereas it is evident the fixed stars have no such tendency towards each other; and, so far is that gravitation from being *essential* to bodies that in some instances a quite contrary principle seems to shew itself; as in the perpendicular growth of plants, and the elasticity of the air. There is nothing necessary or essential in the case[77], but it depends entirely on the will of the Governing Spirit[78], who causes certain bodies to cleave together or tend towards each other according to various laws, whilst He keeps others at a fixed distance; and to some He gives a quite contrary tendency to fly asunder just as He sees convenient.

107. After what has been premised, I think we may lay down the following conclusions. First, it is plain philosophers amuse themselves in vain, when they enquire for any natural efficient cause, distinct from a *mind* or *spirit*. Secondly, considering the whole creation is the workmanship of a *wise and good Agent*, it should

---

[77] According to Sir W. Hamilton, for example, we are *intellectually necessitated* to think that every new phenomenon must have previously existed in *another form* — but not *necessarily* in this, that, or the other particular form; for a knowledge of which we are indebted to experience.

[78] In other words, what *the* preceding form of any new phenomenon actually was, has been determined by the Supreme Will, and is, in that sense, arbitrary. God is the proper cause of the antecedent and consequent forms or phenomena of existence being what we actually find them to be.

seem to become philosophers to employ their thoughts (contrary to what some hold;¹⁹) about the final causes of things; [²⁰ for, besides that this would prove a very pleasing entertainment to the mind, it might be of great advantage, in that it not only discovers to us the attributes of the Creator, but may also direct us in several instances to the proper uses and applications of things;] and I must confess I see no reason why pointing out the various ends to which natural things are adapted, and for which they were originally with unspeakable wisdom contrived, should not be thought one good way of accounting for them, and altogether worthy a philosopher. Thirdly, from what has been premised no reason can be drawn why the history of nature should not still be studied, and observations and experiments made—which, that they are of use to mankind, and enable us to draw any general conclusions, is not the result of any immutable habitudes or relations between things themselves, but only of God's goodness and kindness to men in the administration of the world. See sect. 30 and 31. Fourthly, by a diligent observation of the phenomena within our view, we may discover the general laws of nature, and from them deduce the other phenomena; I do not say *demonstrate*, for all deductions of that kind depend on a supposition that the Author of nature always operates uniformly, and in a constant observance of those rules we take for principles²¹—which we cannot evidently know.

108. [²² It appears from sect. 66, &c. that the steady consistent methods of nature may not unfitly be styled the Language of its Author, whereby He discovers His attributes to our view and directs us how to act for the convenience and felicity of life. And to me] Those men who frame²³ general rules from the phenomena, and afterwards derive²⁴ the phenomena from those rules, seem²⁵ to consider signs rather than causes. ²⁶A man may well understand

---

¹⁹ He probably refers to Bacon.
²⁰ Omitted in second edition.
²¹ Our assumed 'principles,' or supposed *laws of nature*, may be subordinate or special, and therefore variable, associations of sensible signs which, in their ultimate meaning, express a perfect, and therefore necessary, Divine Idea.
²² Omitted in the second edition.
²³ i. e. inductively.
²⁴ i. e. deductively.

²⁵ 'seem to consider signs rather than causes'—'seem to be grammarians, and their art the grammar of nature. Two ways there are of learning a language—either by rule or by practice'—in first edition.
²⁶ 'A man may be well read in the language of nature without understanding the grammar of it, or being able to say.' &c—in first edition.

natural signs without knowing their analogy, or being able to say by what rule a thing is so or so. And, as it is very possible to write improperly, through too strict an observance of general grammar-rules; so, in arguing from general laws of nature, it is not impossible we may extend[87] the analogy too far, and by that means run into mistakes.

109. [[88] To carry on the resemblance.] As in reading other books a wise man will choose to fix his thoughts on the sense and apply it to use, rather than lay them out in grammatical remarks on the language; so, in perusing the volume of nature, methinks it is beneath the dignity of the mind to affect an exactness in reducing each particular phenomenon to general rules, or shewing how it follows from them. We should propose to ourselves nobler views, namely, to recreate and exalt the mind with a prospect of the beauty, order, extent, and variety of natural things: hence, by proper inferences, to enlarge our notions of the grandeur, wisdom, and beneficence of the Creator; and lastly, to make the several parts of the creation, so far as in us lies, subservient to the ends they were designed for, God's glory, and the sustentation and comfort of ourselves and fellow-creatures.

110. [[89]The best key for the aforesaid analogy or natural Science will be easily acknowledged to be a certain celebrated Treatise of *Mechanics*.] In the entrance of which justly admired treatise, Time, Space, and Motion are distinguished into *absolute* and *relative*, *true* and *apparent*, *mathematical* and *vulgar*;—which distinction, as it is at large explained by the author, does suppose those quantities to have an existence without the mind; and that they are ordinarily conceived with relation to sensible things, to which nevertheless in their own nature they bear no relation at all.

111. As for *Time*, as it is there taken in an absolute or ab-

---

[87] 'extend'—'stretch'—In first edition.

[88] Omitted in second edition.

[89] In the first edition, instead of this sentence, the section commences thus: 'The best grammar of the kind we are speaking of will be easily acknowledged to be a treatise of *Mechanics*, demonstrated and applied to nature by a philosopher of a neighbouring nation whom all the world admire. I shall not take upon me to make remarks on the performance of that extraordinary person; only some things he has advanced so directly opposite to the doctrine we have hitherto laid down, that we should be wanting in the regard due to the authority of so great a man did we not take some notice of them.' He refers, of course, to Newton. The first edition was published in Ireland—hence 'neighbouring nation.'— On absolute Space, cf. *Siris*, sect. 170, &c.

stracted sense, for the duration or perseverance of the existence of things, I have nothing more to add concerning it after what has been already said on that subject. Sect. 97 and 98. For the rest, this celebrated author holds there is an *absolute Space*, which, being unperceivable to sense, remains in itself similar and immoveable; and relative space to be the measure thereof, which, being moveable and defined by its situation in respect of sensible bodies, is vulgarly taken for immoveable space. *Place* he defines to be that part of space which is occupied by any body; and according as the space is absolute or relative so also is the place. *Absolute Motion* is said to be the translation of a body from absolute place to absolute place, as relative motion is from one relative place to another. And, because the parts of absolute space do not fall under our senses, instead of them we are obliged to use their sensible measures, and so define both place and motion with respect to bodies which we regard as immoveable. But, it is said in philosophical matters we must abstract from our senses, since it may be that none of those bodies which seem to be quiescent are truly so, and the same thing which is moved relatively may be really at rest; as likewise one and the same body may be in relative rest and motion, or even moved with contrary relative motions at the same time, according as its place is variously defined. All which ambiguity is to be found in the apparent motions, but not at all in the true or absolute, which should therefore be alone regarded in philosophy. And the true we are told are distinguished from apparent or relative motions by the following properties.—First, in true or absolute motion all parts which preserve the same position with respect of the whole, partake of the motions of the whole. Secondly, the place being moved, that which is placed therein is also moved; so that a body moving in a place which is in motion doth participate the motion of its place. Thirdly, true motion is never generated or changed otherwise than by force impressed on the body itself. Fourthly, true motion is always changed by force impressed on the body moved. Fifthly, in circular motion barely relative there is no centrifugal force, which nevertheless, in that which is true or absolute, is proportional to the quantity of motion.

112. But, notwithstanding what has been said, I must confess it does not appear to me that there can be any motion other than

relative[90], so that to conceive motion there must be at least conceived two bodies, whereof the distance or position in regard to each other is varied. Hence, if there was one only body in being it could not possibly be moved. This to me seems very evident, in that the idea I have of motion does necessarily include relation.—[[91] Whether others can conceive it otherwise, a little attention may satisfy them.]

113. But, though in every motion it be necessary to conceive more bodies than one, yet it may be that one only is moved, namely, that on which the force causing the change in the distance or situation of the bodies, is impressed. For, however some may define relative motion, so as to term that body *moved* which changes its distance from some other body, whether the force [[92]or action] causing that change were impressed on it or no, yet as [[91]I cannot assent to this; for, since we are told] relative motion is that which is perceived by sense, and regarded in the ordinary affairs of life, it follows that every man of common sense knows what it is as well as the best philosopher. Now, I ask any one whether, in his sense of motion as he walks along the streets, the stones he passes over may be said to *move*, because they change distance with his feet? To me it appears that though motion includes a relation of one thing to another, yet it is not necessary that each term of the relation be denominated from it. As a man may think of somewhat which does not think, so a body may be moved to or from another body which is not therefore itself in motion, [[91]I mean relative motion, for other I am not able to conceive.]

114. As the place happens to be variously defined, the motion which is related to it varies[93]. A man in a ship may be said to be quiescent with relation to the sides of the vessel, and yet move with relation to the land. Or he may move eastward in respect of the one, and westward in respect of the other. In the common affairs of life men never go beyond the earth to define the place of any body; and what is quiescent in respect of that is accounted *absolutely* to be so. But philosophers, who have a greater extent

---

[90] On motion, cf. *Analyst,* qu. 12, and *De Motu.* See also Malebranche, *Recherche,* l. 8. All attempts to imagine space imply the thoughts of locomotive sense-experience—an unimpeded, as distinguished from an impeded power of locomotion. Cf. sect. 116.

[91] Omitted in second edition.
[92] Added in second edition.
[93] Omitted in second edition.
[94] Omitted in second edition.
[95] See Locke's *Essay,* B. II. 13. § 7—10.

of thought, and juster notions of the system of things, discover even the earth itself to be moved. In order therefore to fix their notions they seem to conceive the corporeal world as finite, and the utmost unmoved walls or shell thereof to be the place whereby they estimate true motions. If we sound our own conceptions, I believe we may find all the absolute motion we can frame an idea of to be at bottom no other than relative motion thus defined. For, as has been already observed, absolute motion, exclusive of all external relation, is incomprehensible; and to this kind of relative motion all the above-mentioned properties, causes, and effects ascribed to absolute motion will, if I mistake not, be found to agree. As to what is said of the centrifugal force, that it does not at all belong to circular relative motion, I do not see how this follows from the experiment which is brought to prove it. See *Philosophiae Naturalis Principia Mathematica, in Schol. Def. VIII.* For the water in the vessel at that time wherein it is said to have the greatest relative circular motion, has, I think, no motion at all; as is plain from the foregoing section.

115. For, to denominate a body *moved* it is requisite, first, that it change its distance or situation with regard to some other body; secondly, that the force occasioning that change be impressed on it. If either of these be wanting, I do not think that, agreeably to the sense of mankind, or the propriety of language, a body can be said to be in motion. I grant indeed that it is possible for us to think a body which we see change its distance from some other to be moved, though it have no force [76]applied to it (in which sense there may be apparent motion), but then it is because the force causing the change of distance is imagined by us to be [77 applied or] impressed on that body thought to move; which indeed shews we are capable of mistaking a thing to be in motion which is not, and that is all, [77 but does not prove that, in the common acceptation of motion, a body is moved merely because it changes distance from another; since as soon as we are undeceived, and find that the moving force was not communicated to it, we no longer hold it to be moved. So, on the other hand, when one only body (the parts whereof preserve a given position between themselves) is imagined to

---

[76] 'applied to'—'impressed on'—in first edition.
[77] Added in second edition.
[78] What follows to the end of this section is omitted in the second edition.

exist, some there are who think that it can be moved all manner of ways, though without any change of distance or situation to any other bodies; which we should not deny if they meant only that it might have an impressed force, which, upon the bare creation of other bodies, would produce a motion of some certain quantity and determination. But that an actual motion (distinct from the impressed force or power productive of change of place in case there were bodies present whereby to define it) can exist in such a single body, I must confess I am not able to comprehend.]

116. From what has been said it follows that the philosophic consideration of motion does not imply the being of an *absolute Space*, distinct from that which is perceived by sense and related to bodies; which that it cannot exist without the mind is clear upon the same principles that demonstrate the like of all other objects of sense. And perhaps, if we enquire narrowly, we shall find we cannot even frame an idea of *pure Space* exclusive of all body. This I must confess seems impossible [99], as being a most abstract idea. When I excite a motion in some part of my body, if it be free or without resistance, I say there is *Space*; but if I find a resistance, then I say there is *Body*: and in proportion as the resistance to motion is lesser or greater, I say the space is more or less *pure*. So that when I speak of pure or empty space, it is not to be supposed that the word 'space' stands for an idea distinct from or conceivable without body and motion—though indeed we are apt to think every noun substantive stands for a distinct idea that may be separated from all others; which has occasioned infinite mistakes. When, therefore, supposing all the world to be annihilated besides my own body, I say there still remains *pure Space*, thereby nothing else is meant but only that I conceive it possible for the limbs of my body to be moved on all sides without the least resistance; but if that too were annihilated then there could be no motion, and consequently no Space [100]. Some, perhaps, may think the sense of seeing does furnish them with the idea of pure space; but it is plain from what we have elsewhere shewn, that the ideas of space and distance are not obtained by that sense. See the *Essay concerning Vision*.

[99] 'seems impossible'—'is above my capacity'—In first edition.
[100] i.e. pure Space, as immediately perceived, is ultimately the sensation of an unresisted motion of the body, or of any of its organs. See this less fully developed in *New Theory of Vision*.

117. What is here laid down seems to put an end to all those disputes and difficulties that have sprung up amongst the learned concerning the nature of *pure Space*. But the chief advantage arising from it is that we are freed from that dangerous dilemma, to which several who have employed their thoughts on that subject imagine themselves reduced, viz. of thinking either that Real Space is God, or else that there is something beside God which is eternal, uncreated, infinite, indivisible, immutable. Both which may justly be thought pernicious and absurd notions. It is certain that not a few divines, as well as philosophers of great note, have, from the difficulty they found in conceiving either limits or annihilation of space, concluded it must be divine. And some of late have set themselves particularly to shew the incommunicable attributes of God agree to it[1]. Which doctrine, how unworthy soever it may seem of the Divine Nature, yet I must confess I do not see how we can get clear of it, so long as we adhere to the received opinions.

118. Hitherto of Natural Philosophy: we come now to make some enquiry concerning that other great branch of speculative knowledge, to wit, Mathematics[2]. These, how celebrated soever they may be for their clearness and certainty of demonstration, which is hardly anywhere else to be found, cannot nevertheless be supposed altogether free from mistakes, if so be that in their principles there lurks some secret error which is common to the professors of those sciences with the rest of mankind. Mathematicians, though they deduce their theorems from a great height of evidence, yet their first principles are limited by the consideration of quantity: and they do not ascend into any enquiry concerning those transcendental maxims which influence all the particular sciences, each part whereof, Mathematics not excepted, does consequently participate of the errors involved in them. That the principles laid down by mathematicians are true, and their way of deduction from those principles clear and incontestible, we do not deny; but, we hold there may be certain erroneous maxims of greater extent than the object of Mathematics, and for that reason not expressly mentioned, though tacitly supposed throughout the

---

[1] Clarke's *Demonstration of the Being and Attributes of God*, which appeared in 1706.
[2] Sect. 118—132.

whole progress of that science; and that the ill effects of those secret unexamined errors are diffused through all the branches thereof. To be plain, we suspect the mathematicians are no less deeply concerned than other men in the errors arising from the doctrine of abstract general ideas, and the existence of objects without the mind.

119. Arithmetic has been thought to have for its object abstract ideas of *Number*; of which to understand the properties and mutual habitudes, is supposed no mean part of speculative knowledge. The opinion of the pure and intellectual nature of numbers in abstract has made them in esteem with those philosophers who seem to have affected an uncommon fineness and elevation of thought. It hath set a price on the most trifling numerical speculations which in practice are of no use, but serve only for amusement; and hath heretofore so far infected the minds of some, that they have dreamed of mighty mysteries involved in numbers, and attempted the explication of natural things by them. But, if we narrowly inquire into our own thoughts, and consider what has been premised, we may perhaps entertain a low opinion of those high flights and abstractions, and look on all inquiries about numbers only as so many *difficiles nugæ*, so far as they are not subservient to practice, and promote the benefit of life.

120. Unity in abstract we have before considered in sect. 13, from which and what has been said in the Introduction, it plainly follows there is not any such idea. But, number being defined a 'collection of units,' we may conclude that, if there be no such thing as unity or unit in abstract, there are no ideas of number in abstract denoted by the numeral names and figures. The theories therefore in Arithmetic, if they are abstracted from the names and figures, as likewise from all use and practice, as well as from the particular things numbered, can be supposed to have nothing at all for their object; hence we may see how entirely the science of numbers is subordinate to practice, and how jejune and trifling it becomes when considered as a matter of mere speculation.

121. However, since there may be some who, deluded by the specious show of discovering abstracted verities, waste their time in arithmetical theorems and problems which have not any use, it will not be amiss if we more fully consider and expose the vanity

of that pretence; and this will plainly appear by taking a view of Arithmetic in its infancy, and observing what it was that originally put men on the study of that science, and to what scope they directed it. It is natural to think that at first, men, for ease of memory and help of computation, made use of counters, or in writing of single strokes, points, or the like, each whereof was made to signify an unit, *i.e.* some one thing of whatever kind they had occasion to reckon. Afterwards they found out the more compendious ways of making one character stand in place of several strokes or points. And, lastly, the notation of the Arabians or Indians came into use, wherein, by the repetition of a few characters or figures, and varying the signification of each figure according to the place it obtains, all numbers may be most aptly expressed; which seems to have been done in imitation of language, so that an exact analogy is observed betwixt the notation by figures and names, the nine simple figures answering the nine first numeral names and places in the former, corresponding to denominations in the latter. And agreeably to those conditions of the simple and local value of figures, were contrived methods of finding, from the given figures or marks of the parts, what figures and how placed are proper to denote the whole, or *vice versa*. And having found the sought figures, the same rule or analogy being observed throughout, it is easy to read them into words; and so the number becomes perfectly known. For then the number of any particular things is said to be known, when we know the name or figures (with their due arrangement) that according to the standing analogy belong to them. For; these signs being known, we can by the operations of arithmetic know the signs of any part of the particular sums signified by them; and, thus computing in signs, (because of the connexion established betwixt them and the distinct multitudes of things whereof one is taken for an unit), we may be able rightly to sum up, divide, and proportion the things themselves that we intend to number.

122. In Arithmetic, therefore, we regard not the *things* but the *signs*, which nevertheless are not regarded for their own sake, but because they direct us how to act with relation to things, and dispose rightly of them. Now, agreeably to what we have before observed of words in general (sect. 19, Introd.) it happens here likewise that abstract ideas are thought to be signified by numeral

names or characters, while they do not suggest ideas of particular things to our minds. I shall not at present enter into a more particular dissertation on this subject, but only observe that it is evident from what has been said, those things which pass for abstract truths and theorems concerning numbers, are in reality conversant about no object distinct from particular numerable things, except only names and characters, which originally came to be considered on no other account but their being signs, or capable to represent aptly whatever particular things men had need to compute. Whence it follows that to study them for their own sake would be just as wise, and to as good purpose as if a man, neglecting the true use or original intention and subserviency of language, should spend his time in impertinent criticisms upon words, or reasonings and controversies purely verbal [1].

123. From numbers we proceed to speak of *Extension* [2], which is the object of Geometry. The *infinite* divisibility of *finite* extension, though it is not expressly laid down either as an axiom or theorem in the elements of that science, yet is throughout the same everywhere supposed and thought to have so inseparable and essential a connexion with the principles and demonstrations in Geometry, that mathematicians never admit it into doubt, or make the least question of it. And, as this notion is the source from whence do spring all those amusing geometrical paradoxes which have such a direct repugnancy to the plain common sense of mankind, and are admitted with so much reluctance into a mind not yet debauched by learning; so is it the principal occasion of all that nice and extreme subtilty which renders the study of Mathematics so very difficult and tedious. Hence, if we can make it appear that no finite extension contains innumerable parts, or is infinitely divisible, it follows that we shall at once clear the science of Geometry from a great number of difficulties and contradictions which have ever been esteemed a reproach to human reason, and withal make the attainment thereof a business of much less time and pains than it hitherto has been.

124. Every particular finite extension which may possibly be the object of our thought is an *idea* existing only in the mind, and consequently each part thereof must be perceived. If, there-

---

[1] Cf. *New Theory of Vision*, sect. 107. &c.
[2] Cf. *New Theory of Vision*, sect. 118—135. 149—160.

fore, I cannot perceive innumerable parts in any finite extension that I consider, it is certain they are not contained in it; but, it is evident that I cannot distinguish innumerable parts in any particular line, surface, or solid, which I either perceive by sense, or figure to myself in my mind: wherefore I conclude they are not contained in it. Nothing can be plainer to me than that the extensions I have in view are no other than my own ideas; and it is no less plain that I cannot resolve any one of my ideas into an infinite number of other ideas, that is, that they are not infinitely divisible⁵. If by finite extension be meant something distinct from a finite idea, I declare I do not know what that is, and so cannot affirm or deny anything of it. But if the terms 'extension,' 'parts,' &c., are taken in any sense conceivable, that is, for ideas, then to say a finite quantity or extension consists of parts infinite in number is so manifest and glaring a contradiction, that every one at first sight acknowledges it to be so; and it is impossible it should ever gain the assent of any reasonable creature who is not brought to it by gentle and slow degrees, as a converted Gentile⁶ to the belief of transubstantiation. Ancient and rooted prejudices do often pass into principles; and those propositions which once obtain the force and credit of a *principle*, are not only themselves, but likewise whatever is deducible from them, thought privileged from all examination. And there is no absurdity so gross, which, by this means, the mind of man may not be prepared to swallow.

125. He whose understanding is prepossessed with the doctrine of abstract general ideas may be [⁷ easily] persuaded that (whatever be thought of the ideas of sense) extension in *abstract* is infinitely divisible. And any one who thinks the objects of sense exist without the mind will perhaps in virtue thereof be brought to admit that⁸ a line but an inch long may contain innumerable parts—really existing, though too small to be discerned. These errors are grafted as well in the minds of geometricians as of other men, and have a like influence on their reasonings; and it were no

---

⁵ Infinitely divisible extension, being unperceived, must be non-existent—if existence necessarily depends on a percipient, and must be actually perceived. The only possible extension is then sensible extension, which cannot be infinitely divided, but only divided down to the point at which its parts become insensible or non-existent.

⁶ 'converted Gentile'—'pagan convert' —in first edition.

⁷ Omitted in second edition.

⁸ 'will perhaps in virtue thereof be brought to admit that,' &c.—'will not stick to affirm that,' &c.—in first edition.

difficult thing to shew how the arguments from Geometry made use of to support the infinite divisibility of extension are bottomed on them. [*But this, if it be thought necessary, we may hereafter find a proper place to treat of in a particular manner.] At present we shall only observe in general whence it is the mathematicians are all so fond and tenacious of that doctrine.

126. It has been observed in another place that the theorems and demonstrations in Geometry are conversant about universal ideas (sect. 15. Introd.); where it is explained in what sense this ought to be understood, to wit, the particular lines and figures included in the diagram are supposed to stand for innumerable others of different sizes; or, in other words, the geometer considers them abstracting from their magnitude—which does not imply that he forms an abstract idea, but only that he cares not what the particular magnitude is, whether great or small, but looks on that as a thing indifferent to the demonstration. Hence it follows that a line in the scheme but an inch long must be spoken of as though it contained ten thousand parts, since it is regarded not in itself, but as it is universal; and it is universal only in its signification, whereby it represents innumerable lines greater than itself, in which may be distinguished ten thousand parts or more, though there may not be above an inch in it. After this manner, the properties of the lines signified are (by a very usual figure) transferred to the sign, and thence, through mistake, thought to appertain to it considered in its own nature.

127. Because there is no number of parts so great but it is possible there may be a line containing more, the inch-line is said to contain parts more than any assignable number; which is true, not of the inch taken absolutely, but only for the things signified by it. But men, not retaining that distinction in their thoughts, slide into a belief that the small particular line described on paper contains in itself parts innumerable. There is no such thing as the ten thousandth part of an inch; but there is of a mile or diameter of the earth, which may be signified by that inch. When therefore I delineate a triangle on paper, and take one side not above an inch, for example, in length to be the radius, this I consider as divided into 10,000 or 100,000 parts or more; for,

---

* Omitted in second edition.

though the ten thousandth part of that line considered in itself is nothing at all, and consequently may be neglected without any error or inconveniency, yet these described lines, being only marks standing for greater quantities, whereof it may be the ten thousandth part is very considerable, it follows that, to prevent notable errors in practice, the radius must be taken of 10,000 parts or more.

128. From what has been said the reason is plain why, to the end any theorem become universal in its use, it is necessary we speak of the lines described on paper as though they contained parts which really they do not. In doing of which, if we examine the matter throughly, we shall perhaps discover that we cannot conceive an inch itself as consisting of, or being divisible into, a thousand parts, but only some other line which is far greater than an inch, and represented by it; and that when we say a line is infinitely divisible, we must mean a line which is infinitely great[n]. What we have here observed seems to be the chief cause why, to suppose the infinite divisibility of finite extension has been thought necessary in geometry.

129. The several absurdities and contradictions which flowed from this false principle might, one would think, have been esteemed so many demonstrations against it. But, by I know not what logic, it is held that proofs *a posteriori* are not to be admitted against propositions relating to infinity—as though it were not impossible even for an infinite mind to reconcile contradictions; or as if anything absurd and repugnant could have a necessary connexion with truth or flow from it. But, whoever considers the weakness of this pretence will think it was contrived on purpose to humour the laziness of the mind which had rather acquiesce in an indolent scepticism than be at the pains to go through with a severe examination of those principles it has ever embraced for true.

130. Of late the speculations about Infinites have run so high, and grown to such strange notions, as have occasioned no small scruples and disputes among the geometers of the present age. Some there are of great note who, not content with holding that finite lines may be divided into an infinite number of parts, do

---

[n] 'we must mean a line,' &c.—' we mean (if we mean anything) a line,' &c.—in first edition.

yet farther maintain that each of those infinitesimals is itself subdivisible into an infinity of other parts or infinitesimals of a second order, and so on *ad infinitum*. These, I say, assert there are infinitesimals of infinitesimals of infinitesimals, &c., without ever coming to an end: so that according to them an inch does not barely contain an infinite number of parts, but an infinity of an infinity of an infinity *ad infinitum* of parts. Others there be who hold all orders of infinitesimals below the first to be nothing at all; thinking it with good reason absurd to imagine there is any positive quantity or part of extension which, though multiplied infinitely, can never equal the smallest given extension. And yet on the other hand it seems no less absurd to think the square, cube, or other power of a positive real root, should itself be nothing at all; which they who hold infinitesimals of the first order, denying all of the subsequent orders, are obliged to maintain.

131. Have we not therefore reason to conclude they are *both* in the wrong, and that there is in effect no such thing as parts infinitely small, or an infinite number of parts contained in any finite quantity? But you will say that if this doctrine obtains it will follow the very foundations of Geometry are destroyed, and those great men who have raised that science to so astonishing a height, have been all the while building a castle in the air. To this it may be replied that whatever is useful in geometry, and promotes the benefit of human life, does still remain firm and unshaken on our principles—that science considered as practical will rather receive advantage than any prejudice from what has been said. But to set this in a due light, and shew how lines and figures may be measured, and their properties investigated, without supposing finite extension to be infinitely divisible, may be the proper business of another place[11]. For the rest, though it should follow that some of the more intricate and subtle parts of Speculative Mathematics may be pared off without any prejudice to truth, yet I do not see what damage will be thence derived to mankind. On the contrary, I think it were highly to be wished that men of great abilities and obstinate application[12] would draw off their

---

[11] See *Analyst*.
[12] 'men of great abilities and obstinate application,' &c.—' men of the greatest abilities and most obstinate application,' &c.—in first edition.

thoughts from those amusements, and employ them in the study of such things as lie nearer the concerns of life, or have a more direct influence on the manners.

132. If it be said that several theorems undoubtedly true are discovered by methods in which infinitesimals are made use of, which could never have been if their existence included a contradiction in it—I answer that upon a thorough examination it will not be found that in any instance it is necessary to make use of or conceive infinitesimal parts of finite lines, or even quantities less than the *minimum sensibile*; nay, it will be evident this is never done, it being impossible. [[13] And, whatever mathematicians may think of fluxions, or the differential calculus and the like, a little reflection will shew them that, in working by those methods, they do not conceive or imagine lines or surfaces less than what are perceivable to sense. They may indeed call those little and almost insensible quantities infinitesimals, or infinitesimals of infinitesimals, if they please; but at bottom this is all, they being in truth finite—nor does the solution of problems require the supposing any other. But this will be more clearly made out hereafter.]

133. By what we have hitherto said, it is plain that very numerous and important errors have taken their rise from those false Principles which were impugned in the foregoing parts of this treatise; and the opposites of those erroneous tenets at the same time appear to be most fruitful Principles, from whence do flow innumerable consequences highly advantageous to true philosophy, as well as to religion. Particularly *Matter*, or *the absolute*[14] *existence of corporeal objects*, hath been shewn to be that wherein the most avowed and pernicious enemies of all knowledge, whether human or divine, have ever placed their chief strength and confidence. And surely, if by distinguishing the real existence of unthinking things from their being perceived, and allowing them a subsistence of their own out of the minds of spirits, no one thing is explained in nature, but on the contrary a great many inexplicable difficulties arise; if the supposition of Matter[15] is barely

---

[13] What follows to the end of this section is omitted in the second edition.

[14] 'absolute,' i.e. unperceived or irrelative existence—supposed to be either something extended, or something of which we have no positive conception at all.

[15] i.e. absolute or unperceived Matter, but not the relative or perceived material world of the senses.

precarious, as not being grounded on so much as one single reason; if its consequences cannot endure the light of examination and free inquiry, but screen themselves under the dark and general pretence of 'infinites being incomprehensible;' if withal the removal of this *Matter*[13] be not attended with the least evil consequence; if it be not even missed in the world, but everything as well, nay much easier conceived without it; if, lastly, both Sceptics and Atheists are for ever silenced upon supposing only spirits and ideas, and this scheme of things is perfectly agreeable both to Reason and Religion —methinks we may expect it should be admitted and firmly embraced, though it were proposed only as an *hypothesis*, and the existence of Matter[15] had been allowed possible, which yet I think we have evidently demonstrated that it is not.

134. True it is that, in consequence of the foregoing principles, several disputes and speculations which are esteemed no mean parts of learning, are rejected as useless [[16]and in effect conversant about nothing at all]. But, how great a prejudice soever against our notions this may give to those who have already been deeply engaged, and made large advances in studies of that nature, yet by others we hope it will not be thought any just ground of dislike to the principles and tenets herein laid down—that they abridge the labour of study, and make human sciences far more clear, compendious, and attainable than they were before.

135. Having despatched what we intended to say concerning the knowledge of IDEAS, the method we proposed leads us in the next place to treat of SPIRITS[17]—with regard to which, perhaps, human knowledge is not so deficient as is vulgarly imagined. The great reason that is assigned for our being thought ignorant of the nature of spirits is—our not having an *idea* of it. But, surely it ought not to be looked on as a defect in a human understanding that it does not perceive the idea of spirit, if it is manifestly

---

[15] See note 18 on previous page.
[16] Omitted in second edition.
[17] Sect. 135—156 treat of the consequences of the new Principles of Human Knowledge, in their application to *Spirit* or *Minds*—the second of the two correlatives in the dualism of Berkeley. This dualism Berkeley does not sufficiently explain. When he speaks of Mind as a Substance, and of minds in the plural, he cannot mean by 'substance' what Spinoza means— that which for its existence needs nothing beyond itself. Mind, with Berkeley, needs ideas, and must be conscious; and finite minds are dependent on God, in a relation which he does not define.

impossible there should be any such idea. And this if I mistake not has been demonstrated in section 27; to which I shall here add —that a spirit has been shewn to be the only substance or support wherein unthinking beings or ideas can exist; but that this *substance* which supports or perceives ideas should itself be an idea or like an idea is evidently absurd.

136. It will perhaps be said that we want a sense (as some have imagined [u]) proper to know substances withal, which, if we had, we might know our own soul as we do a triangle. To this I answer, that, in case we had a new sense bestowed upon us, we could only receive thereby some new sensations or ideas of sense. But I believe nobody will say that what he means by the terms *real* and *substance* is only some particular sort of idea or sensation. We may therefore infer that, all things duly considered, it is not more reasonable to think our faculties defective, in that they do not furnish us with an idea of spirit or active thinking substance, than it would be if we should blame them for not being able to comprehend a *round square*.

137. From the opinion that spirits are to be known after the manner of an idea or sensation have risen many absurd and heterodox tenets, and much scepticism about the nature of the soul. It is even probable that this opinion may have produced a doubt in some whether they had any soul at all distinct from their body, since upon inquiry they could not find they had an idea of it. That an *idea* which is inactive, and the existence whereof consists in being perceived, should be the image or likeness of an agent subsisting by itself, seems to need no other refutation than barely attending to what is meant by those words. But, perhaps you will say that though an idea cannot resemble a spirit in its thinking, acting, or subsisting by itself, yet it may in some other respects; and it is not necessary that an idea or image be in all respects like the original.

138. I answer, if it does not in those mentioned, it is impossible it should represent it in any other thing. Do but leave out the power of willing, thinking, and perceiving ideas, and there remains nothing else wherein the idea can be like a spirit. For, by the word *spirit* we mean only that which thinks, wills, and perceives; this, and this alone, constitutes the signification of that term. If

[u] Locke.

therefore it is impossible that any degree of those powers should be represented in an idea [¹⁹or notion], it is evident there can be no idea [¹⁹or notion] of a spirit.

139. But it will be objected that, if there is no idea signified by the terms *soul*, *spirit*, and *substance*, they are wholly insignificant, or have no meaning in them. I answer, those words do mean or signify a real thing—which is neither an idea nor like an idea, but that which perceives ideas, and wills, and reasons about them. What I am myself—that which I denote by the term *I*—is the same with what is meant by *soul* or *spiritual substance*. [²⁰But if I should say that *I* was nothing, or that *I* was an idea or notion, nothing could be more evidently absurd than either of these propositions.] If it be said that this is only quarrelling at a word, and that, since the immediate significations of other names are by common consent called *ideas*, no reason can be assigned why that which is signified by the name *spirit* or *soul* may not partake in the same appellation. I answer, all the unthinking objects of the mind agree in that they are entirely passive, and their existence consists only in being perceived; whereas a soul or spirit is an active being, whose existence consists, not in being perceived, but in perceiving ideas and thinking²¹. It is therefore necessary, in order to prevent equivocation and confounding natures perfectly disagreeing and unlike, that we distinguish between *spirit* and *idea*. See sect. 27.

140. In a large sense indeed, we may be said to have an idea [²²or rather a notion] of *spirit*; that is, we understand the meaning of the word, otherwise we could not affirm or deny anything of it. Moreover, as we conceive the ideas that are in the minds of other spirits by means of our own, which we suppose to be resemblances of them; so we know other spirits by means of our own soul—which in that sense is the image or idea of them; it having a like respect to other spirits that blueness or heat by me perceived has to those ideas perceived by another²³.

---

[19] Omitted in second edition. Cf. sect. 142.
[20] Ibid.
[21] If the existence of a mind consists in perceiving, it follows that mind is as dependent on ideas (of some sort) as ideas are on mind.
[22] Introduced in second edition, in which be professes to apply the term *notion* exclusively to our knowledge of the Ego, and to our knowledge of relations among our ideas. Sect. 142.
[23] We know other minds or Egos phenomenally, i. e. through phenomena, or by inference from them, but not as ideas or phenomena of which we ourselves are con-

141. [²⁴'The natural immortality of the soul is a necessary consequence of the foregoing doctrine. But before we attempt to prove this, it is fit that we explain the meaning of that tenet.] It must not be supposed that they who assert the natural immortality of the soul²⁵ are of opinion that it is absolutely incapable of annihilation even by the infinite power of the Creator who first gave it being, but only that it is not liable to be broken or dissolved by the ordinary laws of nature or motion. They indeed who hold the soul of man to be only a thin vital flame, or system of animal spirits, make it perishing and corruptible as the body; since there is nothing more easily dissipated than such a being, which it is naturally impossible should survive the ruin of the tabernacle wherein it is inclosed. And this notion has been greedily embraced and cherished by the worst part of mankind, as the most effectual antidote against all impressions of virtue and religion. But it has been made evident that bodies, of what frame or texture soever, are barely passive ideas in the mind—which is more distant and heterogeneous from them than light is from darkness²⁶. We have shewn that the soul is indivisible, incorporeal, unextended, and it is consequently incorruptible. Nothing can be plainer than that the motions, changes, decays, and dissolutions which we hourly see befal natural bodies (and which is what we mean by the *course of nature*) cannot possibly affect an active, simple, uncompounded substance: such a being therefore is indissoluble by the force of nature; that is to say, 'the soul of man is naturally immortal²⁷.'

142. After what has been said, it is, I suppose, plain that our souls are not to be known in the same manner as senseless, inactive objects, or by way of *idea*. *Spirits* and *ideas* are things so wholly different, that when we say 'they exist,' 'they are known,' or the like, these words must not be thought to signify anything

common to both natures[28]. There is nothing alike or common in them; and to expect that by any multiplication or enlargement of our faculties we may be enabled to know a spirit as we do a triangle[29], seems as absurd as if we should hope to see a sound. This is inculcated because I imagine it may be of moment towards clearing several important questions, and preventing some very dangerous errors concerning the nature of the soul. [[30] We may not, I think, strictly be said to have an *idea* of an active being, or of an action[31], although we may be said to have a *notion* of them. I have some knowledge or notion of my mind, and its acts about ideas—inasmuch as I know or understand what is meant by these words. What I know, that I have some notion of. I will not say that the terms *idea* and *notion* may not be used convertibly, if the world will have it so; but yet it conduceth to clearness and propriety that we distinguish things very different by different names. It is also to be remarked that, all relations including an act of the mind[32], we cannot so properly be said to have an idea, but rather a notion of the relations and habitudes between things. But if, in the modern way, the word *idea* is extended to spirits, and relations, and acts, this is, after all, an affair of verbal concern.]

143. It will not be amiss to add, that the doctrine of *abstract ideas* has had no small share in rendering those sciences intricate and obscure which are particularly conversant about spiritual things. Men have imagined they could frame abstract notions of the powers and acts of the mind, and consider them prescinded as well from the mind or spirit itself, as from their respective objects and effects. Hence a great number of dark and ambiguous terms, presumed to stand for abstract notions, have been

---

[28] The objective essence of matter, or the sense-given non-ego, is, with Berkeley, purely phenomenal or ideal; the essence of mind —the Ego—is substantial and causal. Sense-ideas or phenomena are at once dependent on mind, and symbolical of the intentions of mind. Mind and its ideas are, in short, at the opposite poles of existence—being related as subject knowing and object known, as cause and effects, as substance and phenomenon. But he does not say that these poles, thus opposed, are numerically distinguishable as things independent of each other.

[29] I.e. objectively—as an object or idea.

[30] What follows was introduced in the second edition, in which the term *notion* is defined, and assists to express Berkeley's duality in things.

[31] Yet he speaks elsewhere (sect. 1, &c.) of ideas formed by attending to the 'operations' of the mind. He probably refers to the *effects* of the operations, holding that the effects, but not their cause, are ideal.

[32] Here is the germ of Kantism. But Berkeley has not analysed that activity of mind which constitutes *relation*, as distinguished from the personal acting of *will*. Cf. remarkable passages in *Siris*, sect. 297, 308, &c.

introduced into metaphysics and morality, and from these have grown infinite distractions and disputes amongst the learned.

144. But, nothing seems more to have contributed towards engaging men in controversies and mistakes with regard to the nature and operations of the mind, than the being used to speak of those things in terms borrowed from sensible ideas. For example, the will is termed the *motion* of the soul: this infuses a belief that the mind of man is as a ball in motion, impelled and determined by the objects of sense, as necessarily as that is by the stroke of a racket. Hence arise endless scruples and errors of dangerous consequence in morality. All which, I doubt not, may be cleared, and truth appear plain, uniform, and consistent, could but philosophers be prevailed on to [33depart from some received prejudices and modes of speech, and] retire into themselves, and attentively consider their own meaning. [33But the difficulties arising on this head demand a more particular disquisition than suits with the design of this treatise.]

145. From what has been said, it is plain that we cannot know the existence of other spirits otherwise than by their operations, or the ideas by them excited in us. I perceive several motions, changes, and combinations of ideas, that inform me there are certain particular agents, like myself, which accompany them and concur in their production. Hence, the knowledge I have of other spirits is not immediate, as is the knowledge of my ideas; but depending on the intervention of ideas, by me referred to agents or spirits distinct from myself, as effects or concomitant signs [34].

---

[33] Omitted in second edition.

[34] This is one of the most important sections in the book. It has been common (see Reid's *Essays*, VI. 5, &c.) to allege that, on Berkeley's principles, I have no reason to believe in the existence of other minds or wills—a plurality of Egos, or at any rate in other Egos than my own, and the Supreme or Absolute. I can design or intend; all the rest is God's:—my volitions and His determine the phenomenal universe. Now, Berkeley holds that we have the same sort of reason to believe in the existence of other human minds that we have to believe in the existence of God, viz. the sense-symbolism which implies the existence of other finite minds, embodied like our own, is its only reasonable interpretation. Cf. sect.

147, 148. Both are beliefs gathered from the *suggestions* of experience. This enables us to infer the existence not merely of other, and by us, at present, unperceived phenomena, in our own past or future experience; and phenomena in the present, past or future experience of *other minds*; but also, as implied in the latter, the *existence* of other minds—other selfs. His mode of looking at the universe leaves the evidence for the existence of other men as it was before (although our ideas and those of other men are with him not numerically identical, but only in a harmony of similarity); while his theory was believed by him to intensify the evidence of Divine Presence and Providence. See *Alciphron*, Dial. IV., and *Vindication of New Theory of Vision*, sect. 9, 38, &c.

146. But, though there be some things which convince us human agents are concerned in producing them, yet it is evident to every one that those things which are called the Works of Nature, that is, the far greater part of the ideas or sensations perceived by us, are not produced by, or dependent on, the wills of men. There is therefore some other Spirit that causes them; since it is repugnant that they should subsist by themselves. See sect. 29. But, if we attentively consider the constant regularity, order, and concatenation of natural things, the surprising magnificence, beauty and perfection of the larger, and the exquisite contrivance of the smaller parts of the creation, together with the exact harmony and correspondence of the whole, but above all the never-enough-admired laws of pain and pleasure, and the instincts or natural inclinations, appetites, and passions of animals—I say if we consider all these things, and at the same time attend to the meaning and import of the attributes One, Eternal, Infinitely Wise, Good, and Perfect, we shall clearly perceive that they belong to the aforesaid Spirit, 'who works all in all,' and 'by whom all things consist.'

147. Hence, it is evident that God is known as certainly and immediately as any other mind or spirit whatsoever distinct from ourselves. We may even assert that the existence of God is far more evidently perceived than the existence of men; because the effects of nature are infinitely more numerous and considerable than those ascribed to human agents[a]. There is not any one mark that denotes a man, or effect produced by him, which does not more strongly evince the being of that Spirit who is the Author of Nature. For, it is evident that in affecting other persons the will of man has no other object than barely the motion of the limbs of his body; but that such a motion should be attended by, or excite any idea in the mind of another, depends wholly on the will of the Creator. He alone it is who, 'upholding all things by the word of His power,' maintains that intercourse between spirits whereby they are able to perceive the existence of each other[b]. And yet

---

[a] Cf. *Alciphron*, Dial. IV. 8—14; *Vindication of New Theory of Vision*, sect. 8.

[b] God so regulates the sense-given phenomena of ideas of which spirits are individually conscious, as that these phenomena, *while numerically different in each mind*, are nevertheless a practical medium of intercourse between minds. Egoism is seen not to be a necessary result of the fact that no one but myself can be conscious of my own experience, when we recognise that persons only are powers, and that *I* am not the cause of *all* the changes which my ideas or phenomena exhibit. Without being

this pure and clear light which enlightens every one is itself invisible [³⁷to the greatest part of mankind].

148. It seems to be a general pretence of the unthinking herd that they cannot *see* God. Could we but see Him, say they, as we see a man, we should believe that He is, and believing obey His commands. But alas, we need only open our eyes to see the Sovereign Lord of all things, with a more full and clear view than we do any one of our fellow-creatures. Not that I imagine we see God (as some will have it) by a direct and immediate view; or see corporeal things, not by themselves, but by seeing that which represents them in the essence of God, which doctrine is[38], I must confess, to me incomprehensible. But I shall explain my meaning:—A human spirit or person is not perceived by sense, as not being an idea; when therefore we see the colour, size, figure, and motions of a man, we perceive only certain sensations or ideas excited in our own minds; and these being exhibited to our view in sundry distinct collections, serve to mark out unto us the existence of finite and created spirits like ourselves. Hence it is plain we do not see a man—if by *man* is meant that which lives, moves, perceives, and thinks as we do—but only such a certain collection of ideas as directs us to think there is a distinct principle of thought and motion, like to ourselves, accompanying and represented by it. And after the same manner we see God; all the difference is that, whereas some one finite and narrow assemblage of ideas denotes a particular human mind, whithersoever we direct our view, we do at all times and in all places perceive manifest tokens of the Divinity—everything we see, hear, feel, or anywise perceive by sense, being a sign or effect of the power of God; as is our perception of those very motions which are produced by men[39].

themselves conscious of my consciousness, we may infer that other persons or minds are at work to modify it. In short, our experience of power or volition, and of our own limited power, is essential to Berkeley's recognition of a plurality of minds or substances—to his escape from the unity of Absolute Egoism, and to his scientific recognition of his external world.

[37] Omitted in second edition.

[38] Malebranche, as understood by Berkeley. According to Malebranche we see material or sensible things in God, who transcends, and in transcending unites the substantial antithesis of Mind and Matter. See *Recherche*, liv. III. p. ii. ch. 6, &c.

[39] Cf. *Alciphron*, Dial. IV., and *Vindication of New Theory of Vision*, sect. 8, 38, &c. The *eternal* existence of conscious Mind, and the *present* existence of other finite minds than my own, are both inferences, according to Berkeley. The former, however, follows from the assumption that something must be eternal, because something now exists; seeing that this 'something,' as existing, must be a mind conscious of ideas or objects.

149. It is therefore plain that nothing can be more evident to any one that is capable of the least reflection than the existence of God, or a Spirit who is intimately present to our minds, producing in them all that variety of ideas or sensations which continually affect us, on whom we have an absolute and entire dependence, in short 'in whom we live, and move, and have our being.' That the discovery of this great truth, which lies so near and obvious to the mind, should be attained to by the reason of so very few, is a sad instance of the stupidity and inattention of men, who, though they are surrounded with such clear manifestations of the Deity, are yet so little affected by them that they seem, as it were, blinded with excess of light.

150. But you will say, Hath Nature no share in the production of natural things, and must they be all ascribed to the immediate and sole operation of God? I answer, if by *Nature* is meant only the visible *series* of effects or sensations imprinted on our minds, according to certain fixed and general laws, then it is plain that Nature, taken in this sense, cannot produce anything at all [a]. But, if by *Nature* is meant some being distinct from God, as well as from the laws of nature, and things perceived by sense, I must confess that word is to me an empty sound without any intelligible meaning annexed to it. Nature, in this acceptation, is a vain chimera, introduced by those heathens who had not just notions of the omnipresence and infinite perfection of God. But, it is more unaccountable that it should be received among Christians, professing belief in the Holy Scriptures, which constantly ascribe those effects to the immediate hand of God that heathen philosophers are wont to impute to Nature. 'The Lord He causeth the vapours to ascend; He maketh lightnings with rain; He bringeth forth the wind out of his treasures.' Jerem. x. 13. 'He turneth the shadow of death into the morning, and maketh the day dark with night.' Amos v. 8. 'He visiteth the earth, and maketh it soft with showers: He blesseth the springing thereof, and crowneth the year with His goodness; so that the pastures are clothed with flocks, and the valleys are covered over with corn.' See Psal. lxv. But, notwithstanding that is the constant language of Scripture, yet we have I know not what aversion from believing that God concerns Himself so nearly in our affairs.

[a] Cf. sect. 15, 51—53, 60—66, &c.

Fain would we suppose Him at a great distance off, and substitute some blind unthinking deputy in His stead, though (if we may believe Saint Paul) 'He be not far from every one of us.'

151. It will, I doubt not, be objected that the slow, gradual, and roundabout methods observed in the production of natural things do not seem to have for their cause the immediate hand of an Almighty Agent[41]. Besides, monsters, untimely births, fruits blasted in the blossom, rains falling in desert places, miseries incident to human life, and the like, are so many arguments that the whole frame of nature is not immediately actuated and superintended by a Spirit of infinite wisdom and goodness. But the answer to this objection is in a good measure plain from sect. 62; it being visible that the aforesaid methods of nature are absolutely necessary, in order to working by the most simple and general rules, and after a steady and consistent manner; which argues both the wisdom and goodness of God. [[42]For, it doth hence follow that the finger of God is not so conspicuous to the resolved and careless sinner, which gives him an opportunity to harden in his impiety and grow ripe for vengeance. (Vid. sect. 57.)] Such is the artificial contrivance of this mighty machine of nature that, whilst its motions and various phenomena strike on our senses, the hand which actuates the whole is itself unperceivable to men of flesh and blood. 'Verily' (saith the prophet) 'thou art a God that hidest thyself.' Isaiah xlv. 15. But, though the Lord conceal Himself from the eyes of the sensual and lazy, who will not be at the least expense of thought, yet to an unbiassed and attentive mind nothing can be more plainly legible than the intimate presence of an All-wise Spirit, who fashions, regulates, and sustains the whole system of beings[43]. [[44]Secondly.] It is clear, from what we have elsewhere observed, that the operating according to general and stated laws is so necessary for our guidance in the affairs of life, and letting us into the secret of nature, that without it all reach and compass of thought, all human sagacity and design, could serve to no manner of purpose; it were even impossible there should be any such faculties or powers in the mind. See sect. 31. Which one consideration abundantly outbalances whatever particular inconveniences may thence arise.

[41] Cf. sect. 60—66.
[42] Omitted in second edition.
[43] So Pascal in the *Pensées*.
[44] Omitted in second edition.

152. But, we should further consider that the very blemishes and defects of nature are not without their use, in that they make an agreeable sort of variety, and augment the beauty of the rest of the creation, as shades in a picture serve to set off the brighter and more enlightened parts. We would likewise do well to examine whether our taxing the waste of seeds and embryos, and accidental destruction of plants and animals, before they come to full maturity, as an imprudence in the Author of nature, be not the effect of prejudice contracted by our familiarity with impotent and saving mortals[13]. In man indeed a thrifty management of those things which he cannot procure without much pains and industry may be esteemed wisdom. But, we must not imagine that the inexplicably fine machine of an animal or vegetable costs the great Creator any more pains or trouble in its production than a pebble does; nothing being more evident than that an Omnipotent Spirit can indifferently produce everything by a mere *fiat* or act of his will. Hence, it is plain that the splendid profusion of natural things should not be interpreted weakness or prodigality in the agent who produces them, but rather be looked on as an argument of the riches of his power.

153. As for the mixture of pain or uneasiness which is in the world, pursuant to the general laws of nature, and the actions of finite, imperfect spirits, this, in the state we are in at present, is indispensably necessary to our well-being. But our prospects are too narrow. We take, for instance, the idea of some one particular pain into our thoughts, and account it *evil*; whereas, if we enlarge our view, so as to comprehend the various ends, connexions, and dependencies of things, on what occasions and in what proportions we are affected with pain and pleasure, the nature of human freedom, and the design with which we are put into the world; we shall be forced to acknowledge that those particular things which, considered in themselves, appear to be evil, have the nature of good, when considered as linked with the whole system of beings[14].

154. From what has been said, it will be manifest to any considering person, that it is merely for want of attention and comprehensiveness of mind that there are any favourers of Atheism or the Manichean Heresy to be found. Little and unreflecting

---

[14] So Butler, in his *Analogy*. Also cf. sect. 60—66.

souls may indeed burlesque the works of Providence ⁴⁶—the beauty and order whereof they have not capacity, or will not be at the pains, to comprehend; but those who are masters of any justness and extent of thought, and are withal used to reflect, can never sufficiently admire the divine traces of Wisdom and Goodness that shine throughout the Economy of Nature. But what truth is there which glares so strongly on the mind that by an aversion of thought, a wilful shutting of the eyes, we may not escape seeing it, at least with a full and direct view? Is it therefore to be wondered at, if the generality of men, who are ever intent on business or pleasure, and little used to fix or open the eye of their mind, should not have all that conviction and evidence of the Being of God which might be expected in reasonable creatures?

155. We should rather wonder that men can be found so stupid as to neglect, than that neglecting they should be unconvinced of such an evident and momentous truth. And yet it is to be feared that too many of parts and leisure, who live in Christian countries, are, merely through a supine and dreadful negligence, sunk into [⁴⁷a sort of Demy-]Atheism. [⁴⁸They cannot say there is not a God, but neither are they convinced that there is. For what else can it be but some lurking infidelity, some secret misgivings of mind with regard to the existence and attributes of God, which permits sinners to grow and harden in impiety?] Since it is downright impossible that a soul pierced and enlightened with a thorough sense of the omnipresence, holiness, and justice of that Almighty Spirit should persist in a remorseless violation of His laws. We ought, therefore, earnestly to meditate and dwell on those important points; that so we may attain conviction without all scruple 'that the eyes of the Lord are in every place beholding the evil and the good; that He is with us and keepeth us in all places whither we go, and giveth us bread to eat and raiment to

---

⁴⁶ A constant Divine Thought and Providence in the changes of the phenomenal world, rather than the original creation of finite minds and of their ideas or phenomena, is the conception which runs through Berkeley's philosophy, conspicuously in *Siris*.

⁴⁷ Omitted in second edition. Our alleged necessary ignorance of the *ultimate* cause and meaning of the Universe in which we find ourselves is, in the present day, a common objection to the assumption that its phenomena may be interpreted as significant of Supreme or Absolute Mind. As Hume or Comte would have it, the Universe is a singular effect or complement of phenomena, which we can interpret only so far as our secular wants and duties are concerned. They look to the physical or phenomenal, and not to the moral and spiritual evidence.

⁴⁸ Omitted in second edition.

put on;' that He is present and conscious to our innermost thoughts; in fine, that we have a most absolute and immediate dependence on Him. A clear view of which great truths cannot choose but fill our hearts with an awful circumspection and holy fear, which is the strongest incentive to *Virtue*, and the best guard against *Vice*.

156. For, after all, what deserves the first place in our studies is the consideration of GOD and our DUTY; which to promote, as it was the main drift and design of my labours, so shall I esteem them altogether useless and ineffectual if, by what I have said, I cannot inspire my readers with a pious sense of the Presence of God; and, having shewn the falseness or vanity of those barren speculations which make the chief employment of learned men, the better dispose them to reverence and embrace the salutary truths of the Gospel, which to know and to practise is the nighest perfection of human nature.

EDITOR'S PREFACE

TO THE

THREE DIALOGUES BETWEEN HYLAS AND PHILONOUS.

EDITOR'S PREFACE

TO THE

THREE DIALOGUES BETWEEN HYLAS AND PHILONOUS.

THIS work is the gem of British metaphysical literature. Berkeley's claim to be the great modern master of Socratic dialogue rests, indeed, upon *Alciphron*, which surpasses the conversations between Hylas and Philonous in expression of individual character, and in general dramatic effect. Here the conversational form is adopted merely as a convenient way of treating the chief objections to the theory of Matter which is contained in the *Principles of Human Knowledge*. But the clearness of thought and language, the occasional colouring of fancy, and the glow of practical human sympathy and earnestness that pervade the subtle reasonings by which the fallacies of metaphysics are inexorably pursued through these discussions, place the following *Dialogues* almost alone in the modern metaphysical library. Among those who have employed the English language, except perhaps Hume and Ferrier, none approach Berkeley in the art of uniting deep metaphysical thought and ingenious speculation with an easy, graceful, and transparent style. Our surprise and admiration are increased when we recollect that this charming production of reason and imagination came from Ireland, at a time when that country was scarcely known in the world of letters and philosophy.

The *Essay on Vision* and the *Treatise on the Principles of Human Knowledge* may be said to comprehend between them the early metaphysical doctrine of Berkeley. But it appears in these works in a form more suited to scholars and logicians than for obviating popular objections, and promoting the moral purpose their author had in view. His

EDITOR'S PREFACE

Essay on Vision was the precursor of the New Theory of Knowledge contained in his *Principles*. The doctrine regarding sight and touch propounded in the former was meant to be the first movement in a war against the abstractions of metaphysics that was openly proclaimed in the latter. In the preliminary analysis of visual consciousness, the abstraction commonly called Space or Extension was resolved, by psychological analysis, into its original elements, as given in sense, and especially in the sense-symbolism of Sight. But Abstract Space is only a part of the structure of abstractions, reared by metaphysicians, in which Berkeley believed that the current scepticism of his day was finding shelter, and which he wanted to break up, alike in the interest of religion and philosophy. An abstract idea is, with him, a contradiction in terms; and the abstract idea of Matter is, of all others, the parent of doubt and confusion. He argues that the existence of absolute or unperceived Matter is impossible; that all real Matter must be sensible Matter, as all real extension must be sensible extension; that Matter which is neither seen, nor touched, nor heard, nor tasted, nor smelt—of which we are in no way conscious in any of the senses—must be at the best a mere word, an empty abstraction. Whatever actually exists, accordingly, must be either an object of which a mind is conscious—that is to say, an *idea;* or else a *self-conscious mind*, capable of exerting power over ideas. All actual Existence must be dependent on conscious mind, finite or Divine; abstract Existence involves a contradiction in terms, or rather it is a term which contains no meaning.

According to Berkeley, the popular and the philosophical conception of Matter are both absurd—the former because adulterated by the latter. The unreflecting have a confused belief (which can be explained), that what they perceive in the senses exists whether it is perceived or not. The philosophers, granting that what they immediately perceive in the senses is dependent on (embodied) mind, indulge in the irrational hypothesis, that sense-ideas are for us representatives of, or at least substitutes for, an unperceived and unperceivable material world, which exists *per se*, in absolute independence of any perception or imagination of its contents. Berkeley argues against both; against the former for assuming the absolute existence of *the objects of which we are conscious*, which, so far as we know, must be ideas, inasmuch as they can be known to exist only while they are perceived or imagined; against the latter for assuming the abstract or absolute reality of unintelligible *material substance*, existing, as it were, *behind* the immediate objects or ideas of our conscious experience. He infers that sense-ideas themselves, or at least the established combinations of them, are the real things—the only material world; while he warns us that these are not to be confounded with transient personal fancies, in which the real world may be either represented or misrepresented. They are parts in an orderly system. They may be called *external*, if we choose; but not because they have an *absolute*, that is to say, an unperceived and unconceived existence. Their 'externality' consists in their arrangements of perceived co-existence and succession being independent of the will of the finite percipient; and in the fact that, unlike our personal feelings and imaginations, they are virtually objects common to a plurality of minds, and the medium of intercourse between one mind and another. Our sense-consciousness is, on Berkeley's principles, the only material world to which our actions have any reference, or with which either practically or speculatively we can have any concern. Abstract Matter disappears, as Abstract Space or Extension had previously disappeared in the *New Theory of Vision*. Sensible Space and Sensible Matter take their place; and the *esse* of Sensible Space and Sensible Matter is *percipi*, because both are dependent on a percipient.

The paradoxes and paralogisms of pure and mixed mathematics, with regard to Space, Time, Number, Motion, and Infinity, disappear from sciences confined to sensible extension and matter; and the investigation of nature becomes simply an attempt to interpret the arbitrarily established order of co-existence and succession among ideas, in the symbolical world of sense-experience. The prospect of our personal immortality is brightened; for, on these principles, it is metaphysically *impossible* that the sensible world, whether organic or extra-organic, can exist without a conscious mind, while it is at least metaphysically *possible* that created minds may maintain their consciousness of objects without any *sense*-objects to be conscious of. Organisms, along with the whole world of the senses of which our organisms are part, are thus substantially dependent on mind; but minds are not in like absolute dependence on organisms or on any other sensible things—for it is conceivable that the matter of our experience might be exclusive of all sense-objects, and composed of other objects altogether. And, as the common reason of men, tested by their actions, demands the *permanence* of sensible things, even though they are not permanently present to the senses of any one embodied mind, it follows that the very existence of the things of sense (apart from any 'marks of design' in their collocations) implies the permanent existence of Supreme Mind, by whom all real objects are perpetually conceived, and in whom their orderly appearances, disappearances, and reappearances in finite minds may be said to exist potentially. We thus find ourselves living in a sensible world which has its being in Mind.

This was the Philosophy of Substance and Power which Berkeley had proposed in his *Principles*, instead of the old Materialism—the latent Scepticism and Atheism of which last left the sentiments of reverence and love, along with faith and imagination, unsatisfied, deeply rooted as all these are in the nature of man.

The following *Dialogues* discuss what Berkeley regarded as the most plausible Objections, popular and philosophical, to his doctrine of Sensible Things.

The principal aim of the *First Dialogue* is to illustrate the contradictory, or at least unmeaning, nature, and sceptical tendency of the common philosophical opinion—that we perceive in sense a material world which is *real* only inasmuch as it exists in absolute independence of any perceiving or conceiving mind. The absurdity of percipient intercourse with such a world, either in respect of its so-called Secondary or its so-called Primary qualities, and that whether the perception be immediate and presentative, or mediate and representative, is illustrated in detail. Absolute Matter, whether sensible or substantial and abstracted from the senses, cannot, without a contradiction, it is argued, be presented or represented, in or through any sense.

The *Second Dialogue* is first directed against some refined modifications of the philosophical account of absolute Matter, which attribute our knowledge of it to inferences, founded on our experience of sense-ideas assumed to be representative, and not to the senses themselves. The advocates of metaphysical or super-sensible Matter are here assailed in their various hypotheses—that Matter may be the active Cause, or the Instrument, or the Occasion of our sense-experience, or that it is an unknown Something somehow connected with that experience. It is held in this and in the preceding Dialogue, by *Philonous*, who personates Berkeley, that Matter—meaning by that term either an extended, solid, figured, moveable substance; or an unknowing something, existing unperceived and unconceived, of which we cannot affirm extension and solidity, whether identified with the immediate objects of perception, or viewed as capable of being inferred from them—is not merely unproved, but a proved impossibility: it must mean nothing at all, or else mean a contradiction, which virtually comes to the same thing. It cannot be *perceived;* nor *suggested* by what we perceive; nor *demonstrated* by abstract reasoning; nor even *believed in* as an article in the fundamental faith of Common Reason. The only consistent theory of the universe implies, it is maintained, that *things* must be either (a) passive objects of a conscious mind, and controlled by mind, or (b) active minds, conscious of objects, and capable of regulating them. And neither of these two sorts of 'things' is strictly speaking *absolute*, that is to say, independent of the other; though the latter, as identical amid the variations of the phenomena which are the essence of the former, may be regarded as their ground or substance. The *Second Dialogue* ends by substituting, as matter of fact and intelligible Realism, this Theory of the universal dependence of the material world upon Mind, in place of the hypothetical Realism, which requires philosophers to defend, by fallacious reasonings, Absolute Matter, unperceived and unconceived, as the type of objective reality.

In the *Third Dialogue* fresh objections to the New Theory of Sensible Things are discussed. Some of them were treated of in the *Principles of Human Knowledge*.

Is it said that the New Theory is essentially sceptical, and its author another Protagoras, on account of his negation of Absolute Matter—that supposed unchanging essence of the changeable qualities or ideas which we perceive in sense? The answer is, that the *reality* of sensible things, according to the practical conviction of men, does not consist in an abstract *essence* that cannot be perceived, suggested, demonstrated, or even conceived, but in the *facts* that sensible phenomena are actually seen and touched, and that our future may with reasonable confidence be anticipated by the analogy of our present sense-experience.

Is this negation of Absolute Matter assumed to be a mere hypothesis, against which as many objections may be pressed as against the counter hypothesis which affirms its existence? It is answered, that the affirmation of *such* Matter is indeed the affirmation of a mere hypothesis, and one self-convicted by its own contradictions; but that its negation is no hypothesis at all, and only a simple falling back on the facts of experience, without any attempt to explain them.

Is it objected that the *reality* of sensible things involves their permanence during the intervals of our attention to them, and, indeed, their independence of the perceptions and existence of any individual percipient? It is answered, that, according to the New Theory of Real Existence, sensible things are permanently dependent on, or relative to, *a* conscious mind, but not this, that, or the other finite mind.

Is it alleged that the existence of Spiritual Substance or Mind is exposed to all the objections against Absolute Material Substance; and that, if we deny unperceived Matter, we must in consistency allow that Mind can be only a system of floating ideas, without *substance* to support them? The answer is, that there is no parity between conscious or mental substance, and a material substance that is out of all relation to any consciousness. We are aware, in memory, of our own personality and identity; that we are not our ideas, 'but somewhat else'—a thinking, active principle, that perceives, knows, wills, and operates about ideas, and that is revealed as continuous. Each mind is conscious of itself; and, although not conscious of, may reasonably infer the existence of other minds, that can be conceived by us after the analogy of our own. A conceivable Self conscious of objects is thus quite different from abstract and inconceivable Matter.

Is it said that sane people cannot help distinguishing between the *existence* of a thing and its *being perceived?* It is answered, that all they really mean is, to distinguish between being perceived exclusively by the individual percipient, and being independent, as sensible things are, of any one sense-conscious individual.

Does an objector complain that this ideal sense-realism removes the distinction between facts and fancies? He is reminded of the meaning of the word *idea*. That term is not limited by Berkeley to fancies in the world of thought, but is applied also to the immediate objects of our sense experience, which are the test or criterion of physical truth.

Is the supposition that Spirit of which we are conscious is the proper Cause of all the changes in nature declaimed against as extravagant? It is answered, that the supposition of an inert, unconscious Cause of sensible phenomena is still more extravagant.

Is the negation of Absolute Matter said to be repugnant to the common belief of mankind? It is argued in reply, that Absolute Matter is foreign to common belief, which is incapable of even entertaining the conception; and which only requires to reflect upon what it does entertain to be satisfied with a relative or ideal existence of sensible things.

But, if sensible things are the real things, the real moon, for instance, it is alleged, can be only a foot in diameter. It is maintained, in opposition to this, that the term 'real moon' is applied only to what is an inference from the moon, one foot in diameter, which we immediately perceive; and that the former is a part of our previsive experience or *mediate* perception, which is not strictly speaking perceived at all.

The dispute, after all, is merely verbal, it is next objected; and, since all parties refer our sensible ideas and the *things* which they con-

attribute to *a* Power that is external to the percipient mind, why not call that universally acknowledged Power, whatever it may be, Matter, and not Spirit? The reply is, that this would be a ridiculous misapplication of language, and a violation of its commonest usage.

But may we not, it is next suggested, assume the possibility of a third nature—neither idea nor spirit? Not, says Berkeley, if we are to keep to the rule of having meaning in the words we use. We know what is meant by a spirit, or intending and percipient cause, for each of us has immediate experience of one; and we know what is meant by sense-ideas and sensible things, for we have immediate and mediate experience of many. But we have no immediate, and therefore can have no mediate, experience of what is neither an object of a conscious mind, nor a state of conscious activity; and, moreover, 'entia non sunt multiplicanda praeter necessitatem.'

Again, the New Theory of Existence implies, it is said, imperfection, because a sentient nature, in the Supreme Mind. This objection, it is answered, implies a confusion between being actually sentient and merely conceiving what sensations are, or employing them, as God does, as signs for conveying His conceptions to created minds.

The negation of Absolute Matter seems to some objectors to annihilate all the received explanations of physical phenomena given by natural philosophers. But, to be assured that it does not, we have only to recollect what a physical explanation means—that it is the reference of an apparently irregular phenomenon to an acknowledged general rule of co-existence or succession among sense-ideas.

Is the proposed Theory of Existence summarily condemned as a novelty? It can be answered, that all discoveries are novelties at first; or that this theory, when fully understood, is not so much a novelty as a reflective interpretation of common thought and belief.

Yet it seems, at any rate, it is said, to change real things into mere appearances or ideas. Here we have only to consider what we mean when we speak of sensible things as real. It is the changing appearances of which we are conscious in sense, united by custom and association, that are what men mean by 'real sensible things.'

The Theory is inconsistent with the *identity* of material things, it is complained, and also with the acknowledged fact that different persons are percipient of the *same* thing. Not so, Berkeley explains, when we attend to the true meaning of the word 'same,' and dismiss from our thoughts a pretended abstract idea of identity which is nonsensical.

But people exclaim against the supposition that the sensible universe exists in mind, regarding it as a virtual assertion that mind itself is extended, and co-extensive with the sensible universe. Now this proceeds, it is urged, on a forgetfulness of what being 'in mind' means. That form of words is intended to express, being an object or phenomenon of which a mind is cognisant.

Is the Scripture account of the creation of Matter said to be irreconcileable with the negation of absolute material substance? It is answered that the conception of creation being dependent on the existence of finite minds is really most in harmony with the Mosaic account. It is what is seen and felt, and not the cause of what is seen and felt, that is created.

The *Third Dialogue* closes with a statement of Berkeley's doctrine of Matter, in two propositions, which it professes to reconcile—the one-sided proposition of ordinary common sense; and the one-sided proposition of the philosophers.

Most of the objections to Berkeley's doctrine of Matter which have been urged in the last century and a half, by its British, French, and German critics, are discussed by anticipation in these *Dialogues*. The history of objections to the doctrine is very much a history of its misconception. Rightly conceived, or misconceived, it powerfully affected subsequent psychological and metaphysical discussion in these islands, and especially in Scotland.

The first formal criticism of Berkeley by a British author is contained in Andrew Baxter's *Inquiry into the Nature of the Human Soul*, published in 1735. The section is entitled, 'Dean Berkeley's Scheme against the existence of Matter examined, and shown to be inconclusive.' Baxter's most plausible objection is, the tendency of the new doctrine to universal scepticism. To deny Matter, for the reasons given by Berkeley, involves, according to Baxter, the denial of mind, and so a universal denial of what is fixed and substantial. It was thus that, a few years afterwards, Hume sought, in his *Treatise of Human Nature*, to work out Berkeley's theory of Matter into his own universal phenomenalism or positivism—a process against which Berkeley sought to guard his doctrine by anticipation, in a remarkable passage introduced in the last edition of the *Dialogues* (pp. 327—329).

The writings of Reid, Beattie, Oswald, Dugald Stewart, and Thomas Brown are a magazine of objections to the new doctrine. Reid—who curiously seeks to refute Berkeley by refuting, less clearly and conclusively than Berkeley had done before him, the hypothesis of a double or representative perception—urges chiefly the spontaneous belief or common sense of mankind, which obliges us to recognise an external material world. He overlooks what with Berkeley is the only question in debate, namely, the meaning of the term *external*; for, Reid and Berkeley are agreed in holding the existence of a sensible world that is external to, in so far as it is independent of, the will of finite percipients, and a sufficient medium of social intercourse among them. With Berkeley, as with Reid, *this* external existence of sensible things is practically self-evident; and also their sufficiency as symbols for the conveyance of meaning from one mind into another. The same objection, more scientifically defined—that we have a natural belief in the independent existence of Matter, and in our own consciousness of its qualities—is Sir W. Hamilton's assumption against Berkeley; but Hamilton does not define 'the *independent existence* thus claimed for it. 'Men naturally believe,' he says, 'that they themselves exist— because they are conscious of a Self or Ego; they believe that *something different from themselves* exists — because they believe that they are conscious of this Not-self or Non-ego.' (*Discussions*, p. 193.) Now, the existence of *a* Non-ego that is independent of each finite Ego (which alone is affirmed by Hamilton, in his belief of '*something* different from themselves') is deeply rooted in Berkeley's principles; though I do not know that he would say that we are *conscious* of it. According to both, we are conscious of solid and extended phenomena or ideas; but with Berkeley these ideas are dependent on, at the same time that they are 'entirely distinct' from, the percipient. The Divine and finite minds we can infer from our ideas of sense with *their* respective ideas, are Berkeley's Non-ego proper.

That Berkeley's doctrine contains the seeds of Universal Scepticism; that it is virtually a system of Pan-egoism, which deprives us of reasonable belief in a universe of matter and minds external to the phenomena of our individual consciousness; that it is virtually a system of Pantheism, inconsistent with all individuality—these are probably the three most comprehensive objections that have been alleged against it. They are in a measure due to Berkeley's imperfect conception of the distinction between *sense* and *imagination*, notwithstanding the numerous passages which he has devoted to the illustration of this distinction; and to the obscurity in which he has left his doctrine regarding the permanence of sensible things on the one hand, and of persons or minds on the other, as well as the dualism thus involved in his system. Is existence, with Berkeley, the antecedent condition, or is it only the consequence, of being conscious? The empirical basis of the earlier Berkeleian metaphysics, with the mystery which it leaves around the answer to this question, separate his conception of the universe from the Egoistic Idealism of Fichte, and from the logical evolution of mind and matter out of the primitive Hegelian identity of subject and object.

In England the Berkeleian theory, on its negative side, as was natural, received a countenance among the sensational psychologists, which was denied to it in Scotland and Germany. Hartley and Priestley shew various signs of affinity with Berkeley. An anonymous *Essay on the Nature and Existence of the Material World*, dedicated to Dr. Priestley and Dr. Price, which appeared in 1781, is a sceptical argument, on empirical grounds, for the purely sensational nature of Matter. The tendency is now more fully and profoundly developed in the writings of Mr. J. S. Mill.

The *Dialogues between Hylas and Philonous* were published in London in 1713, 'printed by G. James, for Henry Clements, at the Half-Moon, in St. Paul's Churchyard.' The *Essay towards a New Theory of Vision* and the *Treatise on the Principles of Human Knowledge* first appeared in Dublin. Berkeley's subsequent works were published in London.

The *Dialogues* apparently attracted more readers than either the *Essay* or the *Treatise*. The second edition, which is simply a reprint, appeared in 1725, 'printed for William and John Innys, at the West End of St. Paul's.' A third edition, the last in the author's lifetime, 'printed by Jacob Tonson,' which contains some important additions, was published in 1734, conjointly with a new edition of the *Principles*. The *Dialogues* were reprinted in 1776, in the same volume with the edition of the *Principles* which then appeared.

Of Berkeley's earlier metaphysical works, the *Dialogues* alone have been translated into French and German.

The French version appeared at Amsterdam in 1750. The translator's name is not given in the work itself, but it is attributed to the Abbé Jean Paul de Gua de Malves[1], by Barbier, in his *Dictionnaire des Ouvrages anonymes et pseudonymes*, tom. I, p. 283. It contains a Prefatory Note by the translator, along with three curious vignettes (given in the note below) meant to symbolise what, according to the translator, was the leading thought in each Dialogue[2].

---

[1] For some information relative to Gua de Malves, see Quérard's *La France Littéraire*, tom. iii. p. 494.

[2] The following is the translator's Prefatory Note on the objects of the *Dialogues*, and in explanation of three illustrative vignettes:—

'L'Auteur expose dans le premier Dialogue le sentiment du Vulgaire et celui des Philosophes, sur les qualités secondaires et premieres, la nature et l'existence des corps ; et il prétend prouver en même tems l'insuffisance de l'un et de l'autre. La Vignette qu'on voit à la tête du Dialogue, fait allusion à cet objet. Elle représente un Philosophe dans son cabinet, lequel est distrait

EDITOR'S PREFACE. 251

A German translation, by John Christopher Eschenbach, Professor of Philosophy in Rostock, was published at Rostock in 1756. It forms

de son travail par un enfant qu'il aperçoit se voyant lui-même dans un miroir, en tendant les mains pour embrasser sa propre image.

Le Philosophe rit de l'erreur où il croit que tombe l'enfant ; tandis qu'on lui applique à lui-même ces mots tirés d'Horace :

Quid rides ? . . . fabula de te Narratur.

¹ Le second Dialogue est employé à exposer le sentiment de l'Auteur sur le même sujet, a savoir, que les choses corporelles ont une existence réelle dans les esprits qui les aperçoivent; mais qu'elles ne s'auroient exister hors de tous les esprits à la fois, même de l'esprit infini de Dieu ; et que par conséquent la Matière, prise suivant l'acception ordinaire du mot, non seulement n'existe point, mais seroit même absolument impossible. On a tâché de représenter aux yeux ce sentiment dans la Vignette du Dialogue. Le mot grec ΨΥΧΗ qui signifie âme, désigne l'âme : les rayons qui en partent marquent l'attention que l'âme donne à des idées ou objets; les tableaux qu'on a placés aux seuls endroits où les rayons aboutissent, et dont les sujets sont tirés de la description des beautés de la nature, qui se trouve dans le livre, représentent les idées ou objets que l'âme considère, par le secours des facultés qu'elle a reçues de Dieu : et l'action de l'Etre suprême sur l'âme, est figurée par un trait, qui, partant d'un triangle, symbole de la Divinité, et perçant les nuages dont le triangle est environné, s'étend jusqu'à l'âme pour la rivifier, enfin, on a fait ensorte de rendre le même sentiment par ces mots :

Quos nemorum cumque Deus dat, Esse puta.

¹ L'objet du troisième Dialogue est de répondre aux difficultés auxquelles le sentiment qu'on a établi dans les Dialogues précédens, peut être sujet, de l'éclaircir en cette sorte de plus en plus, d'en développer toutes les heureuses conséquences, enfin de faire voir,

EDITOR'S PREFACE.

the larger part of a volume entitled *Sammlung der vornehmsten Schriftsteller die die Würklichkeit ihres eignen Körpers und der ganzen Körperwelt läugnen.* This professed Collection of the most eminent authors who deny the (absolute) existence of their own bodies and of the whole material world consists of Berkeley's *Dialogues*, and Arthur Collier's *Clavis Universalis*, or *Demonstration of the Non-existence or Impossibility of an External World.* The volume contains some annotations, and an Appendix in which a counter demonstration of the existence of Matter is attempted. Eschenbach's principal argument is indirect, and of the nature of a *reductio ad absurdum*. He argues (as so many others have done) that the reasons produced for the merely ideal or dependent existence of Matter are equally conclusive against Mind or Self, assuming, as he does, that we have a like consciousness or intuitive conviction of the independent existence of each.

A curious circumstance connected with the first publication of the *Dialogues between Hylas and Philonous* was the appearance, in the same year, of this *Clavis Universalis*, or Demonstration of the impossibility of Matter, of Arthur Collier, in which a theory is maintained similar to Berkeley's, as regards the merely ideal or phenomenal existence of the sensible world. A more curious coincidence is not to be found in the history of speculative thought than the production, simultaneously, without concert or apparently even knowledge on the part of either author of the opinions of the other, of a theory which implies so great a revolution

qu'étant bien entendu, il revient aux notions les plus communes. Et comme l'Auteur exprime à la fin du livre cette dernière pensée, en comparant ce qu'il vient de dire, à l'eau que les deux Interlocuteurs sont supposés voir jaillir d'un jet, et qu'il remarque que la même force de la gravité fait élever jusqu'à une certaine hauteur et retomber ensuite dans le bassin d'où elle étoit d'abord partie; on a pris cet emblême pour le sujet de la Vignette de ce Dialogue ; on a représenté en conséquence dans cette dernière Vignette les deux Interlocuteurs, se promenant dans le lieu où l'Auteur les suppose, et s'entretenant là-dessus, et pour donner au Lecteur l'explication de l'emblême, on a mis au bas le vers suivant :'

Urget aquas vis sursum, eadem flectitque deorsum.

in the philosophical point of view for such questions. It goes to prove that the intellectual atmosphere of the Lockian epoch in England contained elements favourable to such a result. They are both the genuine produce of the age of Locke and Malebranche. Neither Berkeley nor Collier, both at the time young men, were, when they published their theory, familiar with ancient Greek speculation; that of modern Germany had not even begun to loom in the distance. The Kantian, still more the post-Kantian German philosophy, with its negation of Absolute Matter or 'things in themselves,' and its substitution of an Absolute Knowledge identical with Absolute Existence; the Phenomenalism of Auguste Comte; the advance of the modern interpretation of nature; and the revived study of Plato, have now changed the conditions under which the problem is studied, and are making intelligible to this generation a manner of conceiving the Universe which, for nearly a century and a half, the British critics of Berkeley were unable to realize.

Although Berkeley's *Principles of Human Knowledge* appeared three years before the *Clavis Universalis*, Collier tells us that it was 'after a ten years' pause and deliberation,' that, 'rather than the world should finish its course without once offering to inquire in what manner it exists,' he had 'resolved to put himself upon the trial of the common reader, without pretending to any better art of gaining him than dry reason and metaphysical demonstration.' Mr. Benson, his biographer, says that it was in 1703, at the age of twenty-three, that Collier came to the conclusion that 'there is no such thing as an external world;' and he attributes the premises from which Collier drew this conclusion to his neighbour, Mr. Norris. Among Collier's MSS., there remains the outline of an essay, in three chapters, dated January, 1708, on the non-externality of the *visible* world.

The coincidence between the publication of Berkeley's theory of the relativity of sensible things, and Collier's demonstration of the impossibility of an external or absolute world, is not more curious than the coincidence in their way of unfolding what they taught. Berkeley virtually presented his New Theory of Vision as the first instalment of his New Theory of Knowledge and Existence—thus teaching that *visible* Matter, at any rate, is not, and cannot be, external or independent of perception. Now, the first of the two Parts into which Collier's *Clavis* is divided, consists of experimental proofs that the *visible* world is not, and cannot be, external. Berkeley, moreover, in his *Principles of Human Knowledge*, and in these *Dialogues between Hylas and Philonous*, disposes of the externality not of visible things only but of Matter in general; and maintains that the hypothesis of absolute or external Matter, in every modification of it, is essentially irrational. And in like manner the Second Part of the *Clavis* consists of reasonings in proof of the impossibility of an external world. Finally, in his full-blown theory, as well as in its visual germ, Berkeley takes for granted, as intuitively known, the existence of sensible, including visible, matter; meaning by this, its relative existence, in necessary dependence on a mind. In like manner, what may be called the third proposition of Collier's system asserts the existence of visible matter in particular, and of sensible matter in general.

Berkeley and Collier are not, however, to be identified.

The invisibility of distances, as well as of real magnitudes and situations, and their suggestion by interpretation of visual symbols, propositions which occupy so large a space in Berkeley's Theory of Vision, have no counterpart in Collier's First Part. His proof of the non-externality of the visible world consists of an induction of instances of visible objects, which are allowed by all not to be external, although they seem in visual sense to be as much so as any that are called external.

The Second Part of Collier's Demonstration consists of nine proofs of the impossibility of an external or absolute world, which may be compared with the reasonings and psychological analyses of Berkeley.

Collier's Demonstration concludes with answers to objections, and an application of the theory of a dependent material world to the refutation of the Roman doctrine of the substantial existence of Christ's body in the Eucharist.

The universal sense-symbolism of Berkeley, his broad recognition of the distinction between physical or symbolical, and efficient or proper causation, and his large philosophical insight, are all wanting in the narrow but acute reasonings of Collier. Berkeley's philosophy, owing to its own comprehensiveness, not less than to the humanity of his sympathies and the beauty of his style, is now recognised as a striking expression or solution of problems of modern thought, while Collier is condemned to the obscurity of a mere reasoner of the Schools[1].

A. C. F.

[1] Collier never came fairly out in sight of the philosophical public of last century. He is referred to in Germany by Bilfinger, in his *Dilucidationes Philosophicae* (1746), and also in the *Acta Eruditorum*, Suppl. VI. 244 &c., and in England by Corry in his *Reflections on Liberty and Necessity* (1761), as well as in the *Remarks* on the Reflections, and *Answers* to the Remarks, pp. 7, 8 (1763), where he is described as 'a weak reasoner, and a very dull writer also.' Collier was dragged from his obscurity by Dr. Reid, in his *Essays on the Intellectual Powers*, Essay II. ch. 10. He was a subject of correspondence between Sir James Mackintosh, then at Bombay, and Dr. Parr, and an object of curiosity to Dugald Stewart. A beautiful reprint of the *Clavis* (of the original edition of which only seven copies were then known to exist) appeared in Edinburgh in 1836; and in the following year it was included in a publication of *Metaphysical Tracts by English Philosophers of the Eighteenth Century*, prepared for the press by Dr. Parr.

THREE DIALOGUES

BETWEEN

HYLAS AND PHILONOUS.

THE DESIGN OF WHICH IS PLAINLY TO DEMONSTRATE
THE REALITY AND PERFECTION OF

HUMAN KNOWLEDGE,

THE INCORPOREAL NATURE OF THE

SOUL,

AND THE IMMEDIATE PROVIDENCE OF A

DEITY:

IN OPPOSITION TO

SCEPTICS AND ATHEISTS.

ALSO TO OPEN A METHOD FOR RENDERING THE SCIENCES MORE EASY,
USEFUL, AND COMPENDIOUS.

FIRST PRINTED IN THE YEAR 1713.

TO THE RIGHT HONOURABLE

THE

LORD BERKELEY OF STRATTON[1],

MASTER OF THE ROLLS IN THE KINGDOM OF IRELAND, CHANCELLOR
OF THE DUCHY OF LANCASTER, AND ONE OF THE LORDS OF
HER MAJESTY'S MOST HONOURABLE PRIVY COUNCIL.

MY LORD,

The virtue, learning, and good sense which are acknowledged to distinguish your character, would tempt me to indulge myself the pleasure men naturally take in giving applause to those whom they esteem and honour: and it should seem of importance to the subjects of Great Britain that they knew the eminent share you enjoy in the favour of your sovereign, and the honours she has conferred upon you, have not been owing to any application from your lordship, but entirely to her majesty's own thought, arising from a sense of your personal merit, and an inclination to reward it. But, as your name is prefixed to this treatise with an intention to do honour to myself alone, I shall only say that I am encouraged by the favour you have treated me with, to address these papers to your lordship. And I was the more ambitious of doing this, because a Philosophical Treatise could not so properly be addressed to any one as to a person of your lordship's character, who, to your other valuable distinctions, have added the knowledge and relish of Philosophy.

I am, with the greatest respect,

My Lord,

Your lordship's most obedient and

most humble servant,

GEORGE BERKELEY.

---

[1] William, fourth Lord Berkeley of Stratton, born about 1663, succeeded his brother in 1697, and died in 1741 at Bruton in Somersetshire. The Berkeleys of Stratton were descended from a younger son of Maurice, Lord Berkeley of Berkeley Castle, who died in 1326. His descendant, Sir John Berkeley of Bruton, a zealous Royalist, was created first Lord Berkeley of Stratton in 1658, and in 1669 became Lord Lieutenant of Ireland, an office which he held till 1672, when he was succeeded by the Earl of Essex (see Burke's *Extinct Peerages*). It is said that Bishop Berkeley's father, Collector at Belfast, was his natural son. The Bishop himself was introduced by Dean Swift, in 1713, to the Lord Berkeley of Stratton, to whom the *Dialogues* are dedicated, as 'a cousin of his Lordship.' The title of Berkeley of Stratton became extinct on the death of the fifth Lord in 1773.

THE PREFACE[1].

Though it seems the general opinion of the world, no less than the design of nature and providence, that the end of speculation be Practice, or the improvement and regulation of our lives and actions; yet those who are most addicted to speculative studies, seem as generally of another mind. And, indeed, if we consider the pains that have been taken to perplex the plainest things—that distrust of the senses, those doubts and scruples, those abstractions and refinements that occur in the very entrance of the sciences; it will not seem strange that men of leisure and curiosity should lay themselves out in fruitless disquisitions, without descending to the practical parts of life, or informing themselves in the more necessary and important parts of knowledge.

Upon the common principles of philosophers, we are not assured of the existence of things from their being perceived. And we are taught to distinguish their real nature from that which falls under our senses. Hence arise Scepticism and Paradoxes. It is not enough that we see and feel, that we taste and smell a thing: its true nature, its absolute external entity, is still concealed. For, though it be the fiction of our own brain, we have made it inaccessible to all our faculties. Sense is fallacious, reason defective. We spend our lives in doubting of those things which other men evidently know, and believing those things which they laugh at and despise.

In order, therefore, to divert the busy mind of man from vain researches, it seemed necessary to inquire into the source of its perplexities; and, if possible, to lay down such Principles as, by an easy solution of them, together with their own native evidence, may at once recommend themselves for genuine to the mind, and rescue it from those endless pursuits it is engaged in. Which, with a plain demonstration of the Immediate Providence of an all-seeing God, and the natural Immortality of the soul, should seem the readiest preparation, as well as the strongest motive, to the study and practice of virtue.

This design I proposed in the First Part of a treatise concerning the

[1] This Preface is omitted in the last edition of the *Dialogues*, and in all the collected editions of Berkeley's works.

Principles of Human Knowledge, published in the year 1710. But, before I proceed to publish the Second Part, I thought it requisite to treat more clearly and fully of certain Principles laid down in the First, and to place them in a new light—which is the business of the following *Dialogues*.

In this treatise, which does not presuppose in the reader any knowledge of what was contained in the former, it has been my aim to introduce the notions I advance into the mind in the most easy and familiar manner; especially because they carry with them a great opposition to the prejudices of philosophers, which have so far prevailed against the common sense and natural notions of mankind.

If the principles which I here endeavour to propagate are admitted for true, the consequences which, I think, evidently flow from thence are, that Atheism and Scepticism will be utterly destroyed, many intricate points made plain, great difficulties solved, several useless parts of science retrenched, speculation referred to practice, and men reduced from paradoxes to common sense.

And, although it may, perhaps, seem an uneasy reflection to some that, when they have taken a circuit through so many refined and unvulgar notions, they should at last come to think like other men; yet, methinks, this return to the simple dictates of nature, after having wandered through the wild mazes of philosophy, is not unpleasant. It is like coming home from a long voyage: a man reflects with pleasure on the many difficulties and perplexities he has passed through, sets his heart at ease, and enjoys himself with more satisfaction for the future.

As it was my intention to convince Sceptics and Infidels by reason, so it has been my endeavour strictly to observe the most rigid laws of reasoning. And, to an impartial reader, I hope it will be manifest that the sublime notion of a God, and the comfortable expectation of Immortality, do naturally arise from a close and methodical application of thought—whatever may be the result of that loose, rambling way, not altogether improperly termed Free-thinking, by certain libertines in thought, who can no more endure the restraints of logic than those of religion or government.

It will perhaps be objected to my design that, so far as it tends to ease the mind of difficult and useless inquiries, it can affect only a few speculative persons; but, if by their speculations rightly placed, the study of morality and the law of nature were brought more into fashion among men of parts and genius, the discouragements that draw to Scepticism removed, the measures of right and wrong accurately defined, and the principles of Natural Religion reduced into regular systems, as artfully disposed and clearly connected as those of some other sciences—there are grounds to think these effects would not only have a gradual influence in repairing the too much defaced sense of virtue in the world; but also, by shewing that such parts of revelation as lie within the reach of human inquiry are most agreeable to right reason, would dispose all prudent, unprejudiced persons to a modest and wary treatment of those sacred mysteries which are above the comprehension of our faculties.

It remains that I desire the reader to withhold his censure of these *Dialogues* till he has read them through. Otherwise he may lay them aside, in a mistake of their design, or on account of difficulties or objections which he would find answered in the sequel. A treatise of this nature would require to be once read over coherently, in order to comprehend its design, the proofs, solution of difficulties, and the connexion and disposition of its parts. If it be thought to deserve a second reading, this, I imagine, will make the entire scheme very plain; especially if recourse be had to an Essay I wrote some years since upon *Vision*, and the Treatise concerning the *Principles of Human Knowledge*—wherein divers notions advanced in these *Dialogues* are farther pursued, or placed in different lights, and other points handled which naturally tend to confirm and illustrate them.

THREE DIALOGUES

BETWEEN HYLAS AND PHILONOUS, IN OPPOSITION TO SCEPTICS AND ATHEISTS.

THE FIRST DIALOGUE.

Philonous. Good morrow, *Hylas*: I did not expect to find you abroad so early.

Hylas. It is indeed something unusual; but my thoughts were so taken up with a subject I was discoursing of last night, that finding I could not sleep, I resolved to rise and take a turn in the garden.

Phil. It happened well, to let you see what innocent and agreeable pleasures you lose every morning. Can there be a pleasanter time of the day, or a more delightful season of the year? That purple sky, those wild but sweet notes of birds, the fragrant bloom upon the trees and flowers, the gentle influence of the rising sun, these and a thousand nameless beauties of nature inspire the soul with secret transports; its faculties too being at this time fresh and lively, are fit for these meditations, which the solitude of a garden and tranquillity of the morning naturally dispose us to. But I am afraid I interrupt your thoughts: for you seemed very intent on something.

Hyl. It is true, I was, and shall be obliged to you if you will permit me to go on in the same vein; not that I would by any means deprive myself of your company, for my thoughts always flow more easily in conversation with a friend, than when I am alone: but my request is, that you would suffer me to impart my reflections to you.

Phil. With all my heart, it is what I should have requested myself if you had not prevented me.

Hyl. I was considering the odd fate of those men who have in all ages, through an affectation of being distinguished from the vulgar, or some unaccountable turn of thought, pretended either to believe nothing at all, or to believe the most extravagant things in the world[1]. This however might be borne, if their paradoxes and scepticism did not draw after them some consequences of general disadvantage to mankind. But the mischief lieth here; that when men of less leisure see them who are supposed to have spent their whole time in the pursuits of knowledge professing an entire ignorance of all things, or advancing such notions as are repugnant to plain and commonly received principles, they will be tempted to entertain suspicions concerning the most important truths, which they had hitherto held sacred and unquestionable..

Phil. I entirely agree with you, as to the ill tendency of the affected doubts of some philosophers, and fantastical conceits of others. I am even so far gone of late in this way of thinking, that I have quitted several of the sublime notions I had got in their schools for vulgar opinions. And I give it you on my word, since this revolt from metaphysical notions, to the plain dictates of nature and common sense[2], I find my understanding strangely enlightened, so that I can now easily comprehend a great many things which before were all mystery and riddle.

Hyl. I am glad to find there was nothing in the accounts I heard of you.

Phil. Pray, what were those?

Hyl. You were represented in last night's conversation, as one who maintained the most extravagant opinion that ever entered into the mind of man, to wit, that there is no such thing as *material substance* in the world.

Phil. That there is no such thing as what Philosophers call *material substance*, I am seriously persuaded: but, if I were made to see anything absurd or sceptical in this, I should then have the same reason to renounce this that I imagine I have now to reject the contrary opinion.

---

[1] Cf. *Principles of Human Knowledge*, Introduction. sect. I.

[2] Berkeley's philosophy is professedly a revolt from abstract notions of Matter, Substance, Cause, Space, and Time, to a reflective Common Sense.

Hyl. What! can anything be more fantastical, more repugnant to common sense, or a more manifest piece of Scepticism, than to believe there is no such thing as *matter*?

Phil. Softly, good *Hylas*. What if it should prove, that you, who hold there is, are, by virtue of that opinion, a greater sceptic, and maintain more paradoxes and repugnances to common sense, than I who believe no such thing?

Hyl. You may as soon persuade me, the part is greater than the whole, as that, in order to avoid absurdity and Scepticism, I should ever be obliged to give up my opinion in this point.

Phil. Well then, are you content to admit that opinion for true, which, upon examination, shall appear most agreeable to common sense, and remote from Scepticism?

Hyl. With all my heart. Since you are for raising disputes about the plainest things in nature, I am content for once to hear what you have to say.

Phil. Pray, *Hylas*, what do you mean by a *sceptic*?

Hyl. I mean what all men mean—one that doubts of everything.

Phil. He then who entertains no doubt concerning some particular point, with regard to that point cannot be thought a sceptic.

Hyl. I agree with you.

Phil. Whether doth doubting consist in embracing the affirmative or negative side of a question?

Hyl. In neither; for whoever understands English, cannot but know that *doubting* signifies a suspense between both.

Phil. He then that denieth any point, can no more be said to doubt of it, than he who affirmeth it with the same degree of assurance.

Hyl. True.

Phil. And, consequently, for such his denial is no more to be esteemed a sceptic than the other.

Hyl. I acknowledge it.

Phil. How cometh it to pass then, *Hylas*, that you pronounce me a *sceptic*, because I deny what you affirm, to wit, the existence of Matter? Since, for aught you can tell, I am as peremptory in my denial, as you in your affirmation.

Hyl. Hold, *Philonous*, I have been a little out in my definition; but every false step a man makes in discourse is not to be insisted on. I said indeed that a *sceptic* was one who doubted of everything; but I should have added, or who denies the reality and truth of things.

Phil. What things? Do you mean the principles and theorems of sciences? But these you know are universal intellectual notions, and consequently independent of Matter; the denial therefore of this doth not imply the denying them.

Hyl. I grant it. But are there no other things? What think you of distrusting the senses, of denying the real existence of sensible things, or pretending to know nothing of them. Is not this sufficient to denominate a man a *sceptic*?

Phil. Shall we therefore examine which of us it is that denies the reality of sensible things, or professes the greatest ignorance of them; since, if I take you rightly, he is to be esteemed the greatest *sceptic*?

Hyl. That is what I desire.

Phil. What mean you by Sensible Things?

Hyl. Those things which are perceived by the senses. Can you imagine that I mean anything else?

Phil. Pardon me, *Hylas*, if I am desirous clearly to apprehend your notions, since this may much shorten our inquiry. Suffer me then to ask you this farther question. Are those things only perceived by the senses which are perceived immediately? Or, may those things properly be said to be *sensible* which are perceived mediately, or not without the intervention of others?

Hyl. I do not sufficiently understand you.

Phil. In reading a book, what I immediately perceive are the letters, but mediately, or by means of these, are suggested to my mind the notions of God, virtue, truth, &c. Now, that the letters are truly sensible things, or perceived by sense, there is no doubt: but I would know whether you take the things suggested by them to be so too.

Hyl. No, certainly; it were absurd to think *God* or *virtue* sensible things, though they may be signified and suggested to the mind by sensible marks, with which they have an arbitrary connexion.

Phil. It seems then, that by *sensible things* you mean those only which can be perceived *immediately* by sense?

Hyl. Right.

Phil. Doth it not follow from this, that though I see one part of the sky red, and another blue, and that my reason doth thence evidently conclude there must be some cause of that diversity of colours, yet that cause cannot be said to be a sensible thing, or perceived by the sense of seeing?

Hyl. It doth.

Phil. In like manner, though I hear variety of sounds, yet I cannot be said to hear the causes of those sounds?

Hyl. You cannot.

Phil. And when by my touch I perceive a thing to be hot and heavy, I cannot say, with any truth or propriety, that I feel the cause of its heat or weight?

Hyl. To prevent any more questions of this kind, I tell you once for all, that by *sensible things* I mean those only which are perceived by sense, and that in truth the senses perceive nothing which they do not perceive immediately: for they make no inferences[3]. The deducing therefore of causes or occasions from effects and appearances, which alone are perceived by sense, entirely relates to reason.

Phil. This point then is agreed between us—that *sensible things are those only which are immediately perceived by sense.* You will farther inform me, whether we immediately perceive by sight anything beside light, and colours, and figures; or by hearing, anything but sounds; by the palate, anything beside tastes; by the smell, beside odours; or by the touch, more than tangible qualities.

Hyl. We do not.

Phil. It seems, therefore, that if you take away all sensible qualities, there remains nothing sensible?

Hyl. I grant it.

Phil. Sensible things therefore are nothing else but so many sensible qualities, or combinations of sensible qualities?

Hyl. Nothing else.

Phil. Heat then is a sensible thing?

Hyl. Certainly.

Phil. Doth the reality of sensible things consist in being

---

[3] Cf. *Theory of Vision Vindicated*, sect. 42.

perceived? or, is it something distinct from their being perceived, and that bears no relation to the mind?

Hyl. To *exist* is one thing, and to be *perceived* is another.

Phil. I speak with regard to sensible things only: and of these I ask, whether by their real existence you mean a subsistence exterior to the mind, and distinct from their being perceived?

Hyl. I mean a real absolute being, distinct from, and without any relation to their being perceived.

Phil. Heat therefore, if it be allowed a real being, must exist without the mind?

Hyl. It must.

Phil. Tell me, *Hylas*, is this real existence equally compatible to all degrees of heat, which we perceive; or is there any reason why we should attribute it to some, and deny it to others? and if there be, pray let me know that reason.

Hyl. Whatever degree of heat we perceive by sense, we may be sure the same exists in the object that occasions it.

Phil. What! the greatest as well as the least?

Hyl. I tell you, the reason is plainly the same in respect of both: they are both perceived by sense; nay, the greater degree of heat is more sensibly perceived; and consequently, if there is any difference, we are more certain of its real existence than we can be of the reality of a lesser degree.

Phil. But is not the most vehement and intense degree of heat a very great pain?

Hyl. No one can deny it.

Phil. And is any unperceiving thing capable of pain or pleasure?

Hyl. No certainly.

Phil. Is your material substance a senseless being, or a being endowed with sense and perception?

Hyl. It is senseless without doubt.

Phil. It cannot therefore be the subject of pain?

Hyl. By no means.

Phil. Nor consequently of the greatest heat perceived by sense, since you acknowledge this to be no small pain?

Hyl. I grant it.

Phil. What shall we say then of your external object; is it a material Substance, or no?

Hyl. It is a material substance with the sensible qualities inhering in it.

Phil. How then can a great heat exist in it, since you own it cannot in a material substance? I desire you would clear this point.

Hyl. Hold, *Philonous*, I fear I was out in yielding intense heat to be a pain. It should seem rather, that pain is something distinct from heat, and the consequence or effect of it.

Phil. Upon putting your hand near the fire, do you perceive one simple uniform sensation, or two distinct sensations?

Hyl. But one simple sensation.

Phil. Is not the heat immediately perceived?

Hyl. It is.

Phil. And the pain?

Hyl. True.

Phil. Seeing therefore they are both immediately perceived at the same time, and the fire affects you only with one simple, or uncompounded idea, it follows that this same simple idea is both the intense heat immediately perceived, and the pain; and, consequently, that the intense heat immediately perceived, is nothing distinct from a particular sort of pain.

Hyl. It seems so.

Phil. Again, try in your thoughts, *Hylas*, if you can conceive a vehement sensation to be without pain or pleasure.

Hyl. I cannot.

Phil. Or can you frame to yourself an idea of sensible pain or pleasure, in general, abstracted from every particular idea of heat, cold, tastes, smells? &c.

Hyl. I do not find that I can.

Phil. Doth it not therefore follow, that sensible pain is nothing distinct from those sensations or ideas—in an intense degree?

Hyl. It is undeniable; and, to speak the truth, I begin to suspect a very great heat cannot exist but in a mind perceiving it.

Phil. What! are you then in that *sceptical* state of suspense, between affirming and denying?

Hyl. I think I may be positive in the point. A very violent and painful heat cannot exist without the mind.

Phil. It hath not therefore, according to you, any real being?

Hyl. I own it.

Phil. Is it therefore certain, that there is no body in nature really hot?

Hyl. I have not denied there is any real heat in bodies. I only say, there is no such thing as an intense real heat.

Phil. But, did you not say before that all degrees of heat were equally real; or, if there was any difference, that the greater were more undoubtedly real than the lesser?

Hyl. True: but it was because I did not then consider the ground there is for distinguishing between them, which I now plainly see. And it is this:—because intense heat is nothing else but a particular kind of painful sensation; and pain cannot exist but in a perceiving being; it follows that no intense heat can really exist in an unperceiving corporeal substance. But this is no reason why we should deny heat in an inferior degree to exist in such a substance.

Phil. But how shall we be able to discern those degrees of heat which exist only in the mind from those which exist without it?

Hyl. That is no difficult matter. You know the least pain cannot exist unperceived; whatever, therefore, degree of heat is a pain exists only in the mind. But, as for all other degrees of heat, nothing obliges us to think the same of them.

Phil. I think you granted before that no unperceiving being was capable of pleasure, any more than of pain.

Hyl. I did.

Phil. And is not warmth, or a more gentle degree of heat than what causes uneasiness, a pleasure?

Hyl. What then?

Phil. Consequently, it cannot exist without the mind in an unperceiving substance, or body.

Hyl. So it seems.

Phil. Since, therefore, as well those degrees of heat that are not painful, as those that are, can exist only in a thinking substance; may we not conclude that external bodies are absolutely incapable of any degree of heat whatsoever?

Hyl. On second thoughts, I do not think it so evident that warmth is a pleasure as that a great degree of heat is a pain.

Phil. I do not pretend that warmth is as great a pleasure as heat is a pain. But, if you grant it to be even a small pleasure, it serves to make good my conclusion.

Hyl. I could rather call it an *indolence*. It seems to be nothing more than a privation of both pain and pleasure. And that such a quality or state as this may agree to an unthinking substance, I hope you will not deny.

Phil. If you are resolved to maintain that warmth, or a gentle degree of heat, is no pleasure, I know not how to convince you otherwise, than by appealing to your own sense. But what think you of cold?

Hyl. The same that I do of heat. An intense degree of cold is a pain; for to feel a very great cold, is to perceive a great uneasiness: it cannot therefore exist without the mind; but a lesser degree of cold may, as well as a lesser degree of heat.

Phil. Those bodies, therefore, upon whose application to our own, we perceive a moderate degree of heat, must be concluded to have a moderate degree of heat or warmth in them; and those, upon whose application we feel a like degree of cold, must be thought to have cold in them.

Hyl. They must.

Phil. Can any doctrine be true that necessarily leads a man into an absurdity?

Hyl. Without doubt it cannot.

Phil. Is it not an absurdity to think that the same thing should be at the same time both cold and warm?

Hyl. It is.

Phil. Suppose now one of your hands hot, and the other cold, and that they are both at once put into the same vessel of water, in an intermediate state; will not the water seem cold to one hand, and warm to the other[1]?

Hyl. It will.

Phil. Ought we not therefore, by your principles, to conclude it is really both cold and warm at the same time, that is, according to your own concession, to believe an absurdity?

Hyl. I confess it seems so.

Phil. Consequently, the principles themselves are false, since you have granted that no true principle leads to an absurdity.

Hyl. But, after all, can anything be more absurd than to say, *there is no heat in the fire?*

[1] Cf. *Principles of Human Knowledge*, sect. 14.

Phil. To make the point still clearer; tell me whether, in two cases exactly alike, we ought not to make the same judgment?

Hyl. We ought.

Phil. When a pin pricks your finger, doth it not rend and divide the fibres of your flesh?

Hyl. It doth.

Phil. And when a coal burns your finger, doth it any more?

Hyl. It doth not.

Phil. Since, therefore, you neither judge the sensation itself occasioned by the pin, nor anything like it to be in the pin; you should not, conformably to what you have now granted, judge the sensation occasioned by the fire, or anything like it, to be in the fire.

Hyl. Well, since it must be so, I am content to yield this point, and acknowledge that heat and cold are only sensations existing in our minds. But there still remain qualities enough to secure the reality of external things.

Phil. But what will you say, *Hylas*, if it shall appear that the case is the same with regard to all other sensible qualities[1], and that they can no more be supposed to exist without the mind, than heat and cold?

Hyl. Then indeed you will have done something to the purpose; but that is what I despair of seeing proved.

Phil. Let us examine them in order. What think you of *tastes*—do they exist without the mind, or no?

Hyl. Can any man in his senses doubt whether sugar is sweet, or wormwood bitter?

Phil. Inform me, *Hylas.* Is a sweet taste a particular kind of pleasure or pleasant sensation, or is it not?

Hyl. It is.

Phil. And is not bitterness some kind of uneasiness or pain?

Hyl. I grant it.

Phil. If therefore sugar and wormwood are unthinking corporeal substances existing without the mind, how can sweetness and bitterness, that is, pleasure and pain, agree to them?

Hyl. Hold, *Philonous*, I now see what it was deluded me all this time. You asked whether heat and cold, sweetness and bitterness, were not particular sorts of pleasure and pain; to which I answered simply, that they were. Whereas I should

---

[1] Cf. *Principles of Human Knowledge*, sect. 14, 15.

have thus distinguished:—those qualities, as perceived by us, are pleasures or pains; but not as existing in the external objects. We must not therefore conclude absolutely, that there is no heat in the fire, or sweetness in the sugar, but only that heat or sweetness, as perceived by us, are not in the fire or sugar. What say you to this?

Phil. I say it is nothing to the purpose. Our discourse proceeded altogether concerning sensible things, which you defined to be, *the things we immediately perceive by our senses.* Whatever other qualities, therefore, you speak of, as distinct from these, I know nothing of them, neither do they at all belong to the point in dispute. You may, indeed, pretend to have discovered certain qualities which you do not perceive, and assert those insensible qualities exist in fire and sugar. But what use can be made of this to your present purpose, I am at a loss to conceive. Tell me then once more, do you acknowledge that heat and cold, sweetness and bitterness (meaning those qualities which are perceived by the senses), do not exist without the mind?

Hyl. I see it is to no purpose to hold out, so I give up the cause as to those mentioned qualities. Though I profess it sounds oddly, to say that sugar is not sweet.

Phil. But, for your farther satisfaction, take this along with you: that which at other times seems sweet, shall, to a distempered palate, appear bitter. And, nothing can be plainer than that divers persons perceive different tastes in the same food; since that which one man delights in, another abhors. And how could this be, if the taste was something really inherent in the food?

Hyl. I acknowledge I know not how.

Phil. In the next place, *odours* are to be considered. 'And, with regard to these, I would fain know whether what hath been said of tastes doth not exactly agree to them? Are they not so many pleasing or displeasing sensations?

Hyl. They are.

Phil. Can you then conceive it possible that they should exist in an unperceiving thing?

Hyl. I cannot.

Phil. Or, can you imagine that filth and ordure affect those brute animals that feed on them out of choice, with the same smells which we perceive in them?

Hyl. By no means.

Phil. May we not therefore conclude of smells, as of the other forementioned qualities, that they cannot exist in any but a perceiving substance or mind?

Hyl. I think so.

Phil. Then as to *sounds*, what must we think of them: are they accidents really inherent in external bodies, or not?

Hyl. That they inhere not in the sonorous bodies is plain from hence; because a bell struck in the exhausted receiver of an airpump sends forth no sound. The air, therefore, must be thought the subject of sound.

Phil. What reason is there for that, *Hylas?*

Hyl. Because, when any motion is raised in the air, we perceive a sound greater or lesser, according to the air's motion; but without some motion in the air, we never hear any sound at all.

Phil. And granting that we never hear a sound but when some motion is produced in the air, yet I do not see how you can infer from thence, that the sound itself is in the air.

Hyl. It is this very motion in the external air that produces in the mind the sensation of *sound*. For, striking on the drum of the ear, it causeth a vibration, which by the auditory nerves being communicated to the brain, the soul is thereupon affected with the sensation called *sound*.

Phil. What! is sound then a sensation?

Hyl. I tell you, as perceived by us, it is a particular sensation in the mind.

Phil. And can any sensation exist without the mind?

Hyl. No, certainly.

Phil. How then can sound, being a sensation, exist in the air, if by the *air* you mean a senseless substance existing without the mind?

Hyl. You must distinguish, *Philonous*, between sound as it is perceived by us, and as it is in itself; or (which is the same thing) between the sound we immediately perceive, and that which exists without us. The former, indeed, is a particular kind of sensation, but the latter is merely a vibrative or undulatory motion in the air.

Phil. I thought I had already obviated that distinction, by the answer I gave when you were applying it in a like case before.

But, to say no more of that, are you sure then that sound is really nothing but motion?

Hyl. I am.

Phil. Whatever therefore agrees to real sound, may with truth be attributed to motion?

Hyl. It may.

Phil. It is then good sense to speak of *motion* as of a thing that is *loud, sweet, acute, or grave*.

Hyl. I see you are resolved not to understand me. Is it not evident those accidents or modes belong only to sensible sound, or *sound* in the common acceptation of the word, but not to *sound* in the real and philosophic sense; which, as I just now told you, is nothing but a certain motion of the air?

Phil. It seems then there are two sorts of sound—the one vulgar, or that which is heard, the other philosophical and real?

Hyl. Even so.

Phil. And the latter consists in motion?

Hyl. I told you so before.

Phil. Tell me, *Hylas*, to which of the senses, think you, the idea of motion belongs? to the hearing?

Hyl. No, certainly; but to the sight and touch.

Phil. It should follow then, that, according to you, real sounds may possibly be *seen* or *felt*, but never *heard*.

Hyl. Look you, *Philonous*, you may, if you please, make a jest of my opinion, but that will not alter the truth of things. I own, indeed, the inferences you draw me into, sound something oddly; but common language, you know, is framed by, and for the use of the vulgar: we must not therefore wonder, if expressions adapted to exact philosophic notions seem uncouth and out of the way.

Phil. Is it come to that? I assure you, I imagine myself to have gained no small point, since you make so light of departing from common phrases and opinions; it being a main part of our inquiry, to examine whose notions are widest of the common road, and most repugnant to the general sense of the world. But, can you think it no more than a philosophical paradox, to say that *real sounds are never heard*, and that the idea of them is obtained by some other sense? And is there nothing in this contrary to nature and the truth of things?

Hyl. To deal ingenuously, I do not like it. And, after the concessions already made, I had as well grant that sounds too have no real being without the mind.

Phil. And I hope you will make no difficulty to acknowledge the same of *colours*.

Hyl. Pardon me: the case of colours is very different. Can anything be plainer than that we see them on the objects?

Phil. The objects you speak of are, I suppose, corporeal Substances existing without the mind?

Hyl. They are.

Phil. And have true and real colours inhering in them?

Hyl. Each visible object hath that colour which we see in it.

Phil. How! is there anything visible but what we perceive by sight?

Hyl. There is not.

Phil. And, do we perceive anything by sense which we do not perceive immediately?

Hyl. How often must I be obliged to repeat the same thing? I tell you, we do not.

Phil. Have patience, good *Hylas*, and tell me once more, whether there is anything immediately perceived by the senses, except sensible qualities. I know you asserted there was not; but I would now be informed, whether you still persist in the same opinion.

Hyl. I do.

Phil. Pray, is your corporeal substance either a sensible quality, or made up of sensible qualities?

Hyl. What a question that is! who ever thought it was?

Phil. My reason for asking was, because in saying, *each visible object hath that colour which we see in it*, you make visible objects to be corporeal substances; which implies either that corporeal substances are sensible qualities, or else that there is something beside sensible qualities perceived by sight: but, as this point was formerly agreed between us, and is still maintained by you, it is a clear consequence, that your corporeal substance is nothing distinct from sensible qualities.

Hyl. You may draw as many absurd consequences as you please, and endeavour to perplex the plainest things; but you shall never persuade me out of my senses. I clearly understand my own meaning.

Phil. I wish you would make me understand it too. But, since you are unwilling to have your notion of corporeal substance examined, I shall urge that point no farther. Only be pleased to let me know, whether the same colours which we see exist in external bodies, or some other.

Hyl. The very same.

Phil. What! are then the beautiful red and purple we see on yonder clouds really in them? Or do you imagine they have in themselves any other form than that of a dark mist or vapour?

Hyl. I must own, *Philonous*, those colours are not really in the clouds as they seem to be at this distance. They are only apparent colours.

Phil. Apparent call you them? how shall we distinguish these apparent colours from real?

Hyl. Very easily. Those are to be thought apparent which, appearing only at a distance, vanish upon a nearer approach.

Phil. And those, I suppose, are to be thought real which are discovered by the most near and exact survey.

Hyl. Right.

Phil. Is the nearest and exactest survey made by the help of a microscope, or by the naked eye?

Hyl. By a microscope, doubtless.

Phil. But a microscope often discovers colours in an object different from those perceived by the unassisted sight. And, in case we had microscopes magnifying to any assigned degree, it is certain that no object whatsoever, viewed through them, would appear in the same colour which it exhibits to the naked eye.

Hyl. And what will you conclude from all this? You cannot argue that there are really and naturally no colours on objects: because by artificial managements they may be altered, or made to vanish.

Phil. I think it may evidently be concluded from your own concessions, that all the colours we see with our naked eyes are only apparent as those on the clouds, since they vanish upon a more close and accurate inspection which is afforded us by a microscope. Then, as to what you say by way of prevention: I ask you whether the real and natural state of an object is better discovered by a very sharp and piercing sight, or by one which is less sharp?

Hyl. By the former without doubt.

Phil. Is it not plain from *Dioptrics* that microscopes make the sight more penetrating, and represent objects as they would appear to the eye in case it were naturally endowed with a most exquisite sharpness?

Hyl. It is.

Phil. Consequently the microscopical representation is to be thought that which best sets forth the real nature of the thing, or what it is in itself. The colours, therefore, by it perceived are more genuine and real than those perceived otherwise.

Hyl. I confess there is something in what you say.

Phil. Besides, it is not only possible but manifest, that there actually are animals whose eyes are by nature framed to perceive those things which by reason of their minuteness escape our sight. What think you of those inconceivably small animals perceived by glasses? must we suppose they are all stark blind? Or, in case they see, can it be imagined their sight hath not the same use in preserving their bodies from injuries, which appears in that of all other animals? And if it hath, is it not evident they must see particles less than their own bodies, which will present them with a far different view in each object from that which strikes our senses[a]? Even our own eyes do not always represent objects to us after the same manner. In the *jaundice* every one knows that all things seem yellow. Is it not therefore highly probable those animals in whose eyes we discern a very different texture from that of ours, and whose bodies abound with different humours, do not see the same colours in every object that we do? From all which, should it not seem to follow that all colours are equally apparent, and that none of those which we perceive are really inherent in any outward object?

Hyl. It should.

Phil. The point will be past all doubt, if you consider that, in case colours were real properties or affections inherent in external bodies, they could admit of no alteration without some change wrought in the very bodies themselves: but, is it not evident from what hath been said that, upon the use of microscopes, upon a change happening in the humours of the eye, or a variation of distance, without any manner of real alteration in the thing itself,

---

[a] Cf. *New Theory of Vision*, sect. 80—86.

the colours of any object are either changed, or totally disappear? Nay, all other circumstances remaining the same, change but the situation of some objects, and they shall present different colours to the eye. The same thing happens upon viewing an object in various degrees of light. And what is more known than that the same bodies appear differently coloured by candle-light from what they do in the open day? Add to these the experiment of a prism which, separating the heterogeneous rays of light, alters the colour of any object, and will cause the whitest to appear of a deep blue or red to the naked eye. And now tell me whether you are still of opinion that every body hath its true real colour inhering in it; and, if you think it hath, I would fain know farther from you, what certain distance and position of the object, what peculiar texture and formation of the eye, what degree or kind of light is necessary for ascertaining that true colour, and distinguishing it from apparent ones.

Hyl. I own myself entirely satisfied, that they are all equally apparent, and that there is no such thing as colour really inhering in external bodies, but that it is altogether in the light. And what confirms me in this opinion is that in proportion to the light colours are still more or less vivid; and if there be no light, then are there no colours perceived. Besides, allowing there are colours on external objects, yet, how is it possible for us to perceive them? For no external body affects the mind, unless it acts first on our organs of sense. But the only action of bodies is motion; and motion cannot be communicated otherwise than by impulse. A distant object therefore cannot act on the eye, nor consequently make itself or its properties perceivable to the soul. Whence it plainly follows that it is immediately some contiguous substance, which, operating on the eye, occasions a perception of colours: and such is light.

Phil. How! is light then a substance?

Hyl. I tell you, *Philonous*, external light is nothing but a thin fluid substance, whose minute particles being agitated with a brisk motion, and in various manners reflected from the different surfaces of outward objects to the eyes, communicate different motions to the optic nerves; which, being propagated to the brain, cause therein various impressions; and these are attended with the sensations of red, blue, yellow, &c.

Phil. It seems then the light doth no more than shake the optic nerves.

Hyl. Nothing else.

Phil. And, consequent to each particular motion of the nerves, the mind is affected with a sensation, which is some particular colour.

Hyl. Right.

Phil. And these sensations have no existence without the mind.

Hyl. They have not.

Phil. How then do you affirm that colours are in the light; since by *light* you understand a corporeal substance external to the mind?

Hyl. Light and colours, as immediately perceived by us, I grant cannot exist without the mind. But, in themselves they are only the motions and configurations of certain insensible particles of matter.

Phil. Colours then, in the vulgar sense, or taken for the immediate objects of sight, cannot agree to any but a perceiving substance.

Hyl. That is what I say.

Phil. Well then, since you give up the point as to those sensible qualities which are alone thought colours by all mankind beside; you may hold what you please with regard to those invisible ones of the philosophers. It is not my business to dispute about them; only I would advise you to bethink yourself, whether, considering the inquiry we are upon, it be prudent for you to affirm—*the red and blue which we see are not real colours, but certain unknown motions and figures, which no man ever did or can see, are truly so.* Are not these shocking notions, and are not they subject to as many ridiculous inferences, as those you were obliged to renounce before in the case of sounds?

Hyl. I frankly own, *Philonous*, that it is in vain to stand out any longer. Colours, sounds, tastes, in a word all those termed *secondary qualities*, have certainly no existence without the mind. But, by this acknowledgment I must not be supposed to derogate anything from the reality of Matter or external objects; seeing it is no more than several philosophers maintain, who nevertheless are the farthest imaginable from denying Matter. For the clearer understanding of this, you must know sensible qualities are by philosophers divided into *primary* and *secondary*[7]. The former are Extension, Figure, Solidity, Gravity, Motion, and Rest. And these they hold exist really in bodies. The latter are those above enumerated; or, briefly, all sensible qualities beside the Primary, which they assert are only so many sensations or ideas existing nowhere but in the mind. But all this, I doubt not, you are apprised of. For my part, I have been a long time sensible there was such an opinion current among philosophers, but was never thoroughly convinced of its truth until now.

Phil. You are still then of opinion that *extension* and *figure* are inherent in external unthinking substances?

Hyl. I am.

Phil. But what if the same arguments which are brought against Secondary Qualities will hold good against these also?

Hyl. Why then I shall be obliged to think, they too exist only in the mind.

Phil. Is it your opinion the very figure and extension which you perceive by sense exist in the outward object or material substance?

Hyl. It is.

Phil. Have all other animals as good grounds to think the same of the figure and extension which they see and feel?

Hyl. Without doubt, if they have any thought at all.

Phil. Answer me, *Hylas*. Think you the senses were bestowed upon all animals for their preservation and well-being in life? or were they given to men alone for this end?

Hyl. I make no question but they have the same use in all other animals.

Phil. If so, is it not necessary they should be enabled by them to perceive their own limbs, and those bodies which are capable of harming them?

Hyl. Certainly.

Phil. A mite therefore must be supposed to see his own foot, and things equal or even less than it, as bodies of some considerable dimension; though at the same time they appear to you scarce discernible, or at best as so many visible points[8]?

Hyl. I cannot deny it.

---

[7] On Primary and Secondary Qualities of Matter, cf. *Principles of Human Knowledge*, sect. 9; see also Locke's *Essay*, Bk. II. ch. 8, and Hamilton's edition of Reid, pp. 313—318, also Note D. pp. 825—875.

[8] Cf. *New Theory of Vision*, sect. 80.

Phil. And to creatures less than the mite they will seem yet larger?

Hyl. They will.

Phil. Insomuch that what you can hardly discern will to another extremely minute animal appear as some huge mountain?

Hyl. All this I grant.

Phil. Can one and the same thing be at the same time in itself of different dimensions?

Hyl. That were absurd to imagine.

Phil. But, from what you have laid down it follows that both the extension by you perceived, and that perceived by the mite itself, as likewise all those perceived by lesser animals, are each of them the true extension of the mite's foot; that is to say, by your own principles, you are led into an absurdity.

Hyl. There seems to be some difficulty in the point.

Phil. Again, have you not acknowledged that no real inherent property of any object can be changed without some change in the thing itself?

Hyl. I have.

Phil. But, as we approach to or recede from an object, the visible extension varies, being at one distance ten or a hundred times greater than at another. Doth it not therefore follow from hence likewise that it is not really inherent in the object?

Hyl. I own I am at a loss what to think.

Phil. Your judgment will soon be determined, if you will venture to think as freely concerning this quality as you have done concerning the rest. Was it not admitted as a good argument, that neither heat nor cold was in the water, because it seemed warm to one hand and cold to the other?

Hyl. It was.

Phil. Is it not the very same reasoning to conclude, there is no extension or figure in an object, because to one eye it shall seem little, smooth, and round, when at the same time it appears to the other, great, uneven, and angular?

Hyl. The very same. But does this latter fact ever happen?

Phil. You may at any time make the experiment, by looking with one eye bare, and with the other through a microscope.

Hyl. I know not how to maintain it, and yet I am loath to give up *extension*, I see so many odd consequences following upon such a concession.

Phil. Odd, say you? After the concessions already made, I hope you will stick at nothing for its oddness. [*"But, on the other hand, should it not seem very odd, if the general reasoning which includes all other sensible qualities did not also include extension? If it be allowed that no idea nor anything like an idea can exist in an unperceiving substance, then surely it follows that no figure or mode of extension, which we can either perceive or imagine, or have any idea of, can be really inherent in Matter; not to mention the peculiar difficulty there must be in conceiving a material substance, prior to and distinct from extension, to be the *substratum* of extension. Be the sensible quality what it will—figure, or sound, or colour; it seems alike impossible it should subsist in that which doth not perceive it.*]

Hyl. I give up the point for the present, reserving still a right to retract my opinion, in case I shall hereafter discover any false step in my progress to it.

Phil. That is a right you cannot be denied. Figures and extension being despatched, we proceed next to *motion*. Can a real motion in any external body be at the same time both very swift and very slow?

Hyl. It cannot.

Phil. Is not the motion of a body swift in a reciprocal proportion to the time it takes up in describing any given space? Thus a body that describes a mile in an hour moves three times faster than it would in case it described only a mile in three hours.

Hyl. I agree with you.

Phil. And is not time measured by the succession of ideas in our minds?

Hyl. It is.

Phil. And is it not possible ideas should succeed one another twice as fast in your mind as they do in mine, or in that of some spirit of another kind?

Hyl. I own it.

Phil. Consequently, the same body may to another seem to perform its motion over any space in half the time that it doth to you. And the same reasoning will hold as to any other proportion: that is to say, according to your principles (since the motions perceived are both really in the object) it is possible one and the

---

* What follows, within brackets, is not contained in the first and second editions.

same body shall be really moved the same way at once, both very swift and very slow. How is this consistent either with common sense, or with what you just now granted?

Hyl. I have nothing to say to it.

Phil. Then as for *solidity*, either you do not mean any sensible quality by that word, and so it is beside our inquiry: or if you do, it must be either hardness or resistance. But both the one and the other are plainly relative to our senses: it being evident that what seems hard to one animal may appear soft to another, who hath greater force and firmness of limbs. Nor is it less plain that the resistance I feel is not in the body.

Hyl. I own the very sensation of resistance, which is all you immediately perceive, is not in the *body*; but the cause of that sensation is.

Phil. But the causes of our sensations are not things immediately perceived, and therefore not sensible. This point I thought had been already determined.

Hyl. I own it was; but you will pardon me if I seem a little embarrassed: I know not how to quit my old notions.

Phil. To help you out, do but consider that if *extension* be once acknowledged to have no existence without the mind, the same must necessarily be granted of motion, solidity, and gravity—since they all evidently suppose extension[10]. It is therefore superfluous to inquire particularly concerning each of them. In denying extension, you have denied them all to have any real existence.

Hyl. I wonder, Philonous, if what you say be true, why those philosophers who deny the Secondary Qualities any real existence, should yet attribute it to the Primary. If there is no difference between them, how can this be accounted for?

Phil. It is not my business to account for every opinion of the philosophers. But, among other reasons which may be assigned for this, it seems probable that pleasure and pain being rather annexed to the former than the latter may be one. Heat and cold, tastes and smells, have something more vividly pleasing or disagreeable than the ideas of extension, figure, and motion affect us with. And, it being too visibly absurd to hold that pain or pleasure can be in an unperceiving Substance, men are more easily weaned from believing the external existence of the Secondary

---

[10] What really is Berkeley's theory of the mutual relation of extension and motion?

than the Primary Qualities. You will be satisfied there is something in this, if you recollect the difference you made between an intense and more moderate degree of heat; allowing the one a real existence, while you denied it to the other. But, after all, there is no rational ground for that distinction; for, surely an indifferent sensation is as truly *a sensation* as one more pleasing or painful; and consequently should not any more than they be supposed to exist in an unthinking subject.

Hyl. It is just come into my head, Philonous, that I have somewhere heard of a distinction between absolute and sensible extension[11]. Now, though it be acknowledged that *great* and *small*, consisting merely in the relation which other extended beings have to the parts of our own bodies, do not really inhere in the Substances themselves; yet nothing obliges us to hold the same with regard to *absolute extension*, which is something abstracted from *great* and *small*, from this or that particular magnitude or figure. So likewise as to motion; *swift* and *slow* are altogether relative to the succession of ideas in our own minds. But, it doth not follow, because those modifications of motion exist not without the mind, that therefore absolute motion abstracted from them doth not.

Phil. Pray what is it that distinguishes one motion, or one part of extension, from another? Is it not something sensible, as some degree of swiftness or slowness, some certain magnitude or figure peculiar to each?

Hyl. I think so.

Phil. These qualities, therefore, stripped of all sensible properties, are without all specific and numerical differences, as the schools call them.

Hyl. They are.

Phil. That is to say, they are extension in general, and motion in general.

Hyl. Let it be so.

Phil. But it is a universally received maxim that *Everything which exists is particular*[12]. How then can motion in general, or extension in general, exist in any corporeal Substance?

---

[11] Cf. *New Theory of Vision*, sect. 122—116; *Principles of Human Knowledge*, sect. 113, &c.; *Siris*, sect. 270, &c.

[12] Cf. *Principles of Human Knowledge*, Introduction, sect. 15.

Hyl. I will take time to solve your difficulty.

Phil. But I think the point may be speedily decided. Without doubt you can tell whether you are able to frame this or that idea. Now I am content to put our dispute on this issue. If you can frame in your thoughts a distinct abstract idea of motion or extension; divested of all those sensible modes, as swift and slow, great and small, round and square, and the like, which are acknowledged to exist only in the mind, I will then yield the point you contend for. But, if you cannot, it will be unreasonable on your side to insist any longer upon what you have no notion of.

Hyl. To confess ingenuously, I cannot.

Phil. Can you even separate the ideas of extension and motion from the ideas of all those qualities which they who make the distinction term *secondary*?

Hyl. What! is it not an easy matter to consider extension and motion by themselves, abstracted from all other sensible qualities? Pray how do the mathematicians treat of them?

Phil. I acknowledge, *Hylas*, it is not difficult to form general propositions and reasonings about those qualities, without mentioning any other; and, in this sense, to consider or treat of them abstractedly. But, how doth it follow that, because I can pronounce the word *motion* by itself, I can form the idea of it in my mind exclusive of body? Or, because theorems may be made of extension and figures, without any mention of *great* or *small*, or any other sensible mode or quality, that therefore it is possible such an abstract idea of extension, without any particular [13]size or figure, or sensible quality, should be distinctly formed, and apprehended by the mind? Mathematicians treat of quantity, without regarding what other sensible qualities it is attended with, as being altogether indifferent to their demonstrations. But, when laying aside the words, they contemplate the bare ideas, I believe you will find, they are not the pure abstracted ideas of extension[14].

Hyl. But what say you to *pure intellect*? May not abstracted ideas be framed by that faculty?

Phil. Since I cannot frame abstract ideas at all[15], it is plain

---

[13] 'Size, or figure, or sensible quality'— 'size, colour, &c.,' in the first and second editions.

[14] Cf. *Principles of Human Knowledge,* sect. 118—132.

[15] Cf. *New Theory of Vision,* sect. 123— 126; *Principles of Human Knowledge,* Introduction, sect. 10—20.

I cannot frame them by the help of *pure intellect*; whatsoever faculty you understand by those words. Besides, not to inquire into the nature of pure intellect and its spiritual objects, as *virtue, reason, God,* or the like, thus much seems manifest—that sensible things are only to be perceived by sense, or represented by the imagination. Figures, therefore, and extension, being originally perceived by sense, do not belong to pure intellect: but, for your farther satisfaction, try if you can frame the idea of any figure, abstracted from all particularities of size, or even from other sensible qualities.

Hyl. Let me think a little —— I do not find that I can.

Phil. And can you think it possible that should really exist in nature which implies a repugnancy in its conception?

Hyl. By no means.

Phil. Since therefore it is impossible even for the mind to disunite the ideas of extension and motion from all other sensible qualities, doth it not follow, that where the one exist there necessarily the other exist likewise?

Hyl. It should seem so.

Phil. Consequently, the very same arguments which you admitted as conclusive against the Secondary Qualities are, without any farther application of force, against the Primary too. Besides, if you will trust your senses, is it not plain all sensible qualities coexist, or to them appear as being in the same place? Do they ever represent a motion, or figure, as being divested of all other visible and tangible qualities?

Hyl. You need say no more on this head. I am free to own, if there be no secret error or oversight in our proceedings hitherto, that all sensible qualities are alike to be denied existence without the mind[16]. But, my fear is that I have been too liberal in my former concessions, or overlooked some fallacy or other. In short, I did not take time to think.

Phil. For that matter, *Hylas*, you may take what time you please in reviewing the progress of our inquiry. You are at liberty to recover any slips you might have made, or offer whatever you have omitted which makes for your first opinion.

Hyl. One great oversight I take to be this—that I did not

---

[16] 'without the mind,' i.e. unperceived and unconceived—out of relation to any mind—unintelligible. Cf. *Principles of Human Knowledge,* sect. 3.

sufficiently distinguish the *object* from the *sensation*[17]. Now, though this latter may not exist without the mind, yet it will not thence follow that the former cannot.

Phil. What object do you mean? The object of the senses?

Hyl. The same.

Phil. It is then immediately perceived?

Hyl. Right.

Phil. Make me to understand the difference between what is immediately perceived, and a sensation.

Hyl. The sensation I take to be an act of the mind perceiving; besides which, there is something perceived; and this I call the *object*. For example, there is red and yellow on that tulip. But then the act of perceiving those colours is in me only, and not in the tulip.

Phil. What tulip do you speak of? Is it that which you see?

Hyl. The same.

Phil. And what do you see beside colour, figure, and extension[18]?

Hyl. Nothing.

Phil. What you would say then is that the red and yellow are coexistent with the extension; is it not?

Hyl. That is not all; I would say they have a real existence without the mind, in some unthinking substance.

Phil. That the colours are really in the tulip which I see is manifest. Neither can it be denied that this tulip may exist independent of your mind or mine; but, that any immediate object of the senses—that is, any idea, or combination of ideas—should exist in an unthinking substance, or exterior to all minds, is in itself an evident contradiction. Nor can I imagine how this follows from what you said just now, to wit, that the red and yellow were on the tulip *you saw*, since you do not pretend to *see* that unthinking substance.

Hyl. You have an artful way, *Philonous*, of diverting our inquiry from the subject.

Phil. I see you have no mind to be pressed that way. To return then to your distinction between *sensation* and *object*; if I take you right, you distinguish in every perception two things, the one an action of the mind, the other not.

---

[17] So Reid's *Inquiry*, ch. II. sect. 8, 9; *Essays on the Intellectual Powers*, II. ch. 16. Cf. *New Theory of Vision Vindicated*, sect. 8, &c.

[18] i.e. extended and figured colour. Cf. *New Theory of Vision*, sect. 43, &c.

Hyl. True.

Phil. And this action cannot exist in, or belong to, any unthinking thing[10]; but, whatever beside is implied in a perception may?

Hyl. That is my meaning.

Phil. So that if there was a perception without any act of the mind, it were possible such a perception should exist in an unthinking substance?

Hyl. I grant it. But it is impossible there should be such a perception.

Phil. When is the mind said to be active?

Hyl. When it produces, puts an end to, or changes, anything.

Phil. Can the mind produce, discontinue, or change anything, but by an act of the will?

Hyl. It cannot.

Phil. The mind therefore is to be accounted *active* in its perceptions so far forth as *volitions* is included in them?

Hyl. It is.

Phil. In plucking this flower I am active; because I do it by the motion of my hand, which was consequent upon my volition; so likewise in applying it to my nose. But is either of these smelling?

Hyl. No.

Phil. I act too in drawing the air through my nose; because my breathing so rather than otherwise is the effect of my volition. But neither can this be called *smelling*: for, if it were, I should smell every time I breathed in that manner?

Hyl. True.

Phil. Smelling then is somewhat consequent to all this?

Hyl. It is.

Phil. But I do not find my will concerned any farther. Whatever more there is—as that I perceive such a particular smell, or any smell at all—this is independent of my will, and therein I am altogether passive. Do you find it otherwise with you, Hylas?

Hyl. No, the very same.

Phil. Then, as to seeing, is it not in your power to open your eyes, or keep them shut; to turn them this or that way?

Hyl. Without doubt.

Phil. But, doth it in like manner depend on your will that in looking on this flower you perceive *white* rather than any other

---

[10] Cf. *Principles of Human Knowledge*, sect. 25, 26.

colour? Or, directing your open eyes towards yonder part of the heaven, can you avoid seeing the sun? Or is light or darkness the effect of your volition?

Hyl. No certainly.

Phil. You are then in these respects altogether passive?

Hyl. I am.

Phil. Tell me now, whether *seeing* consists in perceiving light and colours, or in opening and turning the eyes?

Hyl. Without doubt, in the former.

Phil. Since therefore you are in the very perception of light and colours altogether passive, what is become of that action you were speaking of as an ingredient in every sensation? And, doth it not follow from your own concessions, that the perception of light and colours, including no action in it, may exist in an unperceiving substance? And is not this a plain contradiction?

Hyl. I know not what to think of it.

Phil. Besides, since you distinguish the *active* and *passive* in every perception, you must do it in that of pain. But how is it possible that pain, be it as little active as you please, should exist in an unperceiving substance? In short, do but consider the point, and then confess ingenuously, whether light and colours, tastes, sounds, &c. are not all equally passions or sensations in the soul. You may indeed call them *external objects*, and give them in words what subsistence you please. But, examine your own thoughts, and then tell me whether it be not as I say?

Hyl. I acknowledge, *Philonous*, that, upon a fair observation of what passes in my mind, I can discover nothing else but that I am a thinking being, affected with variety of sensations; neither is it possible to conceive how a sensation should exist in an unperceiving substance.—But then, on the other hand, when I look on sensible things in a different view, considering them as so many modes and qualities, I find it necessary to suppose a material *substratum*, without which they cannot be conceived to exist[20].

Phil. Material substratum call you it? Pray, by which of your senses came you acquainted with that being?

Hyl. It is not itself sensible; its modes and qualities only being perceived by the senses.

---

[20] Cf. *Principles of Human Knowledge*, sect. 16-20. &c.—The objections to material Substance, and the disputes to which it had given rise, had been acutely presented by Bayle, in various articles of his Dictionary, some years before.

Phil. I presume then it was by reflection and reason you obtained the idea of it?

Hyl. I do not pretend to any proper positive idea of it. However, I conclude it exists, because qualities cannot be conceived to exist without a support.

Phil. It seems then you have only a relative notion of it, or that you conceive it not otherwise than by conceiving the relation it bears to sensible qualities?

Hyl. Right.

Phil. Be pleased therefore to let me know wherein that relation consists.

Hyl. Is it not sufficiently expressed in the term *substratum*, or *substance*?

Phil. If so, the word *substratum* should import that it is spread under the sensible qualities or accidents?

Hyl. True.

Phil. And consequently under extension?

Hyl. I own it.

Phil. It is therefore somewhat in its own nature entirely distinct from extension?

Hyl. I tell you, extension is only a mode, and Matter is something that supports modes. And is it not evident the thing supported is different from the thing supporting?

Phil. So that something distinct from, and exclusive of, extension is supposed to be the *substratum* of extension?

Hyl. Just so.

Phil. Answer me, *Hylas.* Can a thing be spread without extension? or is not the idea of extension necessarily included in *spreading*?

Hyl. It is.

Phil. Whatsoever therefore you suppose spread under anything must have in itself an extension distinct from the extension of that thing under which it is spread?

Hyl. It must.

Phil. Consequently, every corporeal substance being the *substratum* of extension must have in itself another extension, by which it is qualified to be a *substratum*: and so on to infinity? And I ask whether this be not absurd in itself, and repugnant to what you granted just now, to wit, that the *substratum* was something distinct from and exclusive of extension?

Hyl. Aye but, *Philonous*, you take me wrong. I do not mean that Matter is *spread* in a gross literal sense under extension. The word *substratum* is used only to express in general the same thing with *substance*.

Phil. Well then, let us examine the relation implied in the term *substance*. Is it not that it stands under accidents?

Hyl. The very same.

Phil. But, that one thing may stand under or support another, must it not be extended?

Hyl. It must.

Phil. Is not therefore this supposition liable to the same absurdity with the former?

Hyl. You still take things in a strict literal sense; that is not fair, *Philonous*.

Phil. I am not for imposing any sense on your words: you are at liberty to explain them as you please. Only, I beseech you, make me understand something by them. You tell me Matter supports or stands under accidents. How! is it as your legs support your body?

Hyl. No; that is the literal sense.

Phil. Pray let me know any sense, literal or not literal, that you understand it in. . . . How long must I wait for an answer, *Hylas*?

Hyl. I declare I know not what to say. I once thought I understood well enough what was meant by Matter's supporting accidents. But now, the more I think on it the less can I comprehend it; in short I find that I know nothing of it.

Phil. It seems then you have no idea at all, neither relative nor positive, of Matter; you know neither what it is in itself, nor what relation it bears to accidents?

Hyl. I acknowledge it.

Phil. And yet you asserted that you could not conceive how qualities or accidents should really exist, without conceiving at the same time a material support of them?

Hyl. I did.

Phil. That is to say, when you conceive the real existence of qualities, you do withal conceive something which you cannot conceive?

Hyl. It was wrong I own. But still I fear there is some fallacy or other. Pray what think you of this? It is just come into my head that the ground of all our mistake lies in your treating of each quality by itself. Now, I grant that each quality cannot singly subsist without the mind. Colour cannot without extension, neither can figure without some other sensible quality. But, as the several qualities united or blended together form entire sensible things, nothing hinders why such things may not be supposed to exist without the mind.

Phil. Either, *Hylas*, you are jesting, or have a very bad memory. Though indeed we went through all the qualities by name one after another; yet my arguments, or rather your concessions, nowhere tended to prove that the Secondary Qualities did not subsist each alone by itself; but, that they were not *at all* without the mind. Indeed, in treating of figure and motion we concluded they could not exist without the mind, because it was impossible even in thought to separate them from all secondary qualities, so as to conceive them existing by themselves. But then this was not the only argument made use of upon that occasion. But (to pass by all that hath been hitherto said, and reckon it for nothing, if you will have it so) I am content to put the whole upon this issue. If you can conceive it possible for any mixture or combination of qualities, or any sensible object whatever, to exist without the mind, then I will grant it actually to be so [21].

Hyl. If it comes to that the point will soon be decided. What more easy than to conceive a tree or house existing by itself, independent of, and unperceived by, any mind whatsoever? I do at this present time conceive them existing after that manner.

Phil. How say you, *Hylas*, can you see a thing which is at the same time unseen?

Hyl. No, that were a contradiction.

Phil. Is it not as great a contradiction to talk of *conceiving* a thing which is *unconceived* [22]?

Hyl. It is.

Phil. The tree or house therefore which you think of is conceived by you?

Hyl. How should it be otherwise?

---

[21] Cf. *Principles of Human Knowledge*, sect. 23.

[22] Cf. *Principles of Human Knowledge*, sect. 23; Ferrier's *Theory of Knowing and Being*, Prop. III. obs. 15—18.

Phil. And what is conceived is surely in the mind?

Hyl. Without question, that which is conceived is in the mind.

Phil. How then came you to say, you conceived a house or tree existing independent and out of all minds whatsoever?

Hyl. That was I own an oversight; but stay, let me consider what led me into it.—It is a pleasant mistake enough. As I was thinking of a tree in a solitary place where no one was present to see it, methought that was to conceive a tree as existing unperceived or unthought of—not considering that I myself conceived it all the while. But now I plainly see that all I can do is to frame ideas in my own mind. I may indeed conceive in my own thoughts the idea of a tree, or a house, or a mountain, but that is all. And this is far from proving that I can conceive them *existing out of the minds of all Spirits*.

Phil. You acknowledge then that you cannot possibly conceive how any one corporeal sensible thing should exist otherwise than in a mind?

Hyl. I do.

Phil. And yet you will earnestly contend for the truth of that which you cannot so much as conceive?

Hyl. I profess I know not what to think; but still there are some scruples remain with me. Is it not certain I *see* things at a distance? Do we not perceive the stars and moon, for example, to be a great way off? Is not this, I say, manifest to the senses?

Phil. Do you not in a dream too perceive those or the like objects?

Hyl. I do.

Phil. And have they not then the same appearance of being distant?

Hyl. They have.

Phil. But you do not thence conclude the apparitions in a dream to be without the mind?

Hyl. By no means.

Phil. You ought not therefore to conclude that sensible objects are without the mind, from their appearance or manner wherein they are perceived.

Hyl. I acknowledge it. But doth not my sense deceive me in those cases?

Phil. By no means. The idea or thing which you immediately perceive, neither sense nor reason informs you that it actually exists without the mind. By sense you only know that you are affected with such certain sensations of light and colours, &c. And these you will not say are without the mind.

Hyl. True: but, beside all that, do you not think the sight suggests something of *outness* or *distance*?

Phil. Upon approaching a distant object, do the visible size and figure change perpetually, or do they appear the same at all distances?

Hyl. They are in a continual change.

Phil. Sight therefore doth not suggest or any way inform you that the visible object you immediately perceive exists at a distance [24], or will be perceived when you advance farther onward; there being a continued series of visible objects succeeding each other during the whole time of your approach.

Hyl. It doth not; but still I know, upon seeing an object, what object I shall perceive after having passed over a certain distance: no matter whether it be exactly the same or no: there is still something of distance suggested in the case.

Phil. Good *Hylas*, do but reflect a little on the point, and then tell me whether there be any more in it than this:—From the ideas you actually perceive by sight, you have by experience learned to collect what other ideas you will (according to the standing order of nature) be affected with, after such a certain succession of time and motion.

Hyl. Upon the whole, I take it to be nothing else.

Phil. Now, is it not plain that if we suppose a man born blind was on a sudden made to see, he could at first have no experience of what may be suggested by sight?

Hyl. It is.

Phil. He would not then, according to you, have any notion of distance annexed to the things he saw; but would take them for a new set of sensations existing only in his mind?

Hyl. It is undeniable.

Phil. But, to make it still more plain: is not *distance* a line turned endwise to the eye?

---

[24] (See the *Essay towards a New Theory of Vision*, and its *Vindication*.) Note by the Author in the 1734 edition. Cf. with what follows *New Theory of Vision*, sect. 3, &c.; *Principles of Human Knowledge*, sect. 43, 14; *Alciphron*, Dial. IV. 8.

Hyl. It is.

Phil. And can a line so situated be perceived by sight?

Hyl. It cannot.

Phil. Doth it not therefore follow that distance is not properly and immediately perceived by sight?

Hyl. It should seem so.

Phil. Again, is it your opinion that colours are at a distance?

Hyl. It must be acknowledged they are only in the mind.

Phil. But do not colours appear to the eye as coexisting in the same place with extension and figures?

Hyl. They do.

Phil. How can you then conclude from sight that figures exist without, when you acknowledge colours do not; the sensible appearance being the very same with regard to both?

Hyl. I know not what to answer.

Phil. But, allowing that distance was truly and immediately perceived by the mind, yet it would not thence follow it existed out of the mind. For, whatever is immediately perceived is an idea: and can any *idea* exist out of the mind?

Hyl. To suppose that were absurd: but, inform me, Philonous, can we perceive or know nothing beside our ideas?

Phil. As for the rational deducing of causes from effects, that is beside our inquiry. And, by the senses you can best tell whether you perceive anything which is not immediately perceived. And I ask you, whether the things immediately perceived are other than your own sensations or ideas? You have indeed more than once, in the course of this conversation, declared yourself on those points; but you seem, by this last question, to have departed from what you then thought.

Hyl. To speak the truth, *Philonous,* I think there are two kinds of objects:—the one perceived immediately, which are likewise called *ideas*; the other are real things or external objects, perceived by the mediation of ideas, which are their images and representations. Now, I own ideas do not exist without the mind; but the latter sort of objects do. I am sorry I did not think of this distinction sooner; it would probably have cut short your discourse.

Phil. Are those external objects perceived by sense, or by some other faculty?

Hyl. They are perceived by sense.

Phil. How! is there anything perceived by sense which is not immediately perceived?

Hyl. Yes, *Philonous*, in some sort there is. For example, when I look on a picture or statue of Julius Cæsar, I may be said after a manner to perceive him (though not immediately) by my senses.

Phil. It seems then you will have our ideas, which alone are immediately perceived, to be pictures of external things: and that these also are perceived by sense, inasmuch as they have a conformity or resemblance to our ideas?

Hyl. That is my meaning.

Phil. And, in the same way that Julius Cæsar, in himself invisible, is nevertheless perceived by sight; real things, in themselves imperceptible, are perceived by sense.

Hyl. In the very same.

Phil. Tell me, *Hylas*, when you behold the picture of Julius Cæsar, do you see with your eyes any more than some colours and figures, with a certain symmetry and composition of the whole?

Hyl. Nothing else.

Phil. And would not a man who had never known anything of Julius Cæsar see as much?

Hyl. He would.

Phil. Consequently he hath his sight, and the use of it, in as perfect a degree as you?

Hyl. I agree with you.

Phil. Whence comes it then that your thoughts are directed to the Roman emperor, and his are not? This cannot proceed from the sensations or ideas of sense by you then perceived; since you acknowledge you have no advantage over him in that respect. It should seem therefore to proceed from reason and memory: should it not?

Hyl. It should.

Phil. Consequently, it will not follow from that instance that anything is perceived by sense which is not immediately perceived. Though I grant we may, in one acceptation, be said to perceive [*] sensible things mediately by sense—that is, when, from a frequently

---

[*] Mark here the meaning assigned to the term 'perception;' and the distinction between immediate or proper perception, and mediate perception, in which conception is implied —a distinction so important in the interpretation of Berkeley.

perceived connexion, the immediate perception of ideas by one sense suggests to the mind others, perhaps belonging to another sense, which are wont to be connected with them. For instance, when I hear a coach drive along the streets, immediately I perceive only the sound; but, from the experience I have had that such a sound is connected with a coach, I am said to hear the coach. It is nevertheless evident that, in truth and strictness, nothing can be *heard* but *sound*; and the coach is not then properly perceived by sense, but suggested from experience. So likewise when we are said to see a red-hot bar of iron; the solidity and heat of the iron are not the objects of sight, but suggested to the imagination by the colour and figure which are properly perceived by that sense. In short, those things alone are actually and strictly perceived by any sense, which would have been perceived in case that same sense had then been first conferred on us. As for other things, it is plain they are only suggested to the mind by experience, grounded on former perceptions. But, to return to your comparison of Cæsar's picture, it is plain, if you keep to that, you must hold the real things or archetypes of our ideas are not perceived by sense, but by some internal faculty of the soul, as reason or memory. I would therefore fain know what arguments you can draw from reason for the existence of what you call *real things* or *material objects*. Or, whether you remember to have seen them formerly as they are in themselves; or, if you have heard or read of any one that did.

Hyl. I see, *Philonous*, you are disposed to raillery; but that will never convince me.

Phil. My aim is only to learn from you the way to come at the knowledge of *material beings*. Whatever we perceive is perceived immediately or mediately: by sense; or by reason and reflection. But, as you have excluded sense, pray shew me what reason you have to believe their existence; or what *medium* you can possibly make use of to prove it, either to mine or your own understanding.

Hyl. To deal ingenuously, *Philonous*, now I consider the point, I do not find I can give you any good reason for it. But, thus much seems pretty plain, that it is at least possible such things may really exist. And, as long as there is no absurdity in supposing them, I am resolved to believe as I did, till you bring good reasons to the contrary.

Phil. What! is it come to this, that you only believe the existence of material objects, and that your belief is founded barely on the possibility of its being true? Then you will have me bring reasons against it: though another would think it reasonable the proof should lie on him who holds the affirmative. And, after all, this very point which you are now resolved to maintain, without any reason, is in effect what you have more than once during this discourse seen good reason to give up. But, to pass over all this; if I understand you rightly, you say our ideas do not exist without the mind; but that they are copies, images, or representations, of certain originals that do?

Hyl. You take me right.

Phil. They are then like external things[a]?

Hyl. They are.

Phil. Have those things a stable and permanent nature, independent of our senses; or are they in a perpetual change, upon our producing any motions in our bodies—suspending, exerting, or altering, our faculties or organs of sense?

Hyl. Real things, it is plain, have a fixed and real nature, which remains the same notwithstanding any change in our senses, or in the posture and motion of our bodies; which indeed may affect the ideas in our minds, but it were absurd to think they had the same effect on things existing without the mind.

Phil. How then is it possible that things perpetually fleeting and variable as our ideas should be copies or images of anything fixed and constant? Or, in other words, since all sensible qualities, as size, figure, colour, &c., that is, our ideas, are continually changing upon every alteration in the distance, medium, or instruments of sensation; how can any determinate material objects be properly represented or painted forth by several distinct things, each of which is so different from and unlike the rest? Or, if you say it resembles some one only of our ideas, how shall we be able to distinguish the true copy from all the false ones?

Hyl. I profess, *Philonous*, I am at a loss. I know not what to say to this.

Phil. But neither is this all. Which are material objects in themselves—perceptible or imperceptible?

Hyl. Properly and immediately nothing can be perceived but

[a] Cf. *Principles of Human Knowledge*, sect. 8.

ideas. All material things, therefore, are in themselves insensible, and to be perceived only by our ideas.

Phil. Ideas then are sensible, and their archetypes or originals insensible?

Hyl. Right.

Phil. But how can that which is sensible be like that which is insensible? Can a real thing, in itself *invisible*, be like a *colour*; or a real thing, which is not *audible*, be like a *sound?* In a word, can anything be like a sensation or idea, but another sensation or idea?

Hyl. I must own, I think not.

Phil. Is it possible there should be any doubt on the point? Do you not perfectly know your own ideas?

Hyl. I know them perfectly; since what I do not perceive or know can be no part of my idea[a].

Phil. Consider, therefore, and examine them, and then tell me if there be anything in them which can exist without the mind? or if you can conceive anything like them existing without the mind?

Hyl. Upon inquiry, I find it is impossible for me to conceive or understand how anything but an idea can be like an idea. And it is most evident that *no idea can exist without the mind.*

Phil. You are therefore, by your principles, forced to deny the reality of sensible things; since you made it to consist in an absolute existence exterior to the mind. That is to say, you are a downright sceptic. So I have gained my point, which was to shew your principles led to Scepticism.

Hyl. For the present I am, if not entirely convinced, at least silenced.

Phil. I would fain know what more you would require in order to a perfect conviction. Have you not had the liberty of explaining yourself all manner of ways? Were any little slips in discourse laid hold and insisted on? Or were you not allowed to retract or reinforce anything you had offered, as best served your purpose? Hath not everything you could say been heard and examined with all the fairness imaginable? In a word, have you not in every point been convinced out of your own mouth? and, if you can at present discover any flaw in any of your former

---

[a] Cf. *Principles of Human Knowledge,* sect. 25.

concessions, or think of any remaining subterfuge, any new distinction, colour, or comment whatsoever, why do you not produce it?

Hyl. A little patience, *Philonous.* I am at present so amazed to see myself ensnared, and as it were imprisoned in the labyrinths you have drawn me into, that on the sudden it cannot be expected I should find my way out. You must give me time to look about me and recollect myself.

Phil. Hark; is not this the college bell?

Hyl. It rings for prayers.

Phil. We will go in then, if you please, and meet here again to-morrow morning. In the meantime, you may employ your thoughts on this morning's discourse, and try if you can find any fallacy in it, or invent any new means to extricate yourself.

Hyl. Agreed.

THE SECOND DIALOGUE.

Hylas. I beg your pardon, *Philonous*, for not meeting you sooner. All this morning my head was so filled with our late conversation that I had not leisure to think of the time of the day, or indeed of anything else.

Philonous. I am glad you were so intent upon it, in hopes if there were any mistakes in your concessions, or fallacies in my reasonings from them, you will now discover them to me.

Hyl. I assure you I have done nothing ever since I saw you but search after mistakes and fallacies, and, with that view, have minutely examined the whole series of yesterday's discourse: but all in vain, for the notions it led me into, upon review, appear still more clear and evident; and, the more I consider them, the more irresistibly do they force my assent.

Phil. And is not this, think you, a sign that they are genuine, that they proceed from nature, and are conformable to right reason? Truth and beauty are in this alike, that the strictest survey sets them both off to advantage; while the false lustre of error and disguise cannot endure being reviewed, or too nearly inspected.

Hyl. I own there is a great deal in what you say. Nor can any one be more entirely satisfied of the truth of those odd consequences, so long as I have in view the reasonings that lead to them. But, when these are out of my thoughts, there seems, on the other hand, something so satisfactory, so natural and intelligible, in the modern way of explaining things that, I profess, I know not how to reject it.

Phil. I know not what way you mean.

Hyl. I mean the way of accounting for our sensations or ideas.

Phil. How is that?

Hyl. It is supposed the soul makes her residence in some part of the brain, from which the nerves take their rise, and are thence extended to all parts of the body; and that outward objects, by the different impressions they make on the organs of sense, communicate certain vibrative motions to the nerves; and these being filled with spirits propagate them to the brain or seat of the soul, which, according to the various impressions or traces thereby made in the brain, is variously affected with ideas.

Phil. And call you this an explication of the manner whereby we are affected with ideas?

Hyl. Why not, *Philonous*; have you anything to object against it?

Phil. I would first know whether I rightly understand your hypothesis. You make certain traces in the brain to be the causes or occasions of our ideas. Pray tell me whether by the *brain* you mean any sensible thing.

Hyl. What else think you I could mean?

Phil. Sensible things are all immediately perceivable; and those things which are immediately perceivable are ideas; and these exist only in the mind. Thus much you have, if I mistake not, long since agreed to.

Hyl. I do not deny it.

Phil. The brain therefore you speak of, being a sensible thing, exists only in the mind[1]. Now, I would fain know whether you think it reasonable to suppose that one idea or thing existing in the mind occasions all other ideas. And, if you think so, pray how do you account for the origin of that primary idea or brain itself?

Hyl. I do not explain the origin of our ideas by that brain which is perceivable to sense—this being itself only a combination of sensible ideas—but by another which I imagine.

Phil. But are not things imagined as truly *in the mind* as things perceived[2]?

Hyl. I must confess they are.

Phil. It comes, therefore, to the same thing; and you have been all this while accounting for ideas by certain motions or impressions of the brain, that is, by some alterations in an idea, whether sensible or imaginable it matters not.

Hyl. I begin to suspect my hypothesis.

---

[1] With Berkeley, the human body, including of course the brain, exists in the mind, and not the mind in the body;—for brain and body (if we apply the term existence to them in any intelligible meaning) depend on being perceived or imagined; while mind may, at least conceivably, exist independently of its sensible organisation, and of sensible things. Cf. *Siris*, sect. 285, 295, &c.

[2] Cf. *Principles of Human Knowledge*, sect. 23; also pp. 291, 292.

Phil. Besides spirits, all that we know or conceive are our own ideas. When, therefore, you say all ideas are occasioned by impressions in the brain, do you conceive this brain or no? If you do, then you talk of ideas imprinted in an idea causing that same idea, which is absurd. If you do not conceive it, you talk unintelligibly, instead of forming a reasonable hypothesis.

Hyl. I now clearly see it was a mere dream. There is nothing in it.

Phil. You need not be much concerned at it; for after all, this way of explaining things, as you called it, could never have satisfied any reasonable man. What connexion is there between a motion in the nerves, and the sensations of sound or colour in the mind? Or how is it possible these should be the effect of that?

Hyl. But I could never think it had so little in it as now it seems to have.

Phil. Well then, are you at length satisfied that no sensible things have a real³ existence; and that you are in truth an arrant *sceptic*?

Hyl. It is too plain to be denied.

Phil. Look! are not the fields covered with a delightful verdure? Is there not something in the woods and groves, in the rivers and clear springs, that soothes, that delights, that transports the soul? At the prospect of the wide and deep ocean, or some huge mountain whose top is lost in the clouds, or of an old gloomy forest, are not our minds filled with a pleasing horror? Even in rocks and deserts is there not an agreeable wildness? How sincere a pleasure is it to behold the natural beauties of the earth! To preserve and renew our relish for them, is not the veil of night alternately drawn over her face, and doth she not change her dress with the seasons? How aptly are the elements disposed! What variety and use [⁴in the meanest productions of nature!] What delicacy, what beauty, what contrivance, in animal and vegetable bodies! How exquisitely are all things suited, as well to their particular ends, as to constitute opposite parts of the whole! And, while they mutually aid and support, do they not also set off and illustrate each other? Raise now your thoughts from this ball of earth to all those glorious luminaries that adorn the high arch of heaven. The motion and situation of the planets, are they

---

³ If by *real* we mean an existence absolute, i.e. unperceived and unimagined in any mind.

⁴ 'in stones and minerals,' in first and second editions.

not admirable for use and order? Were those (miscalled *erratic*) globes ever known to stray, in their repeated journeys through the pathless void? Do they not measure areas round the sun ever proportioned to the times? So fixed, so immutable are the laws by which the unseen Author of nature actuates the universe. How vivid and radiant is the lustre of the fixed stars! How magnificent and rich that negligent profusion with which they appear to be scattered throughout the whole azure vault! Yet, if you take the telescope, it brings into your sight a new host of stars that escape the naked eye. Here they seem contiguous and minute, but to a nearer view immense orbs of light at various distances, far sunk in the abyss of space. Now you must call imagination to your aid. The feeble narrow sense cannot descry innumerable worlds revolving round the central fires; and in those worlds the energy of an all-perfect Mind displayed in endless forms. But, neither sense nor imagination are big enough to comprehend the boundless extent, with all its glittering furniture. Though the labouring mind exert and strain each power to its utmost reach, there still stands out ungrasped a surplusage immeasurable. Yet all the vast bodies that compose this mighty frame, how distant and remote soever, are by some secret mechanism, some Divine art and force, linked in a mutual dependence and intercourse with each other, even with this earth, which was almost slipt from my thoughts and lost in the crowd of worlds. Is not the whole system immense, beautiful, glorious beyond expression and beyond thought! What treatment, then, do those philosophers deserve, who would deprive these noble and delightful scenes of all reality? How should those Principles be entertained that lead us to think all the visible beauty of the creation a false imaginary glare? To be plain, can you expect this Scepticism of yours will not be thought extravagantly absurd by all men of sense?

Hyl. Other men may think as they please; but for your part you have nothing to reproach me with. My comfort is, you are as much a sceptic as I am.

Phil. There, Hylas, I must beg leave to differ from you.

Hyl. What! have you all along agreed to the premises, and do you now deny the conclusion, and leave me to maintain those paradoxes by myself which you led me into? This surely is not fair.

Phil. I deny that I agreed with you in those notions that led to

Scepticism. You indeed said the *reality* of sensible things consisted in an *absolute existence* out of the minds of spirits, or distinct from their being perceived. And, pursuant to this notion of reality, you are obliged to deny sensible things any real existence: that is, according to your own definition, you profess yourself a sceptic. But I neither said nor thought the reality of sensible things was to be defined after that manner. To me it is evident, for the reasons you allow of, that sensible things cannot exist otherwise than in a mind or spirit. Whence I conclude, not that they have no real existence, but that, seeing they depend not on my thought, and have an existence distinct from being perceived by me[1], *there must be some other mind wherein they exist*. As sure, therefore, as the sensible world really exists, so sure is there an infinite omnipresent Spirit, who contains and supports it.

Hyl. What! this is no more than I and all Christians hold; nay, and all others too who believe there is a God, and that He knows and comprehends all things.

Phil. Aye, but here lies the difference. Men commonly believe that all things are known or perceived by God, because they believe the being of a God; whereas I, on the other side, immediately and necessarily conclude the being of a God, because all sensible things must be perceived by Him.

Hyl. But, so long as we all believe the same thing, what matter is it how we come by that belief?

Phil. But neither do we agree in the same opinion. For philosophers, though they acknowledge all corporeal beings to be perceived by God, yet they attribute to them an absolute subsistence distinct from their being perceived by any mind whatever, which I do not. Besides, is there no difference between saying, *There is a God, therefore He perceives all things*; and saying, *Sensible things do really exist; and, if they really exist*[1], *they are necessarily perceived by an infinite mind: therefore there is an infinite mind, or God?* This furnishes you with a direct and immediate demonstration, from a most evident principle[2], of the *being of a God*.

---

[1] Cf. *Principles of Human Knowledge*, sect. 29—33; also sect. 90.—The permanence of sensible things, during the intervals of their being perceived or imagined by finite minds, is here assumed, as a conviction of Common Sense. This permanence involves, according to Berkeley, the existence of Supreme Mind and a constant Providence.

[2] The 'principle' is that of the reality, which implies the *permanence* and *externality* (in Berkeley's meaning of the term 'external') of sensible things. Cf. *Principles*

Divines and philosophers had proved beyond all controversy, from the beauty and usefulness of the several parts of the creation, that it was the workmanship of God. But that—setting aside all help of astronomy and natural philosophy, all contemplation of the contrivance, order, and adjustment of things—an infinite mind should be necessarily inferred from the bare *existence* of the sensible world, is an advantage to them only who have made this easy reflection: that the sensible world is that which we perceive by our several senses; and that nothing is perceived by the senses beside ideas; and that no idea or archetype of an idea can exist otherwise than in a mind. You may now, without any laborious search into the sciences, without any subtlety of reason, or tedious length of discourse, oppose and baffle the most strenuous advocate for Atheism; those miserable refuges, whether in an eternal succession of unthinking causes and effects, or in a fortuitous concourse of atoms; those wild imaginations of Vanini, Hobbes, and Spinoza: in a word, the whole system of Atheism, is it not entirely overthrown, by this single reflection on the repugnancy included in supposing the whole, or any part, even the most rude and shapeless, of the visible world, to exist without a mind? Let any one of those abettors of impiety but look into his own thoughts, and there try if he can conceive how so much as a rock, a desert, a chaos, or confused jumble of atoms; how anything at all, either sensible or imaginable, can exist independent of a mind, and he need go no farther to be convinced of his folly. Can anything be fairer than to put a dispute on such an issue, and leave it to a man himself to see if he can conceive, even in thought, what he holds to be true in fact, and from a notional to allow it a real existence¹?

Hyl. It cannot be denied there is something highly serviceable to religion in what you advance. But do you not think it looks very like a notion entertained by some eminent moderns², of *seeing all things in God?*

---

of *Human Knowledge*, sect. 90. A permanent or external material world of this sort is, on Berkeley's principles, necessarily grounded on Supreme Mind, because absolutely dependent on mind, and nevertheless only partially and at intervals sustained by finite or created minds.

¹ The present existence of Something implies the eternal existence of Mind, if Something must exist eternally, and if Being, as such, involves Mind. Berkeley's Natural Theology comes to this, grounded as it is in the very existence of sensible things, apart from marks of design.

² He refers of course to Malebranche, whose Divine Vision was an attempt to

Phil. I would gladly know that opinion: pray explain it to me.

Hyl. They conceive that the soul, being immaterial, is incapable of being united with material things, so as to perceive them in themselves; but that she perceives them by her union with the substance of God, which, being spiritual, is therefore purely intelligible, or capable of being the immediate object of a spirit's thought. Besides, the Divine essence contains in it perfections correspondent to each created being; and which are, for that reason, proper to exhibit or represent them to the mind.

Phil. I do not understand how our ideas, which are things altogether passive and inert, can be the essence, or any part (or like any part) of the essence or substance of God, who is an impassive, indivisible, pure, active being. Many more difficulties and objections there are which occur at first view against this hypothesis; but I shall only add that it is liable to all the absurdities of the common hypothesis, in making a created world exist otherwise than in the mind of a Spirit. Beside all which it hath this peculiar to itself—that it makes that material world serve to no purpose. And, if it pass for a good argument against other hypotheses in the sciences that they suppose nature or the Divine wisdom to make something in vain, or do that by tedious roundabout methods which might have been performed in a much more easy and compendious way, what shall we think of that hypothesis which supposes the whole world made in vain?

Hyl. But what say you, are not you too of opinion that we see all things in God? If I mistake not, what you advance comes near it.

Phil. [⁹Few men think, yet all have opinions. Hence men's opinions are superficial and confused. It is nothing strange that tenets, which in themselves are ever so different, should nevertheless be confounded with each other by those who do not consider them attentively. I shall not therefore be surprised if some men imagine that I run into the enthusiasm of Malebranche; though in truth,I am very remote from it. He builds on the most abstract general ideas, which I entirely disclaim. He asserts an absolute external world, which I deny. He maintains that we are deceived by our senses, and know not the real natures or the

---

reconcile the Cartesian duality in Being, with the unity of Perception, through God, in whom all things are ideally or intellectually represented.

⁹ The passage within brackets is not contained in the first and second editions.

true forms and figures of extended beings; of all which I hold the direct contrary. So that upon the whole there are no principles more fundamentally opposite than his and mine. It must be owned that] I entirely agree with what the holy Scripture saith, 'That in God we live and move and have our being.' But that we see things in His essence, after the manner above set forth, I am far from believing. Take here in brief my meaning.—It is evident that the things I perceive are my own ideas, and that no idea can exist unless it be in a mind. Nor is it less plain that these ideas or things by me perceived, either themselves or their archetypes[10], exist independently of my mind; since I know myself not to be their author, it being out of my power to determine at pleasure what particular ideas I shall be affected with upon opening my eyes or ears. They must therefore exist in some other mind, whose will it is they should be exhibited to me[11]. The things, I say, immediately perceived are ideas or sensations, call them which you will. But how can any idea or sensation exist in, or be produced by, anything but a mind or spirit? This indeed is inconceivable[12]; and to assert that which is inconceivable is to talk nonsense: is it not?

Hyl. Without doubt.

Phil. But, on the other hand, it is very conceivable that they should exist in and be produced by a Spirit[13]; since this is no more than I daily experience in myself, inasmuch as I perceive numberless ideas; and, by an act of my will, can form a great variety of them, and raise them up in my imagination: though, it must be confessed, these creatures of the fancy are not altogether so distinct, so strong, vivid, and permanent, as those perceived by my senses[11]—which latter are called *real things*. From all which

---

[10] He does not affirm that our individual percepts themselves have an existence that is independent of any mind, even of the mind of the percipient. They may be only signs of external and independent existence or power—in other minds, and ultimately in the Supreme Mind.

[11] Cf. *Principles of Human Knowledge,* sect. 29—33.

[12] Cf. *Principles of Human Knowledge,* sect. 3—14.

[13] I can represent in imagination another mind, either finite or Divine, perceiving and conceiving sensible things; because I have an example of this in the experience of my own mind. I cannot represent to myself sensible things existing absolutely unperceived and unimagined; because I cannot, without a contradiction, have an example of this in my own experience.

[14] That is to say, the *existence* of Supreme Mind is inferred from our common-sense belief in the permanent existence of a material world; the *character* of the Supreme Will is inferred from the manner in which sensible phenomena coexist and succeed one another—from the language of nature—the sense-symbolism which we are constantly trying to interpret. Cf. *New Theory of Vision Vindicated,* passim.

I conclude, *there is a Mind which affects me every moment with all the sensible impressions I perceive.* And, from the variety, order, and manner of these, I conclude the Author of them to be *wise, powerful, and good, beyond comprehension*[15]. Mark it well; I do not say, I see things by perceiving that which represents them in the intelligible Substance of God. This I do not understand; but I say, the things by me perceived are known by the understanding, and produced by the will of an infinite Spirit. And is not all this most plain and evident? Is there any more in it than what a little observation in our own minds, and that which passeth in them, not only enableth us to conceive, but also obligeth us to acknowledge?

Hyl. I think I understand you very clearly; and own the proof you give of a Deity seems no less evident than surprising. But, allowing that God is the supreme and universal Cause of all things, yet, may there not be still a third nature besides Spirits and Ideas? May we not admit a subordinate and limited cause of our ideas? In a word, may there not for all that be *Matter*?

Phil. How often must I inculcate the same thing? You allow the things immediately perceived by sense to exist nowhere without the mind; but there is nothing perceived by sense which is not perceived immediately: therefore there is nothing sensible that exists without the mind. The Matter, therefore, which you still insist on is something intelligible, I suppose; something that may be discovered by reason[16], and not by sense.

Hyl. You are in the right.

Phil. Pray let me know what reasoning your belief of Matter is grounded on; and what this Matter is in your present sense of it.

Hyl. I find myself affected with various ideas, whereof I know I am not the cause; neither are they the cause of themselves, or of one another, or capable of subsisting by themselves, as being altogether inactive, fleeting, dependent beings. They have therefore some cause distinct from me and them: of which I pretend to know no more than that it is *the cause of my ideas*[17]. And this thing, whatever it be, I call Matter.

---

[15] Cf. *Principles of Human Knowledge*, sect. 30.

[16] 'reason,' i.e. by reasoning or necessary inference.

[17] Cf. *Principles of Human Knowledge*, sect. 51—33.—An important objection (though not suggested by Hylas) is, that the cause of our sense-experience is unknown, and unknowable by human reasoning—that we cannot either affirm or deny that it is an intelligent voluntary Agent. We know the sensible *effects*, as matter of fact, it is said, but we can tell nothing about their *cause*—a matter of science at any rate.

Phil. Tell me, Hylas, hath every one a liberty to change the current proper signification attached to a common name in any language? For example, suppose a traveller should tell you that in a certain country men pass unhurt through the fire; and, upon explaining himself, you found he meant by the word *fire* that which others call *water*: or, if he should assert that there are trees that walk upon two legs, meaning men by the term *trees*. Would you think this reasonable?

Hyl. No, I should think it very absurd. Common custom is the standard of propriety in language. And for any man to affect speaking improperly is to pervert the use of speech, and can never serve to a better purpose than to protract and multiply disputes where there is no difference in opinion.

Phil. And doth not *Matter*, in the common current acceptation of the word, signify an extended, solid, moveable, unthinking, inactive Substance?

Hyl. It doth.

Phil. And, hath it not been made evident that no such substance can possibly exist[18]? And, though it should be allowed to exist, yet how can that which is *inactive* be a *cause*; or that which is *unthinking* be a *cause of thought*? You may, indeed, if you please, annex to the word *Matter* a contrary meaning to what is vulgarly received; and tell me you understand by it—an unextended, thinking, active being, which is the cause of our ideas. But what else is this than to play with words, and run into that very fault you just now condemned with so much reason? I do by no means find fault with your reasoning, in that you collect a cause from the *phænomena*: but I deny that the cause deducible by reason[19] can properly be termed Matter.

Hyl. There is indeed something in what you say. But I am afraid you do not thoroughly comprehend my meaning. I would by no means be thought to deny that God, or an infinite Spirit, is the Supreme Cause of all things. All I contend for is, that subordinate

---

[18] Berkeley's *material substance* is the synthesis of extended, solid, moveable, unthinking, inactive *ideas* or *phænomena*, in a word the bundle of qualities which is commonly called a 'sensible thing,' and which is presented, or conditionally presentable, in a finite sense-experience, but is ultimately dependent on or substantiated in Supreme Mind.

[19] Inasmuch as, according to Berkeley, it must be a Rational Will—which it would be absurd to call Matter. But he overlooks the objection already mentioned, that no ultimate cause at all of sensible phænomena can be determined by science, which cannot transcend the phænomena themselves, and their order as contemporaneous and successive.

to the Supreme Agent, there is a cause of a limited and inferior nature, which concurs in the production of our ideas, not by any act of will or spiritual efficiency, but by that kind of action which belongs to Matter, viz. *motion*.

Phil. I find you are at every turn relapsing into your old exploded conceit, of a moveable, and consequently an extended, substance existing without the mind. What! have you already forgotten you were convinced, or are you willing I should repeat what has been said on that head? In truth this is not fair dealing in you, still to suppose the being of that which you have so often acknowledged to have no being. But, not to insist farther on what has been so largely handled, I ask whether all your ideas are not perfectly passive and inert, including nothing of action in them[20].

Hyl. They are.

Phil. And are sensible qualities anything else but ideas?

Hyl. How often have I acknowledged that they are not.

Phil. But is not motion a sensible quality?

Hyl. It is.

Phil. Consequently it is no action?

Hyl. I agree with you. And indeed it is very plain that when I stir my finger it remains passive; but my will which produced the motion is active.

Phil. Now, I desire to know, in the first place, whether, motion being allowed to be no action, you can conceive any action besides volition: and, in the second place, whether to say something and conceive[21] nothing be not to talk nonsense: and, lastly, whether, having considered the premises, you do not perceive that to suppose any efficient or active cause of our ideas, other than *Spirit*, is highly absurd and unreasonable?

Hyl. I give up the point entirely. But, though Matter may not be a cause, yet what hinders its being an *instrument* subservient to the supreme Agent in the production of our ideas?

Phil. An instrument say you; pray what may be the figure, springs, wheels, and motions, of that instrument?

---

[20] Cf. *Principles of Human Knowledge*, sect. 25.

[21] It is here argued that as volition is the only cause of which we have any experience, and which consequently alone conveys for us any meaning into the term Cause, to employ that term when volition is absent is to make it equivalent to the term nothing—at least to meaninglessness or unintelligibility.

Hyl. Those I pretend to determine nothing of, both the substance and its qualities being entirely unknown to me.

Phil. What! You are then of opinion it is made up of unknown parts, that it hath unknown motions, and an unknown shape?

Hyl. I do not believe that it hath any figure or motion at all, being already convinced, that no sensible qualities can exist in an unperceiving substance.

Phil. But what notion is it possible to frame of an instrument void of all sensible qualities, even extension itself?

Hyl. I do not pretend to have any notion of it.

Phil. And what reason have you to think this unknown, this inconceivable Somewhat doth exist? Is it that you imagine God cannot act as well without it; or that you find by experience the use of some such thing, when you form ideas in your own mind?

Hyl. You are always teasing me for reasons of my belief. Pray what reasons have you not to believe it?

Phil. It is to me a sufficient reason not to believe the existence of anything, if I see no reason for believing it. But, not to insist on reasons for believing, you will not so much as let me know what it is you would have me believe; since you say you have no manner of notion of it. After all, let me entreat you to consider whether it be like a philosopher, or even like a man of common sense, to pretend to believe you know not what, and you know not why.

Hyl. Hold, *Philonous*. When I tell you matter is an *instrument*, I do not mean altogether nothing. It is true I know not the particular kind of instrument; but, however, I have some notion of *instrument in general*, which I apply to it.

Phil. But what if it should prove that there is something, even in the most general notion of *instrument*, as taken in a distinct sense from *cause*, which makes the use of it inconsistent with the Divine attributes?

Hyl. Make that appear and I shall give up the point.

Phil. What mean you by the general nature or notion of *instrument*?

Hyl. That which is common to all particular instruments composeth the general notion.

Phil. Is it not common to all instruments, that they are applied to the doing those things only which cannot be performed by the mere act of our wills? Thus, for instance, I never use an instrument to move my finger, because it is done by a volition. But I should use one if I were to remove part of a rock, or tear up a tree by the roots. Are you of the same mind? Or, can you shew any example where an instrument is made use of in producing an effect immediately depending on the will of the agent?

Hyl. I own I cannot.

Phil. How therefore can you suppose that an all-perfect Spirit, on whose will all things have an absolute and immediate dependence, should need an instrument in his operations, or, not needing it, make use of it? Thus, it seems to me that you are obliged to own the use of a lifeless inactive instrument to be incompatible with the infinite perfection of God; that is, by your own confession, to give up the point.

Hyl. It doth not readily occur what I can answer you.

Phil. But, methinks you should be ready to own the truth, when it hath been fairly proved to you. We indeed, who are beings of finite powers, are forced to make use of instruments. And the use of an instrument sheweth the agent to be limited by rules of another's prescription, and that he cannot obtain his end but in such a way, and by such conditions. Whence it seems a clear consequence, that the supreme unlimited Agent useth no tool or instrument at all. The will of an Omnipotent Spirit is no sooner exerted than executed, without the application of means—which, if they are employed by inferior agents, it is not upon account of any real efficacy that is in them, or necessary aptitude to produce any effect, but merely in compliance with the laws of nature, or those conditions prescribed to them by the First Cause, who is Himself above all limitation or prescription whatsoever.

Hyl. I will no longer maintain that Matter is an instrument. However, I would not be understood to give up its existence neither; since, notwithstanding what hath been said, it may still be an *occasion*[22].

Phil. How many shapes is your Matter to take? Or, how often must it be proved not to exist, before you are content to part with it? But, to say no more of this (though by all the laws of disputation I may justly blame you for so frequently changing the

[22] Cf. *Principles of Human Knowledge*, sect. 68—79.

signification of the principal term)—I would fain know what you mean by affirming that matter is an occasion, having already denied it to be a cause. And, when you have shewn in what sense you understand *occasion*, pray, in the next place, be pleased to shew me what reason induceth you to believe there is such an occasion of our ideas?

Hyl. As to the first point: by *occasion* I mean an inactive unthinking being, at the presence whereof God excites ideas in our minds.

Phil. And what may be the nature of that inactive unthinking being?

Hyl. I know nothing of its nature.

Phil. Proceed then to the second point, and assign some reason why we should allow an existence to this inactive, unthinking, unknown thing.

Hyl. When we see ideas produced in our minds after an orderly and constant manner, it is natural to think they have some fixed and regular occasions, at the presence of which they are excited.

Phil. You acknowledge then God alone to be the cause of our ideas, and that He causes them at the presence of those occasions.

Hyl. That is my opinion.

Phil. Those things which you say are present to God, without doubt He perceives.

Hyl. Certainly; otherwise they could not be to Him an occasion of acting.

Phil. Not to insist now on your making sense of this hypothesis, or answering all the puzzling questions and difficulties it is liable to: I only ask whether the order and regularity observable in the series of our ideas, or the course of nature, be not sufficiently accounted for by the wisdom and power of God; and whether it doth not derogate from those attributes, to suppose He is influenced, directed, or put in mind, when and what He is to act, by an unthinking substance? And, lastly, whether, in case I granted all you contend for, it would make anything to your purpose—it not being easy to conceive how the external or absolute existence of an unthinking substance, distinct from its being perceived, can be inferred from my allowing that there are certain things perceived by the mind of God, which are to Him the occasion of producing ideas in us?

Hyl. I am perfectly at a loss what to think, this notion of *occasion* seeming now altogether as groundless as the rest.

Phil. Do you not at length perceive that in all these different acceptations of *Matter*, you have been only supposing you know not what, for no manner of reason, and to no kind of use?

Hyl. I freely own myself less fond of my notions since they have been so accurately examined. But still, methinks, I have some confused perception that there is such a thing as *Matter*.

Phil. Either you perceive[21] the being of Matter immediately, or mediately. If immediately, pray inform me by which of the senses you perceive it. If mediately, let me know by what reasoning it is inferred from those things which you perceive immediately. So much for the perception.—Then for the Matter itself, I ask whether it is object, *substratum*, cause, instrument, or occasion? You have already pleaded for each of these, shifting your notions, and making Matter to appear sometimes in one shape, then in another. And what you have offered hath been disapproved and rejected by yourself. If you have anything new to advance I would gladly hear it.

Hyl. I think I have already offered all I had to say on those heads. I am at a loss what more to urge.

Phil. And yet you are loath to part with your old prejudice. But, to make you quit it more easily, I desire that, beside what has been hitherto suggested, you will farther consider whether, upon supposition that Matter exists, you can possibly conceive how you should be affected by it? Or, supposing it did not exist, whether it be not evident you might for all that be affected with the same ideas you now are, and consequently have the very same reasons to believe its existence that you now can have[22]?

Hyl. I acknowledge it is possible we might perceive all things just as we do now, though there was no Matter in the world; neither can I conceive, if there be Matter, how it should produce any idea in our minds. And, I do farther grant you have entirely satisfied me that it is impossible there should be such a thing as Matter in any of the foregoing acceptations. But still I cannot

---

[21] Mark here again the double meaning of the terms *perceive*, *perception*, &c.; they are in some places equivalent to consciousness, and in others to inference from what we are conscious of.

[22] Cf. *Principles of Human Knowledge*, sect. 20.

help supposing that there is *Matter* in some sense or other. What that is I do not indeed pretend to determine.

Phil. I do not expect you should define exactly the nature of that unknown being. Only be pleased to tell me whether it is a Substance—and if so, whether you can suppose a substance without accidents; or, in case you suppose it to have accidents or qualities, I desire you will let me know what those qualities are, at least what is meant by Matter's supporting them?

Hyl. We have already argued on those points. I have no more to say to them. But, to prevent any farther questions, let me tell you I at present understand by *Matter* neither substance nor accident, thinking nor extended being, neither cause, instrument, nor occasion, but something entirely unknown, distinct from all these[a].

Phil. It seems then you include in your present notion of Matter nothing but the general abstract idea of *entity*.

Hyl. Nothing else, save only that I superadd to this general idea the negation of all those particular things, qualities, or ideas, that I perceive, imagine, or in anywise apprehend.

Phil. Pray where do you suppose this unknown Matter to exist?

Hyl. Oh *Philonous*! now you think you have entangled me; for, if I say it exists in place then you will infer that it exists in the mind, since it is agreed that place or extension exists only in the mind: but I am not ashamed to own my ignorance. I know not where it exists; only I am sure it exists not in place. There is a negative answer for you. And you must expect no other to all the questions you put for the future about Matter.

Phil. Since you will not tell me where it exists, be pleased to inform me after what manner you suppose it to exist, or what you mean by its *existence*?

Hyl. It neither thinks nor acts, neither perceives nor is perceived.

Phil. But what is there positive in your abstracted notion of its existence?

Hyl. Upon a nice observation, I do not find I have any positive notion or meaning at all. I tell you again, I am not ashamed to own my ignorance. I know not what is meant by its *existence*, or how it exists.

[a] Cf. *Principles of Human Knowledge*, sect. 80, 81.

Phil. Continue, good *Hylas*, to act the same ingenuous part, and tell me sincerely whether you can frame a distinct idea of Entity in general, prescinded from and exclusive of all thinking and corporeal beings [a], all particular things whatsoever.

Hyl. Hold, let me think a little——I profess, *Philonous*, I do not find that I can. At first glance, methought I had some dilute and airy notion of pure Entity in abstract; but, upon closer attention, it hath quite vanished out of sight. The more I think on it, the more am I confirmed in my prudent resolution of giving none but negative answers, and not pretending to the least degree of any positive knowledge or conception of Matter, its *where*, its *how*, its *entity*, or anything belonging to it.

Phil. When, therefore, you speak of the existence of Matter, you have not any notion in your mind?

Hyl. None at all.

Phil. Pray tell me if the case stands not thus:—at first, from a belief of material substance, you would have it that the immediate objects existed without the mind; then that they are archetypes; then causes; next instruments; then occasions: lastly, *something in general*, which being interpreted proves *nothing*. So Matter comes to nothing [b]. What think you, *Hylas*, is not this a fair summary of your whole proceeding?

Hyl. Be that as it will, yet I still insist upon it, that our not being able to conceive a thing is no argument against its existence [c].

Phil. That from a cause, effect, operation, sign, or other circumstance there may reasonably be inferred the existence of a thing not immediately perceived; and that it were absurd for any man to argue against the existence of that thing, from his having no direct and positive notion of it, I freely own. But, where there is nothing of all this; where neither reason nor revelation induces us to believe the existence of a thing; where we have not even a relative notion of it; where an abstraction is made from perceiving and being perceived, from Spirit and idea: lastly, where there is not so much as the most inadequate or faint idea pretended to—I will not indeed thence conclude

---

[a] I.e. all Spirits and Ideas.
[b] Cf. *Principles of Human Knowledge*, sect. 14, 80.
[c] So Sir W. Hamilton in his *Discussions* and *Lectures*.

against the reality of any notion, or existence of anything; but my inference shall be, that you mean nothing at all; that you employ words to no manner of purpose, without any design or signification whatsoever. And I leave it to you to consider how mere jargon should be treated.

Hyl. To deal frankly with you, *Philonous*, your arguments seem in themselves unanswerable; but they have not so great an effect on me as to produce that entire conviction, that hearty acquiescence, which attends demonstration[19]. I find myself still relapsing into an obscure surmise of I know not what, *matter*.

Phil. But, are you not sensible, *Hylas*, that two things must concur to take away all scruple, and work a plenary assent in the mind? Let a visible object be set in never so clear a light, yet, if there is any imperfection in the sight, or if the eye is not directed towards it, it will not be distinctly seen. And, though a demonstration be never so well grounded and fairly proposed, yet, if there is withal a stain of prejudice, or a wrong bias on the understanding, can it be expected on a sudden to perceive clearly and adhere firmly to the truth? No, there is need of time and pains: the attention must be awakened and detained by a frequent repetition of the same thing placed oft in the same, oft in different lights. I have said it already, and find I must still repeat and inculcate, that it is an unaccountable licence you take, in pretending to maintain you know not what, for you know not what reason, to you know not what purpose. Can this be paralleled in any art or science, any sect or profession of men? Or is there anything so barefacedly groundless and unreasonable to be met with even in the lowest of common conversation? But, perhaps you will still say, Matter may exist; though at the same time you neither know what is meant by *Matter*, or by its *existence*. This indeed is surprising, and the more so because it is altogether voluntary [20and of your own head], you not being led to it by

---

[19] This, according to Hume (who somehow takes for granted that Berkeley's reasonings can produce no conviction) is the natural effect of Berkeley's philosophy.—'Most of the writings of that very ingenious author (Berkeley) form the best lessons of scepticism which are to be found either among the ancient or modern philosophers, Bayle not excepted. . . . That all his arguments, though otherwise intended, are, in reality, merely sceptical appears from this—*that they admit of no answer, and produce no conviction*. Their only effect is to cause that momentary amazement and irresolution and confusion, which is the result of scepticism.' (Hume's *Essays*, vol. II, Note N., p. 554.)

[20] Omitted in last edition.

any one reason; for I challenge you to shew me that thing in nature which needs Matter to explain or account for it.

Hyl. The reality of things cannot be maintained without supposing the existence of Matter. And is not this, think you, a good reason why I should be earnest in its defence?

Phil. The reality of things! What things, sensible or intelligible?

Hyl. Sensible things.

Phil. My glove for example?

Hyl. That or any other thing perceived by the senses.

Phil. But to fix on some particular thing;—is it not a sufficient evidence to me of the existence of this *glove*, that I see it, and feel it, and wear it? Or, if this will not do, how is it possible I should be assured of the reality of this thing, which I actually see in this place, by supposing that some unknown thing, which I never did or can see, exists after an unknown manner, in an unknown place, or in no place at all? How can the supposed reality of that which is intangible be a proof that anything tangible really exists? Or, of that which is invisible, that any visible thing, or, in general of anything which is imperceptible, that a perceptible exists? Do but explain this and I shall think nothing too hard for you.

Hyl. Upon the whole, I am content to own the existence of Matter is highly improbable; but the direct and absolute impossibility of it does not appear to me.

Phil. But, granting Matter to be possible, yet, upon that account merely, it can have no more claim to existence than a golden mountain or a centaur.

Hyl. I acknowledge it; but still you do not deny it is possible; and that which is possible, for aught you know, may actually exist.

Phil. I deny it to be possible; and have, if I mistake not, evidently proved, from your own concessions, that it is not. In the common sense of the word *Matter*, is there any more implied than an extended, solid, figured, moveable substance existing without the mind? And have not you acknowledged, over and over, that you have seen evident reason for denying the possibility of such a substance?

Hyl. True, but that is only one sense of the term *Matter*.

Phil. But, is it not the only proper genuine received sense? and, if Matter in such a sense be proved impossible, may it not be thought with good grounds absolutely impossible? Else how could anything be proved impossible? Or, indeed, how could there be any proof at all one way or other, to a man who takes the liberty to unsettle and change the common signification of words?

Hyl. I thought philosophers might be allowed to speak more accurately than the vulgar, and were not always confined to the common acceptation of a term.

Phil. But this now mentioned is the common received sense among philosophers themselves. But, not to insist on that, have you not been allowed to take Matter in what sense you pleased? And have you not used this privilege in the utmost extent, sometimes entirely changing, at others leaving out or putting into the definition of it whatever, for the present, best served your design, contrary to all the known rules of reason and logic? And hath not this shifting, unfair method of yours spun out our dispute to an unnecessary length; Matter having been particularly examined, and by your own confession refuted in each of those senses? And can any more be required to prove the absolute impossibility of a thing, than the proving it impossible in every particular sense that either you or any one else understands it in?

Hyl. But I am not so thoroughly satisfied that you have proved the impossibility of matter, in the last most obscure abstracted and indefinite sense.

Phil. When is a thing shewn to be impossible?

Hyl. When a repugnancy is demonstrated between the ideas comprehended in its definition.

Phil. But where there are no ideas, there no repugnancy can be demonstrated between ideas?

Hyl. I agree with you.

Phil. Now, in that which you call the obscure indefinite sense of the word *Matter*, it is plain, by your own confession, there was included no idea at all, no sense except an unknown sense, which is the same thing as none. You are not, therefore, to expect I should prove a repugnancy between ideas, where there are no ideas; or the impossibility of Matter taken in an *unknown* sense, that is, no sense at all. My business was only to shew you meant *nothing*; and this you were brought to own. So that, in all your various senses, you have been shewed either to mean nothing at all, or, if anything, an absurdity[1]. And if this be not sufficient to prove the impossibility of a thing, I desire you will let me know what is.

Hyl. I acknowledge you have proved that Matter is impossible; nor do I see what more can be said in defence of it. But, at the same time that I give up this, I suspect all my other notions. For surely none could be more seemingly evident than this once was: and yet it now seems as false and absurd as ever it did true before. But I think we have discussed the point sufficiently for the present. The remaining part of the day I would willingly spend in running over in my thoughts the several heads of this morning's conversation, and to-morrow shall be glad to meet you here again about the same time.

Phil. I will not fail to attend you.

---

[1] Cf. *Principles of Human Knowledge*, sect. 13, 14, where, as well as in other places, Berkeley argues, not merely that the absolute existence of Matter is unproved, but that such existence is impossible — every attempt at a positive conception of it being inconsistent with intelligibility.

THE THIRD DIALOGUE.

Philonous. ¹Tell me, *Hylas,* what are the fruits of yesterday's meditation? Hath it confirmed you in the same mind you were in at parting? or have you since seen cause to change your opinion?

Hylas. Truly my opinion is that all our opinions are alike vain and uncertain. What we approve to-day, we condemn to-morrow. We keep a stir about knowledge, and spend our lives in the pursuit of it, when, alas! we know nothing all the while: nor do I think it possible for us ever to know anything in this life. Our faculties are too narrow and too few. Nature certainly never intended us for Speculation.

Phil. What! say you we can know nothing, *Hylas?*

Hyl. There is not that single thing in the world whereof we can know the real nature, or what it is in itself.

Phil. Will you tell me I do not really know what fire or water is?

Hyl. You may indeed know that fire appears hot, and water fluid; but this is no more than knowing what sensations are produced in your own mind, upon the application of fire and water to your organs of sense. Their internal constitution, their true and real nature, you are utterly in the dark as to *that*.

Phil. Do I not know this to be a real stone that I stand on, and that which I see before my eyes to be a real tree?

Hyl. Know? No, it is impossible you or any man alive should know it. All you know is, that you have such a certain idea or appearance in your own mind. But what is this to the real tree or stone? I tell you that colour, figure, and hardness, which you perceive, are not the real natures of those things, or in the least like them. The same may be said of all other real things or corporeal substances which compose the world. They have none of them anything of themselves, like those sensible qualities by

¹ 'So Hylas'—in first and second editions.

us perceived. We should not therefore pretend to affirm or know anything of them, as they are in their own nature.

Phil. But surely, *Hylas*, I can distinguish gold, for example, from iron: and how could this be, if I knew not what either truly was?

Hyl. Believe me, *Philonous*, you can only distinguish between your own ideas. That yellowness, that weight, and other sensible qualities, think you they are really in the gold? They are only relative to the senses, and have no absolute existence in nature. And in pretending to distinguish the species of real things, by the appearances in your mind, you may perhaps act as wisely as he that should conclude two men were of a different species, because their clothes were not of the same colour.

Phil. It seems, then, we are altogether put off with the appearances of things, and those false ones too. The very meat I eat, and the cloth I wear, have nothing in them like what I see and feel.

Hyl. Even so.

Phil. But is it not strange the whole world should be thus imposed on, and so foolish as to believe their senses? And yet I know not how it is, but men eat, and drink, and sleep, and perform all the offices of life, as comfortably and conveniently as if they really knew the things they are conversant about.

Hyl. They do so: but you know ordinary practice does not require a nicety of speculative knowledge. Hence the vulgar retain their mistakes, and for all that make a shift to bustle through the affairs of life. But philosophers know better things.

Phil. You mean, they know that they *know nothing*.

Hyl. That is the very top and perfection of human knowledge[1].

Phil. But are you all this while in earnest, *Hylas*; and are you seriously persuaded that you know nothing real in the world? Suppose you are going to write, would you not call for pen, ink, and paper, like another man; and do you not know what it is you call for?

Hyl. How often must I tell you, that I know not the real nature of any one thing in the universe? I may indeed upon occasion make use of pen, ink, and paper. But, what any one of them is in its own true nature, I declare positively I know not. And the same is true with regard to every other corporeal thing. And, what is more, we are not only ignorant of the true and real nature of things, but even of their existence. It cannot be denied that we

---

[1] See Hamilton's *Discussions*, pp. 634—649.

perceive such certain appearances or ideas; but it cannot be concluded from thence that bodies really exist. Nay, now I think on it, I must, agreeably to my former concessions, farther declare that it is impossible any real corporeal thing should exist in nature.

Phil. You amaze me. Was ever anything more wild and extravagant than the notions you now maintain: and is it not evident you are led into all these extravagances by the belief of *material substance*? This makes you dream of those unknown natures[2] in everything. It is this occasions your distinguishing between the reality and sensible appearances of things. It is to this you are indebted for being ignorant of what everybody else knows perfectly well. Nor is this all: you are not only ignorant of the true nature of everything, but you know not whether anything really exists, or whether there are any true natures at all; forasmuch as you attribute to your material beings an absolute or external existence, wherein you suppose their reality consists. And, as you are forced in the end to acknowledge such an existence means either a direct repugnancy, or nothing at all, it follows that you are obliged to pull down your own hypothesis of material Substance, and positively to deny the real existence of any part of the universe. And so you are plunged into the deepest and most deplorable *Scepticism* that ever man was[3]. Tell me, *Hylas*, is it not as I say?

Hyl. I agree with you. *Material substance* was no more than an hypothesis, and a false and groundless one too. I will no longer spend my breath in defence of it. But, whatever hypothesis you advance, or whatsoever scheme of things you introduce in its stead, I doubt not it will appear every whit as false: let me but be allowed to question you upon it. That is, suffer me to serve you in your own kind, and I warrant it shall conduct you through as many perplexities and contradictions, to the very same state of Scepticism that I myself am in at present.

---

[2] Variously called *noumena*, 'things-in-themselves,' absolute or unknown Substance &c.—all which Berkeley's philosophy banishes from existence, on the ground of their unintelligibility, and thus annihilates all questions concerning them. Existence and reality are confined by Berkeley within the conscious experience of Minds—finite and Divine.

[3] Berkeley of course claims that his doctrine supersedes scepticism, and excludes the possibility of fallacy in sense—in excluding a representative perception. He assumes nevertheless our trust in the language of nature—in the reality and constancy of natural law. When we see an orange, for instance, the visual sense guarantees only its colour. The other phenomena, which we associate with its colour—its other 'qualities'—are, when we merely look at the orange, believed in by suggestion or unsuggested inference. Cf. *Theory of Vision Vindicated*, sect. 9—11.

Phil. I assure you, *Hylas*, I do not pretend to frame any hypothesis at all¹. I am of a vulgar cast, simple enough to believe my senses, and leave things as I find them. To be plain, it is my opinion that the real things are those very things I see and feel, and perceive² by my senses. These I know, and, finding they answer all the necessities and purposes of life, have no reason to be solicitous about any other unknown beings. A piece of sensible bread, for instance, would stay my stomach better than ten thousand times as much of that insensible, unintelligible, real bread you speak of. It is likewise my opinion that colours and other sensible qualities are on the objects. I cannot for my life help thinking that snow is white, and fire hot. You indeed, who by *snow* and *fire* mean certain external, unperceived, unperceiving substances, are in the right to deny whiteness or heat to be affections inherent in them. But I, who understand by those words the things I see and feel, am obliged to think like other folks. And, as I am no sceptic with regard to the nature of things, so neither am I as to their existence. That a thing should be really perceived by my senses³, and at the same time not really exist, is to me a plain contradiction; since I cannot prescind or abstract, even in thought, the existence of a sensible thing from its being perceived. Wood, stones, fire, water, flesh, iron, and the like things, which I name and discourse of, are things that I know. And I should not have known them but that I perceived them by my senses; and things perceived by the senses are immediately perceived; and things immediately perceived are ideas; and ideas cannot exist without the mind; their existence therefore consists in being perceived; when, therefore, they are actually perceived there can be no doubt of their existence. Away then with all that Scepticism, all those ridiculous philosophical doubts. What a jest is it for a philosopher to question the existence of sensible things, till he hath it proved to him from the veracity of God⁴; or to pretend our knowledge in this point falls short of

---

¹ He assumes the common belief on which all interpretation of natural language proceeds—that sensible phenomena are evolved in a uniform and rational order, which is independent of, and in that respect external to, the will of the percipient.

² Mediately as well immediately perceive.

³ We can hardly be said to have an *immediate* sense-perception of any 'thing'—meaning by 'thing' a congeries of sense-ideas or phenomena, presented in the different senses. We immediately perceive some of its qualities, and infer the others which these suggest. See the last three notes.

⁴ He probably refers to Des Cartes.

intuition or demonstration⁸! I might as well doubt of my own being, as of the being of those things I actually see and feel.

Hyl. Not so fast, *Philonous:* you say you cannot conceive how sensible things should exist without the mind. Do you not?

Phil. I do.

Hyl. Supposing you were annihilated, cannot you conceive it possible that things perceivable by sense may still exist⁹?

Phil. I can; but then it must be in another mind. When I deny sensible things an existence out of the mind, I do not mean my mind in particular, but all minds. Now, it is plain they have an existence exterior to my mind; since I find them by experience to be independent of it [10]. There is therefore some other mind wherein they exist [11], during the intervals between the times of my perceiving them: as likewise they did before my birth, and would do after my supposed annihilation. And, as the same is true with regard to all other finite created spirits, it necessarily follows there is an *omnipresent eternal Mind,* which knows and comprehends all things, and exhibits them to our view in such a manner, and according to such rules, as He Himself hath ordained, and are by us termed the *laws of nature.*

Hyl. Answer me, *Philonous.* Are all our ideas perfectly inert beings? Or have they any agency included in them?

Phil. They are altogether passive and inert [12].

---

⁸ As Locke does. See *Essay,* B. IV. ch. 11.

⁹ Cf. *Principles of Human Knowledge,* sect. 18—48.—'You ask me whether we are not in the wrong in imagining things to exist when they are not perceived by the senses. I answer no. The existence of our ideas consists in their being sensibly perceived, imagined, or thought on. Whenever they are imagined or thought on they do exist. Whenever they are mentioned, they are imagined or thought on.... Bodies, taken for powers, do exist when not perceived; but this existence is not actual. When I say a *power* exists, no more is meant than that *if,* in the light, I open my eyes, and look that way, I shall see the body.... Bodies do exist whether we think of them or no:—they being taken in a twofold sense for (1) collections of thoughts or perceptions; (2) collections of powers to cause these thoughts. These *latter exist;* though perhaps it may be one simple perfect power—the Divine Will.' (Berkeley's *MS. Common Place Book.*)

[10] This is Berkeley's argument for the real or external existence of his sensible world—in his meaning of the terms real and external. Cf. *Principles of Human Knowledge,* sect. 90.

[11] It is in the assumptions involved in this proposition that Berkeley differs, for example, from Hume and Comte and Mr. J. S. Mill; who accept sense-given phenomena, and assume the orderly constancy of their reappearances, *as a matter of fact,* while they profess ignorance of the *ultimate cause* of that steady order. The ground of sensible things, which Berkeley refers to Supreme Mind, Mr. Mill expresses by the term '*permanent possibility of sensations.*' (See his *Examination of Hamilton,* ch. 11.) Our belief in the continued existence of a sensible thing *in our absence* merely means, with him, our conviction, derived from custom, that we should perceive it if our circumstances were different from what, at the time, they happen to be.

[12] Cf. *Principles of Human Knowledge,* sect. 25.

Hyl. And is not God an agent, a being purely active?

Phil. I acknowledge it.

Hyl. No idea therefore can be like unto, or represent the nature of God?

Phil. It cannot.

Hyl. Since therefore you have no idea of the mind of God, how can you conceive it possible that things should exist in His mind? Or, if you can conceive the mind of God, without having an idea of it, why may not I be allowed to conceive the existence of Matter, notwithstanding I have no idea of it?

Phil. As to your first question: I own I have properly no *idea*, either of God or any other spirit; for these being active, cannot be represented by things perfectly inert, as our ideas are. I do nevertheless know that I, who am a spirit or thinking substance, exist as certainly as I know my ideas exist [13]. Farther, I know what I mean by the terms *I* and *myself*; and I know this immediately or intuitively, though I do not perceive it as I perceive a triangle, a colour, or a sound. The Mind, Spirit, or Soul is that indivisible unextended thing which thinks, acts, and perceives. I say *indivisible*, because unextended; and *unextended*, because extended, figured, moveable things are ideas; and that which perceives ideas, which thinks and wills, is plainly itself no idea, nor like an idea. Ideas are things inactive, and perceived. And Spirits a sort of beings altogether different from them. I do not therefore say my soul is an idea, or like an idea. However, taking the word *idea* in a large sense, my soul may be said to furnish me with an idea, that is, an image or likeness of God—though indeed extremely inadequate. For, all the notion I have of God is obtained by reflecting on my own soul, heightening its powers, and removing its imperfections. I have, therefore, though not an inactive idea, yet in *myself* some sort of an active thinking image of the Deity. And, though I perceive Him not by sense, yet I have a notion of Him, or know Him by reflection and reasoning. My own mind and my own ideas I have an immediate knowledge of; and, by the help of these, do mediately apprehend the possibility of the existence of other spirits and ideas [14]. Farther, from my

---

[13] Cf. *Principles of Human Knowledge*, sect. 2, 27, 135—142.

[14] Mark that, with Berkeley, while I am conscious of myself, I can only infer, or rather inductively the existence of other finite minds. I cannot of course be conscious

own being, and from the dependency I find in myself and my ideas, I do, by an act of reason [15], necessarily infer the existence of a God, and of all created things in the mind of God. So much for your first question. For the second: I suppose by this time you can answer it yourself. For you neither perceive Matter objectively, as you do an inactive being or idea [16]; nor know it, as you do yourself, by a reflex act [17]; neither do you mediately apprehend it by similitude of the one or the other [18]; nor yet collect it by reasoning from that which you know immediately [19]. All which makes the case of *Matter* widely different from that of the *Deity*.

[20 *Hyl.* You say your own soul supplies you with some sort of an idea or image of God. But, at the same time, you acknowledge you have, properly speaking, no *idea* of your own soul. You even affirm that spirits are a sort of beings altogether different from ideas. Consequently that no idea can be like a spirit. We have therefore no idea of any spirit. You admit nevertheless that there is spiritual Substance, although you have no idea of it; while you deny there can be such a thing as material Substance, because you have no notion or idea of it. Is this fair dealing? To act consistently, you must either admit Matter or reject Spirit. What say you to this?

Phil. I say, in the first place, that I do not deny the existence of material substance, merely because I have no notion of it, but because the notion of it is inconsistent; or, in other words, because it is repugnant that there should be a notion of it. Many things, for ought I know, may exist, whereof neither I nor any other man

---

of another consciousness than my own; yet Berkeley has by some been erroneously supposed to say the contrary.

[15] 'reason,' i.e. reasoning or necessary inference—founded here on our sense of personal dependence, and not merely on our faith in the permanent existence of those synthesss of sense-given phenomena which we call sensible things. Our inductive inference of the existence of finite minds is a subordinate and contingent application of the same general belief.

[16] Cf. *Principles of Human Knowledge*, sect. 135—138.

[17] Does this imply that with Berkeley the notion of self, as distinguished from the *ideas* of not-self, is not an original datum, but the result of reflection upon experience—the *subjective* or permanent, so to speak, as distinguished from its *objective* or variable phase of experience? Yet he says in many places that we are conscious of 'our own being.' Cf. *Principles of Human Knowledge*, sect. 89.

[18] Cf. *Ibid.* sect. 8.

[19] Cf. *Ibid.* sect. 20.

[20] This, perhaps the most important passage in the *Dialogues* (pp. 327—329), printed within brackets, is not contained in the first and second editions. It is, by anticipation, Berkeley's answer to Hume's application of the objections to the reality and possibility of Absolute or Unknown Matter, to the reality and possibility of the Ego or Self of which we are aware through memory, as identical amid the changes of its ideas or successive states.

hath or can have any idea or notion whatsoever. But then those things must be possible, that is, nothing inconsistent must be included in their definition. I say, secondly, that, although we believe things to exist which we do not perceive, yet we may not believe that any particular thing exists, without some reason for such belief: but I have no reason for believing the existence of Matter. I have no immediate intuition thereof: neither can I immediately from my sensations, ideas, notions, actions, or passions, infer an unthinking, unperceiving, inactive Substance—either by probable deduction, or necessary consequence. Whereas the being of my Self, that is, my own soul, mind, or thinking principle, I evidently know by reflection[21]. You will forgive me if I repeat the same things in answer to the same objections. In the very notion or definition of *material Substance*, there is included a manifest repugnance and inconsistency. But this cannot be said of the notion of Spirit. That ideas should exist in what doth not perceive, or be produced by what doth not act, is repugnant. But, it is no repugnancy to say that a perceiving thing should be the subject of ideas, or an active thing the cause of them. It is granted we have neither an immediate evidence nor a demonstrative knowledge of the existence of other finite spirits; but it will not thence follow that such spirits are on a foot with material substances: if to suppose the one be inconsistent, and it be not inconsistent to suppose the other; if the one can be inferred by no argument, and there is a probability for the other; if we see signs and effects indicating distinct finite agents like ourselves, and see no sign or symptom whatever that leads to a rational belief of Matter. I say, lastly, that I have a notion of Spirit, though I have not, strictly speaking, an idea of it[22]. I do not perceive it as an idea, or by means of an idea, but know it by reflection.

Hyl. Notwithstanding all you have said, to me it seems that, according to your own way of thinking, and in consequence of your own principles, it should follow that *you* are only a system of floating ideas, without any substance to support them. Words are not to be used without a meaning. And, as there is no more meaning in *spiritual Substance* than in *material Substance*, the one is to be exploded as well as the other.

Phil. How often must I repeat, that I know or am conscious of

---

[21] See note [20] on preceding page. [22] Cf. *Principles of Human Knowledge*, sect. 142.

my own being; and that *I myself* am not my ideas, but somewhat else[20], a thinking, active principle that perceives, knows, wills, and operates about ideas. I know that I, one and the same self, perceive both colours and sounds: that a colour cannot perceive a sound, nor a sound a colour: that I am therefore one individual principle, distinct from colour and sound; and, for the same reason, from all other sensible things and inert ideas. But, I am not in like manner conscious either of the existence or essence of Matter[21]. On the contrary, I know that nothing inconsistent can exist, and that the existence of Matter implies an inconsistency. Farther, I know what I mean when I affirm that there is a spiritual substance or support of ideas, that is, that a spirit knows and perceives ideas. But, I do not know what is meant when it is said that an unperceiving substance hath inherent in it and supports either ideas or the archetypes of ideas. There is therefore upon the whole no parity of case between Spirit and Matter.]

Hyl. I own myself satisfied in this point. But, do you in earnest think the real existence of sensible things consists in their being actually perceived? If so; how comes it that all mankind distinguish between them? Ask the first man you meet, and he shall tell you, *to be perceived* is one thing, and *to exist* is another.

Phil. I am content, *Hylas*, to appeal to the common sense of the world for the truth of my notion. Ask the gardener why he thinks yonder cherry-tree exists in the garden, and he shall tell you, because he sees and feels it; in a word, because he perceives it by his senses. Ask him why he thinks an orange-tree not to be there, and he shall tell you, because he does not perceive it. What he perceives by sense, that he terms a real being, and saith it *is* or *exists*; but, that which is not perceivable, the same, he saith, hath no being.

Hyl. Yes, *Philonous*, I grant the existence of a sensible thing consists in being perceivable, but not in being actually perceived.

Phil. And what is perceivable but an idea? And can an idea exist without being actually perceived? These are points long since agreed between us.

---

[20] Cf. *Principles of Human Knowledge*, sect. 2. Does he suppose that this Self exists when it is not actually conscious or cognisant of any ideas—sensible or other? Or, does he allow that mind is ever unconscious?

[21] That is of material Substance existing independently of any mind. Berkeley refers here to a consciousness of matter, i.e. consciousness of a belief in material Substance.

Hyl. But, be your opinion never so true, yet surely you will not deny it is shocking, and contrary to the common sense of men[25]. Ask the fellow whether yonder tree hath an existence out of his mind: what answer think you he would make?

Phil. The same that I should myself, to wit, that it doth exist out of his mind. But then to a Christian it cannot surely be shocking to say, the real tree, existing without his mind, is truly known and comprehended by (that is *exists in*) the infinite mind of God. Probably he may not at first glance be aware of the direct and immediate proof there is of this; inasmuch as the very being of a tree, or any other sensible thing, implies a mind wherein it is. But the point itself he cannot deny. The question between the Materialists and me is not, whether things have a *real* existence out of the mind of this or that person, but, whether they have an *absolute* existence, distinct from being perceived by God, and exterior to all minds[26]. This indeed some heathens and philosophers have affirmed, but whoever entertains notions of the Deity suitable to the Holy Scriptures will be of another opinion.

Hyl. But, according to your notions, what difference is there between real things, and chimeras formed by the imagination, or the visions of a dream—since they are all equally in the mind[27]?

Phil. The ideas formed by the imagination are faint and indistinct; they have, besides, an entire dependence on the will. But the ideas perceived by sense, that is, real things, are more vivid and clear; and, being imprinted on the mind by a spirit distinct from us, have not the like dependence on our will. There is therefore no danger of confounding these with the foregoing: and there is as little of confounding them with the visions of a dream, which are dim, irregular, and confused. And, though they should happen to be never so lively and natural, yet, by their not being connected, and of a piece with the preceding and subsequent transactions of our lives, they might easily be distinguished from realities. In short, by whatever method you distinguish *things* from *chimeras* on your scheme, the same, it is evident, will hold

---

[25] Cf. *Principles of Human Knowledge*, sect. 54—57.

[26] This one sentence expresses the whole question between Berkeley and his antagonists—the negative and the positive side of his doctrine.

[27] Cf. *Principles of Human Knowledge*, sect. 29—41.

also upon mine. For, it must be, I presume, by some perceived difference; and I am not for depriving you of any one thing that you perceive.

Hyl. But still, *Philonous*, you hold, there is nothing in the world but spirits and ideas. And this, you must needs acknowledge, sounds very oddly.

Phil. I own the word *idea*, not being commonly used for *thing*, sounds something out of the way. My reason for using it was, because a necessary[18] relation to the mind is understood to be implied by that term; and it is now commonly used by philosophers to denote the immediate objects of the understanding. But, however oddly the proposition may sound in words, yet it includes nothing so very strange or shocking in its sense; which in effect amounts to no more than this, to wit, that there are only things perceiving, and things perceived; or that every unthinking being is necessarily, and from the very nature of its existence, perceived by some mind; if not by a finite created mind, yet certainly by the infinite mind of God, in whom 'we live, and move, and have our being.' Is this as strange as to say, the sensible qualities are not on the objects: or that we cannot be sure of the existence of things, or know anything of their real natures—though we both see and feel them, and perceive them by all our senses?

Hyl. And, in consequence of this, must we not think there are no such things as physical or corporeal causes; but that a Spirit is the immediate cause of all the phenomena in nature? Can there be anything more extravagant than this?

Phil. Yes, it is infinitely more extravagant to say—a thing which is inert operates on the mind, and which is unperceiving is the cause of our perceptions, [19 without any regard either to consistency, or the old known axiom, *Nothing can give to another that which it hath not itself*]. Besides, that which to you, I know not for what reason, seems so extravagant is no more than the Holy Scriptures assert in a hundred places. In them God is represented as the sole and immediate Author of all those effects

---

[18] 'necessary'—see what Berkeley says at the close of the *Second Dialogue*, and elsewhere, as to the impossibility of the existence of Matter; and of the unmeaning nature of propositions which pretend to express an existence of things sensible, that is external to or independent of all sentient and intelligent being.

[19] The words within brackets are omitted in the last edition.

which some heathens and philosophers are wont to ascribe to Nature, Matter, Fate, or the like unthinking principle. This is so much the constant language of Scripture that it were needless to confirm it by citations.

Hyl. You are not aware, *Philonous*, that, in making God the immediate Author of all the motions in nature, you make Him the Author of murder, sacrilege, adultery, and the like heinous sins.

Phil. In answer to that, I observe, first, that the imputation of guilt is the same, whether a person commits an action with or without an instrument. In case therefore you suppose God to act by the mediation of an instrument, or occasion, called *Matter*, you as truly make Him the author of sin as I, who think Him the immediate agent in all those operations vulgarly ascribed to Nature. I farther observe that sin or moral turpitude doth not consist in the outward physical action or motion, but in the internal deviation of the will from the laws of reason and religion. This is plain, in that the killing an enemy in a battle, or putting a criminal legally to death, is not thought sinful; though the outward act be the very same with that in the case of murder. Since, therefore, sin doth not consist in the physical action, the making God an immediate cause of all such actions is not making Him the Author of sin. Lastly, I have nowhere said that God is the only agent who produces all the motions in bodies. It is true I have denied there are any other agents besides spirits; but this is very consistent with allowing to thinking rational beings, in the production of motions, the use of limited powers, ultimately indeed derived from God, but immediately under the direction of their own wills[30], which is sufficient to entitle them to all the guilt of their actions.

Hyl. But the denying Matter, *Philonous*, or corporeal Substance; there is the point. You can never persuade me that this is not repugnant to the universal sense of mankind. Were our dispute to be determined by most voices, I am confident you would give up the point, without gathering the votes.

Phil. I wish both our opinions were fairly stated and submitted to the judgment of men who had plain common sense, without the prejudices of a learned education. Let me be represented as one

---

[*] The existence of secondary causes is recognised by Berkeley only in the form of finite minds or spirits.

who trusts his senses, who thinks he knows the things he sees and feels, and entertains no doubts of their existence; and you fairly set forth with all your doubts, your paradoxes, and your scepticism about you, and I shall willingly acquiesce in the determination of any indifferent person. That there is no substance wherein ideas can exist beside spirit is to me evident. And that the objects immediately perceived are ideas, is on all hands agreed. And that sensible qualities are objects immediately perceived no one can deny. It is therefore evident there can be no *substratum* of those qualities but spirit; in which they exist, not by way of mode or property, but as a thing perceived in that which perceives it [31]. I deny therefore that there is any unthinking *substratum* of the objects of sense, and in that acceptation that there is any material substance. But if by *material substance* is meant only sensible body, that which is seen and felt (and the unphilosophical part of the world, I dare say, mean no more), then I am more certain of matter's existence than you or any other philosopher pretend to be. If there be anything which makes the generality of mankind averse from the notions I espouse, it is a misapprehension that I deny the reality of sensible things: but, as it is you who are guilty of that and not I, it follows that in truth their aversion is against your notions and not mine. I do therefore assert that I am as certain as of my own being, that there are bodies or corporeal substances (meaning the things I perceive by my senses); and that, granting this, the bulk of mankind will take no thought about, nor think themselves at all concerned in the fate of those unknown natures and philosophical quiddities which some men are so fond of.

Hyl. What say you to this? Since, according to you, men judge of the reality of things by their senses, how can a man be mistaken in thinking the moon a plain lucid surface, about a foot in diameter; or a square tower, seen at a distance, round; or an oar, with one end in the water, crooked [32]?

Phil. He is not mistaken with regard to the ideas he actually perceives, but in the inferences he makes from his present perceptions. Thus, in the case of the oar, what he immediately perceives by sight is certainly crooked; and so far he is in the right. But, if he thence conclude that upon taking the oar out of the water he shall perceive the same crookedness; or that it

---

[31] Cf. *Principles of Human Knowledge*, sect. 49.   [32] Cf. *Alciphron*, Dial. IV. 9.

would affect his touch as crooked things are wont to do: in that he is mistaken. In like manner, if he shall conclude from what he perceives in one station, that, in case he advances towards the moon or tower, he should still be affected with the like ideas, he he is mistaken. But his mistake lies not in what he perceives immediately and at present (it being a manifest contradiction to suppose he should err in respect of that), but in the wrong judgment he makes concerning the ideas he apprehends to be connected with those immediately perceived: or, concerning the ideas that, from what he perceives at present, he imagines would be perceived in other circumstances. The case is the same with regard to the Copernican system. We do not here perceive any motion of the earth: but it were erroneous thence to conclude, that, in case we were placed at as great a distance from that as we are now from the other planets, we should not then perceive its motion [30].

Hyl. I understand you; and must needs own you say things plausible enough: but, give me leave to put you in mind of one thing. Pray, *Philonous*, were you not formerly as positive that Matter existed, as you are now that it does not?

Phil. I was. But here lies the difference. Before, my positiveness was founded, without examination, upon prejudice; but now, after inquiry, upon evidence.

Hyl. After all, it seems our dispute is rather about words than things. We agree in the thing, but differ in the name. That we are affected with ideas from without is evident; and it is no less evident that there must be (I will not say archetypes, but) powers without the mind, corresponding to those ideas. And, as these powers cannot subsist by themselves, there is some subject of them necessarily to be admitted, which I call *Matter*, and you call *Spirit*. This is all the difference.

Phil. Pray, *Hylas*, is that powerful being, or subject of powers, extended?

Hyl. It hath not extension; but it hath the power to raise in you the idea of extension.

Phil. It is therefore itself unextended?

Hyl. I grant it.

Phil. Is it not also active?

---

[30] Cf. *Principles of Human Knowledge*, sect. 58.

Hyl. Without doubt: otherwise, how could we attribute powers to it?

Phil. Now let me ask you two questions: *First,* whether it be agreeable to the usage either of philosophers or others to give the name *Matter* to an unextended active being? And, *Secondly,* whether it be not ridiculously absurd to misapply names contrary to the common use of language?

Hyl. Well then, let it not be called Matter, since you will have it so, but some *third nature* distinct from Matter and Spirit. For what reason is there why you should call it spirit? Does not the notion of spirit imply that it is thinking, as well as active and unextended?

Phil. My reason is this: because I have a mind to have some notion of meaning in what I say; but I have no notion of any action distinct from volition, neither can I conceive volition to be anywhere but in a spirit; therefore, when I speak of an active being, I am obliged to mean a spirit. Beside, what can be plainer than that a thing which hath no ideas in itself cannot impart them to me; and, if it hath ideas, surely it must be a spirit. To make you comprehend the point still more clearly if it be possible— I assert as well as you that, since we are affected from without, we must allow powers to be without, in a being distinct from ourselves. So far we are agreed. But then we differ as to the kind of this powerful being [14]. I will have it to be spirit, you Matter, or I know not what (I may add too, you know not what) third nature. Thus, I prove it to be spirit. From the effects I see produced I conclude there are actions; and, because actions, volitions; and, because there are volitions, there must be a will. Again, the things I perceive must have an existence, they or their archetypes, out of my mind: but, being ideas, neither they nor their archetypes can exist otherwise than in an understanding; there is therefore an understanding. But will and understanding constitute in the strictest sense a mind or spirit. The powerful cause, therefore, of my ideas is in strict propriety of speech a *spirit.*

---

[14] This is the gist of the whole question. According to the Materialists, sensible phenomena are due to *Material Substance*, or to some unknown 'third nature;' according to Berkeley, to Rational Will; according to Hume and the Positivists, their origin is absolutely unknown, and we can only generalize them inductively, through customs, as facts. For Berkeley's vindication of his Theism, see *Alciphron*, Dial. IV., and *New Theory of Vision Vindicated.* Also *Principles of Human Knowledge*, sect. 29—33.

Hyl. And now I warrant you think you have made the point very clear, little suspecting that what you advance leads directly to a contradiction. Is it not an absurdity to imagine any imperfection in God?

Phil. Without a doubt.

Hyl. To suffer pain is an imperfection?

Phil. It is.

Hyl. Are we not sometimes affected with pain and uneasiness by some other being?

Phil. We are.

Hyl. And have you not said that being is a spirit, and is not that spirit God?

Phil. I grant it.

Hyl. But you have asserted that whatever ideas we perceive from without are in the mind which affects us. The ideas, therefore, of pain and uneasiness are in God; or, in other words, God suffers pain: that is to say, there is an imperfection in the Divine nature, which, you acknowledge, was absurd. So you are caught in a plain contradiction[35].

Phil. That God knows or understands all things, and that He knows, among other things, what pain is, even every sort of painful sensation, and what it is for His creatures to suffer pain, I make no question. But, that God, though He knows and sometimes causes painful sensations in us, can Himself suffer pain, I positively deny. We, who are limited and dependent spirits, are liable to impressions of sense, the effects of an external agent, which, being produced against our wills, are sometimes painful and uneasy. But God, whom no external being can affect, who perceives nothing by sense as we do, whose will is absolute and independent, causing all things, and liable to be thwarted or resisted by nothing; it is evident, such a Being as this can suffer nothing, nor be affected with any painful sensation, or indeed any sensation at all. We are chained to a body, that is to say, our perceptions are connected with corporeal motions. By the law of our nature, we are affected upon every alteration in the nervous parts of our sensible body; which sensible body, rightly considered, is nothing but a complexion of such qualities or ideas

---

[35] A similar objection is urged by Erdmann, in the criticism of Berkeley in his *Grundriss der Geschichte der Philosophie*.

as have no existence distinct from being perceived by a mind: so that this connexion of sensations with corporeal motions means no more than a correspondence in the order of nature between two sets of ideas, or things immediately perceivable. But God is a pure spirit, disengaged from all such sympathy or natural ties. No corporeal motions are attended with the sensations of pain or pleasure in His mind. To know everything knowable is certainly a perfection; but to endure, or suffer, or feel anything by sense, is an imperfection. The former, I say, agrees to God, but not the latter. God knows or hath ideas; but His ideas are not conveyed to Him by sense, as ours are. Your not distinguishing, where there is so manifest a difference, makes you fancy you see an absurdity where there is none.

Hyl. But, all this while you have not considered that the quantity of Matter hath been demonstrated to be proportioned to the gravity of bodies[m]. And what can withstand demonstration?

Phil. Let me see how you demonstrate that point.

Hyl. I lay it down for a principle that the moments or quantities of motion in bodies are in a direct compounded reason of the velocities and quantities of Matter contained in them. Hence, where the velocities are equal, it follows the moments are directly as the quantity of Matter in each. But it is found by experience that all bodies (bating the small inequalities, arising from the resistance of the air) descend with an equal velocity; the motion therefore of descending bodies, and consequently their gravity, which is the cause or principle of that motion, is proportional to the quantity of Matter; which was to be demonstrated.

Phil. You lay it down as a self-evident principle that the quantity of motion in any body is proportional to the velocity and *Matter* taken together; and this is made use of to prove a proposition from whence the existence of *Matter* is inferred. Pray is not this arguing in a circle?

Hyl. In the premise I only mean that the motion is proportional to the velocity, jointly with the extension and solidity.

Phil. But, allowing this to be true, yet it will not thence follow that gravity is proportional to *Matter*, in your philosophic sense of the word; except you take it for granted that unknown *substratum*, or whatever else you call it, is proportional to those

---

[m] Cf. *Principles of Human Knowledge*, sect. 50; *Siris*, sect. 319.

sensible qualities; which to suppose is plainly begging the question. That there is magnitude and solidity, or resistance, perceived by sense, I readily grant; as likewise, that gravity may be proportional to those qualities I will not dispute. But that either these qualities as perceived by us, or the powers producing them, do exist in a *material substratum*,—this is what I deny, and you indeed affirm, but, notwithstanding your demonstration, have not yet proved.

Hyl. I shall insist no longer on that point. Do you think, however, you shall persuade me the natural philosophers have been dreaming all this while? Pray what becomes of all their hypotheses and explications of the phenomena, which suppose the existence of Matter[a]?

Phil. What mean you, *Hylas*, by the *phenomena*?

Hyl. I mean the appearances which I perceive by my senses.

Phil. And the appearances perceived by sense, are they not ideas?

Hyl. I have told you so a hundred times.

Phil. Therefore, to explain the phenomena is to shew how we come to be affected with ideas, in that manner and [b] order wherein they are imprinted on our senses. Is it not?

Hyl. It is.

Phil. Now, if you can prove that any philosopher hath explained the production of any one idea in our minds by the help of *Matter*, I shall for ever acquiesce, and look on all that hath been said against it as nothing; but, if you cannot, it is vain to urge the explication of phenomena. That a Being endowed with knowledge and will should produce or exhibit ideas is easily understood. But, that a Being which is utterly destitute of these faculties should be able to produce ideas, or in any sort to affect an intelligence, this I can never understand. This I say—though we had some positive conception of Matter, though we knew its qualities, and could comprehend its existence—would yet be so far from explaining things, that it is itself the most inexplicable thing in the world. And yet, for all this, it will not follow that philosophers have been doing nothing; for, by observing and reasoning upon the connexion of ideas, they discover the laws

---

[a] Cf. *Principles of Human Knowledge*, sect. 50.   [b] 'order'—'series'—in first and second editions.

and methods of nature, which is a part of knowledge both useful and entertaining.

Hyl. After all, can it be supposed God would deceive all mankind? Do you imagine He would have induced the whole world to believe the being of Matter, if there was no such thing?

Phil. That every epidemical opinion arising from prejudice, or passion, or thoughtlessness may be imputed to God, as the Author of it, I believe you will not affirm. Whatsoever opinion we father on Him, it must be either because He has discovered it to us by supernatural revelation; or because it is so evident to our natural faculties, which were framed and given us by God, that it is impossible we should withhold our assent from it. But where is the revelation? or where is the evidence that extorts the belief of Matter? Nay, how does it appear, that Matter, taken for something distinct from what we perceive by our senses, is thought to exist by all mankind; or, indeed, by any except a few philosophers, who do not know what they would be at? Your question supposes these points are clear; and, when you have cleared them, I shall think myself obliged to give you another answer. In the meantime let it suffice that I tell you, I do not suppose God has deceived mankind at all.

Hyl. But the novelty, *Philonous*, the novelty! There lies the danger. New notions should always be discountenanced; they unsettle men's minds, and nobody knows where they will end.

Phil. Why the rejecting a notion that hath no foundation, either in sense, or in reason, or in Divine authority, should be thought to unsettle the belief of such opinions as are grounded on all or any of these, I cannot imagine. That innovations in government and religion are dangerous, and ought to be discountenanced, I freely own. But, is there the like reason why they should be discouraged in philosophy? The making anything known which was unknown before is an innovation in knowledge: and, if all such innovations had been forbidden, men would have made a notable progress in the arts and sciences. But it is none of my business to plead for novelties and paradoxes. That the qualities we perceive are not on the objects: that we must not believe our senses: that we know nothing of the real nature of things, and can never be assured even of their existence: that real colours and sounds are nothing but certain unknown figures and motions: that motions are in themselves neither swift nor slow: that there are in bodies absolute extensions, without any particular magnitude or figure: that a thing stupid, thoughtless, and inactive, operates on a spirit: that the least particle of a body contains innumerable extended parts:—these are the novelties, these are the strange notions which shock the genuine uncorrupted judgment of all mankind; and being once admitted, embarrass the mind with endless doubts and difficulties. And it is against these and the like innovations I endeavour to vindicate Common Sense. It is true, in doing this, I may perhaps be obliged to use some *ambages*, and ways of speech not common. But, if my notions are once thoroughly understood, that which is most singular in them will, in effect, be found to amount to no more than this:—that it is absolutely impossible, and a plain contradiction, to suppose any unthinking being should exist without being perceived by a mind. And, if this notion be singular, it is a shame it should be so at this time of day, and in a Christian country.

Hyl. As for the difficulties other opinions may be liable to, those are out of the question. It is your business to defend your own opinion. Can anything be plainer than that you are for changing all things into ideas? You, I say, who are not ashamed to charge me with *scepticism*. This is so plain, there is no denying it.

Phil. You mistake me. I am not for changing things into ideas, but rather ideas into things [39]; since those immediate objects of perception, which, according to you, are only appearances of things, I take to be the real things themselves.

Hyl. Things! you may pretend what you please; but it is certain you leave us nothing but the empty forms of things, the outside only which strikes the senses.

Phil. What you call the empty forms and outside of things seem to me the very things themselves. Nor are they empty or incomplete, otherwise than upon your supposition—that Matter [10] is an essential part of all corporeal things. We both, therefore,

---

[39] Cf. *Principles of Human Knowledge*, sect. 38. Berkeley is not for making things *subjective*, but ideas *objective*.
[10] i.e. Absolute Matter.

agree in this, that we perceive only sensible forms; but herein we differ, you will have them to be empty appearances, I real beings. In short, you do not trust your senses, I do.

Hyl. You say you believe your senses; and seem to applaud yourself that in this you agree with the vulgar. According to you, therefore, the true nature of a thing is discovered by the senses. If so, whence comes that disagreement? Why, is not the same figure, and other sensible qualities, perceived all manner of ways? And why should we use a microscope the better to discover the true nature of a body, if it were discoverable to the naked eye?

Phil. Strictly speaking, *Hylas*, we do not see the same object that we feel[41]; neither is the same object perceived by the microscope which was by the naked eye[42]. But, in case every variation was thought sufficient to constitute a new kind or individual, the endless number or confusion of names would render language impracticable. Therefore, to avoid this as well as other inconveniences which are obvious upon a little thought, men combine together several ideas, apprehended by divers senses, or by the same sense at different times, or in different circumstances, but observed, however, to have some connexion in nature, either with respect to co-existence or succession—all which they refer to one name, and consider as one thing. Hence, it follows that when I examine by my other senses a thing I have seen, it is not in order to understand better the same object which I had perceived by sight—the object of one sense not being perceived by the other senses. And, when I look through a microscope, it is not that I may perceive more clearly what I perceived already with my bare eyes; the object perceived by the glass being quite different from the former. But, in both cases, my aim is only to know what ideas are connected together; and the more a man knows of the connexion of ideas[43], the more he is said to know of the nature of things. What, therefore, if our ideas are variable; what if our senses are not in all circumstances affected with the same appearances? It will not thence follow they are not to be trusted, or that they are inconsistent either with themselves or anything else; except it be with your preconceived

---

[41] Cf. *New Theory of Vision*, sect. 49; and *Theory of Vision Vindicated*, sect. 9, 10, 11, &c.

[42] Cf. *New Theory of Vision*, sect. 84—86.

[43] I. e. sense-ideas or presentations.

notion of (I know not what) one single, unchanged, unperceivable, real nature, marked by each name: which prejudice seems to have taken its rise from not rightly understanding the common language of men, speaking of several distinct ideas as united into one thing by the mind. And, indeed, there is cause to suspect several erroneous conceits of the philosophers are owing to the same original: while they began to build their schemes not so much on notions as words, which were framed by the vulgar, merely for conveniency and dispatch in the common actions of life, without any regard to speculation[14].

Hyl. Methinks I apprehend your meaning.

Phil. It is your opinion the ideas we perceive by our senses are not real things, but images or copies of them. Our knowledge, therefore, is no farther real than as our ideas are the true representations of those originals. But, as these supposed originals are in themselves unknown, it is impossible to know how far our ideas resemble them; or whether they resemble them at all[15]. We cannot, therefore, be sure we have any real knowledge. Farther, as our ideas are perpetually varied, without any change in the supposed real things, it necessarily follows they cannot all be true copies of them: or, if some are and others are not, it is impossible to distinguish the former from the latter. And this plunges us yet deeper in uncertainty. Again, when we consider the point, we cannot conceive how any idea, or anything like an idea, should have an absolute existence out of a mind: nor consequently, according to you, how there should be any real thing in nature[16]. The result of all which is that we are thrown into the most hopeless and abandoned Scepticism. Now, give me leave to ask you, First, Whether your referring ideas to certain absolutely existing unperceived substances, as their originals, be not the source of all this Scepticism[17]? Secondly, whether you are informed, either by sense or reason[18], of the existence of those unknown originals? And, in case you are not, whether it be not absurd to suppose them? Thirdly, Whether, upon inquiry, you find there is anything distinctly conceived or meant by the *absolute or external existence of unperceiving substances*[19]? Lastly, Whether,

---

[14] Cf. *Principles of Human Knowledge*, Introduction, sect. 23—25.
[15] Cf. *Principles of Human Knowledge*, sect. 8—10, 86, 87.
[16] Cf. *Ibid.* sect. 6.
[17] Cf. *Ibid.* sect. 87—90.
[18] Cf. *Ibid.* sect. 18.
[19] Cf. *Ibid.* sect. 24.

the premises considered, it be not the wisest way to follow nature, trust your senses, and, laying aside all anxious thought about unknown natures or substances[30], admit with the vulgar those for real things which are perceived by the senses?

Hyl. For the present, I have no inclination to the answering part. I would much rather see how you can get over what follows. Pray are not the objects perceived by the senses of one, likewise perceivable to others present? If there were a hundred more here, they would all see the garden, the trees, and flowers, as I see them. But they are not in the same manner affected with the ideas I frame in my imagination. Does not this make a difference between the former sort of objects and the latter?'

Phil. I grant it does. Nor have I ever denied a difference between the objects of sense and those of imagination[31]. But what would you infer from thence? You cannot say that sensible objects exist unperceived, because they are perceived by many.

Hyl. I own I can make nothing of that objection: but it hath led me into another. Is it not your opinion that by our senses we perceive only the ideas existing in our minds?

Phil. It is.

Hyl. But the same idea which is in my mind cannot be in yours, or in any other mind. Doth it not therefore follow, from your principles, that no two can see the same thing[32]? And is not this highly absurd?

Phil. If the term *same* be taken in the vulgar acceptation, it is certain (and not at all repugnant to the principles I maintain) that different persons may perceive the same thing; or the same thing or idea exist in different minds. Words are of arbitrary imposition; and, since men are used to apply the word *same* where no distinction or variety is perceived, and I do not pretend to alter their perceptions, it follows that, as men have said before, *several saw the same thing*, so they may, upon like occasions, still continue to use

---

[30] i. e. *noumena*, 'things-in-themselves,' &c.

[31] Cf. *Principles of Human Knowledge*, sect. 29—41.

[32] See Hamilton's Reid, p. 284; also Collier's *Clavis Universalis*, p. 6, where Collier says that he does not mean that the world, or any object in it which is perceived, for example, by John, is dependent on any other mind except John's. 'Two or more persons who are present at a concert of music may indeed in some measure be said to hear the *same* notes; yet the sound which the one hears is not the very same with the sound which another hears, because the souls or persons are supposed to be different; therefore the sound which Peter hears is external to, or independent on, the soul of John.'

the same phrase, without any deviation either from propriety of language, or the truth of things. But, if the term *same* be used in the acceptation of philosophers, who pretend to an abstracted notion of identity, then, according to their sundry definitions of this notion (for it is not yet agreed wherein that philosophic identity consists), it may or may not be possible for divers persons to perceive the same thing [a]. But whether philosophers shall think fit to call a thing the *same* or no, is, I conceive, of small importance. Let us suppose several men together, all endued with the same faculties, and consequently affected in like sort by their senses, and who had yet never known the use of language; they would, without question, agree in their perceptions. Though perhaps, when they came to the use of speech, some regarding the uniformness of what was perceived, might call it the *same* thing: others, especially regarding the diversity of persons who perceived, might choose the denomination of *different* things. But who sees not that all the dispute is about a word? to wit, whether what is perceived by different persons may yet have the term *same* applied to it? Or, suppose a house, whose walls or outward shell remaining unaltered, the chambers are all pulled down, and new ones built in their place; and that you should call this the *same*, and I should say it was not the *same* house:—would we not, for all this, perfectly agree in our thoughts of the house, considered in itself? And would not all the difference consist in a sound? If you should say, We differ in our notions; for that you superadded to your idea of the house the simple abstracted idea of identity, whereas I did not; I would tell you, I know not what you mean by the *abstracted idea of identity*; and should desire you to look into your own thoughts, and be sure you understood yourself.—— Why so silent, *Hylas*? Are you not yet satisfied men may dispute about identity and diversity, without any real difference in their thoughts and opinions, abstracted from names? Take this farther reflection with you—that whether Matter be allowed to exist or no, the case is exactly the same as to the point in hand. For, the Materialists themselves acknowledge what we immediately perceive by our senses to be our own ideas. Your difficulty,

---

[a] Berkeley seems to hold that there is no identity other than perfect similarity in any individuals besides persons. As to personal identity he is obscure. Cf. *Siris*, sect. 347. &c.

therefore, that no two see the same thing, makes equally against the Materialists and me.

Hyl. [*Ay, Philonous,*] But they suppose an external archetype, to which referring their several ideas they may truly be said to perceive the same thing.

Phil. And (not to mention your having discarded those archetypes) so may you suppose an external archetype on my principles;—*external*, I mean, to your own mind; though indeed it must be supposed to exist in that mind which comprehends all things; but then, this serves all the ends of *identity*, as well as if it existed out of a mind. And I am sure you yourself will not say it is less intelligible.

Hyl. You have indeed clearly satisfied me—either that there is no difficulty at bottom in this point; or, if there be, that it makes equally against both opinions.

Phil. But that which makes equally against two contradictory opinions can be a proof against neither.

Hyl. I acknowledge it. But, after all, *Philonous*, when I consider the substance of what you advance against *Scepticism*, it amounts to no more than this:—We are sure that we really see, hear, feel; in a word, that we are affected with sensible impressions.

Phil. And how are we concerned any farther? I see this *cherry*, I feel it, I taste it: and I am sure *nothing* cannot be seen, or felt, or tasted: it is therefore *real*[55]. Take away the sensations of softness, moisture, redness, tartness, and you take away the *cherry*. Since it is not a being distinct from sensations; a *cherry*, I say, is nothing but a congeries of sensible impressions, or ideas perceived by various senses: which ideas are united into one thing (or have one name given them) by the mind;—because they are observed to attend each other. Thus, when the palate is affected with such a particular taste, the sight is affected with a red colour, the touch with roundness, softness, &c. Hence, when I see, and feel, and taste, in sundry certain manners, I am sure the *cherry* exists, or is real; its reality being in my opinion nothing abstracted from those sensations. But if, by the word *cherry*, you mean an unknown nature, distinct from all those sensible qualities,

---

[54] Omitted in last edition.

[55] But I am not actually sentient of all its qualities simultaneously. My notion of the cherry includes ideas suggested to imagination, and not actually given in sense, when I merely see or touch it, e.g. its taste, odour, &c.

and by its *existence* something distinct from its being perceived; then, indeed, I own, neither you nor I, nor any one else, can be sure it exists.

Hyl. But, what would you say, *Philonous*, if I should bring the very same reasons against the existence of sensible things in a mind, which you have offered against their existing in a material *substratum?*

Phil. When I see your reasons, you shall hear what I have to say to them.

Hyl. Is the mind extended or unextended?

Phil. Unextended, without doubt.

Hyl. Do you say the things you perceive are in your mind?

Phil. They are.

Hyl. Again, have I not heard you speak of sensible impressions?

Phil. I believe you may.

Hyl. Explain to me now, O *Philonous!* how it is possible there should be room for all those trees and houses to exist in your mind. Can extended things be contained in that which is unextended? Or, are we to imagine impressions made on a thing void of all solidity? You cannot say objects are in your mind, as books in your study: or that things are imprinted on it, as the figure of a seal upon wax. In what sense, therefore, are we to understand those expressions? Explain me this if you can: and I shall then be able to answer all those queries you formerly put to me about my *substratum.*

Phil. Look you, *Hylas,* when I speak of objects as existing in the mind, or imprinted on the senses, I would not be understood in the gross literal sense—as when bodies are said to exist in a place, or a seal to make an impression upon wax. My meaning is only that the mind comprehends or perceives them; and that it is affected from without, or by some being distinct from itself[36]. This is my explication of your difficulty; and how it can serve to make your tenet of an unperceiving material *substratum* intelligible, I would fain know.

Hyl. Nay, if that be all, I confess I do not see what use can be made of it. But are you not guilty of some abuse of language in this?

---

[36] This explanation of what is meant by existence 'in mind,' or intelligible existence, is continually overlooked by Berkeley's critics.

Phil. None at all. It is no more than common custom, which you know is the rule of language, hath authorized: nothing being more usual, than for philosophers to speak of the immediate objects of the understanding as things existing in the mind. Nor is there anything in this but what is conformable to the general analogy of language; most part of the mental operations being signified by words borrowed from sensible things; as is plain in the terms *comprehend, reflect, discourse, &c.*, which, being applied to the mind, must not be taken in their gross original sense.

Hyl. You have, I own, satisfied me in this point. But there still remains one great difficulty, which I know not how you will get over. And, indeed, it is of such importance that if you could solve all others, without being able to find a solution for this, you must never expect to make me a proselyte to your principles.

Phil. Let me know this mighty difficulty.

Hyl. The Scripture account of the creation is what appears to me utterly irreconcilable with your notions [37]. Moses tells us of a creation: a creation of what? of ideas? No certainly, but of things, of real things, solid corporeal substances. Bring your principles to agree with this, and I shall perhaps agree with you.

Phil. Moses mentions the sun, moon, and stars, earth and sea, plants and animals. That all these do really exist, and were in the beginning created by God, I make no question. If by *ideas* you mean fictions and fancies of the mind [38], then these are no ideas. If by *ideas* you mean immediate objects of the understanding, or sensible things which cannot exist unperceived, or out of a mind [39], then these things are ideas. But whether you do or do not call them *ideas*, it matters little. The difference is only about a name. And, whether that name be retained or rejected, the sense, the truth, and reality of things continues the same. In common talk, the objects of our senses are not termed *ideas* but *things*. Call them so still—provided you do not attribute to them any absolute external existence—and I shall never quarrel with you for a word. The creation, therefore, I allow to have been a creation of things, of *real* things. Neither is this in the least inconsistent with my principles, as is evident from what I

---

[37] Cf. *Principles of Human Knowledge*, sect. 81—84.
[38] I.e. if you take the term *idea* in its restricted popular meaning.
[39] I.e. if you take the term *idea* in its philosophical meaning.

have now said; and would have been evident to you without this, if you had not forgotten what had been so often said before. But as for solid corporeal substances, I desire you to shew where Moses makes any mention of them; and, if they should be mentioned by him, or any other inspired writer, it would still be incumbent on you to shew those words were not taken in the vulgar acceptation, for things falling under our senses, but in the philosophic acceptation, for Matter, or *an unknown quiddity, with an absolute existence*. When you have proved these points, then (and not till then) may you bring the authority of Moses into our dispute.

Hyl. It is in vain to dispute about a point so clear. I am content to refer it to your own conscience. Are you not satisfied there is some peculiar repugnancy between the Mosaic account of the creation and your notions?

Phil. If all possible sense which can be put on the first chapter of Genesis may be conceived as consistently with my principles as any other, then it has no peculiar repugnancy with them. But there is no sense you may not as well conceive, believing as I do. Since, besides spirits, all you conceive are ideas; and the existence of these I do not deny. Neither do you pretend they exist without the mind.

Hyl. Pray let me see any sense you can understand it in.

Phil. Why, I imagine that if I had been present at the creation, I should have seen things produced into being—that is become perceptible—in the order prescribed by the sacred historian. I ever before believed the Mosaic account of the creation, and now find no alteration in my manner of believing it. When things are said to begin or end their existence, we do not mean this with regard to God, but His creatures. All objects are eternally known by God, or, which is the same thing, have an eternal existence in His mind: but when things, before imperceptible to creatures, are, by a decree of God, perceptible to them, then are they said to begin a relative existence, with respect to created minds. Upon reading therefore the Mosaic account of the creation, I understand that the several parts of the world became gradually perceivable to finite spirits, endowed with proper faculties; so that, whoever such were present, they were in truth perceived by them. This is the literal obvious sense suggested to me by the words of the Holy Scripture: in which is included no mention or no thought, either of *substratum*, instrument, occasion, or absolute existence. And, upon inquiry, I doubt not it will be found that most plain honest men, who believe the creation, never think of those things any more than I. What metaphysical sense you may understand it in, you only can tell.

Hyl. But, *Philonous*, you do not seem to be aware that you allow created things, in the beginning, only a relative, and consequently hypothetical being: that is to say, upon supposition there were men to perceive them, without which they have no actuality of absolute existence wherein creation might terminate. Is it not, therefore, according to you, plainly impossible the creation of any inanimate creatures should precede that of man? And is not this directly contrary to the Mosaic account?

Phil. In answer to that, I say, first, created beings might begin to exist in the mind of other created intelligences beside men. You will not therefore be able to prove any contradiction between Moses and my notions, unless you first shew there was no other order of finite created spirits in being before man. I say farther, in case we conceive the creation, as we should at this time a parcel of plants or vegetables of all sorts produced, by an invisible power, in a desert where nobody was present—that this way of explaining or conceiving it is consistent with my principles, since they deprive you of nothing, either sensible or imaginable; that it exactly suits with the common, natural, and undebauched notions of mankind; that it manifests the dependence of all things on God; and consequently hath all the good effect or influence, which it is possible that important article of our faith should have in making men humble, thankful, and resigned to their [*great] Creator. I say, moreover, that, in this naked conception of things, divested of words, there will not be found any notion of what you call the *actuality of absolute existence*. You may indeed raise a dust with those terms, and so lengthen our dispute to no purpose. But I entreat you calmly to look into your own thoughts, and then tell me if they are not a useless and unintelligible jargon.

Hyl. I own I have no very clear notion annexed to them. But what say you to this? Do you not make the existence of sensible things consist in their being in a mind? And were not all things

---

* In first and second editions only.

eternally in the mind of God? Did they not therefore exist from all eternity, according to you? And how could that which was eternal be created in time? Can anything be clearer or better connected than this?

Phil. And are not you too of opinion, that God knew all things from eternity?

Hyl. I am.

Phil. Consequently they always had a being in the Divine intellect.

Hyl. This I acknowledge.

Phil. By your own confession, therefore, nothing is new, or begins to be, in respect of the mind of God. So we are agreed in that point.

Hyl. What shall we make then of the creation?

Phil. May we not understand it to have been entirely in respect of finite spirits; so that things, with regard to us, may properly be said to begin their existence, or be created, when God decreed they should become perceptible to intelligent creatures, in that order and manner which He then established, and we now call the laws of nature? You may call this a *relative*, or *hypothetical existence* if you please. But so long as it supplies us with the most natural, obvious, and literal sense of the Mosaic history of the creation; so long as it answers all the religious ends of that great article; in a word, so long as you can assign no other sense or meaning in its stead; why should we reject this? Is it to comply with a ridiculous sceptical humour of making everything nonsense and unintelligible? I am sure you cannot say it is for the glory of God. For, allowing it to be a thing possible and conceivable that the corporeal world should have an absolute existence extrinsical to the mind of God, as well as to the minds of all created spirits; yet how could this set forth either the immensity or omniscience of the Deity, or the necessary and immediate dependence of all things on Him? Nay, would it not rather seem to derogate from those attributes?

Hyl. Well, but as to this decree of God's, for making things perceptible, what say you, *Philonous*—is it not plain, God did either execute that decree from all eternity, or at some certain time began to will what He had not actually willed before, but only designed to will? If the former, then there could be no creation or beginning of existence in finite things. If the latter, then we must acknowledge something new to befall the Deity; which implies a sort of change: and all change argues imperfection.

Phil. Pray consider what you are doing. Is it not evident this objection concludes equally against a creation in any sense; nay, against every other act of the Deity, discoverable by the light of nature? None of which can we conceive, otherwise than as performed in time, and having a beginning. God is a Being of transcendent and unlimited perfections: His Nature, therefore, is incomprehensible to finite spirits. It is not, therefore, to be expected, that any man, whether *Materialist* or *Immaterialist*, should have exactly just notions of the Deity, His attributes, and ways of operation. If then you would infer anything against me, your difficulty must not be drawn from the inadequateness of our conceptions of the Divine nature—which is unavoidable on any scheme, but from the denial of Matter, of which there is not one word, directly or indirectly, in what you have now objected.

Hyl. I must acknowledge the difficulties you are concerned to clear are such only as arise from the non-existence of Matter, and are peculiar to that notion. So far you are in the right. But I cannot by any means bring myself to think there is no such peculiar repugnancy between the creation and your opinion: though indeed where to fix it, I do not distinctly know.

Phil. What would you have? Do I not acknowledge a twofold state of things—the one ectypal or natural, the other archetypal and eternal? The former was created in time; the latter existed from everlasting in the mind of God[a]. Is not this agreeable to the common notions of divines? Or is any more than this necessary in order to conceive the creation? But you suspect some peculiar repugnancy, though you know not where it lies. To take away all possibility of scruple in the case, do but consider this one point. Either you are not able to conceive the creation on any hypothesis whatsoever; and, if so, there is no ground for dislike or complaint against any particular opinion on that score: or you are able to conceive it; and, if so, why not on my principles, since thereby nothing conceivable is taken away? You have all along been allowed the full scope of sense, imagination, and reason. Whatever, therefore, you could before

[a] Cf. *Siris*. sect. 347—349.

apprehend, either immediately or mediately by your senses, or by ratiocination from your senses; whatever you could perceive, imagine, or understand, remains still with you. If, therefore, the notion you have of the creation by other principles be intelligible, you have it still upon mine; if it be not intelligible, I conceive it to be no notion at all; and so there is no loss of it. And indeed it seems to me very plain that the supposition of Matter, that is a thing perfectly unknown and inconceivable, cannot serve to make us conceive anything. And, I hope it need not be proved to you that if the existence of Matter doth not make the creation conceivable, the creation's being without it inconceivable can be no objection against its non-existence.

Hyl. I confess, Philonous, you have almost satisfied me in this point of the creation.

Phil. I would fain know why you are not quite satisfied. You tell me indeed of a repugnancy between the Mosaic history and Immaterialism: but you know not where it lies. Is this reasonable, *Hylas*? Can you expect I should solve a difficulty without knowing what it is? But, to pass by all that, would not a man think you were assured there is no repugnancy between the received notions of Materialists and the inspired writings?

Hyl. And so I am.

Phil. Ought the historical part of Scripture to be understood in a plain obvious sense, or in a sense which is metaphysical and out of the way?

Hyl. In the plain sense, doubtless.

Phil. When Moses speaks of herbs, earth, water, &c. as having been created by God; think you not the sensible things commonly signified by those words are suggested to every unphilosophical reader?

Hyl. I cannot help thinking so.

Phil. And are not all ideas, or things perceived by sense, to be denied a real existence by the doctrine of the Materialist?

Hyl. This I have already acknowledged.

Phil. The creation, therefore, according to them, was not the creation of things sensible, which have only a relative being, but of certain unknown natures, which have an absolute being, wherein creation might terminate?

Hyl. True.

Phil. Is it not therefore evident the assertors of Matter destroy the plain obvious sense of Moses, with which their notions are utterly inconsistent; and instead of it obtrude on us I know not what, something equally unintelligible to themselves and me?

Hyl. I cannot contradict you.

Phil. Moses tells us of a creation. A creation of what? of unknown quiddities, of occasions, or *substratum?* No, certainly; but of things obvious to the senses. You must first reconcile this with your notions, if you expect I should be reconciled to them.

Hyl. I see you can assault me with my own weapons.

Phil. Then as to *absolute existence*,—was there ever known a more jejune notion than that? Something it is so abstracted and unintelligible that you have frankly owned you could not conceive it, much less explain anything by it. But, allowing Matter to exist, and the notion of absolute existence to be as clear as light, yet, was this ever known to make the creation more credible? Nay, hath it not furnished the atheists and infidels of all ages with the most plausible arguments against a creation? That a corporeal substance, which hath an absolute existence without the minds of spirits, should be produced out of nothing, by the mere will of a Spirit, hath been looked upon as a thing so contrary to all reason, so impossible and absurd, that not only the most celebrated among the ancients, but even divers modern and Christian philosophers have thought Matter co-eternal with the Deity. Lay these things together, and then judge you whether Materialism disposes men to believe the creation of things.

Hyl. I own, *Philonous,* I think it does not. This of the *creation* is the last objection I can think of; and I must needs own it hath been sufficiently answered as well as the rest. Nothing now remains to be overcome but a sort of unaccountable backwardness that I find in myself towards your notions.

Phil. When a man is swayed, he knows not why, to one side of the question, can this, think you, be anything else but the effect of prejudice, which never fails to attend old and rooted notions? And indeed in this respect I cannot deny the belief of Matter to have very much the advantage over the contrary opinion, with men of a learned education.

Hyl. I confess it seems to be as you say.

The Third Dialogue

Phil. As a balance, therefore, to this weight of prejudice, let us throw into the scale the great advantages[a] that arise from the belief of Immaterialism, both in regard to religion and human learning. —The being of a God, and incorruptibility of the soul, those great articles of religion, are they not proved with the clearest and most immediate evidence? When I say the being of a *God*, I do not mean an obscure general cause of things, whereof we have no conception, but *God*, in the strict and proper sense of the word; a Being whose spirituality, omnipresence, providence, omniscience, infinite power and goodness, are as conspicuous as the existence of sensible things, of which (notwithstanding the fallacious pretences and affected scruples of Sceptics) there is no more reason to doubt than of our own being.—Then, with relation to human sciences: in Natural Philosophy, what intricacies, what obscurities, what contradictions hath the belief of Matter led men into! To say nothing of the numberless disputes about its extent, continuity, homogeneity, gravity, divisibility, &c.—do they not pretend to explain all things by bodies operating on bodies, according to the laws of motion? and yet, are they able to comprehend how one body should move another? Nay, admitting there was no difficulty in reconciling the notion of an inert being with a cause, or in conceiving how an accident might pass from one body to another; yet, by all their strained thoughts and extravagant suppositions, have they been able to reach the mechanical production of any one animal or vegetable body? Can they account, by the laws of motion, for sounds, tastes, smells, or colours, or for the regular course of things? Have they accounted, by physical principles, for the aptitude and contrivance even of the most inconsiderable parts of the universe? But laying aside Matter and corporeal causes, and admitting only the efficiency of an All-perfect Mind, are not all the effects of nature easy and intelligible? If the *phenomena* are nothing else but *ideas*; God is a *spirit*, but Matter an unintelligent, unperceiving being. If they demonstrate an unlimited power in their cause; God is active and omnipotent, but Matter an inert mass. If the order, regularity, and usefulness of them can never be sufficiently admired; God is infinitely wise and provident, but Matter destitute of all contrivance and design. These surely

---

[a] Cf. *Principles of Human Knowledge*, sect. 85—156, in which the religious and scientific advantages of Immaterialism are illustrated.

are great advantages in *physics*. Not to mention that the apprehension of a distant Deity naturally disposes men to a negligence in their moral actions, which they would be more cautious of, in case they thought Him immediately present, and acting on their minds, without the interposition of Matter, or unthinking second causes.—Then in *metaphysics*: what difficulties concerning entity in abstract, substantial forms, hylarchic principles, plastic natures, [60]substance and accident, principle of individuation, possibility of Matter's thinking, origin of ideas, the manner how two independent substances so widely different as *Spirit* and *Matter*, should mutually operate on each other? what difficulties, I say, and endless disquisitions, concerning these and innumerable other the like points, do we escape, by supposing only Spirits and ideas?—Even the *mathematics* themselves, if we take away the absolute existence of extended things, become much more clear and easy; the most shocking paradoxes and intricate speculations in those sciences depending on the infinite divisibility of finite extension, which depends on that supposition.—But what need is there to insist on the particular sciences? Is not that opposition to all science whatsoever, that frenzy of the ancient and modern Sceptics, built on the same foundation? Or can you produce so much as one argument against the reality of corporeal things, or in behalf of that avowed utter ignorance of their natures, which doth not suppose their reality to consist in an external absolute existence? Upon this supposition, indeed, the objections from the change of colours in a pigeon's neck, or the appearance of the broken oar in the water, must be allowed to have weight. But these and the like objections vanish, if we do not maintain the being of absolute external originals, but place the reality of things in ideas, fleeting indeed, and changeable;—however, not changed at random, but according to the fixed order of nature. For, herein consists that constancy and truth of things which secures all the concerns of life, and distinguishes that which is *real* from the irregular visions of the fancy [61].

Hyl. I agree to all you have now said, and must own that

---

[60] 'substance and accident'—'subjects and adjuncts,'—in first and second editions.
[61] Cf. *Principles of Human Knowledge*, sect. 28—41; also *Siris*, sect. 294—297. 300—318. 335. 359—368, where we have glimpses of a more transcendental doctrine, allied to Platonism and Hegelianism.

nothing can incline me to embrace your opinion more than the advantages I see it is attended with. I am by nature lazy; and this would be a mighty abridgment in knowledge. What doubts, what hypotheses, what labyrinths of amusement, what fields of disputation, what an ocean of false learning may be avoided by that single notion of *Immaterialism*!

Phil. After all, is there anything farther remaining to be done? You may remember you promised to embrace that opinion which upon examination should appear most agreeable to Common Sense and remote from Scepticism. This, by your own confession, is that which denies Matter, or the absolute existence of corporeal things. Nor is this all; the same notion has been proved several ways, viewed in different lights, pursued in its consequences, and all objections against it cleared. Can there be a greater evidence of its truth? or is it possible it should have all the marks of a true opinion and yet be false?

Hyl. I own myself entirely satisfied for the present in all respects. But, what security can I have that I shall still continue the same full assent to your opinion, and that no unthought-of objection or difficulty will occur hereafter?

Phil. Pray, Hylas, do you in other cases, when a point is once evidently proved, withhold your consent on account of objections or difficulties it may be liable to? Are the difficulties that attend the doctrine of incommensurable quantities, of the angle of contact, of the asymptotes to curves, or the like, sufficient to make you hold out against mathematical demonstration? Or will you disbelieve the Providence of God, because there may be some particular things which you know not how to reconcile with it? If there are difficulties attending *Immaterialism*, there are at the same time direct and evident proofs of it. But for the existence of Matter there is not one proof, and far more numerous and insurmountable objections lie against it. But where are those mighty difficulties you insist on? Alas! you know not where or what they are; something which may possibly occur hereafter. If this be a sufficient pretence for withholding your full assent, you should never yield it to any proposition, how free soever from exceptions, how clearly and solidly soever demonstrated.

Hyl. You have satisfied me, Philonous.

Phil. But, to arm you against all future objections, do but consider—that which bears equally hard on two contradictory opinions can be proof against neither. Whenever, therefore, any difficulty occurs, try if you can find a solution for it on the hypothesis of the *Materialists*. Be not deceived by words; but sound your own thoughts. And in case you cannot conceive it easier by the help of *Materialism*, it is plain it can be no objection against *Immaterialism*. Had you proceeded all along by this rule, you would probably have spared yourself abundance of trouble in objecting; since of all your difficulties I challenge you to shew one that is explained by Matter: nay, which is not more unintelligible with than without that supposition, and consequently makes rather *against* than *for* it. You should consider, in each particular, whether the difficulty arises from the *non-existence of Matter*. If it doth not, you might as well argue from the infinite divisibility of extension against the Divine prescience, as from such a difficulty against *Immaterialism*. And yet, upon recollection, I believe you will find this to have been often if not always the case. You should likewise take heed not to argue on a *petitio principii*. One is apt to say, the unknown substances ought to be esteemed real things, rather than the ideas in our minds: and who can tell but the unthinking external substance may concur as a cause or instrument in the productions of our ideas? But, is not this proceeding on a supposition that there are such external substances? And to suppose this, is it not begging the question? But, above all things, you should beware of imposing on yourself by that vulgar sophism which is called *ignoratio elenchi*. You talked often as if you thought I maintained the non-existence of Sensible Things:—whereas in truth no one can be more thoroughly assured of their existence than I am: and it is you who doubt; I should have said, positively deny it. Everything that is seen, felt, heard, or any way perceived by the senses, is, on the principles I embrace, a real being, but not on yours. Remember, the Matter you contend for is an unknown somewhat (if indeed it may be termed *somewhat*), which is quite stripped of all sensible qualities, and can neither be perceived by sense, nor apprehended by the mind. Remember, I say, that it is not any object which is hard or soft, hot or cold, blue or white, round or square, &c.;—for all these things I affirm do exist. Though indeed I deny they have an existence distinct from being perceived; or that they exist out of all minds whatsoever. Think on these points; let them be attentively considered and still kept in view. Otherwise you will not comprehend the state of the question; without which your objections will always be wide of the mark, and, instead of mine, may possibly be directed (as more than once they have been) against your own notions.

Hyl. I must needs own, Philonous, nothing seems to have kept me from agreeing with you more than this same *mistaking the question*. In denying Matter, at first glimpse I am tempted to imagine you deny the things we see and feel: but, upon reflection, find there is no ground for it. What think you, therefore, of retaining the name *Matter*, and applying it to *sensible things?* This may be done without any change in your sentiments: and, believe me, it would be a means of reconciling them to some persons who may be more shocked at an innovation in words than in opinion.

Phil. With all my heart: retain the word *Matter*, and apply it to the objects of sense, if you please; provided you do not attribute to them any subsistence distinct from their being perceived. I shall never quarrel with you for an expression. *Matter*, or *material substance*, are terms introduced by philosophers; and, as used by them, imply a sort of independency, or a subsistence distinct from being perceived by a mind: but are never used by common people; or, if ever, it is to signify the immediate objects of sense. One would think, therefore, so long as the names of all particular things, with the terms *sensible*, *substance*, *body*, *stuff*, and the like, are retained, the word *Matter* should be never missed in common talk. And in philosophical discourses it seems the best way to leave it quite out: since there is not, perhaps, any one thing that hath more favoured and strengthened the depraved bent of the mind towards Atheism than the use of that general confused term.

Hyl. Well but, Philonous, since I am content to give up the notion of an unthinking substance exterior to the mind, I think you ought not to deny me the privilege of using the word *Matter* as I please, and annexing it to a collection of sensible qualities subsisting only in the mind. I freely own there is no other substance, in a strict sense, than *Spirit*. But I have been so long

accustomed to the term *Matter* that I know not how to part with
it. To say, there is no *Matter* in the world, is still shocking
to me. Whereas to say—There is no *Matter*, if by that term be
meant an unthinking substance existing without the mind; but
if by *Matter* is meant some sensible thing, whose existence
consists in being perceived, then there is *Matter*:—this distinction
gives it quite another turn; and men will come into your notions
with small difficulty, when they are proposed in that manner.
For, after all, the controversy about *Matter* in the strict acceptation
of it, lies altogether between you and the philosophers: whose
principles, I acknowledge, are not near so natural, or so agreeable
to the common sense of mankind, and Holy Scripture, as yours.
There is nothing we either desire or shun but as it makes,
or is apprehended to make, some part of our happiness or misery.
But what hath happiness or misery, joy or grief, pleasure or pain,
to do with Absolute Existence; or with unknown entities, abstracted from all relation to us? It is evident, things regard us
only as they are pleasing or displeasing: and they can please
or displease only so far forth as they are perceived. Farther,
therefore, we are not concerned; and thus far you leave things
as you found them. Yet still there is something new in this
doctrine. It is plain, I do not now think with the philosophers,
nor yet altogether with the vulgar. I would know how the case
stands in that respect; precisely, what you have added to, or
altered in my former notions.

Phil. I do not pretend to be a setter-up of new notions. My
endeavours tend only to unite and place in a clearer light that
truth which was before shared between the vulgar and the philosophers:—the former being of opinion, that *those things they immediately perceive are the real things*; and the latter, that *the things
immediately perceived are ideas which exist only in the mind*[a]. Which

---

[a] These two propositions are a summary of Berkeley's theory of *sensible things*. The second is, at least superficially, at vari- ance with Natural Realism, according, for instance, to Hamilton and Dr. Mansel. 'The (immediate) objects of sense are real,' says the latter, 'as having an existence independently of the act of perception; while the phantasms of the imagination may be called unreal, as existing only as modi- fications of the Ego.' (*Prolegomena Logica*, p. 298.) But, with Berkeley, the immediate objects of sense, substantially dependent on *perception*, are independent of the *will* of the percipient, and thus external to his proper personality. Berkeley's 'external world,' resulting from two factors, Divine and human, is causally independent of each finite mind; but neither causally nor substan- tially independent of Mind. And in what other meaning of the term is 'Independ- ence' of the percipient act intelligible?

two notions put together, do, in effect, constitute the substance of what I advance.

Hyl. I have been a long time distrusting my senses; methought I saw things by a dim light and through false glasses. Now the glasses are removed and a new light breaks in upon my understanding. I am clearly convinced that I see things in their native forms, and am no longer in pain about their *unknown natures* or *absolute existence*. This is the state I find myself in at present; though, indeed, the course that brought me to it I do not yet thoroughly comprehend. You set out upon the same principles that Academics, Cartesians, and the like sects usually do, and for a long time it looked as if you were advancing their Philosophical Scepticism; but, in the end, your conclusions are directly opposite to theirs.

Phil. You see, Hylas, the water of yonder fountain, how it is forced upwards, in a round column, to a certain height; at which it breaks, and falls back into the basin from whence it rose: its ascent as well as descent proceeding from the same uniform law or principle of *gravitation*. Just so, the same principles which, at first view, lead to Scepticism, pursued to a certain point, bring men back to Common Sense.

THE END.

EDITOR'S PREFACE

TO THE

THEORY OF VISION, OR VISUAL LANGUAGE, VINDICATED AND EXPLAINED.

EDITOR'S PREFACE

TO THE

THEORY OF VISION, OR VISUAL LANGUAGE, VINDICATED AND EXPLAINED.

THIS Tract, ostensibly a 'Vindication' of the New Theory of Vision, is a summary of the principles in which Berkeley's early metaphysical and theological philosophy originated. It was published twenty years later than the *Dialogues between Hylas and Philonous*, and twenty-four years later than the original *Essay* on Vision.

Alciphron, which was Berkeley's chief polemic against Free-thinkers, on behalf of fundamental beliefs in Ethics, Natural Theology, and Christianity, appeared in March 1732. The Fourth Dialogue defends faith in the present existence, intelligence, and goodness of God, by resting it upon the Theory of Visual Symbolism, conjoined with the proof of the impossibility of abstract or substantial Matter.

A new edition of the *Essay towards a New Theory of Vision* was appended to *Alciphron*.

On the 9th September, 1732, the 'Anonymous Letter' placed at the end of the following Tract, appeared in the Dublin *Daily Post-Boy*, with its eight objections to the New Theory that Vision is 'the sole language of God.'

This 'Anonymous Letter' was the immediate occasion of the 'Vindication,' which was published in London, 'printed for J. Tonson in the Strand,' in March 1733.

The fortune of the 'Vindication' illustrates the chronic tendency to misconceive and neglect Berkeley's philosophy. A brief and ingenious summary of his speculation, in one of its most interesting applications—it was at first misunderstood and then overlooked, and has since been unaccountably omitted in all the collected editions of Berkeley's Works.

For nearly a hundred years after its publication it obtained only slight and unappreciative recognition. It was the subject of a reference in Smith's *Optics*, in 1738; and, in the present century, it is alluded to by Sir J. Mackintosh in his *Dissertation* (art. *Shaftesbury*, note), and by Sir W. Hamilton in his *Discussions* (*Idealism; with reference to the Scheme of Arthur Collier*, &c.). An annotated edition was published in 1860, by Mr. H. V. H. Cowell, Associate of King's College, London, which has made the Tract familiar to recent students in metaphysics.

The opening sections of the 'Vindication' suggest the theological value of the Theory that Vision is a Divine Language. It was offered as a new and striking evidence of the perpetual presence and providence of God, in an age of Atheistical and Pantheistical free-thought.

Sect. 9—18 determine the meanings of certain terms apt to be misconceived in the discussion, and explain the scope of the New Theory. In particular, the distinction between the *immediate objects* of consciousness in the five senses (to which objects the names *idea* and *sensation* are also applied) and their *Cause* is insisted on, as of prime importance in the Theory of Vision. The immediate objects given in any one of the senses are (in themselves, and abstracted from their Cause) antithetical to the objects presented in the other senses. Experience assures us of this. We can find nothing common to the sensation of colour and the sensation of hardness, for example; for we are conscious of an antithesis between these two kinds of sensation. Notwithstanding, a sensation previously given in one of the senses may be suggested in imagination by a present sensation in another—under the associative law according to which signs suggest meanings in artificial language. What we are visually conscious of 'suggests' what we have been tactually conscious of; while neither of these two kinds of sensation contains *in itself* any revelation of its external Substance, or its external Cause.

Now, the ontological problem of Substance and Cause must not, Berkeley warns us, be confused with the psychological study of the different sorts of sensation; and of the laws under which these suggest one another as sign and signification, in Natural Language. The reflex study of our various sense-consciousnesses should precede that of the problem of externality, at least in the Theory of pure Vision—which Theory indeed is exhausted when it has reached the conception that visible objects or sensations are signs in a language of Nature; although it opens the way to the still higher conception of the world of presented sensations, regarded as a system of signs in a Divine Language, and of the entire phenomenal universe of the senses, as a collection of objects and effects in which Mind is the only Substance and Cause.

For the effectual expression of the distinction between what we are actually conscious of, and the cause of what we are thus conscious of, the contrasting terms *immediate object, sensation, idea, phenomenon, sensible effect,* &c. on the one hand; and *substance, cause, power, external existence,* &c. on the other, are, it is argued, indispensable.

Answers in succession to the eight objections of the 'Anonymous Letter,' and a general statement of the intended scope of the New Theory of Vision, are given in sect. 19—34, on the basis of the preliminary verbal explanations in the preceding sections.

Sect. 35—47 contain an exposition of the New Theory, arrived at in the early *Essay* by analytical research, with a view to apply it in this 'Vindication' deductively as the solution of questions in psychological Optics. The tendency of the previous analysis was to dissolve prejudices produced in the human mind by the constant association of visual and tactual experience; to exhibit the essential antithesis of these two sorts of sensation; and to explain the fact of their subsequent synthesis—a task, in the author's view, at least as necessary to a comprehensive or philosophical theory of Optics as is either the physiological examination of the material organ of sight, or an attempt to explain our visual judgments by the aid of geometry.

In these sections, as well as in those which follow, the order of the original *Essay* is reversed. The conclusion in which that *Essay* issues is here assumed at the outset, and is applied, in the sections which follow, to explain our judgments of the situations, signs, and distances of the things we seem to see—in short, our acquired faculty or habit of seeing. This conclusion involves the assumption that human imagination is governed by an associative law of accidental but constant concomitance (sect 39). There need be no resemblance, or necessary connexion between the phenomena given in sight and those given in the other senses, especially touch; for there is none between the meanings in an artificial language and the signs by which they are expressed. In Visual Language the signs are light and colour (sect. 42). Colour in its varieties is, *on this principle of suggestion, and on this alone,* sufficient to reproduce in imagination the correlative modifications of tactual, muscular, and locomotive sensation with which it is associated in the constitution of the sensible universe. Physiological questions regarding the mechanism of the eye have nothing to do with the psychological laws which explain how the mind learns to 'see,' i.e. to interpret visual signs (sect. 49). The pervading principles of the New Theory are stated to be, the absolute heterogeneity of the visible and the tangible; the presumption of man's inability, either by instinct or by reasoning, apart from experience, to comprehend the tactual and practical meaning of visual signs; and the proof that constant association in the senses, in conjunction with faith in the permanence of that association, is able to infuse a real meaning into the sensations of our visual consciousness (sect 41—47).

In sect. 48—52, the law of suggestion by constant sensible association is applied to explain our habit of interpreting aright the visual signs of real or tangible Situation, i.e. the visible, tactual, muscular, and locomotive sensations into which Locality may be analysed; and, in particular, to solve the difficulty, long a puzzle to inquirers in Optics, of vision by means of inverted images on the retina.

The same Theory of suggestion or association is applied, in sect. 53—61, to explain our acquired visual discernment of real Magnitude, as well as certain subordinate problems involved in this.

Sect. 62—69 employ the New Theory to explain, by means of visible signs, our visual judgment of real Distance, and of the distances of particular things from the eye. These signs are enumerated and verified in detail.

In these applications and verifications of the Theory (sect. 48—69), its purely psychological character is sustained throughout, by a steady appeal to what we are conscious of, unadulterated by facts in physiology, or demonstrations in geometry. The structure and functions of the eye cannot, it is assumed, throw any light upon the question of the origin —whether instinctive, ratiocinative, or experiential—of our visual judgments of Extension in its three dimensions, and of the relations of material things to Space. The physiology of the eye is, in short, irrelevant to the New Theory of Vision; which disposes, accordingly, for the purposes of this 'Vindication,' of investigations like those of Mr. Wheatstone, and reasonings like those of Mr. Abbott.

The 'Vindication' closes (sect. 70) with an allusion to Cheselden's since celebrated record, in the *Philosophical Transactions*, of the case of a person born blind, and afterwards made to see. As he was, of course, previously to the experiment, in possession of tactual, muscular, and locomotive experience, the case does not prove—what requires no proof—that pure visional sensation of colour is not the sensation of resistance. Cases like that of Cheselden are, however, appealed to in support of that part of the Theory which assumes that our power of interpreting the real.or tactual meaning of purely visual signs is not due to an Original Instinct, and that it may be explained by the known laws of Suggestion, under a divinely-established association of the visible and tangible worlds.

The ultimate aim of the Theory of Vision, as here vindicated, is to restore belief in the Divine—by teaching us that even the sensible forms of nature are the expression of Deity; that man is so constituted that he cannot help interpreting them; and that he may, by reflection, find in them a perpetual reminder of that Divine Essence in Existence of which he is always apt otherwise to lose the consciousness. A similar aim is manifest in *Siris*. This philosophy virtually implies that the Sensible World is, for each of us, the phenomenal expression of an external *Will* and of Absolute *Intelligence*.

A. C. F.

THE

THEORY OF VISION,

OR

VISUAL LANGUAGE,

SHEWING THE IMMEDIATE PRESENCE AND PROVIDENCE
OF A DEITY,

VINDICATED AND EXPLAINED.

BY THE AUTHOR OF
Alciphron, or, The Minute Philosopher.

Acts xvii. 28.
In Him we live, and move, and have our being.

1733.

a b

THE
THEORY OF VISION
VINDICATED AND EXPLAINED:

In answer to an Anonymous Writer.

1. AN ill state of health, which permits me to apply myself but seldom and by short intervals to any kind of studies, must be my apology, Sir, for not answering your Letter[1] sooner. This would have altogether excused me from a controversy upon points either personal or purely speculative, or from entering the lists with declaimers, whom I leave to the triumph of their own passions. And indeed to one of this character, who contradicts himself and misrepresents me, what answer can be made more than to desire his readers not to take his word for what I say, but to use their own eyes, read, examine, and judge for themselves? And to their Common Sense I appeal. For such a writer, such an answer may suffice. But argument, I allow, hath a right to be considered, and, where it doth not convince, to be opposed with reason. And being persuaded that the *Theory of Vision*, annexed to *The Minute Philosopher*, affords to thinking men a new and unanswerable proof of the Existence and immediate Operation of God, and the constant condescending care of His Providence, I think myself concerned, as well as I am able, to defend and explain it, at a time wherein Atheism hath made a greater progress than some are willing to own, or others to believe.

2. [2]He who considers that the present avowed enemies of

---

[1] [Published in the (Dublin) 'Daily Post-Boy' of September the 9th, 1732; which see in the Appendix]—AUTHOR.

[2] Sect. 2—8 contain observations upon the growth of Atheism out of English Deism, in the early part of last century. Cf. *Alciphron*, Dial. I. sect. 7—9, &c.

Christianity began their attacks against it under the specious pretext of defending the Christian Church and its rights[1], when he observes the same men pleading for Natural Religion, will be tempted to suspect their views, and judge of their sincerity in one case from what they have shewed in the other. Certainly the notion of a watchful, active, intelligent, free Spirit, with whom we have to do, and in whom we live and move and have our being, is not the most prevailing in the books and conversation even of those who are called Deists. Besides, as their schemes take effect, we may plainly perceive moral virtue and the religion of nature to decay, and see, both from reason and experience, that the destroying the Revealed Religion must end in Atheism or Idolatry. It must be owned, many minute philosophers would not like at present to be accounted Atheists. But how many, twenty years ago, would have been affronted to be thought Infidels, who would now be much more affronted to be thought Christians! As it would be unjust to charge those with Atheism who are not really tainted with it; so it will be allowed very uncharitable and imprudent to overlook it in those who are, and suffer such men, under specious pretexts, to spread their principles, and in the event to play the same game with Natural Religion that they have done with Revealed.

3. It must, without question, shock some innocent admirers of a certain plausible pretender to Deism and Natural Religion[2], if a man should say, there are strong signatures of Atheism and irreligion in every sense, natural as well as revealed, to be found even in that admired writer:—and yet, to introduce taste instead of duty, to make man a necessary agent, to deride a future judgment, seem to all intents and purposes atheistical, or subversive of all religion whatsoever. And these every attentive reader may plainly discover to be his principles; although it be not always easy to fix a determinate sense on such a loose and incoherent writer. There seems to be a certain way of writing, whether good or bad, tinsel or sterling, sense or nonsense, which, being suited to that size of understanding that qualifies its owners for the Minute Philosophy, doth marvellously strike and dazzle those ingenious men, who are

---

[1] The allusion is to Matthew Tindal. His *Rights of the Christian Church asserted against the Romish and other Priests* was published in 1706. Cf. p. 374, note 9.
[2] Shaftesbury, against whom the Third Dialogue in *Alciphron* is directed.

by this means conducted they know not how, and they know not whither. Doubtless that Atheist who gilds, and insinuates, and, even while he insinuates, disclaims his principles, is the likeliest to spread them. What availeth it, in the cause of Virtue and Natural Religion, to acknowledge the strongest traces of wisdom and power throughout the structure of the universe, if this wisdom is not employed to observe, nor this power to recompense our actions; if we neither believe ourselves accountable, nor God our Judge?

4. All that is said of a vital principle, of order, harmony, and proportion; all that is said of the natural decorum and fitness of things; all that is said of taste and enthusiasm, may well consist and be supported, without a grain even of Natural Religion, without any notion of Law or Duty, any belief of a Lord or Judge, or any religious sense of a God;—the contemplation of the mind upon the ideas of beauty, and virtue, and order, and fitness, being one thing, and a sense of religion another. So long as we admit no principle of good actions but natural affection, no reward but natural consequences; so long as we apprehend no judgment, harbour no fears, and cherish no hopes of a future state, but laugh at all these things, with the author of the *Characteristics*, and those whom he esteems the liberal and polished part of mankind[5], how can we be said to be religious in any sense? Or what is here that an Atheist may not find his account in as well as a Theist? To what moral purpose might not Fate or Nature serve as well as a Deity, on such a scheme? And is not this, at bottom, the amount of all those fair pretences?

5. Certainly that atheistical men, who hold no principles of any religion, natural or revealed, are an increasing number, and this too among people of no despicable rank, hath long since been expressly acknowledged[6] by one who will be allowed a proper judge, even this same plausible pretender himself to Deism and enthusiasm. But if any well-meaning persons, deluded by artful writers

---

[5] [*Characteristics*, vol. III. Miscel. 3. ch. 2]—AUTHOR. 'The fortune of the *Characteristics*,' says Sir J. Mackintosh, 'has been singular. For a time the work was admired more undistinguishably than its literary character warrants. In the succeeding period it was justly criticised, but too severely condemned. Of late, more unjustly than in either of the two former cases, it has been generally neglected. It seemed to have the power of changing the temper of its critics. It provoked the amiable Berkeley to a harshness equally unwonted and unwarranted; while it softened the rugged Warburton so far as to dispose the fierce yet not altogether ungenerous polemic to praise an enemy in the very heat of conflict.'—*Dissertation on the Progress of Ethical Philosophy*, sect. V.

[6] [*Moralists*, part II. sect. 3]—AUTHOR.

in the Minute Philosophy, or wanting the opportunity of any unreserved conversation with some ingenious men of that sect, should think that *Lysicles*[7] hath overshot the mark, and misrepresented their principles;—to be satisfied of the contrary, they need only cast an eye on the *Philosophical Dissertation upon Death*[8], lately published by a minute philosopher. Perhaps some man of leisure may think it worth while to trace the progress and unfolding of their principles, down from the writer In defence of the *Rights of the Christian Church*[9], to this plain dealer, the admirable author upon *Death*. During which period of time, I think one may observe a laid design gradually to undermine the belief of the Divine Attributes and Natural Religion; which scheme runs parallel with their gradual, covert, insincere proceedings, in respect of the Gospel.

6. That atheistical principles have taken deeper root, and are farther spread than most people are apt to imagine, will be plain to whoever considers that Pantheism, Materialism, Fatalism are nothing but Atheism a little disguised; that the notions of *Hobbes*, *Spinoza*, *Leibnitz*[10], and *Bayle* are relished and applauded; that as they who deny the Freedom and Immortality of the soul in effect deny its being, even so they do, as to all moral effects and natural religion, deny the being of God, who deny Him to be an observer, judge, and rewarder of human actions; that the course of arguing pursued by infidels leads to Atheism as well as Infidelity.

[An instance of this may be seen in the proceeding of the author of a book[11] intituled, *A Discourse of Free-thinking occasioned by*

---

[7] One of the Interlocutors in *Alciphron*, on the free-thinking side.

[8] *A Philosophical Dissertation upon Death, composed for the Consolation of the Unhappy. By a Friend to Truth.* London, 1732. This work is attributed to A. Radicati, Conti de Passerano, and the translation to John (Thomas?) Morgan. The fear of death, as well as the moral feelings and judgments of men, are referred in this Essay to habit and education; and the licence of a morality according to circumstances is vindicated, as well as the lawfulness and occasional expediency of suicide.

[9] *The Rights of the Christian Church asserted against the Romish and other Priests who claim an independent power over it. With a Preface concerning the Government of the Church of England as by Law established.* London, 1706. The author, as is well known, was Matthew Tindal, one of the English Deists. The work called forth a host of controversial pamphlets. It was defended, however, by Le Clerc and others as simply an attack on Sacerdotalism. In 1731, Tindal published *Christianity as old as the Creation: or the Gospel a republication of the Religion of Nature*.

[10] Leibnitz is here associated with Hobbes, Spinoza, and Bayle, his professed antagonists, probably on the ground of his Necessarianism, more or less developed in his *Theodicée*, and in his *Correspondence* with Dr. Samuel Clarke.

[11] Anthony Collins, whose *Discourse* appeared in 1713, and was the occasion of much controversy. See in particular *Remarks upon a late Discourse of Free-thinking:*

the Rise and Growth of a Sect called Free-thinkers, who, having insinuated his infidelity from men's various pretences and opinions concerning revealed religion, in like manner appears to insinuate his Atheism from the differing notions of men concerning the nature and attributes of God—particularly from the opinion of our knowing God by Analogy (see p. 42 of the mentioned book), as it hath been misunderstood and misinterpreted by some of late years. Such is the ill effect of untoward defences and explanations of our faith; and such advantage do incautious friends give its enemies. If there be any modern well-meaning writer, who (perhaps from not having considered the Fifth Book of *Euclid*) writes much of Analogy without understanding it, and thereby hath slipped his foot into this snare, I wish him to slip it back again, and, instead of causing scandal to good men and triumph to Atheists, discreetly explain away his first sense, and return to speak of God and His attributes in the style of other Christians; allowing that knowledge and wisdom do, in the proper sense of the words, belong to God, and that we have some notion, though infinitely inadequate, of these Divine attributes, yet still more than a man blind from his birth can have of sight and colours[12].]

But to return, if I see it in their writings, if they own it in their conversation, if their ideas imply it, if their ends are not answered but by supposing it, if their leading author[13] hath pretended to demonstrate Atheism, but thought fit to conceal his Demonstration from the public; if this was known in their clubs, and yet that author was nevertheless followed, and represented to the world as a believer of Natural Religion; if these things are

in *a Letter to T. H., D.D.* (Dr. Hare, afterwards Bishop of Chichester), *by Phileleutherus Lipsiensis* (Dr. Bentley). London, 1713. It was in 1713 that the Essays against the Free-thinkers, attributed to Berkeley, appeared in the 'Guardian.'

[12] Cf. *Alciphron*, Dialogue IV. sect. 16—22. In which the nature of man's notion of God, and the insufficiency of the analogical hypothesis to account for our theological knowledge is discussed. This alleged heresy is defended with acuteness and learning in the *Divine Analogy* of Bishop Browne, which appeared in 1733, almost contemporaneously with *Alciphron*. Besides Berkeley and Browne, both Irish bishops, and opposed on this question of an analogical knowledge of 'things Divine and Supernatural,' two archbishops of Dublin and three English prelates, are associated with it. See Archbishop King's discourse on *The Right Method of interpreting Scripture, in what relates to the Nature of the Deity*, edited with notes by Archbishop Whately; Bishop Law's Notes on Archbishop King's *Essay on the Origin of Evil*; Bishop Copleston's *Inquiry into the Doctrines of Necessity and Predestination*; and Bishop Hampden's Bampton Lectures on *The Scholastic Philosophy in its relation to Christian Theology*; to which may be added Dr. Mansel's well-known Bampton Lectures on *The Limits of Religious Thought*.

[13] Anthony Collins. Cf. *Alciphron*—'Advertisement,' note.

so (and I know them to be so), surely what the favourers of their schemes would palliate, it is the duty of others to display and refute.

7. And although the characters of Divinity are large and legible throughout the whole creation to men of plain sense and common understanding, yet it must be considered that we have other adversaries to oppose, other proselytes to make—men prejudiced to false systems and proof against vulgar arguments, who must be dealt with on a different footing. Conceited, metaphysical, disputing men must be paid in another coin; we must shew that truth and reason in all shapes are equally against them, except we resolve to give them up, what they are very fond of being thought to engross, all pretensions to philosophy, science, and speculation.

8. Meanwhile thus much is evident: those good men who shall not care to employ their thoughts on this *Theory of Vision* have no reason to find fault. They are just where they were, being left in full possession of all other arguments for a God, none of which are weakened by this. And as for those who shall be at the pains to examine and consider this subject, it is hoped they may be pleased to find, in an age wherein so many schemes of Atheism are restored or invented, a new argument of a singular nature in proof of the immediate Care and Providence of a God, present to our minds, and directing our actions. As these considerations convince me that I cannot employ myself more usefully than in contributing to awaken and possess men with a thorough sense of the Deity inspecting, concerning, and interesting itself in human actions and affairs: so, I hope it will not be disagreeable to you that, in order to this, I make my appeal to Reason, from your remarks upon what I have wrote concerning Vision; since men who differ in the means may yet agree in the end, and in the same candour and love of truth.

9. [14]By a sensible *object* I understand that which is properly perceived by sense. Things properly perceived by sense are immediately perceived[15]. Besides things properly and immediately per-

---

[14] Sect. 9—13 contain Berkeley's explanation of the term *sensible object*, i.e. sensible idea or sensation; and enforce the, with him, essential distinction between perceivable objects (i. e. sensations) and their unperceivable cause.

[15] i.e. our percepts proper are sensations (or *ideas*, as Berkeley calls them) which we

ceived by any sense, there may be also other things suggested to the mind by means of those proper and immediate objects;—which things so suggested are not objects of that sense, being in truth only objects of the imagination, and originally belonging to some other sense or faculty. Thus, sounds are the proper object of hearing, being properly and immediately perceived by that, and by no other sense. But, by the mediation of sounds or words, all other things may be suggested to the mind; and yet things so suggested are not thought the object of hearing.

10. The peculiar objects of each sense, although they are truly or strictly perceived by that sense alone, may yet be suggested to the imagination by some other sense. The objects therefore of all the senses may become objects of imagination, which faculty represents all sensible things. A colour, therefore, which is truly perceived by sight alone, may, nevertheless, upon hearing the words blue or red, be apprehended by the imagination. It is in a primary and peculiar manner the object of sight; in a secondary manner it is the object of imagination: but cannot properly be supposed the object of hearing.

11. The objects of sense, being things immediately perceived, are otherwise called *ideas*. The *cause* of these ideas, or the power of producing them, is not the object of sense—not being itself perceived, but only inferred by reason from its effects, to wit, those objects or ideas which are perceived by sense. From our ideas of sense the inference of reason is good to Power, Cause, Agent. But we may not therefore infer that our ideas are like unto this Power, Cause, or Active Being. On the contrary, it seems evident that an idea can be only like another idea, and that in our ideas or immediate objects of sense, there is nothing of Power, Causality, or Agency included [16].

12. Hence it follows that the Power or Cause of ideas is not an object of sense, but of reason. Our knowledge of the cause is measured by the effect; of the power, by our idea. To the absolute nature, therefore, of outward causes or powers, we have nothing to say: they are no objects of our sense or perception.

are conscious of in our actual sense-experience, and not mere representations which we are induced to believe by suggestion, or by inductive inference founded on the sensations. What is suggested is not an object of sense, but of imagination, when imagination ministers to belief.

[16] Cf. *Principles of Human Knowledge*, sect. 15—38.

Whenever, therefore, the appellation of sensible *object* is used in a determined intelligible sense, it is not applied to signify the absolutely existing outward cause or power, but the ideas[17] themselves produced thereby.

13. Ideas which are observed to be connected together are vulgarly considered under the relation of cause and effect, whereas, in strict and philosophic truth, they are only related as the sign to the thing signified[18]. For, we know our ideas, and therefore know that one idea cannot be the cause of another. We know that our ideas of sense are not the cause of themselves. We know also that *we* do not cause them. Hence we know they must have some other efficient cause, distinct from them and us[19].

14. [20]In treating of Vision, it was my purpose to consider the effects and appearances, the objects[20] perceived by my senses, the ideas[21] of sight as connected with those of touch; to inquire how one idea comes to suggest another belonging to a different sense, how things visible suggest things tangible, how present things suggest things more remote and future, whether by likeness, by necessary connexion, by geometrical inference, or by arbitrary institution[22].

15. It hath indeed been a prevailing opinion and undoubted principle among mathematicians and philosophers that there were certain ideas common to both senses: whence arose the distinction of primary and secondary qualities. But, I think it hath been demonstrated that there is no such thing as a common object—as an idea, or kind of idea perceived both by sight and touch[23].

16. In order to treat with due exactness on the nature of Vision,

---

[17] i. e. sensations.
[18] The whole theory of (physical) causation, as developed by Hume, Dr. Thomas Brown, Mr. J. S. Mill, and other recent theorists on the methods of positive science, is involved in this sentence. Cf. *Principles of Human Knowledge*, sect. 25, 26. 51—53. 65, 66, &c.
[19] This is Berkeley's explanation of our notion and belief of externality. The external world is essentially dependent on mind, but actually independent of each finite will or efficient cause, and thus impersonal. Cf. *Principles of Human Knowledge*, sect. 56, 57, &c.
[20] Sect. 14—18 explain the design and scope of the *Essay towards a New Theory of Vision*, published twenty-four years previously.
[21] i. e. the *sensible objects* (called *ideas* by Berkeley) of which we are conscious, as distinguished from their causes, of which we are not, and cannot be, immediately percipient. This corresponds to the distinction between perception proper and mediate or suggested perception.
[22] The doctrine of visual suggestion, by the synthesis of arbitrary association, is the essence of the New Theory of Vision, which is founded upon the phenomenal heterogeneity of the visible and tangible worlds.
[23] [*Theory of Vision*, sect. 127, &c.]—AUTHOR.

it is necessary in the first place accurately to consider our own ideas"; to distinguish where there is a difference; to call things by their right names; to define terms, and not confound ourselves and others by their ambiguous use; the want or neglect whereof hath so often produced mistakes. Hence it is that men talk as if one idea was the efficient cause of another; hence they mistake inferences of reason for perceptions of sense; hence they confound the power residing in somewhat external with the proper object of sense—which is in truth no more than our own idea.

17. When we have well understood and considered the nature of Vision", we may, by reasoning from thence, be better able to collect some knowledge of the external, unseen Cause of our ideas; whether it be one or many, intelligent or unintelligent, active or inert, body or spirit. But, in order to understand and comprehend this Theory, and discover the true principles thereof, we should consider the likeliest way is not to attend to unknown substances, external causes, agents, or powers, nor to reason or infer anything about or from things obscure, unperceived, and altogether unknown.

18. As in this inquiry we are concerned with what objects we perceive, or our own ideas, so, upon them our reasonings must proceed. To treat of things utterly unknown as if we knew them, and so lay our beginning in obscurity, would not surely seem the properest means for the discovering of truth. Hence it follows, that it would be wrong if one about to treat of the nature of Vision, should, instead of attending to visible ideas, define the object of sight to be that obscure cause, that invisible power or agent, which produced visible ideas in our minds. Certainly such cause or power does not seem to be the *object* either of the sense or the science of Vision, inasmuch as what we know thereby we know only of the effects.—Having premised thus much, I now proceed to consider the principles laid down in your Letter, which I shall take in order as they lie.

" In other words, a theory of vision implies preliminary reflection upon the objects of which we are conscious in the various senses—the sensations given in each sense.

" I. e. the objects we are actually conscious of in seeing—in themselves, apart from extreme substances or causes. This *purified* sense-consciousness is Berkeley's foundation for his theory of externality in another consciousness than our own; in contrast to the theory of an unknowable externality, independent of any mind—his philosophy of substances and causes as necessarily Mind, or at least dependent on Divine and finite Minds.

19. [25]In your *first paragraph* or *section*, you say that 'whatever it is without which is the cause of any idea within, you call the object of sense;' and you tell us soon after this[27], 'that we cannot possibly have an idea of any object without.'—Hence it follows that by an *object* of sense you mean something that we can have no manner of idea of. This making the objects of sense to be things utterly insensible seems to me contrary to common sense and the use of language. That there is nothing in the reason of things to justify such a definition is, I think, plain from what has been premised[28]. And that it is contrary to received custom and opinion, I appeal to the experience of the first man you meet, who I suppose will tell you that by an object of sense he means that which is perceived by sense[29], and not a thing utterly unperceivable and unknown. The beings, substances, powers which exist without may indeed concern a treatise on some other science, and may there become a proper subject of inquiry. But, why they should be considered as objects of the visive faculty, in a treatise of Optics, I do not comprehend.

20. The real objects of sight we see, and what we see we know. And these true objects of sense and knowledge, to wit, our own ideas, are to be considered, compared, distinguished, in order to understand the true Theory of Vision. As to the outward cause of these ideas, whether it be one and the same, or various and manifold, whether it be thinking or unthinking, spirit or body, or whatever else we conceive or determine about it, the visible appearances do not alter their nature—our ideas are still the same. Though I may have an erroneous notion of the cause, or though I may be utterly ignorant of its nature, yet this does not hinder my making true and certain judgments about my ideas; my knowing which are the same, and which different; wherein they

---

[25] Sect. 19—34 contain answers to the special objections of the *Anonymous Writer*, and general remarks upon his *Letter*.

[26] [Sect. 4]—AUTHOR.

[27] [*Supra*, sect. 9, 11, 12]—AUTHOR. Berkeley and his critic use the term *object* differently, which must be remembered in what follows.

[28] I. e. *immediately* perceived, or of which we have a sense-consciousness. Here, as elsewhere, Berkeley insists upon the distinction between the sensations of which we are actually conscious (which he calls objects or ideas), on the one hand, and, on the other hand, (a) what, as conceivable, may be, indeed is, suggested by the sensation, whether called physical substance or physical cause —which he accepts; as well as (b) abstract or inconceivable substances and cause— which he absolutely rejects. The contrast between *objects-proper*, and their *causes* (whether unintelligible or spiritual), is the cardinal fact in these sections. The former alone, he says, belong to the Theory of Vision.

agree, and wherein they disagree; which are connected together, and wherein this connexion consists; whether it be founded in a likeness of nature, in a geometrical necessity, or merely in experience and custom[30].

21. In your *second section*, you say 'that if we had but one sense, we might be apt to conclude there were no objects at all without us; but that, since the same object is the cause of ideas by different senses, thence we infer its existence.'—Now, in the first place, I observe, that I am at a loss concerning the point which is here assumed, and would fain be informed how we come to know that the same object causeth ideas by different senses. In the next place, I must observe that, if I had only one sense, I should nevertheless infer and conclude there was some cause without me (which you, it seems, define to be an *object*), producing the sensations or ideas perceived by that sense. For, if I am conscious that I do not cause them, and know that they are not the cause of themselves, both which points seem very clear, it plainly follows that there must be some other third cause distinct from me and them[31].

22. In your *third section*, you acknowledge with me 'that the connexion between ideas of different senses ariseth only from experience.'—Herein we are agreed. In your *fourth section* you say 'that a word denoting an external object, is the representative of no manner of idea. Neither can we possibly have an idea of what is solely without us.'—What is here said of an external unknown object hath been already considered[32].

23. In the *following section* of your Letter, you declare 'that our ideas have only an arbitrary connexion with outward objects, that they are nothing like the outward objects, and that a variation in our ideas doth not imply or infer a change in the objects, which may still remain the same.'—Now, to say nothing about the confused use of the word 'object,' which hath been more than once already observed, I shall only remark that the points asserted in this section do not seem to consist with some others that follow.

24. For, in the *sixth section*, you say 'that in the present

---

[30] To which last it is referred by Berkeley.

[31] Hence, an external or independent world (of some sort) may be inferred from the sensations of which we are conscious in any one of the senses—our conviction of our own personal agency, and of its limits, being of course assumed.

[32] [*Supra*, sect. 19]—AUTHOR.

situation of things, there is an infallible certain connexion between the idea and the object.'—But how can we perceive this connexion, since, according to you, we never perceive such object, nor can have any idea of it? or, not perceiving it, how can we know this connexion to be infallibly certain?

25. In the *seventh section*, it is said 'that we may, from our infallible experience, argue from our idea of one sense to that of another.'—But, I think it is plain that our experience of the connexion between ideas of sight and touch is not infallible; since, if it were, there could be no *deceptio visus*, neither in painting, perspective, dioptrics, nor any otherwise.

26. In the *last section*, you affirm 'that experience plainly teaches us that a just proportion is observed in the alteration of the ideas of each sense, from the alteration of the object.'—Now, I cannot possibly reconcile this section with the fifth, or comprehend how experience should shew us that the alteration of the object produceth a proportionable alteration in the ideas of different senses; or how indeed it should shew us anything at all either from or about the alteration of an object utterly unknown, of which we neither have nor can have any manner of idea. What I do not perceive or know, how can I perceive or know to be altered? And, knowing nothing of its alterations, how can I compute anything by them, deduce anything from them, or be said to have any experience about them [33]?

27. From the observations you have premised, rightly understood and considered, you say it follows 'that my *New Theory of Vision* must in great measure fall to the ground; and the laws of Optics will be found to stand upon the old unshaken bottom.' —But, though I have considered and endeavoured to understand your remarks, yet I do not in the least comprehend how this conclusion can be inferred from them. The reason you assign for such inference is, 'because, although our ideas in one sense are entirely different from our ideas in another, yet we may

---

[33] In the preceding sections, Berkeley is virtually arguing against the possibility of an ultimately representative perception or intelligence of the supposed material substance and cause. We can imagine and infer only what we have had examples of in our previous presentative experience. He here and elsewhere anticipates objections of Reid and Hamilton to a representative perception of things whose externality consists in an absolute divorce from mind, and which, therefore, have not been previously, through the senses, in presentative relation to the mind in which, nevertheless, they are assumed to be represented.

justly argue from one to the other, as they have one common cause without; of which, you say, we cannot possibly have even the faintest idea.'—Now, my theory nowhere supposeth that we may not justly argue from the ideas of one sense to those of another, by analogy and by experience; on the contrary, this very point is affirmed, proved, or supported throughout[34].

28. Indeed I do not see how the inferences which we make from visible to tangible ideas include any consideration of one common unknown external cause, or depend thereon, but only on mere custom or habit. The experience which I have had that certain ideas of one sense are attended or connected with certain ideas of a different sense is, I think, a sufficient reason why the one may suggest the other.

29. In the next place, you affirm 'that something without, which is the cause of all the variety of ideas within, in one sense, is the cause also of the variety in another: and, as they have a necessary connexion with it, we very justly demonstrate, from our ideas of feeling of the same object, what will be our ideas of seeing.'—As to which, give me leave to remark that to inquire whether that *unknown something* be the same in both cases, or different, is a point foreign to Optics; inasmuch as our perceptions by the visive faculty will be the very same, however we determine that point. Perhaps[35] I think that the same Being[36] which causeth our ideas of sight doth cause not only our ideas of touch likewise, but also all our ideas of all the other senses, with all the varieties thereof. But this, I say, is foreign to the purpose[37].

30. As to what you advance, that our ideas have a *necessary* connexion with such cause, it seems to me *gratis dictum*: no reason is produced for this assertion; and I cannot assent to it without a reason. The ideas or effects I grant are evidently perceived: but the cause you say is utterly unknown[38]. How then can you tell whether such unknown cause acts arbitrarily or necessarily? I see the effects or appearances: and I know that effects must

---

[34] [*Theory of Vision*, sect. 38 and 78, &c.]—AUTHOR.

[35] Does this 'perhaps' imply any hesitation on Berkeley's part as to the essence of his early philosophy—the substantiality and causality of sensible things in God, as opposed to their substantiality and causality in an unknown and incognisable essence, out of all relation to Mind.

[36] God.

[37] For, in Optics we are concerned exclusively, according to Berkeley, with the *effects* (i. e. our sensations or sense-ideas); and their relations to one another, as immediately-perceived sign and mediately-perceived meaning.

[38] [*Letter*, sect. 1 and 4]—AUTHOR.

have a cause: but I neither see nor know that their connexion with that cause is necessary. Whatever there may be, I am sure I see no such necessary connexion, nor, consequently, can demonstrate by means thereof from ideas of one sense to those of another.

31. You add that although to talk of seeing by tangible angles and lines be direct nonsense, yet, to demonstrate from angles and lines in feeling to the ideas in seeing that arise from the same common object is very good sense. If by this no more is meant than that men might argue and compute geometrically by lines and angles in Optics, it is so far from carrying in it any opposition to my theory that I have expressly declared the same thing[9]. This doctrine, as admitted by me, is indeed subject to certain limitations; there being divers cases wherein the writers of Optics thought we judged by lines and angles, or by a sort of natural geometry, with regard to which I think they were mistaken, and I have given my reasons for it. And those reasons, as they are untouched in your letter, retain their force with me.

32. I have now gone through your reflexions, which the conclusion intimates to have been written in haste, and, having considered them with all the attention I am master of, must now leave it to the thinking reader to judge whether they contain anything that should oblige me to depart from what I have advanced in my *Theory of Vision*. For my own part, if I were ever so willing, it is not on this occasion in my power to indulge myself in the honest satisfaction it would be frankly to give up a known error; a thing so much more right and reputable to denounce than to defend. On the contrary, it should seem that the Theory will stand secure; since you agree with me that men do not see by lines and angles; since I, on the other hand, agree with you that we may nevertheless compute in Optics by lines and angles, as I have expressly shewed; since all that is said in your Letter about the object, the same object, the alteration of the object, is quite foreign to the theory, which considereth our ideas[10] as the object of sense, and hath nothing to do with that unknown, unperceived, unintelligible thing which you signify by the word *object*[11]. Certainly the laws of Optics will not stand on the old, unshaken

[9] [*Theory of Vision*, sect. 78]—AUTHOR.
[10] [*Supra*, sect. 14]—AUTHOR.
[11] I. e. our sensations.

bottom, if it be allowed that we do not see by geometry [a]; if it be evident that explications of phenomena given by the received theories in Optics are insufficient and faulty; if other principles are found necessary for explaining the nature of vision; if there be no idea, nor kind of idea, common to both senses [b], contrary to the old received universal supposition of optic writers.

33. We not only impose on others but often on ourselves, by the unsteady or ambiguous use of terms. One would imagine that an *object* should be perceived. I must own, when that word is employed in a different sense, that I am at a loss for its meaning, and consequently cannot comprehend any arguments or conclusions about it. And I am not sure that, on my own part, some inaccuracy of expression, as well as the peculiar nature of the subject, not always easy either to explain or conceive, may not have rendered my Treatise concerning Vision difficult to a cursory reader. But, to one of due attention, and who makes my words an occasion of his own thinking, I conceive the whole to be very intelligible: and, when it is rightly understood, I scarce doubt but it will be assented to. One thing at least I can affirm, that, if I am mistaken, I can plead neither haste nor inattention, having taken true pains and much thought about it.

34. And had you, Sir, thought it worth while to have dwelt more particularly on the subject, to have pointed out distinct passages in my Treatise, to have answered any of my objections to the received notions, refuted any of my arguments in behalf of mine, or made a particular application of your own; I might without doubt have profited by your reflections. But it seems to me we have been considering, either different things, or else the same things in such different views as the one can cast no light on the other. I shall, nevertheless, take this opportunity to make a review of my Theory, in order to render it more easy and clear; and the rather because, as I had applied myself betimes to this subject, it became familiar—and in treating of things familiar to ourselves, we are too apt to think them so to others.

35. "It seemed proper, if not unavoidable, to begin in the

---

[a] [*Letter*, sect. 8]—AUTHOR.
[b] [*Theory of Vision*, sect. 127]—AUTHOR.
[c] Sect. 35—47 contain a restatement of the *New Theory* of a Divine Language in

accustomed style of optic writers—admitting divers things as true, which, in a rigorous sense, are not such, but only received by the vulgar and admitted as such. There hath been a long and close connexion in our minds between the ideas[15] of sight and touch. Hence they are considered as one thing—which prejudice suiteth well enough with the purpose of life; and language is suited to this prejudice. The work of science and speculation is to unravel our prejudices and mistakes, untwisting the closest connexions, distinguishing things that are different; instead of confused or perplexed, giving us distinct views; gradually correcting our judgment, and reducing it to a philosophical exactness. And, as this work is the work of time, and done by degrees, it is extremely difficult, if at all possible, to escape the snares of popular language, and the being betrayed thereby to say things strictly speaking neither true nor consistent[16]. This makes thought and candour more especially necessary in the reader. For, language being accommodated to the prænotions of men and use of life, it is difficult to express therein the precise truth of things, which is so distant from their use, and so contrary to our prænotions.

36. In the contrivance of Vision, as that of other things, the wisdom of Providence seemeth to have consulted the operation rather than the theory of man; to the former things are admirably fitted, but, by that very means, the latter is often perplexed. For, as useful as these immediate suggestions and constant connexions are to direct our actions; so is our distinguishing between things confounded, and as it were blended together, no less necessary to the speculation and knowledge of truth.

37. The knowledge of these connexions, relations, and differences of things visible and tangible, their nature, force, and significancy hath not been duly considered by former writers on Optics, and seems to have been the great *desideratum* in that science, which for want thereof was confused and imperfect. A Treatise, therefore, of this philosophical kind, for the understanding of Vision, is at least as necessary as the physical consideration of the eye, nerve, coats, humours; refractions, bodily nature, and motion of light; or the geometrical application of lines

---

Vision, conveyed to us by suggestion.—In sect. 48—70 this Theory is employed to explain deductively our visual discernment of the real Situation, Size, and Distance of sensible things.

[a] i.e. sensations.
[b] Cf. *Principles of Human Knowledge*—'Introduction.'

and angles for *praxis* or theory, in dioptric glasses and mirrors, for computing and reducing to some rule and measure our judgments, so far as they are proportional to the objects of geometry. In these three lights Vision should be considered, in order to a complete Theory of Optics.

38. It is to be noted that, in considering the Theory of Vision, I observed a certain known method, wherein, from false and popular suppositions, men do often arrive at truth. Whereas in the synthetical method of delivering science or truth already found, we proceed in an inverted order, the conclusions in the analysis being assumed as principles in the synthesis. I shall therefore now begin with that conclusion—That *Vision is the Language of the Author of Nature*, from thence deducing theorems and solutions of phenomena, and explaining the nature of visible things and the visive faculty[17].

39. Ideas which are observed to be connected with other ideas come to be considered as signs, by means whereof things not actually perceived by sense are signified or suggested to the imagination; whose objects they are, and which alone perceives them. And, as sounds suggest other things, so characters suggest other sounds; and, in general, all signs suggest the things signified, there being no idea which may not offer to the mind another idea which hath been frequently joined with it. In certain cases a sign may suggest its correlate as an image, in others as an effect, in others as a cause. But, where there is no such relation of similitude or causality, nor any necessary connexion whatsoever, two things, by their mere coexistence, or two ideas, merely by being perceived together, may suggest or signify one the other—their connexion being all the while arbitrary; for it is the connexion only, as such, that causeth this effect[18].

---

[17] In the original *Essay towards a New Theory of Vision*, Berkeley proceeds analytically; whereas, in the following synopsis, he first hypothetically assumes the Theory of a Visual Language—with which the earlier treatise concludes, and then verifies it, by shewing synthetically how it explains the phenomena of Vision; and in particular solves difficulties contained in our judgments of the situation, sizes, and distances of things. See Editor's Preface to the *Essay*, p. 6, note.

[18] This doctrine of 'suggestion' is the constructive principle of the New Theory; which is an application, on a great scale, of the law of constant association, regulating imagination and belief in individuals, in established harmony with the Divine Associations among sensations, common to a plurality of individuals, and which express the order of external nature. It should be compared with Kant's theory of perception, according to which sensations, received into the necessary forms of space and time, are constructed or made intelligible by the cate-

40. A great number of arbitrary signs, various and opposite, do constitute a Language. If such arbitrary connexion be instituted by men, it is an artificial Language; if by the Author of Nature, it is a Natural Language. Infinitely various are the modifications of light and sound, whence they are each capable of supplying an endless variety of signs, and, accordingly, have been each employed to form languages; the one by the arbitrary appointment of mankind, the other by that of God Himself[19]. A connexion established by the Author of Nature, in the ordinary course of things, may surely be called natural, as that made by men will be named artificial. And yet this doth not hinder but the one may be as arbitrary as the other. And, in fact, there is no more likeness to exhibit, or necessity to infer, things tangible from the modifications of light, than there is in language to collect the meaning from the sound[20]. But, such as the connexion is of the various tones and articulations of voice with their several meanings, the same is it between the various modes of light and their respective correlates, or, in other words, between the ideas of sight and touch.

41. As to light, and its several modes or colours, all thinking men are agreed that they are ideas peculiar only to sight; neither common to the touch, nor of the same kind with any that are perceived by that sense. But herein lies the mistake, that, beside these, there are supposed other ideas common to both senses, being equally perceived by sight and touch—such as Extension, Size, Figure, and Motion. But that there are in reality no such common ideas, and that the objects[31] of sight, marked by these words, are entirely different and heterogeneous from whatever is the object[32] of feeling, marked by the same names, hath been proved in the *Theory*[33], and seems by you admitted; though I cannot conceive how you should in reason admit this, and at the same time contend for the received theories, which are so much ruined as mine is established by this main part and pillar thereof.

42. To perceive is one thing; to judge is another. So likewise,

---

gories. Cf. *Siris*, sect. 318, where Berkeley says that space is neither an intellectual notion, nor perceived by any of the senses.

[19] [*Minute Philosopher*, Dial. IV. sect. 7, 11]—AUTHOR.

[20] [*Theory of Vision*, sect. 144 and 147] —AUTHOR.

[31] i.e. the immediate objects, or sensations, of which we are visually conscious.

[32] i.e. the immediate objects, or sensations, of which we are tactually and muscularly conscious.

[33] [*Theory of Vision*, sect. 117]—AUTHOR.

to be suggested is one thing, and to be inferred another. Things are suggested and perceived by sense. We make judgments and inferences by the understanding. What we immediately and properly perceive by sight is its primary object—light and colours. What is suggested, or perceived by mediation thereof, are tangible ideas—which may be considered as secondary and improper objects of sight. We infer causes from effects, effects from causes, and properties one from another, where the connexion is necessary. But, how comes it to pass that we apprehend by the ideas of sight certain other ideas, which neither resemble them, nor cause them, nor are caused by them, nor have any necessary connexion with them?—the solution of this problem, in its full extent, doth comprehend the whole Theory of Vision[14]. This stating of the matter placeth it on a new foot, and in a different light from all preceding theories.

43. To explain how the mind or soul of man simply sees is one thing, and belongs to Philosophy. To consider particles as moving in certain lines, rays of light as refracted or reflected, or crossing, or including angles, is quite another thing, and appertaineth to Geometry. To account for the sense of vision by the mechanism of the eye is a third thing, which appertaineth to Anatomy and experiments. These two latter speculations are of use in practice, to assist the defects and remedy the distempers of sight, agreeably to the natural laws contained in this mundane system. But the former Theory is that which makes us understand the true nature of Vision, considered as a faculty of the soul. Which Theory, as I have already observed[15], may be reduced to this simple question, to wit, How comes it to pass that a set of ideas, altogether different from tangible ideas, should nevertheless suggest them to us—there being no necessary connexion between them? To which the proper answer is—That this is done in virtue of an arbitrary connexion, instituted by the Author of Nature.

44. The proper, immediate object of vision is light, in all its

---

[14] According to Berkeley, the Theory of Vision involves merely the two elements of *immediate perception* (of the proper objects or sensations of each sense); and *suggestion in imagination* (of what had previously been perceived simultaneously in another of the senses). Judgment and reasoning are assigned to the Understanding, as conversant with necessary truth, and not with arbitrary associations, either in the subjective imagination of individual men, or in that objective Providence of God by which the sense-experience, and consequently the imagination, of individuals is determined.

[15] See preceding section.

modes and variations, various colours in kind, in degree, in quantity; some lively, others faint; more of some and less of others; various in their bounds or limits; various in their order and situation[36]. A blind man, when first made to see, might perceive these objects[37], in which there is an endless variety; but he would neither perceive nor imagine any resemblance or connexion between these visible objects and those perceived by feeling[38]. Lights, shades, and colours would suggest nothing to him about bodies, hard or soft, rough or smooth: nor would their quantities, limits, or order suggest to him geometrical figures, or extension, or situation—which they must do upon the received supposition, that these objects are common to sight and touch.

45. All the various sorts, combinations, quantities, degrees, and dispositions of light and colours, would, upon the first perception thereof, be considered in themselves only as a new set of sensations and ideas. As they are wholly new and unknown, a man born blind[39] would not, at first sight, give them the names of things formerly known and perceived by his touch. But, after some experience, he would perceive[40] their connexion with tangible things, and would, therefore, consider them as signs, and give them (as is usual in other cases) the same names with the things signified.

46. More and less, greater and smaller, extent, proportion, interval are all found in Time as in Space; but it will not therefore follow that these are homogeneous quantities. No more will it follow, from the attribution of common names, that visible ideas are homogeneous with those of feeling. It is true that terms denoting tangible extension, figure, location, motion, and the like, are also applied to denote the quantity, relation, and order of the proper visible objects, or ideas of sight. But this proceeds only from experience and analogy. There is a *higher* and *lower* in the notes of music; men speak in a high or a low key. And this, it is plain, is no more than metaphor or analogy. So likewise, to express the order of visible ideas, the words *situation*, *high* and *low*,

---

[36] Cf. *Essay towards a New Theory of Vision*, sect. 43.
[37] I.e. be conscious of these sensations.
[38] [*Theory of Vision*, sect. 41 and 106]—ATTY'S E.
[39] Cf. *Essay*, sect. 41, and various other passages in which the experience of the 'born blind,' when they first receive sight, is inferred.
[40] I.e. mediately, or through suggestion, but not by the immediate perception involved in his original experience in seeing.

up and *down*, are made use of; and their sense, when so applied, is analogical.

47. But, in the case of Vision we do not rest in a supposed analogy between different and heterogeneous natures. We suppose an identity of nature, or one and the same object common to both senses. And this mistake we are led into; forasmuch as the various motions of the head, upward and downward, to the right and to the left, being attended with a diversity in the visible ideas, it cometh to pass that those motions and situations of the head, which in truth are tangible, do confer their own attributes and appellations on visible ideas wherewith they are connected, and which by that means come to be termed *high* and *low*, *right* and *left*, and to be marked by other names betokening the modes of position[61]; which, antecedently to such experienced connexion, would not have been attributed to them, at least not in the primary and literal sense.

48. From hence we may see how the mind is enabled to discern by sight the Situation[60] of distant objects. Those immediate objects whose mutual respect and order come to be expressed by terms relative to tangible place, being connected with the real objects of touch, what we say and judge of the one, we say and judge of the other—transferring our thought or apprehension from the signs to the things signified; as it is usual, in hearing or reading a discourse, to overlook the sounds or letters, and instantly pass on to the meaning[61].

49. But there is a great difficulty relating to the situation of objects, as perceived by sight. For, since the pencils of rays issuing from any luminous object do, after their passage through the pupil, and their refraction by the crystalline, delineate inverted pictures in the *retina*—which pictures are supposed the immediate proper objects of sight, how comes it to pass that the objects whereof the pictures are thus inverted do yet seem erect and in their natural situation? For, the objects not being perceived otherwise than by their pictures, it should follow that, as these are inverted, those should seem so too. But this difficulty, which is inexplicable on

---

[60] [*Theory of Vision*, sect. 90]—AUTHOR.
[61] Sect. 48—53 treat of our visual discernment of Situation by suggestion, and may be compared with sect. 88—119 in the *Essay*, which correspond to them.
[62] [*Minute Philosopher*, Dial. IV. sect. 11] —AUTHOR.

all the received principles and theories, admits of a most natural solution, if it be considered that the *retina*, crystalline, pupil, rays, crossing refracted, and reunited in distinct images, correspondent and similar to the outward objects, are things altogether of a *tangible* nature.

50. The pictures, so called, being formed by the radious pencils, after their above-mentioned crossing and refraction, are not so truly pictures as images, or figures, or projections—tangible figures projected by tangible rays on a tangible *retina*, which are so far from being the proper objects of sight that they are not at all perceived thereby, being by nature altogether of the tangible kind, and apprehended by the Imagination alone, when we suppose them actually taken in by the eye. These tangible images on the *retina* have some resemblance unto the tangible objects from which the rays go forth; and in respect of those objects I grant they are inverted. But then I deny that they are, or can be, the proper immediate objects of sight. This, indeed, is vulgarly supposed by the writers of Optics: but it is a vulgar error; which being removed, the forementioned difficulty is removed with it, and admits a just and full solution, being shown to arise from a mistake.

51. Pictures, therefore, may be understood in a twofold sense, or as two kinds quite dissimilar and heterogeneous—the one consisting of light, shade, and colours; the other not properly pictures, but images projected on the *retina*. Accordingly, for distinction, I shall call those *pictures*, and these *images*. The former are visible, and the peculiar objects of sight. The latter are so far otherwise, that a man blind from his birth may perfectly imagine, understand, and comprehend them. And here it may not be amiss to observe that figures and motions which cannot be actually felt by us, but only imagined, may nevertheless be esteemed tangible ideas; forasmuch as they are of the same kind with the objects of touch, and as the imagination drew them from that sense.

52. Throughout this whole affair the mind is wonderfully apt to be deluded by the sudden suggestions of Fancy, which it confounds with the Perceptions of Sense, and is prone to mistake a close and habitual connexion between the most distinct and different things for an identity of nature[61]. The solution of this

---

[61] [*Theory of Vision*, sect. 144]—AUTHOR. In truth the so-called 'images,' or concurrent rays on the retina, are not themselves what we see: they are merely organic conditions

knot about inverted images seems the principal point in the whole Optic Theory; the most difficult perhaps to comprehend, but the most deserving of our attention, and, when rightly understood, the surest way to lead the mind into a thorough knowledge of the true nature of Vision.

53. It is to be noted of these inverted images on the *retina* that, although they are in kind altogether different from the proper objects of sight or pictures, they may nevertheless be proportional to them; as indeed the most different and heterogeneous things in nature may, for all that, have analogy, and be proportional each to other. And although those images, when the distance is given, should be simply as the radiating surfaces; and although it be consequently allowed that the pictures are in that case proportional to those radiating surfaces, or the tangible real magnitude of things; yet it will not thence follow that in common sight we perceive or judge of those tangible real magnitudes simply by the visible magnitudes of the pictures; for, therein the distance is not given, tangible objects being placed at various distances; and the diameters of the images, to which images the pictures are proportional, are inversely as those distances, which distances are not immediately perceived by sight[a]. And, admitting they were, it is nevertheless certain that the mind, in apprehending the magnitudes of tangible objects of sight, doth not compute them by means of the inverse proportion of the distances, and the direct proportion of the pictures. That no such inference or reasoning attends the common act of seeing, every one's experience may inform him.

54. To know how we perceive or apprehend by sight the real Magnitude[b] of tangible objects, we must consider the immediate visible objects, and their properties or accidents. These immediate objects are the pictures. These pictures are some more lively, others more faint. Some are higher, others are lower in their own order or peculiar location; which, though in truth quite distinct, and altogether different from that of tangible objects, hath nevertheless a relation and connexion with it, and thence comes

---

of visual consciousness by means of which we see.

[a] [*Theory of Vision*, sect. 2]—AUTHOR.
[b] Sect. 54—61 treat of the (mediate) perception of Magnitude by suggestion. Cf.

sect. 81—87 in the *Essay*. See record of experiments by Wheatstone, *Philosophical Transactions* (1852), in explanation of the visual discernment of Magnitude.

to be signified by the same terms, *high*, *low*, and so forth. Now, by the greatness of the pictures, their faintness and their situation, we perceive the magnitude of tangible objects—the greater, the fainter, and the upper pictures suggesting the greater tangible magnitude.

55. For the better explication of this point, we may suppose a diaphanous plain erected near the eye, perpendicular to the horizon, and divided into small equal squares. A straight line from the eye to the utmost limit of the horizon, passing through this diaphanous plain, will mark a certain point or height to which the horizontal plain, as projected or represented in the perpendicular plain, would rise. The eye sees all the parts and objects in the horizontal plain, through certain corresponding squares of the perpendicular diaphanous plain. Those that occupy most squares have a greater visible extension, which is proportional to the squares. But the tangible magnitudes of objects are not judged proportional thereto. For, those that are seen through the upper squares shall appear vastly bigger than those seen through the lower squares, though occupying the same, or a much greater number of those equal squares in the diaphanous plain.

56. Rays issuing from every point of each part or object in the horizontal plain, through the diaphanous plain to the eye, do to the imagination exhibit an image of the horizontal plain and all its parts, delineated in the diaphanous plain, and occupying the squares thereof to a certain height marked out by a right line reaching from the eye to the farthest limit of the horizon. A line drawn through the foremost height or mark, upon the diaphanous plain, and parallel to the horizon, I call the horizontal line. Every square contains an image of some corresponding part of the horizontal plain. And this entire image we may call the horizontal image, and the picture answering to it the horizontal picture. In which representation, the upper images suggest much greater magnitudes than the lower. And these images suggesting the greater magnitudes are also fainter as well as upper. Whence it follows that faintness and situation concur with visible magnitude to suggest tangible magnitude. For the truth of all which I appeal to the experience and attention of the reader who shall add his own reflexion to what I have written.

57. It is true this diaphanous plain, and the images supposed to

be projected thereon, are altogether of a tangible nature[67]. But then there are pictures[68] relative to those images[68]; and those pictures have an order among themselves, answering to the situation of the images, in respect of which order they are said to be higher and lower[69]. These pictures also are more or less faint; they, and not the images, being in truth the visible objects. Therefore, what hath been said of the images must in strictness be understood of the corresponding pictures, whose faintness, situation, and magnitude, being immediately perceived by sight, do all three concur in suggesting the magnitude of tangible objects, and this only by an experienced connexion.

58. The magnitude of the picture will perhaps be thought by some to have a *necessary* connexion with that of the tangible object, or (if not confounded with it) to be at least the sole means of suggesting it. But so far is this from being true, that of two visible pictures, equally large, the one, being fainter and upper, shall suggest an hundred times greater tangible magnitude than the other[70]; which is an evident proof that we do not judge of the tangible magnitude merely by the visible, but that our judgment or apprehension is to be rated rather by other things, which yet, not being conceived to have so much resemblance with tangible magnitude, may therefore be overlooked.

59. It is farther to be observed that, beside this magnitude, situation, and faintness of the pictures, our prænotions concerning the kind, size, shape, and nature of things do concur in suggesting to us their tangible magnitudes. Thus, for instance, a picture equally great, equally faint, and in the very same situation, shall in the shape of a man suggest a lesser magnitude than it would in the shape of a tower.

60. Where the kind, faintness, and situation of the horizontal pictures[71] are given, the suggested tangible magnitude will be as the visible. The distances and magnitudes that we have been accustomed to measure by experience of touch, lying in the horizontal plain, it thence comes to pass that situations of the horizontal pictures suggest the tangible magnitudes, which are not in like manner suggested by vertical pictures. And it is to be noted that, as an object gradually ascends from the horizon towards the zenith,

---

[67] [*Theory of Vision*, sect. 158]—AUTHOR.
[68] Cf. sect. 51, for the distinction between *pictures* and *images*.
[69] [*Supra*, sect. 46]—AUTHOR.
[70] [*Theory of Vision*, sect. 78]—AUTHOR.
[71] [*Supra*, sect. 56]—AUTHOR.

our judgment concerning its tangible magnitude comes by degrees to depend more entirely on its visible magnitude. For the faintness is lessened as the quantity of intercepted air and vapours is diminished. And as the object riseth the eye of the spectator is also raised above the horizon: so that the two concurring circumstances, of faintness and horizontal situation, ceasing to influence the suggestion of tangible magnitudes, this same suggestion or judgment doth, in proportion thereto, become the sole effect of the visible magnitude and the prænotions. But, it is evident that if several things (for instance, the faintness, situation, and visible magnitude) concur to enlarge an idea, upon the gradual omission of some of those things, the idea will be gradually lessened. This is the case of the moon[72], when she ascends above the horizon, and gradually diminisheth her apparent dimension, as her altitude increaseth.

61. It is natural for mathematicians to regard the visual angle and the apparent magnitude as the sole or principal means of our apprehending the tangible magnitude of objects. But, it is plain from what hath been premised, that our apprehension is much influenced by other things[73], which have no similitude or necessary connexion therewith.

62. And these same means, which suggest the magnitude of tangible things, do also suggest their Distance[74]; and in the same manner, that is to say, by experience alone, and not by any necessary connexion or geometrical inference. The faintness, therefore, and vividness, the upper and lower situations, together with the visible size of the pictures, and our prænotions concerning the shape and kind of tangible objects, are the true medium by which we apprehend the various degrees of tangible distance[75]. Which follows from what hath been premised, and will indeed be evident to whoever considers that those visual angles, with their arches or subtenses, are neither perceived by sight, nor by experience of any other sense. Whereas it is certain that the pictures, with their

---

[71] [*Theory of Vision*, sect. 73.]—AUTHOR.
[72] [*Supra*, sect. 58.]—AUTHOR.
[74] [*Theory of Vision*, sect. 77.]—AUTHOR. The invisibility of real Distance, and the Theory of the suggestion of the distances of objects by experience or custom, are expressly treated in sect. 2—51 of the *Essay towards a New Theory of Vision*. Sect. 77 refers to Distance in connexion with Magnitude.

[75] Note that Berkeley's problem refers to *tangible* or *real* distance, and not to its visible signs.

magnitudes, situations, and degrees of faintness, are alone the proper objects of sight; so that whatever is perceived[76] by sight must be perceived by means thereof. To which perception the prænotions also, gained by experience of touch, or of sight and touch conjointly, do contribute.

63. And indeed we need only reflect on what we see to be assured that the less the pictures are, the fainter they are, and the higher (provided still they are beneath the horizontal[77] line or its picture), by so much the greater will the distance seem to be. And this upper situation of the picture is in strictness what must be understood when, after a popular manner of speech, the eye is said to *perceive* fields, lakes, and the like, interjacent[78] between it and the distant object—the pictures corresponding to them being only perceived to be lower than that of the object[79]. Now, it is evident that none of these things have in their own nature any *necessary* connexion with the various degrees of distance. It will also appear, upon a little reflexion, that sundry circumstances of shape, colour, and kind, do influence our judgments or apprehensions of distance; all which follows from our prænotions, which are merely the effect of experience.

64. As it is natural for mathematicians to reduce things to the rule and measure of geometry, they are prone to suppose that the apparent magnitude hath a greater share than we really find, in forming our judgment concerning the distance of things from the eye. And, no doubt, it would be an easy and ready rule to determine the apparent place of an object, if we could say that its distance was inversely as the diameter of its apparent magnitude, and so judge by this alone, exclusive of every other circumstance. But that this would be no true rule is evident, there being certain cases in vision, by refracted or reflected light, wherein the diminution of the apparent magnitude is attended with an apparent diminution of distance[80].

65. But further to satisfy us that our judgments or apprehensions, either of the greatness or distance of an object, do not depend absolutely on the apparent magnitude, we need only ask the first painter we meet, who, considering Nature rather than

---

[76] i. e. perceived mediately, or through suggestion.
[77] [*Supra*, sect. 56]—AUTHOR.
[78] [*Theory of Vision*, sect. 3]—AUTHOR.
[79] [*Supra*, sect. 55]—AUTHOR.
[80] Cf. *New Theory of Vision*, sect. 39.

Geometry, well knows that several other circumstances contribute thereto: and, since art can only deceive us as it imitates nature, we need but observe pieces of perspective and landscapes to be able to judge of this point.

66. When the object is so near that the interval between the pupils beareth some sensible proportion to it, the sensation which attends the turning or straining of the eyes, in order to unite the two optic axes therein, is to be considered as one means of our perceiving distance[a]. It must be owned, this sensation belongeth properly to the sense of feeling; but, as it waits upon and hath a regular connexion with distinct vision of near distance (the nearer this, the greater that), so it is natural that it should become a sign thereof, and suggest it to the mind[b]. And that it is so in fact follows from that known experiment of hanging up a ring edge-wise to the eyes, and then endeavouring, with one eye shut, by a lateral motion, to insert into it the end of a stick; which is found more difficult to perform than with both eyes open, from the want of this means of judging by the sensation attending the nearer meeting or crossing of the two optic axes.

67. True it is that the mind of man is pleased to observe in nature rules or methods, simple, uniform, general, and reducible to mathematics, as a means of rendering its knowledge at once easy and extensive. But we must not, for the sake of uniformities or analogies, depart from truth and fact, nor imagine that in all cases the apparent place or distance of an object must be suggested by the same means. And, indeed, it answers the end of vision to suppose that the mind should have certain additional means or helps, for judging more accurately of the distance of those objects which are the nearest, and consequently most concern us.

68. It is also to be observed that when the distance is so small that the breadth of the pupil bears a considerable proportion to it, the object appears confused. And this confusion being constantly observed in poring on such near objects, and increasing as the distance lessens, becomes thereby a means of suggesting the place of an object[c]. For, one idea is qualified to suggest another, merely by being often perceived with it. And, if the one increaseth

---

[a] [*Theory of Vision*, sect. 16, 17]—AUTHOR.
[b] [*Supra*, sect. 39]—AUTHOR.
[c] [*Theory of Vision*, sect. 21]—AUTHOR.

either directly or inversely as the other, various degrees of the former will suggest various degrees of the latter, by virtue of such habitual connexion, and proportional increase or diminution. And thus the gradual changing confusedness of an object may concur to form our apprehension of near distance, when we look only with one eye. And this alone may explain Dr. Barrow's difficulty, the case as proposed by him regarding only one visible point[14]. And when several points are considered, or the image supposed an extended surface, its increasing confusedness will, in that case, concur with the increasing magnitude to diminish its distance, which will be inversely as both.

69. Our experience in Vision is got by the naked eye. We apprehend or judge from this same experience, when we look through glasses. We may not, nevertheless, in all cases, conclude from the one to the other; because that certain circumstances, either excluded or added, by the help of glasses, may sometimes alter our judgments, particularly as they depend upon prænotions.

70. What I have here written may serve as a commentary on my *Essay towards a New Theory of Vision*; and, I believe, will make it plain to thinking men. In an age wherein we hear so much of thinking and reasoning, it may seem needless to observe, how useful and necessary it is to think, in order to obtain just and accurate notions, to distinguish things that are different, to speak consistently, to know even our own meaning. And yet, for want of this, we may see many, even in these days, run into perpetual blunders and paralogisms. No friend, therefore, to truth and knowledge would lay any restraint or discouragement on thinking. There are, it must be owned, certain general maxims, the result of ages, and the collected sense of thinking persons, which serve instead of thinking, for a guide or rule to the multitude, who, not caring to think for themselves, it is fit they should be conducted by the thoughts of others. But those who set up for themselves, those who depart from the public rule, or those who would reduce them to it, if they do not think, what will men think of them? As I pretend not to make any discoveries which another might not as well have made, who should have thought it worth his pains: so I must needs say that without pains and thought

[14] [*Theory of Vision*, sect. 29]—AUTHOR.

no man will ever understand the true nature of Vision, or comprehend what I have wrote concerning it.

71. [55]Before I conclude, it may not be amiss to add the following extract from the *Philosophical Transactions*, relating to a person blind from his infancy, and long after made to see:—'When he first saw, he was so far from making any judgment about distances that he thought all objects whatever touched his eyes (as he expressed it) as what he felt did his skin, and thought no objects so agreeable as those which were smooth and regular, though he could form no judgment of their shape, or guess what it was in any object that was pleasing to him. He knew not the shape of anything, nor any one thing from another, however different in shape or magnitude: but upon being told what things were, whose form he before knew from Feeling, he would carefully observe them that he might know them again; but having too many objects to learn at once, he forgot many of them; and (as he said) at first he learned to know, and again forgot, a thousand things in a day. Several weeks after he was couched, being deceived by pictures, he asked which was the lying sense—Feeling or Seeing? He was never able to imagine any lines beyond the bounds he saw. The room he was in, he said, he knew to be part of the house, yet he could not conceive that the whole house could look bigger. He said every new object was a new delight, and the pleasure was so great that he wanted ways to express it[56].'—Thus, by fact and experiment, those points of the theory which seem the most remote from common apprehension were not a little confirmed, many years after I had been led into the discovery of them by reasoning.

---

[55] Sect. 71 contains Berkeley's principal reference to external observation and experiment, as distinguished from reflection upon what we are conscious of—in verification of the New Theory, and especially in verification of the principle that our power of interpreting the real or tangible meaning of visual signs is due, not to an original instinct, but to the suggestion of custom.

[56] [*Philosophical Transactions*, No. 402]—AUTHOR. This is Berkeley's only allusion to the famous experiment of Cheselden, recorded in the *Philosophical Transactions* for 1728. This original record is given at full length in a supplementary note at the end of this volume.

FINIS.

A Letter from an Anonymous Writer to the Author of the Minute Philosopher[1].

REVEREND SIR,

I have read over your treatise called *Alciphron*, in which the Free-thinkers of the present age, in their various shifted tenets, are pleasantly, elegantly, and solidly confuted. The style is easy, the language plain, and the arguments are nervous. But upon the Treatise annexed thereto[2], and upon that part where you seem to intimate that Vision is the sole Language of God[3], I beg leave to make these few observations, and offer them to your's and your readers' consideration.

1. Whatever it is without that is the cause of any idea within, I call the *object* of sense; the sensations arising from such objects, I call *ideas*. The objects, therefore, that cause such sensations are without us, and the ideas within.

2. Had we but one sense, we might be apt to conclude that there were no objects at all without us, but that the whole scene of ideas which passed through the mind arose from its internal operations; but since the same object is the cause of ideas by different senses, thence we infer its existence. But, though the object be one and the same, the ideas that it produces in different senses have no manner of similitude with one another. Because,

3. Whatever connexion there is betwixt the idea of one sense and the idea of another, produced by the same object, arises only from experience. To explain this a little familiarly, let us suppose a man to have such an exquisite sense of feeling given him that he could perceive plainly and distinctly the inequality of the surface of two objects, which, by its reflecting and refracting the rays of light, produces

---

[1] This 'Letter' appeared in the *Daily Post-Boy*, September 9, 1732. The first edition of *Alciphron, or The Minute Philosopher*, was published in Dublin six months before, and the *Theory of Vision Vindicated and Explained* four months after its appearance. The 'Letter' is appended to the latter.

[2] The *Essay towards a New Theory of Vision*—which was annexed to *Alciphron*, on account of its connexion with the Fourth Dialogue.

[3] e.g. *Essay*, sect. 147; with which cf. *Alciphron*, Dial. IV. sect. 7—15.

the ideas of colours. At first, in the dark, though he plainly perceived a difference by his touch, yet he could not possibly tell which was red and which was white, whereas a little experience would make him feel a colour in the dark, as well as see it in the light.

4. The same word in languages stands very often for the object without, and the ideas it produces within, in the several senses. When it stands for any object without, it is the representative of no manner of idea; neither can we possibly have any idea of what is solely without us. Because,

5. Ideas within have no other connexion with the objects without than from the frame and make of our bodies, which is by the arbitrary appointment of God; and, though we cannot well help imagining that the objects without are something like our ideas within, yet a new set of senses, or the alteration of the old ones, would soon convince us of our mistake; and, though our ideas would then be never so different, yet the objects might be the same.

6. However, in the present situation of affairs, there is an infallible certain connexion betwixt the idea and the object; and, therefore, when an object produces an idea in one sense, we know, but from experience only, what idea it will produce in another sense.

7. The alteration of an object may produce a different idea in one sense from what it did before, which may not be distinguished by another sense. But, where the alteration occasions different ideas in different senses, we may, from our infallible experience, argue from the idea of one sense to that of the other; so that, if a different idea arises in two senses from the alteration of an object, either in situation or distance, or any other way, when we have the idea in one sense, we know from use what idea the object so situated will produce in the other.

8. Hence, as the operations of Nature are always regular and uniform, where the same alteration of the object occasions a smaller difference in the ideas of one sense, and a greater in the other, a curious observer may argue as well from exact observations as if the difference in the ideas was equal; since experience plainly teaches us that a just proportion is observed in the alteration of the ideas of each sense, from the alteration of the object. Within this sphere is confined all the judicious observations and knowledge of mankind.

Now, from these observations, rightly understood and considered, your *New Theory of Vision* must in a great measure fall to the ground, and the laws of Optics will be found to stand upon the old unshaken bottom. For, though our ideas of magnitude and distance in one sense are entirely different from our ideas of magnitude and distance in another, yet we may justly argue from one to the other, as they have one common cause without, of which, as without, we cannot possibly have the faintest idea. The ideas I have of distance and magnitude by feeling are widely different from the ideas I have of them by seeing; but that *something without* which is the cause of all the variety of the ideas within, in one sense, is the cause also of the variety in the other; and, as they have a necessary connexion with it, we may very justly demonstrate from our ideas of feeling of the same object what will be our ideas in seeing. And, though to talk of seeing by tangible angles and tangible lines be, I agree with you, direct nonsense, yet to demonstrate from angles and lines in feelings, to the ideas in seeing that arise from the same common object, is very good sense, and so *vice versâ*.

From these observations, thus hastily laid together, and a thorough digestion thereof, a great many useful corollaries in all philosophical disputes might be collected.

I am,

Your humble servant, &c.

APPENDIX.

A.

BERKELEY'S ROUGH DRAFT OF THE INTRODUCTION TO THE PRINCIPLES OF HUMAN KNOWLEDGE.

[AFTER the *Principles of Human Knowledge* had passed through the press, I found Berkeley's autograph of a rough draft of the Introduction, in the manuscript department of the Library of Trinity College, Dublin. It seems to have been written in November and December, 1708. I here present it to the reader, who will find that it varies considerably from the published version, besides containing erasures and interlineations which have a biographical and literary, as well as a philosophical interest. As this Introduction forms Berkeley's early attack upon metaphysical abstractions, and his reasoned exposition of what has since been called his Nominalism, it may be well to have so important a part of his philosophy placed before us in various verbal forms which it successively assumed when it was struggling into the final expression. The student of his mind may like also to compare these with still earlier illustrative fragments in the *Commonplace Book*, appended to his *Life and Letters*, as well as with the theory of universals in *Alciphron* and especially in *Siris*. What Berkeley here means to deny is the existence of any *physical* reality, corresponding to general names, apart from actual or imagined sensible phenomena. In this early attack upon 'abstract ideas,' his characteristic ardour carried him in appearance to the extreme of rejecting the universalizing element, by which Mind constitutes and gives objectivity to things, and of resting knowledge on the shifting foundation of phenomena or ideas—particular, contingent, and subjective. But if he seems to do this in the Introduction, he virtually proceeds in the body of the *Principles* upon the assumption that personal substantiality and efficient or voluntary causality are universal and uncreated necessities of Being—axiomatic truths involved in all concrete consciousness of phenomena. This assumption (along with the assumed general fact of established cosmical order) redeems his philosophy from subjectivity, and gives cohesion and fixedness to knowledge. This stable intellectuality is more manifest in *Siris*. But he everywhere leans on living acts, not verbal formulas.

A. C. F.]

Appendix A.

Philosophy being nothing else but the study of wisdom and truth, it may seem strange that they who have spent much time and pains in it, do usually find themselves embarrass'd with more doubts and difficulties than they were before they [¹came to that study. There is nothing these men can [²touch] with their hands or behold with their eyes but has its inaccessible and dark sides. Something] they imagine to be in every drop of water, every grain of sand which can puzzle [³and confound] the most clear and [⁴elevated] understanding, and are often by their principles led into a necessity of admitting the most irreconcilable opinions for true, or (which is worse) of sitting down in a forlorn scepticism.

The cause of this is thought to be the obscurity of things, together with the natural weakness and imperfection of our understanding. It is said the senses we have are few, and these design'd by nature only for the support of life, and not to penetrate into the constitution and inward essence of things. Besides, the mind of man being finite when it treats of things which partake of infinity, it is not to be wonder'd at if it run into absurdities⁵ and contradictions, out of which it is [³absolutely] impossible it should ever extricate itself, it being of the nature of Infinite not to be comprehended by that which is finite⁶.

But I cannot think our faculties are so weak and inadequate in respect of things, as these men would make us believe. I cannot be brought to suppose that right deductions from true principles should ever end⁷ in consequences which cannot be maintain'd or made consistent. We should believe that God has dealt more bountifully with the sons of men than to give them a strong desire for that which he had placed quite out of their reach, and so made it impossible for them to obtain. Surely our wise and good Creatour would never have made us so eager in the search of truth meerly to baulk and perplex us, to make us blame our faculties,

---

¹ On the opposite page of the MS., instead of what follows within brackets—'meddled with that study. To them the most common and familiar things appear intricate and perplex'd, there's nothing but has its dark sides. Somewhat'

² 'handle.'

³ Erased.

⁴ 'comprehensive.'

⁵ 'absurdities' instead of 'inconsistencys' erased.

⁶ on the margin of this paragraph is written—'Nov. 15, 1708.'

⁷ 'end' instead of 'terminate' erased.

and bewail our inevitable ignorance. This were not agreeable to the wonted indulgent methods of Providence, which, whatever appetites it may have implanted in the creatures, doth usually furnish them with such means as, if rightly made use of, will not fail to satisfy them. Upon the whole my opinion is, that the far greatest part, if not all, of those difficultys which have hitherto amus'd philosophers, and block'd up the way to knowledge, are entirely owing to themselves. That they have first rais'd a dust, and then complain they cannot see.

My purpose therefore is, to [^8 try if I can] discover [^9 and point out] what those principles are which have introduc'd all that doubtfulness and uncertainty, those absurditys and contradictions into the several sects of philosophy, insomuch that the wisest men have thought our ignorance incurable, conceiving it to arise from the natural dulness and limitation of our faculties. And at the same time to establish such principles in their stead, as shall be free from the like consequences, and lead the mind into a clear view of truth. And surely it is a work well deserving of our pains, to try to extend the limits of our knowledge, and [^10 do right to] human understanding, by making it to appear that those lets and difficultys which stay and embarrass the mind in its enquirys [^11 after truth] do not spring from any darkness and intricacy in the objects, or [^12 natural] defect in the intellectual powers, so much as from false principles which have been insisted on, and might have been avoided.

How difficult and discouraging soever this attempt may seem, when I consider what a number of men of very great and extraordinary abilitys have gone before me, [^9 and miscarry'd] in the like [^13 designs, yet] I am not without some hopes, upon the consideration that the largest views are not always the clearest, and that he who is shortsighted will be apt to draw the object nearer, and by a close and narrow survey may perhaps discern that which had escaped far better eyes.

[^14 In my entrance upon this work] I think it necessary to take

---

[^8] Instead of 'endeavour to.' [^9] Erased.
[^10] Instead of 'beat down those mounds and barriers that have been put to.'
[^11] Within brackets in the MS.
[^12] Instead of 'incurable' erased.
[^13] Instead of 'undertakings.'
[^14] Instead of 'But here in the entrance, before I proceed any further.' On the blank page opposite we have—'In my entrance upon this work (before I descend to more particular subjects) [and] (to more particular enquirys).'

notice of [[15] that wch seems to have been the source of a great many errours, and to have made the way to knowledge very intricate and perplex'd, that wch seems to have had a chiefe part in rendering speculation intricate and perplex'd, and to have been the source of innumerable errours and difficulties in almost all parts of knowledge]—and that is the opinion that there are Abstract Ideas or General Conceptions of Things. He who is not a perfect stranger to the writings and [[16] notions] of philosophers must needs acknowledge that [[17] no small] part of [[18] them] are spent [19] about Abstract Ideas. These are, in a more special manner, thought to be the objects of those sciences that go by the name of logic and metaphysics, and of all that which passes under the notion of the most abstracted and sublime philosophy. In all which [[20] speculative sciences] you shall scarce find any question handled [[20] by the philosophers] in such a manner as does not suppose their existence in the mind, and that it is very well acquainted with them; [[20] so that these parts of learning must of necessity be overrun with [very much] useles wrangling and jargon, [innumerable] absurdities and contradictions [opinions], if so be that Abstract General Ideas are perfectly inconceivable, as I am well assur'd they [never were—cannot be] conceived by me, [[21] nor do I think it possible they should be conceiv'd by any one else].]

By abstract idea, genera, species, universal notions, all which amount to the same thing, as I find these terms explain'd by the best and clearest writers, we are to understand ideas which equally represent the particulars of any sort, and are made by the mind which, observing that the individuals of each kind agree in some things and differ in others, takes out and singles from the rest that which is common to all, making thereof one abstract general idea; which [[20] general idea] contains all those ideas wherein the particulars of that kind agree [[20] and partake], separated from and exclusive of all those other concomitant ideas

---

[15] Instead of—'y^t wch seem to me [one] very powerful and universal cause of error and confusion throughout the philosophy of all sects and ages'—and the opposite page, 'that which seems to me a wide-spread (in philosophical enquirys] throughout the philosophy of all sects and ages.'

[16] Brackets in the MS.

[17] Instead of 'very great.'

[18] Instead of 'their disputes and contemplations [speculations].'

[19] 'concerning' instead of 'about' erased.

[20] Erased.

[21] On opposite page—'and I very much question whether they ever were or can be by any one else.'

whereby they [⁷² individuals] are distinguished [⁸¹ from each other] one from another. [⁸⁰ To this abstract general idea thus framed the mind gives a general name, and lays it up and uses it as a standard whereby to judge what particulars are and what are not to be accounted of that sort, those onely which contain every part of the general idea having a right to be admitted into that sort and called by that name.]

For example, the mind having observed that Peter, James, and John, &c. resemble each other in certain common agreements of shape and other quality, leaves out of the complex idea it has of Peter, James, &c. that which is peculiar to each, retaining onely that which is common to all. And so it makes one [⁸³ abstract] complex idea, wherein all the particulars partake, abstracting entirely from and cutting off all those circumstances and differences which might determine it to any particular existence: and after this manner you come by [⁸¹ the] precise abstract idea of [⁷² a] man. In which [⁸¹ idea] it is true there is included colour, because there is no man but hath some colour, but then it can be neither white [⁹⁸ colour] nor black [⁸² colour] nor any particular colour, but colour in general, because there is no one particular colour wherein all men partake. In like manner you will tell me there is included stature, but it is neither tall stature nor low stature, nor yet middling stature, but stature in general. And so of the rest. [²³ Suppose now I should ask whether you comprehended, in this your abstract idea of man, the ideas of eyes, or ears, or nose, or legs, or arms, [this might perhaps put you to a stand for an answer, for] you will own it to be an odd and mutilated idea of a man wᶜʰ is without all these. Yet it must be so to make it consistent with the doctrine of abstract ideas, there being particular men that want, some arms, some legs, [some] noses, &c.]

[⁹² But supposing the abstract idea of man to be very conceivable, let us proceed to see [²⁶ how] it comes to be enlarg'd into the more general and comprehensive idea of animal.] There being a great variety of other creatures [⁷³ as birds] that partake in some parts, but not all, of the complex idea of man, the mind leaving

---

⁷² Erased.   ⁸³ Instead of 'general.'
⁷¹ Instead of 'a clear.'
⁸⁰ Erased. On opposite page, but erased, are the words—' an odd and mutilated idea, that of man without all these.' And on the same page—' it must needs [make an odd and frightful figure the idea] of (a) man without all these,' also erased.

⁹⁶ Instead of ' by what steps and abstractions.'

out those parts which are peculiar to men, and retaining those onely which are common to all the living creatures, frames the idea of animal, [²⁵ which is more general than that of man, it comprehending not only all particular men, but also all birds, beasts, fishes, and insects.] The constituent parts whereof [²⁶ of the complex idea of animal] are body, life, sense, and spontaneous motion. By body is meant body [²⁷ in general], without any particular shape or figure, there being no one shape or figure common to all animals, without covering either of hair, or feathers, or [²⁸ scales], and yet it is not naked. Hair, feathers, [²⁸ scales], and nakedness being peculiar distinguishing properties of [²⁷ the] particular animals, and for that reason left out of the [²⁹ abstract] idea. Upon the same account, the spontaneous motion must be neither walking nor flying nor creeping, it is nevertheless a motion, but what that motion is it is not easy to say.

In like manner a man [²⁷ having seen several lines] by leaving out of his idea of a line [³⁰ the particular colour and length], comes by the idea of a line, which is neither black, nor white, nor red, &c., nor long nor short, which he calls the abstract idea of a line, and which, for ought that I can see, is just nothing. [²⁷ For I ask whether a line has any more than one particular colour and one particular length, which [when they are] being left out, I beseech any ³¹ one to consider what it is that remains.]

Whether others have this [³² wonderful] faculty of abstracting their ideas, they can [³³ best] tell. For myself, I dare be confident I have it not; [²⁷ and I am apt to think that some of those who fancy themselves to enjoy that privilege, would, upon looking narrowly into their own thoughts, find they wanted it as much as I. For there was a time when, being banter'd and abus'd by words, I did not in the least doubt my having it. But upon a strict survey of my abilitys, I not only discover my own deficiency in that point, but also cannot conceive it possible that such a person should be even in the most perfect and exalted understanding.] I find I have a faculty of imagining, conceiving, or representing to myself the ideas of those particular things I have

---

²⁵ Erased. ²⁶ Instead of 'him.' ³¹ 'one' instead of 'man.'
²⁷ Instead of 'general.' ³² Instead of 'marvellous.'
³⁰ Instead of 'all particular colour, and all particular length.' ³³ Instead of 'better.'

perceiv'd, and of variously compounding and dividing them.
I can imagine a man with two heads, or the upper parts of a
man joyn'd to the body of a horse. I can consider the hand,
the eye, the nose each by itself [³⁴ abstracted or] separated from
the rest of the body. But then whatever eye or nose I imagine,
they must have some particular shape and colour. The idea of
man that I frame to myself must be either of a white, or a black,
or a tawny, a straight or a crooked, a tall or a low or a middling
sized man. I cannot by any effort of [³⁵ thought] frame to myself
an idea of man [³⁶ prescinding from all particulars] that shall have
nothing particular in it. [³⁶ For my life I cannot comprehend
abstract ideas ³⁷.]

And there are grounds to think [³⁸ most] men will acknowledge themselves to be in my case. The generality of men, which
are simple and illiterate, never pretend to abstract notions. It is
said they are difficult and not to be attained without much study
and speculation, we may therefore reasonably conclude that, if
such there be, they are altogether confin'd to the learned.

But it must be confess'd, I do not see what great advantage they
give them above the rest of mankind. He who considers that
whatever has any existence in nature and can any wise affect or
concern [³⁶ is] him is particular, will not find great cause to be
discontent with his facultys, if [³⁹ they] cannot reach a piece of
knowledge as useless as it is refin'd; [³⁶ and] which whether it
be to be found even in those deep thinkers may well be made
a question.

For besides the [⁴⁰ incomprehensibleness] of abstract ideas to
my understanding (which may pass for an argument, since those
gentlemen do not pretend to any new facultys distinct from those
of ordinary men), there are not wanting other proofs against them.
[⁴¹ It is, I think, a receiv'd axiom that an impossibility cannot
be conceiv'd. For what created intelligence will pretend to

---

³⁴ Instead of 'singled out and.'
³⁵ Instead of 'Imagination.'
³⁶ Erased.
³⁷ On opposite page the words—'I can conceive well enough what is meant by adequate and inadequate, clear and obscure, distinct and confus'd [ideas], but'—are written and erased.
³⁸ Instead of 'the far greatest part of.'
³⁹ Instead of 'he.'

⁴⁰ Instead of 'incomprehensibility,' and on opposite page, but erased—'incomprehensibleness to my understanding by any [intellect—understanding] whatsoever.'
⁴¹ Erased. On opposite page—'That a contradiction cannot be conceiv'd by any human understanding whatsoever is, I think, agreed on all hands. And to me it is no less clear that the description of an abstract idea doth include a contradiction in it.'

conceive that which God cannot cause to be? Now it is on all hands agreed, that nothing abstract or general can be made really to exist; whence it should seem to follow, that it cannot have so much as an ideal existence in the understanding.]

[⁴¹ I do not think it necessary to insist on any more proofs, against the doctrine of abstraction in this place, especially for that the absurditys, which in the progress of this work I shall observe to have sprung from that doctrine, will yield plenty of arguments a posteriori against it.] I proceed [⁴² therefore] to examine what can be alledged in defence [⁴³ of the doctrine of abstraction], and try if I can discover what it is that [⁴⁴ inclines] the men of speculation to embrace an opinion so pregnant of absurditys, and so remote from common sense as that seems to be.

There has been a late excellent and deservedly esteem'd philosopher, to whose judgment, so far as authority is of any weight with me, I would pay the utmost deference. This great man, no doubt, has very much countenanc'd the doctrine of abstraction by seeming to think [⁴⁵ it] is that which puts the widest difference in point of understanding betwixt man and beast. Thus speaks he: 'The having of general ideas is that which puts a perfect distinction betwixt man and brutes, and is an excellency which the facultys of brutes do by no means attain unto. For it is evident we observe no footsteps in them of making use of general signs for [⁴⁶ making] universal ideas; from which we have reason to imagine that they have not the faculty of abstracting, or making general ideas, since they have no use of words or any other general signs.' And a little lower: 'Therefore I think we may suppose that 'tis in this that the species of brutes are discriminated from men, and 'tis that proper difference wherein they are wholly separated, and which at last widens to so wide a distance. For if they have any ideas at all and are not bare machines (as some would have them), we cannot deny them to have some reason. It seems as evident to me, that they do some of them in certain instances reason, as that they have sense, but it is only in particular ideas, just as they receiv'd them from their senses. They are the best of them tied up within those

---

⁴¹ Erased. ⁴³ Instead of 'thereof.' ⁴⁵ Instead of 'the having abstract ideas.'
⁴² Instead of 'has inclined.' ⁴⁶ Within brackets in the MS.

narrow bounds, and have not (as I think) the faculty to enlarge them by any kind of abstraction.' (*Essay on Human Understanding*, Book 2. chap 11. s. 10, 11.) I readily agree with this authour that the faculties of brutes can by no means attain to the making of abstract general ideas. But then if that inability to abstract be made the distinguishing property of that sort of animals, I fear a great many of those that now pass for men must be reckon'd into their number.

The reason which is here assign'd why we have no grounds to think that brutes have general ideas, is that we observe in them no use of words or any other general signs—which is built on this supposition—that the making use of words implys the having of general ideas, and that [[47] on the other hand] those who have general ideas fail not to make use of words, or other universal signs, [[48] whereby] to express [[48] and signify them], [[*] That this is the] From which it must follow, that men who use language are able to abstract and generalize their ideas, but brutes [[49] that] use it not are destitute of that faculty. That this is the sense and arguing of the authour of the *Essay*, will farther appear, by his answering the question he in another place puts. Since all things that exist are only particulars, how come we by general terms? His answer is—'Words become general by being made the signs of general ideas.' (*Essay on Human Understanding*, b. 3. c. 3. s. 6.) From which assertion I must crave leave to dissent, being of opinion that a word becomes general by being [[50] the] made the sign, not of a general idea, but of many particular ideas. Sure I am, as to what concerns myself, when I say the word Socrates is a proper [[*] or particular] name, and the word man an appellative or general name, I mean no more than this, viz. that the one is peculiar and appropriated to one particular person, the other common to a great many particular persons, each [[51] of which] has an equall right in propriety of language to be called by the name man. [[*] This, I say, is the whole truth of the matter, and not that I make any incomprehensible abstract idea whereunto I annex the name man. That were to [make] my words stand for I know not what.]

That great man seems to think the necessary ends of language

[47] Instead of 'reciprocally.' [50] Within brackets in the MS.
[48] Erased.   [49] Instead of 'who.'   [51] Instead of 'whereof.'

could not be attain'd [⁵² to] without the use of abstract ideas. B. 3. c. 6. s. 39 [⁵⁰ he shews it] and elsewhere he shews it to be his opinion that they are made in order to naming. B. 3. c. 1. s. 3 he has these words: 'It is not enough for the perfection of language that sounds can be made signs of ideas, unless those signs can be so made use of as to comprehend several particular things: for the multiplication of words would have perplex'd their use, had every particular thing need of a distinct name to be signified by. To remedy this inconvenience language had yet a farther improvement in the use of general terms whereby one word was made to mark a number of particular existences, which advantageous use of sounds was obtained only by the difference of the ideas they were made signs of. Those names becoming general which are made to stand for general ideas, and those remaining particular where the ideas they are used for are particular.' Now I would fain know why a word may not be made to comprehend a great number of particular things in its signification, without the [⁵³ help] of a general idea? Is it not possible to give the name [⁵⁴ colour to black, white, and red, &c.] without having first made that strange and to me incomprehensible idea of [⁵⁶ colour in abstract]? Or must we imagine that a child upon sight of a particular body, and being told it is called an apple, must first frame to himself an abstract general idea [⁵⁶ exclusive of] all particular colour, tast, and figure before he can attain to the use of the word apple, and apply it to all the particulars of that sort of fruit that come in his way? [⁵⁹ This surely is a task too hard and metaphysical to be perform'd by an infant just beginning to speak.] Nay, I appeal to the experience of any grown man, whether this be the course he takes in acquainting himself with the [⁵⁷ right] use and signification of any word? Let any man take a fair and impartial view of his own thoughts, and then determine whether his general words do not become so only by being made to mark a number of particular existences, without any the least thought of abstraction. For what, I pray, are words but signs of our thoughts? and how are

---

⁵² Erased.
⁵³ Instead of 'interposition.'
⁵⁴ Instead of 'man to Peter, James, and John.'
⁵⁵ Instead of 'man which shall have nothing particular in it.'
⁵⁶ Instead of 'thereof, abstracting from.'
⁵⁷ Instead of 'proper.'

signs of any sort render'd universal otherwise than by being made to signify, or represent indifferently, a multitude of particular things?

The ideas that are in every man's mind ly hid[50 den], and cannot of themselves be brought into the view of another. It was therefore necessary, for discourse and communication, that men should institute sounds to be signs of their ideas, which being [59 excited] in the mind of the hearer [60 might] bring along with them [58 into his understanding] such ideas as in the propriety of any language were annex'd to them. But because of the almost infinite number and variety of our [61 ideas], it is impossible, and if it were possible would yet be a useless thing, to appropriate a particular [54 word to a] sign or name to every one of them. From which it must necessarily follow, that one word be made the sign of a great number of particular ideas, between which there is some likeness and which are said to be of the same sort. [61 But then these sorts are not determin'd and set out by nature, as was thought by most philosophers. Nor yet are they limited by any precise abstract ideas settl'd in the mind, with the general name annexed to them, as is the opinion of the authour of the *Essay*, nor do they in truth seem to me to have any precise bounds or limits at all. For if [there were] they had I do not see how there could be those doubts and scruples about the sorting of particular beings which [that authour insists on as a good proof] are observ'd sometimes to have happen'd. Neither do I think it necessary the kinds or species of things should be so very accurately bounded and marked out, language being made by and for the common use of men, who do not ordinarily take notice of the minuter and less considerable differences of things.] From [58 all] which to me it seems evident that the having of general names does not imply the having of general ideas, but barely the marking by them a number of particular ideas, and that all the ends of language

---

58 Erased. 59 Instead of 'raised.'
60 Instead of 'shall.'
61 Instead of 'thoughts.'
54 Erased. On the opposite page we have —' Every one's experience may convince him that this is all that's meant by general names, and that they do not stand either for universal natures distinct from our conceptions as was held by the Peripateticks and generality of the Schoolmen, nor yet for universal notions or ideas as is the opinion of that sort of Schoolmen called Nominals and of the authour of the *Essay*.'

may be and are attain'd without the help of any such faculty as abstraction.

Which will be made yet more manifest if we consider the different manners wherein words [*² and ideas [are] do stand for and represent things] represent ideas, and ideas things. There is no similitude or resemblance betwixt words and the ideas that are marked by them. Any name may be used indifferently for the sign of any idea, or any number of ideas, it not being determin'd by any likeness to represent one more than another. But it is not so with ideas in respect of things, of which they are suppos'd to be the copies and images. They are not thought to represent them [*³ any] otherwise than as they resemble them. Whence it follows that an idea is not capable of representing indifferently anything [*⁴ whatsoever], it being limited by the likeness it beares to some particular [*⁵ thing] to represent it rather than any other. The word man may equally be put to signify any particular man I can think of. But I cannot frame an idea of man which shall equally represent and correspond to each particular of that sort of creatures that may possibly exist.

I shall [*⁶ only] add one more passage out of the *Essay on Human Understanding*, which is as follows: 'Abstract ideas are not so obvious or easy to children or the yet unexercised mind as particular ones. If they seem so to grown men 'tis only because by constant and familiar use they are made so. For when we nicely reflect upon them we shall find that general ideas are fictions and contrivances of the mind that carry difficulty with them and do not so easily offer themselves as we are apt to imagine. For example, does it not require some pains and skill to form the general idea of a triangle (which is yet none of the most abstract, comprehensive and difficult), for it must be neither oblique nor rectangle, neither equilateral, equicrural, nor scalenon, but all and none of these at once? In effect, it is something imperfect, that cannot exist; an idea wherein some parts of several different and inconsistent ideas are put together. 'Tis true the mind in this imperfect state has need of such ideas, and makes all the hast to them it can, for the conveniency of communication and enlargement of knowledge, to both which

---

* Erased.   ⁶² Instead of ' or number of things.'   ⁶³ Instead of 'existence.'

it is naturally very much enclin'd; but yet one has reason to suspect such ideas are marks of our imperfection. At least this is enough to shew that the most abstract and general ideas are not those that the mind is first and most easily acquainted with, nor such as its earliest knowledge is conversant about.' B. 4. c. 7. s. 9. If any man has the faculty of framing in his mind such an idea of a triangle as is here describ'd, it is in vain to pretend to dispute him out of it, nor would I go about it. All I desire is that every one would fully and certainly inform himself whether he has such an idea or no. And this, methinks, can be no hard task for any one to perform. What more easy than for any one to look a little into his own understanding, and there try whether he has, or can attain to have, an idea that shall correspond with the description here given of the general idea of a triangle which is neither oblique nor rectangle, neither equilateral, equicrural, nor scalenon, but all and none of these at once? He that can conceive such manifest contradictions and inconsistencys, 'tis fit he enjoy his privilege. For my part [66 I am well assur'd] 67 I have not the power of so doing, nor consequently of making to myself these general ideas; neither do I find that I have any need of them either for the conveniency of communication or the enlargement of knowledge [66 for the conveniency of communication and enlargement of knowledge. For which I am not sorry, because it is here said one has reason to suspect such ideas are marks of our *imperfection*. Tho', I must own, I do not see how this agrees with what has been above quoted [out of the same authour], viz. the having of general ideas is that which puts a perfect distinction betwixt man and brutes, and is an *excellency* which the faculties of brutes do by no means attain unto.]

It is observable [66 what it is here said] of the difficulty that abstract ideas carry with them, and the pains and skill that is requisite to the forming [66 of] them. To the same purpose Aristotle (who was certainly a great admirer and promoter of the doctrine of abstraction) has these words: χεδὸν δὲ καὶ χαλεπώτατα γνωρίζειν τοῖς ἀνθρώποις 'ότι τὰ μάλιστα καθόλου πορρωτάτω γὰρ τῶν αἰσθήσεών 'ότι. There is scarce anything so incomprehensible to men as

---

66 Erased.
67 On opposite page—erased —'I must own I have so much of the brute in my understanding, that.'
68 Instead of ' that which is [here] said by that authour on this occasion.'

the most universal notions, because they are most remote from sense. *Metaph.* lib. i. cap. 2 [69]. It is on all hands agreed, that there is need of great pains and toil and labour of the mind, to emancipate [70 our thoughts] from particular ideas such as are taken in by the senses, and raise [70 them] to those lofty speculations [71 which] are conversant about abstract and universal ones.

From all which the natural consequence should seem to be, that so difficult a thing as the forming of abstract ideas is not necessary for communication, which is so easy and familiar to all sorts of men, even the most barbarous and unreflecting. But we are told, if they seem obvious and easy to grown men, 'tis only because by constant and familiar use they are made so. Now I would fain know at what time it is men are employ'd in surmounting that difficulty, and furnishing themselves with those necessary [74 materials] of discourse. It cannot be when they are grown up, for then they are not conscious of any such pains-taking. It remains therefore to be the business of their childhood. And surely the great and multiply'd labour of framing general notions will be found a hard task for that tender age. Is it not a hard thing to imagine that a couple of children cannot commune one with another of their sugar-plumbs and rattles, and the rest of their little trinkets, till they have first tack'd together numberless inconsistencys, and so framed in their minds general abstract ideas, and annex'd them to every common name they make use of?

Nor do I think they are a whit more needful for enlargement of knowledge, than for communication. For tho' it be a point much insisted on in the Schools that all knowledge is about universals, yet I [73 can by no means see the necessity of] this doctrine. It is acknowledg'd that nothing has a fairer title to the name of knowledge or science than geometry. Now I appeal to any man's thoughts whether, upon the entrance into that study, the first thing to be done is to try to conceive a circle that is neither great nor small, nor of any determinate radius, or to make ideas of triangles and parallelograms that are neither rectangular

---

[69] Text as in Schwegler—σχεδὸν δὲ καὶ χαλεπώτατα ταῦτα γνωρίζειν τοῖς ἀνθρώποις, τὰ μάλιστα καθόλου πορρωτάτω γὰρ τῶν αἰσθήσεών ἐστιν.

[70] Instead of 'it.'

[71] Instead of 'that.'

[72] Instead of 'preliminary.'

[73] Instead of '[could never] bring myself to comprehend.'

nor obliquangular, &c.? It is [⁷⁴ true] one thing for a proposition to be universally true, and another for it to be about universal natures or notions. [⁷⁵ Because] that the three angles of a triangle are equal to two right ones is granted to be a proposition universally true, it will not therefore follow that we are to understand it of universal triangles, or universal angles. It will suffice that it be true of [⁷⁴ any particular tri] the particular angles of any particular triangle whatsoever.

But here it will be demanded, how we can know any proposition to be true of all particular triangles, except we have first seen it demonstrated of the general idea of a triangle, which equally agrees to and represents them all? For because a property may be demonstrated to belong to some one particular triangle, it will not thence follow that it equally belongs to [⁷⁴ some] any other triangle which in all respects is not the same with the former. For instance, having demonstrated that the three angles of an isosceles, rectangular triangle are equal to two right ones, I cannot therefore conclude this affection agrees to all other triangles which have neither a right angle nor two equal sides. It seems therefore, that to be certain this proposition is universally true, we must either make a particular demonstration for every particular triangle, which is impossible, or else we must, once for all, demonstrate it of the general idea of a triangle in which all the particulars do indifferently partake, and by which they are all equally represented.

To which I answer, that notwithstanding the idea I have in my mind, whilst I make the demonstration, be that of some particular triangle, e.g. an isosceles, rectangular ones whose sides are of a determinate length, I may nevertheless be certain that it extends to all other rectilinear triangles of what sort or bigness soever. And that because neither the right angle, nor the equality, nor determinate length of the legs are at all concern'd in the demonstration. 'Tis true the diagram I have in my view does include these particulars, but then there is not the least mention made of them in the proof of the proposition. It is not said the three angles are equal to two right ones, because one of them is a right angle, or because the legs comprehending it are [⁷⁴ equal]

---

⁷⁴ Erased.   ⁷⁵ Instead of 'Thus [notwithstanding].'

of the same length; which sufficiently shews that the right angle might have been oblique and the sides unequal, and yet the demonstration have held good. And for this reason it is that I conclude that to be true of any obliquangular or scalenon which I had demonstrated of a particular right angled equicrural triangle; and not because I demonstrated the proposition of the general idea of a triangle which was all and none, it not being possible for me to conceive any triangle whereof I cannot delineate the like on paper. But I believe no man, whatever he may conceive, will pretend to describe a general triangle with his pencill. This being rightly consider'd, I believe we shall not be found to have any great [76 want] need of those eternal, immutable, universal ideas about which the philosophers keep such a stir, and without which they think there can be no silence at all.

But what becomes of these general maxims, these first principles of knowledge, [77 so frequently in the mouths] of [76 the] metaphysicians, all wch are suppos'd to be about abstract and universal ideas? To which all the answer I can make is, that whatsoever proposition is made up of terms standing for general notions or ideas, the same is to me, so far forth, [76 absolutely] unintelligible: and whether it be that those speculative gentlemen have by earnest and profound study attain'd to an elevation of thought above the reach of ordinary capacities and endeavours, or whatever else be the cause, sure I am there are in their writings many things which I now find myself unable to understand. Tho' being accustom'd to those forms of speech, I once thought there was no difficulty in them. But this one thing seems [76 to me] pretty plain and certain. How high soever that goodly fabrick of metaphysics might have been rais'd, and by what venerable names soever it may be supported, yet if [76 withall] it be built on [78 no other] foundation [79 than] inconsistency and contradictions, it is after all but a castle in the air [80].

It were an endless as well as an useless thing to trace the Schoolmen, those great masters of abstraction, and all others whether ancient or modern logicians and metaphysicians, thro' those numerous inextricable labyrinths of errour and dispute,

---

[76] Erased.
[77] Instead of 'these curious speculations.'
[78] Instead of 'the sandy.'
[79] Instead of 'of.'
[80] On margin, 'Dec. 1.'

which their doctrine of abstract natures and notions seems to have led them into. What bickerings and controversys, and what a learned dust has been rais'd about those matters, and what [⁸¹ great] mighty advantage has been from thence deriv'd to mankind, are things at this day too clearly known to need to be insisted on by me. Nor has that doctrine been confin'd to those two sciences, that make the most avowed profession of it. The contagion thereof has spread through[⁸¹ out] all the parts of philosophy. It has invaded and overrun those usefull studys of physic and divinity, and even the mathematicians themselves have had their full share of it.

When men consider the great pain, industry and parts that have [⁸¹ in] for so many ages been lay'd out on the cultivation and advancement of the sciences, and that [⁸² notwithstanding] all this, the far greatest part of them remain full of doubts and uncertainties, and disputes that are like never to have an end, and even those that are thought to be supported by the most clear and cogent demonstrations do contain in them paradoxes that are perfectly irreconcilable to the understandings of men, and that taking all together a very small portion of them does supply any real benefit to mankind, otherwise than by being an innocent diversion and amusement—I say upon the consideration of all this, men are wont to be cast into an amazement and despondency, and perfect contempt of all study. But that wonder and despair may perhaps cease upon a view of the false principles and wrong foundations of science [⁸¹ which] that have been made use of. Amongst all which there is none, methinks, of a more wide and universal sway over the thoughts of studious men than that we have been endeavouring to detect and overthrow. [⁸³ To me certainly it does not seem strange that unprofitable debates and absurd and extravagant opinions should abound in the writings of those men who, disdaining the vulgar and obvious informations of sense, do in the depth of their understanding contemplate abstract ideas ⁸³.]

I come now to consider the [⁸¹ source] of this prevailing [⁸³ notion], and that seems to me most evidently to be language.

---

⁸¹ Erased.
⁸² Instead of 'for.'
⁸³ On margin—'Dec. 2.'
⁸¹ Instead of 'cause.'
⁸³ Instead of 'imagination in the minds of men.'

And surely nothing of less extent than reason itself could have been the source of an opinion, as epidemical as it is absurd. That [86 words are] the conceit of abstract idea ows its birth and origine to words, will appear, as from other reasons, so also from the plain confession of the ablest patrons of y^t doctrine, who [86 do] acknowledge that they are made in order to naming; from which it is a clear consequence that there had been no such thing as speech, or universal signs, there never had been [86 abstract ideas] any thought of abstract ideas. I find it also declared in express terms that general truths can never be well made known, and are very seldom apprehended but as conceived and expressed in words; all which doth plainly set forth the inseparable connexion and mutual dependence [86 on each other] that is thought to be between words and abstract ideas. For whereas it is elsewhere said [86 there could be no communication by general names [87 without there being] also general ideas of which they were to be signs; we are here, on the other hand, told that] that general ideas [88 are] necessary for communication by general names; here, on the other hand, we are told that names are needfull for the understanding of [86 abstract notions] general truths. Now by the bye, I would fain know how it is possible for words to make a man apprehend that which he cannot apprehend without them. I do not deny they are necessary for communication, and so making me know the ideas that are in the mind of another. But when any truth, whether [86 about general or part] about general or particular ideas, is once made known to me by words, [86 I cannot see any manner of] so that I rightly apprehend the ideas contained in it, I see no manner of reason why I may not omit the words, and yet retain as full and clear a conception of the ideas themselves, as I had [86 of them] while they were cloathed with words. Words being, so far as I can see, of use only for recording and communicating, but not absolutely apprehending [86 of] ideas. [86 I know there be some things which pass for truths that will not bear this [stripping—being stript] of the attire of words, but this I always took for a sure and certain sign that there were no clear and determinate ideas underneath.] I proceed to show the manner wherein words have contributed to the growth and origine of that mistake.

⁸⁶ Erased.   ⁸⁷ Instead of 'except there were.'   ⁸⁸ Instead of 'were.'

That which seems [⁸⁹ to me principally] in a great measure to have drove men into the conceit of [⁹⁰ abstract] ideas, is the opinion, that every name has, or ought to have, one only precise and settl'd signification: which inclines [⁹¹ men] them to think there are certain abstract, determinate, general ideas that make the true and only immediate signification of each general name, and that it is by the mediation of these abstract ideas that a general name comes to signify any particular thing. Whereas there is in truth [⁹¹ a] diversity of significations in every general name whatsoever [⁸⁹ except only the proper names]. Nor is there any such thing as one precise and definite signification annexed to each [⁹² appellative] name. All which does evidently follow from what has been already said, and will [⁸⁹ be] clearly appear to any one by a little reflexion.

But [⁸⁹ here] to this, I doubt not, it will be objected that every name that has a definition is thereby tied down and restrain'd to [⁹³ one certain] signification, e. g. a triangle is defin'd to be a plain surface comprehended by three right lines, by which that name is limited to denote one certain idea, and no other. To which I answer, that in the definition it is not said, whether the surface be great or small, black or white or transparent, or whether the sides are long or short, equal or unequal, or with what angles they are inclin'd to each other. In all which there may be great variety, and consequently there is no one settled idea which limits the signification of the word triangle. 'Tis one thing for to keep a word [⁹⁰ everywhere] constantly to the same definition, and another to make it stand everywhere for the same idea: [⁹³ that] is necessary, but [⁹⁴ this] is useless and impracticable. [⁸⁹ Nor does it avail to say the abstract idea of a triangle, which bounds the signification of that name, is itself determin'd, tho' the angles, sides, &c. are not. For besides the absurdity of such an idea, which has been already shown, it is evident that if the simple ideas or parts, i. e. the lines, angles, and surface, are themselves various and undetermin'd, the complex idea or whole triangle cannot be one settled determinate idea.]

⁸⁹ Erased.
⁹⁰ Instead of 'general.'
⁹¹ Instead of 'an homonomy or.'
⁹² Instead of 'a particular.'
⁹³ Instead of 'the former.'
⁹⁴ Instead of 'the latter.'

[⁸⁵ But to give a farther account, how words came to introduce the doctrine of universal ideas, it will be necessary to observe there is a notion current among those that pass for the deepest thinkers, that every significant name stands for an idea. It is said by them that a proposition cannot otherwise be understood than by perceiving [⁸⁶ the agreement or disagreement of] the ideas marked by the terms [⁸⁷ thereof] of it. Whence it follows, that according to those men every proposition that is not jargon must consist of terms or names that carry along with them each a determinate idea. This being so, and it being [certain] withall certain that names which yet are not thought altogether insignificant do not always mark out particular ideas, it is straightway concluded that they stand for general ones.

In answer to this I say, that names, significant names, do not always stand for ideas, but that they may be and are often used to good purpose [tho' they are] without being suppos'd to stand for or represent any idea at all. And as to what we are told of understanding propositions by [perceiving] the agreement or disagreement of the ideas marked by their terms, this to me in many cases seems absolutely false. For the better clearing and demonstrating of all which I shall make use of some particular instances. Suppose I have the idea of some one particular dog to which I give the name Melampus, and then frame this proposition—Melampus is an animal. Where 'tis evident the name Melampus denotes one particular idea. And as for the other name or term of the proposition, there are a sort of philosophers will tell you thereby is meant not only a universal conception, but also [corresponding thereto] a universal nature or essence really existing without the mind, whereof Melampus doth partake, as tho' it were possible that even things themselves could be universal. And [But] this with reason is exploded as nonsensical and absurd. But then those men who have so clearly and fully detected the emptyness and insignificancy of that wretched jargon [of S.G.W. (?)], are themselves to me equally unintelligible. For they will have it that if I understand what I say I must make the name animal stand for an abstract general idea which agrees to and corresponds with the particular idea marked by the name Melampus. But if a man may be allow'd to know his own meaning, I do declare that in my thoughts the word animal is neither suppos'd to stand for an universal nature, nor yet for an abstract idea, which to me is at least as absurd and incomprehensible as the other. Nor does it indeed in that proposition stand for any idea [at all] at all. All that I intend to signify thereby being only this—that the particular [creature] thing I call Melampus has a right to be called by the name animal. And I do intreat any one to make this easy tryal. Let him but cast out of his [thoughts] the words of the proposition, and then see whether two clear and determinate ideas remain [** in his understanding] whereof he finds one to be conformable to the other. I perceive it evidently in myself that upon laying aside all thought of the words 'Melampus is an animal,' I have remaining in my mind one only naked and bare idea, viz. that particular one to which I gave the name Melampus. Tho' some there be that pretend they have also a general idea signified by the word animal, which they perceive to agree with the particular idea signified by the word Melampus, [which idea is made up of inconsistencys and contradictions, as has been already shown.] Whether this or that be the truth of the matter, I desire every particular person to consider and conclude for himself.]

And this methinks may pretty clearly inform us how men might first have come to think there was a general idea of animal.

* Erased.

For in the proposition we have instanc'd in, it is plain the word animal is not suppos'd to stand for the idea of any one particular [anima] [creature] animal. For if it be made stand for another different from that is marked by the name Melampus, the proposition is false and includes a contradiction; and if it be made signify the very same individual that Melampus doth, it is a tautology. But it is presumed that every name stands for an Idea. It remains therefore that the word animal stands for [the] general abstract idea [of animal]. In like manner we may be able with a little attention to discover how other general ideas [of all sorts] might at first have stolen into the thoughts of man.

But farther to make it evident that words may be used to good purpose without bringing into the mind determinate ideas, I shall add this instance. We are told [that] the good things which God hath prepared for them that love him are such as eye hath not seen nor ear heard, nor hath it enter'd into the heart of man to conceive. What man will pretend to say these words of the inspir'd writer are empty and [ses (?)] insignificant? And yet who is there that can say they bring into his mind [determi] clear and determinate ideas, or in truth any ideas at all [ideas] of the good things [pre] in store for them that love God? It may perhaps be said that those words lay before us the clear and determinate abstract ideas of good in general and thing in general; but I am afraid it will be found that those very abstract ideas are every whit as remote from the comprehension of men as the particular pleasures of the saints in heaven. But, say you, those words of the Apostle must have some import. They cannot be suppos'd to have been utter'd without all meaning and design whatsoever. I answer, the saying is very weighty, and carrys with it a great design, but it is not to raise in the minds of men the abstract ideas of thing or good, nor yet the particular ideas of the joys of the blessed. The design is to make them more chearfull and fervent in their duty; and how this may be compass'd without making the words good things [to be] stand for and mark out to our understandings any ideas either general or particular, I proceed to show.

Upon mention of a reward to a man for his pains and perseverance in any occupation whatsoever, it seems to me that

divers things do ordinarily ensue. For there may be excited in
his understanding an idea of the particular good thing to him
proposed for a reward. There may also ensue thereupon an
alacrity and steddiness in fulfilling those conditions on which
it is to be obtain'd, together with a zealous desire of serving
and pleasing the person in whose power it is to bestow that
good thing. All these things, I say, may and often do follow
upon the pronunciation of those words that declare the recompence.
Now I do not see any reason why the latter may not happen
without the former. What is it that hinders why a man may
not be stirr'd up to diligence and zeal in his duty, by being told
he shall have a good thing for his reward, tho' at the same time
there be excited in his mind no other idea than barely those
of sounds or characters? When he was a child he had frequently heard those words used to him to create in him an
obedience to the commands of those that spoke them, and as
he grew up he has found by experience that upon the mentioning
of those words by an honest man it has been his interest to
have doubled his zeal and activity for the service of that person.
Thus there having grown up in his mind a customary connexion
betwixt the hearing that proposition and being disposed to obey
with cheerfulness the injunctions that accompany it, methinks
it might be made use of, tho' not to introduce into his mind
any idea marked by the words good thing, yet to excite in him
a willingness to perform that which is requir'd of him. And
this seems to me all that is design'd by the speaker, except
only when he intends those words shall [be the mark of] signifie
the idea of some particular thing: e. g. in the case I mention'd
'tis evident the Apostle never intended the words [good things]
should [mark out to] our understandings the ideas of those
particular things our faculties never attain'd to. And yet I
cannot think that he used them at random and without design; on
the contrary, it is my opinion that he used them to very good
purpose, namely, to beget in us a cheerfulness and zeal and
perseverance in well-doing, without any thought of introducing
into our minds the abstract idea of a good thing. If any one
will joyn ever so little reflexion of his own to what has been
said, I doubt not it will evidently appear to him that general
names are often used in the propriety of language without the

speaker's designing them for marks of ideas in his own which he would [them] have them raise in the understanding of the hearer.

[⁹⁹ Even] proper names themselves are not always spoken with a design to bring into our view the ideas of those particular things that are suppos'd to be annex'd to them. For example, when a Schoolman tells you that Aristotle hath said it, think you that he intends [¹ thereby] to [ra] excite in your imagination the idea of that particular man? All he means by it is only to dispose you to receive his opinion with that deference and submission that custom has annex'd to that name. When a man that has been accustom'd to resign his judgment [of] to the authority of that philosopher [shall] [upon] in reading of a book meet with the letters that compose his name, he forthwith yields his assent to the doctrine it was brought to support, and that with such a quick and sudden [² glance of thought] as it is impossible any idea either of the person or writings of that man should go before—so close and immediate a connexion has long custom establish'd betwixt the very word Aristotle and the motions of assent and reverence in the minds of some men.

I intreat the reader to reflect with himself, and see if it does not oft happen, either in hearing, or reading a discourse, that the passions of delight, love, hatred, admiration, disdain, &c. [¹ do not] arise immediately in his mind upon the perception of certain words without any ideas coming between. At first, indeed, the words might have occasion'd ideas that may be apt to produce those emotions of mind. But if I mistake not, it will be found that when language is once grown familiar, ³ to a man the hearing of the sound or sight of the characters is oft immediately attended with those passions which at first were wont to be produc'd by the intervention of ideas that are now quite omitted.

[⁴ Further], the communicating of ideas marked by words is not the chief and only end of language, as is commonly suppos'd. There are other ends, as the raising of some passion, the exciting to or deterring from an action⁵. To which the former

---

⁹⁹ 'Nor is it less certain that' erased.
¹ Erased.
² 'action of the mind'—on opposite page.
³ 'to a man' erased.
⁴ 'From which it follows, that' erased.
⁵ On opposite page—'the putting the mind in some particular disposition. Hence

is in many cases barely subservient, and sometimes ⁶entirely omitted when these can be obtain'd without it, as I think does not infrequently happen in the familiar use of language.

I ask any man whether [⁷ every time] he tells another that such an action is honourable and vertuous, with an ⁸ intention to excite him to the performance of it, he has at that instant ideas of honour and virtue ⁹ in his [thoug] view, and whether in reality his intention be to raise [¹⁰ that] idea, together with their agreement to the [¹¹ particular] idea of that particular action, in the understanding of him he speaks to [¹¹ or rather whether this be not his full purpose, namely, that those words should excite in the mind of the hearer an esteem of that particular action, and stir him up to the performance of it].

[¹¹ Upon hearing the words lie [&] rascal, indignation, revenge, and the suddain motions of anger do instantly [ensue] in the minds of some men, without our attending to the definition of those names or concerning the ideas they are suppos'd to stand for—all that passion and resentment having been by custom connected to those very sounds themselves and the manner of their utterance ¹⁰.]

It is plain therefore that a man may understand what is said to him without having a clear and determinate idea annexed to and marked by every particular [¹³ word] in the discourse he hears. Nay, he may perfectly understand it. For what is it, I pray, to understand perfectly, but only to understand all that is meant by the person that speaks? which very oft is nothing more than barely to excite in [¹⁴ his mind] certain emotions without any thought of those ideas so much talk'd of and so little understood. For the truth whereof I appeal to every [man's] one's experience.

I know not how this doctrine will go down with those [philosophers] who may be apt to give the titles of gibberish and jargon

---

we may conceive how it is possible for the promise that is made us of the good things of another life excite in us suitable dispositions, tho' the words good things do not bring into our minds particular ideas of the pleasures of heaven, nor yet the ideas of good in general or things in general.

⁶ ' entirely ' erased.
⁷ ' when' erased.
⁸ ' vertuous with an' substituted for ' vertuous.'

⁹ ' virtue' substituted for ' vertue.'
¹⁰ ' those abstract' erased.
¹¹ Erased.
¹² On opposite page —' Innumerable instances of this kind may be given—else. But why should I be tedious in enumerating these things, which every one's observation will, I doubt not, plentifully suggest unto him ?'
¹³ ' name '—on opposite page.
¹⁴ ' the hearer'—on opposite page.

to all discourse whatsoever so far forth as the words contained in it are not made the signs of clear and determinate ideas, who think it nonsense for a man to assent to any proposition each term whereof doth not bring into his mind a clear and distinct idea, and tell us [15 over and over] that every pertinent [16 word] [17 hath an idea annexed unto] which never fails to accompany it where 'tis rightly understood. Which opinion of theirs, how plausibly soever it might have been maintain'd by some, seems to me to have introduced a great deal of difficulty and nonsense into the reasonings of men. Certainly nothing could be fitter to bring forth and cherish the doctrine of abstract ideas. For when men were indubitably conscious to themselves that many [18 words] they used did not denote any particular ideas, lest they should be thought altogether insignificant, they were of necessity driven into the opinion that they stood for [19 general ones].

But more effectually to show the absurdity of an opinion that carrys with it so great an appearance of [clearness and strength of] reason, but is [20 in fact] most dangerous and destructive both to reason and religion, I shall, if I mistake not, in the progress of this work demonstrate there be names well known and familiar to men, which tho' they mark and [stand] and signify things, cannot be suppos'd to signifie ideas of any sort, either general or particular, without the greatest nonsense and contradiction; it being absolutely impossible, and a direct repugnancy, that any intellect, how exalted and comprehensive soever, should frame ideas of these things.

We have, I think, shown the impossibility of abstract ideas. We have consider'd what has been said in behalf of them by their ablest patrons, and endeavour'd to demonstrate they are of no use for those ends to which they [21 are] thought necessary. And, lastly, we have traced them to the source from whence they flow, which appears evidently to be language.

Since therefore words have been discover'd to be so very apt to impose on the understandings of men, I am resolv'd in my [22 inquiries] to make as little use of them as possibly I can.

---

15 Erased.
16 'name'—on opposite page.
17 'in the mark of an idea'—on opposite page.
18 'names'—on opposite page.
19 'good sense and sound'—on opposite page.
20 Instead of 'withall.'
21 'are' instead of 'were.'
22 Instead of 'reasonings.'

Whatever ideas I consider, I shall endeavour to take them bare and naked into my view, keeping out of my thoughts, so far as I am able, those names which long and constant use hath so strictly united to them.

Let us conceive a solitary man, one born and bred in such a place of the world, and in such circumstances, as he shall never have had occasion to make use of universal signs for his ideas. That man shall have a constant train of particular ideas passing in his mind. Whatever he sees, hears, imagines, or anywise conceives, is on all hands, even by the patrons of abstract ideas, granted to be particular. Let us withall suppose him under no necessity of labouring to secure himself from hunger and cold, but at full ease, naturally of good facultys, [23 and] contemplative. Such a one I should take to be nearer the discovery of certain great and excellent truths yet unknown, than he that has had the education of schools, [24 has been instructed in the ancient and modern philosophy], and by much reading and conversation has [furnish'd his head] attain'd to the knowledge of those arts and sciences that make so great a noise in the [24 learned] world. It is true, the knowledge of our solitary philosopher is not like to be so very wide and extended, it being confin'd to those few particulars that come within his own observation. But then, if he is like to have less knowledge, he is withall like to have fewer mistakes than other men.

It cannot be deny'd that words are of excellent use, in that by their means all that stock of knowledge, which has been purchas'd by the joynt labours of inquisitive men in all ages and nations, may be drawn into the view, and made the possession of one [24 particular] single person. But there [25 are some] parts of learning which contain the knowledge of things the most noble and important of any within the reach of human reason, that have had the ill fate to be so signally perplex'd and darken'd by the abuse of words and general ways of speech wherein they are deliver'd, that in the study [26 of them] a man cannot be too much upon his guard, [27 whether] in his private meditations, or in reading the writings or hearing the discourses of other men, to prevent his being cheated [28 by the glibness and familiarity

---

[23] 'but' erased. [25] Erased. [26] Instead of 'thereof.'
[24] Instead of 'is one.' [27] Instead of 'either.'

of speech] into a belief that those words stand for ideas which, in truth, stand for none at all: which grand mistake it is almost incredible what a mist and darkness it has cast over the understandings of men, otherwise the most rational and clear-sighted.

I shall therefore endeavour, so far as I am able, [²⁸ to put myself in the posture of the solitary philosopher. I will confine my thoughts and enquiries to the naked scene of my own particular ideas,] from which I may expect to derive the following advantages.

First. I shall be sure to get clear of all [²⁹ verbal] controversies purely verbal. The [³⁰ springing up of] which weeds in almost all the sciences has been [³¹ the] a most fatal obstruction to the growth of true and sound knowledge: and accordingly is at this day esteem'd as such, and made the great and just complaint of the wisest men.

Secondly. 'Tis reasonable to expect that [³¹ by this] the trouble of sounding, or examining, or comprehending any notion may be very much abridg'd. For it oft happens that a notion, when it is cloathed with words, seems tedious and operose, and hard to be conceiv'd, which yet being stript of that garniture, the ideas shrink into a narrow compass, and are view'd almost by one glance of thought.

Thirdly. I shall have fewer objects to consider than other men seem to have had. [³² Because] I find myself to want several of those supposed ideas, in contemplating of which the philosophers do usually spend much pains and study. [³⁹ nay, even of those (which without doubt will appear very surprising) that pass for simple, particular ideas. It [is inconceivable what] cannot be believ'd what a wonderfull emptyness and scarcity of ideas that man shall descry who will lay aside all use of words in his meditations.

Fourthly. Having remov'd the veil of words, I may expect to have a clearer prospect of the ideas that remain in my understanding. To behold the deformity of errour we need only undress it.]

---

²⁸ Erased. On the opposite page—' to take off the mask of words, and obtain a naked view of my own particular ideas.'
²⁹ Erased.
³⁰ Instead of 'insisting on.'
³¹ Instead of 'hereby.'
³² Instead of 'For that.'

Fifthly. This seemeth to be a sure [33 way] to extricate myself out of that fine and subtile net of abstract ideas; which has so miserably perplex'd and entangled the minds of men, and that with this peculiar circumstance, that by how much the finer and the more curious was the wit of any man, by so much the deeper was he like to be ensnar'd and faster held therein.

Sixthly. So long as I confine my [34 thoughts] to my own ideas divested of words, I do not see how I can easily be mistaken. The objects I consider I [35 clearly] and adequately know. I cannot be deceiv'd in thinking I have an idea which I have not. Nor, on the other hand, can I be ignorant of any idea that I have. It is not possible for me to think any of my own ideas are alike or unlike which are not truly so. To discern the agreements and disagreements there are between my ideas, to see what simple ideas are included in any [36 compound] idea, and what not, [37 there is nothing requisite but] an attentive perception of what passes in my own understanding.

But the attainment of all these advantages does presuppose an entire deliverance from the deception of words, which I dare scarce promise myself. So difficult a thing it is to dissolve a union so early begun, and confirm'd by so long a habit, as that betwixt words and ideas.

Which difficulty seems to have been very much encreas'd by the [38 doctrine of abstraction]. For so long as men thought abstract ideas were annex'd to their words, it does not seem strange they should use words for ideas. It being found an impracticable thing to lay aside the word and retain the abstract idea in the mind, which in itself was perfectly inconceivable. This made it necessary for them to reason and meditate about words, to which they suppos'd abstract ideas were connected, and by means whereof they thought those ideas could be conceiv'd, tho' they could not without them. [39 But surely those

---

[33] Instead of 'means whereby.'
[34] Instead of 'contemplations.'
[35] Instead of 'perfectly.'
[36] Instead of 'complex.'
[37] Erased here—'all this I can do without being taught by [another], there being requisite thereto nothing more than.' Also—

[' the writings and discoveries of other men or without having any great parts of my own] there is nothing more requisite.'
[38] Instead of 'opinion of abstract ideas.'
[39] Erased.

ideas ought to be suspected that cannot endure the light without a covering.]

Another thing which makes words and ideas thought much [⁴⁰ harder to separate] than in truth they are, is the opinion that every name stands for an idea. [⁴¹ For] it is no wonder that men should fatigue themselves in vain, and find it a very difficult undertaking, when they endeavour'd to [⁴² obtain a clear and naked] view of [⁴³ those] the ideas marked by those words, which in truth mark none at all; [⁴³ as I have already shown many names often do not, even when they are not altogether [insignificant], and I shall more fully show it hereafter].

[⁴⁴ This] seems to me the principal cause why those men that have so emphatically recommended to others the laying aside the use of words in their meditations, and contemplating their bare ideas, have yet been so little able to perform it themselves. Of late many have been very sensible of the absurd opinions, and insignificant disputes, that grow out of the abuse of words. In order to redress these evils, they advise well that we attend to the ideas that are signified, and draw off our attention from the words that signify them. But how good soever this advice may be that they have given others ⁴⁵ men, it is plain they little regarded it themselves, so long as they thought the only immediate use of words was to signifie ideas, and that the immediate signification of every general name was a determinate abstract idea.

Which having been shown to be mistakes, a man may now, with much greater ease, deliver himself from the imposture of words. He that knows he hath no other than particular ideas, will not puzzle himself in vain to find out and conceive the abstract idea annexed to any name. And he that knows names [⁴⁵ when made use of in the propriety of language] do not always stand for ideas, will spare himself the labour of looking for ideas where there are none to be had. Those obstacles being now remov'd, I earnestly desire that every one would use his utmost endeavour to attain a clear and naked view of [⁴⁶ the] ideas he would consider [⁴⁷ by separating] from them all that varnish and mist of words,

---

⁴⁰ Instead of 'more inseparable.'
⁴¹ Instead of 'Now.'
⁴² Instead of 'strip and take a.'
⁴³ Erased.
⁴⁴ Instead of 'These.'
⁴⁵ 'men' erased.
⁴⁶ Instead of 'his own.'
⁴⁷ Instead of 'having separated.'

which so fatally blinds the judgment and dissipates the attention of men.

This is, I am confident, the shortest way to knowledge, and cannot cost too much pains in coming at. In vain do we extend our view into the heavens, and rake into the entrails of the earth. In vain do we consult the writings and discourses of learned men, and trace the dark footsteps of antiquity. We need only draw the curtain of words, to behold the fairest tree of knowledge, whose fruit is excellent and within the reach of [48 our hand].

Unless we take care to clear the first principles of knowledge from the [49 incumbrance and delusion] of words, [50 the consequences we draw from them] we may make infinite reasonings upon them to no purpose. We may [51 deduce consequences from] consequences, and be never the wiser. The farther we go, we shall only lose ourselves the more irrecoverably, and be the deeper entangled in difficulties and mistakes.

I do therefore intreat whoever designs to read the following sheets, that he would make my words the occasion of his own thinking, and endeavour to attain the same train of thoughts in reading that I had in writing them. By this means it will be easy for him [58 to discover the truth or falsity of what I say]. He will be out of all danger of being deceiv'd by my words. And I do not see what inducement he can have to err in considering his own naked, undisguised ideas.

That I may contribute, so far as in me lies, to expose my thoughts [50 to the] fairly to the understanding of the reader, I shall throughout endeavour to express myself in the clearest, plainest, and most familiar 53 manner, abstaining from [50 all flourish and pomp of words], all hard and unusual terms which are [50 commonly] pretended by those that use them to cover a sense [50 intricate and] abstracted and sublime.

[50 I pretend not to treat of anything but what is obvious and [50 accommodated to] the understanding of every reasonable man.]

---

48 Instead of ' [say man] to pluck it.'
49 Instead of ' cheat.'
50 Erased.
51 Instead of ' lose ourselves in.'

52 Instead of ' whatever mistakes I might have committed.'
53 After ' manner ' ' I shall ' erased.

B.

ARTHUR COLLIER.

The simultaneous publication of a conception of the nature of sensible reality so far accordant as that of Berkeley and Collier has been considered by historians of philosophy so curious that I am induced here to reprint the Introduction to Collier's *Clavis Universalis: or, a new Inquiry after Truth, being a Demonstration of the Non-existence, or Impossibility, of an External World*[1]. The reader of Berkeley may thus conveniently compare, with what Berkeley taught, Collier's thesis regarding the inexistence of the material world.

Arthur Collier was born on the 12th of October, 1680—more than four years before Berkeley—at the rectory of Langford Magna in Wiltshire. He entered Pembroke College, Oxford, in July 1697. He succeeded his father as rector of Langford Magna in 1704, and continued to hold that living till his death in 1732. One of his near neighbours, during the first years of his incumbency, was John Norris, the English Malebranche, rector of Bemerton, author of *An Essay towards the Theory of the Ideal or Intelligible World* (1701–4), who died in 1711.

From his own account, Collier seems to have adopted his new thought regarding the meaning of sensible existence or reality about 1703, though he did not publish it till 1713, in the early part of which year the *Clavis Universalis* appeared.

Five interesting letters of Collier, in exposition and defence of his notion of Matter, are given in Benson's *Memoirs*. Two of them were written in 1714, and the others in 1715, 1720, and 1722. That written in 1715 is addressed to Dr. Samuel Clarke. Two of the others are to Samuel Low, a grammarian; another was sent to Dr. Waterland; and the last is addressed to Mr. Shepherd, Fellow of Trinity College, Oxford.

---

[1] The motto of this work, taken from Malebranche, is *Vulgi assensum et approbatio, circa materiam difficilem, est certum argumentum falsitatis istius opinionis cui assentitur.*—De Inquis. Verit. Lib. III. p. 194.

Collier seems to have been more disposed than Berkeley to apply philosophical speculation directly to Christian theology. His theological speculations occupied a considerable share of his life, and involved a subtle modification of Arianism—according to which the sensible world exists in the mind of man; the mind of man exists in Christ; and Christ exists in God—all exemplifying what he calls 'in-existence,' or dependent existence. This chain of *inexistent* being he deduces from speculative reason, and also from the words of Scripture. Collier was a friend and correspondent of Whiston, whose theory of 'Primitive Christianity' was discussed about that time.

Collier was a Tory and High Churchman, and curiously, like Berkeley, he published a sermon on the Christian obligation of submission to the higher powers, founded on Romans xiii. 1.

It does not appear that Berkeley and Collier ever met, nor is he once named by Berkeley, though Berkeley is more than once named by him.

THE INTRODUCTION TO THE CLAVIS UNIVERSALIS,

'Wherein the Question in General is explained and stated, and the whole subject divided into two particular heads.

Though I am verily persuaded that, in the whole course of the following treatise, I shall or can have no other adversary but prejudice; yet, having by me no mechanical engine proper to remove it; nor being able to invent any other method of attacking it, besides that of fair reason and argument; rather than the world should finish its course without once offering to enquire in what manner it exists, (and for one reason more, which I need not name, unless the end desired were more hopeful); I am at last, after a ten years pause and deliberation, content to put myself upon the trial of the common reader, without pretending to any better art of gaining him on my side, than that of dry reason and metaphysical demonstration.

. The Question I am concerned about is in general this—Whether there be any such thing as an External World. And my title will suffice to inform my reader, that the *negative* of this question is the point I am to demonstrate.

In order to which, let us first explain the terms.

Accordingly, by *World*, I mean whatsoever is usually understood by the terms body, extension, space, matter, quantity, &c., if there be any other word in our English tongue which is synonymous with all or any of these terms.

And now nothing remains but the explication of the word *External*.

By this, in general, I understand the same as is usually understood by the words, absolute, self-existent, independent &c.; and this is what I deny of all matter, body, extension, &c.

If this, you will say, be all that I mean by the word external, I am like to meet with no adversary at all, for who has ever affirmed, that matter is self-existent, absolute, or independent?

To this I answer, What others hold, or have held in times past, I shall not here inquire. On the contrary, I should be glad to find by the event, that all mankind were agreed in that which I contend for as the truth, viz. that matter is not, cannot be, independent, absolute, or self-existent. In the mean time, whether they are so or no, will be tried by this.

Secondly, and more particularly, That by not independent, not absolutely existent, not external, I mean and contend for nothing less than that all matter, body, extension, &c. exists in, or in dependence on, mind, thought, or perception; and that it is not capable of an existence, which is not thus dependent.

This perhaps may awaken another to demand of me, How? to which I as readily answer—just how my reader pleases, provided it be somehow. As for instance, we usually say, An *accident* exists in, or in dependence on, its proper subject; and that its very essence, or reality of its existence, is *so* to exist. Will this pass for an explication of my assertion? If so, I am content to stand by it, in this sense of the words. *Again*, we usually say (and fancy too we know what we mean in saying,) that a body exists in, and also in dependence on, its proper *place*, so as to exist necessarily in some place or other. Will this description of dependence please my inquisitive reader? If so, I am content to join issue with him, and contend that all matter exists in, or as much dependently on, mind, thought, or perception, to the full, as any body exists in place. Nay, I hold the description to be so just and apposite as if a man should say, A thing is like itself: for, I suppose I need not tell my reader that when I affirm that all matter exists in mind, after the same manner as body exists in place, I mean the very same as if I had said, that mind itself is the place of body, and so its place, as that it is not capable of existing in any other place, or in place after any other manner. *Again, lastly*, it is a common saying, that an object of perception exists in, or in dependence on, its respective *faculty*. And of these objects there are many who will reckon with me, light, sounds, colours, and even some material things, such as trees, houses, &c., which are seen, as we say, *in* a looking-glass, but which are, or ought to be, owned to have no existence but *in*, or *respectively on*, the minds or faculties of those who perceive them. But, to please all parties at once, I affirm that I know of no manner in which an object of perception exists in, or on, its respective faculty, which I will not admit in this place to be a just description of that manner of *in-existence* after which all matter that exists is affirmed by me to *exist in mind*. Nevertheless, were I to speak my mind freely I should choose to compare it to the in-existence of some, rather than some other objects of perception—particularly such as are objects of the sense of vision; and of these, those more especially which are allowed by others to exist wholly in the mind or visive faculty;

such as objects seen in a looking-glass, by men distempered, light-headed, ecstatic, &c., where not only colours, but entire bodies, are perceived or seen. For these cases are exactly parallel with that existence which I affirm of all matter, body, or extension whatsoever.

Having endeavoured, in as distinct terms as I can, to give my reader notice of what I mean by the proposition I have undertaken the defence of, it will be requisite in the next place, to declare in as plain terms, what I do not mean by it.

Accordingly, I declare in the *first* place, That in affirming that there is no external world, I make no doubt or question of the *existence* of bodies, or whether the bodies which are seen exist or not. It is with me a first principle, that *whatsoever is seen*, is. To deny or doubt of this is errant scepticism, and at once unqualifies a man for any part or office of a disputant, or philosopher; so that it will be remembered from this time, that my enquiry is not concerning the existence, but altogether concerning the *extra*-existence of certain things or objects; or, in other words, what I affirm and contend for, is not that bodies do not exist, or that the external world does not exist, but that such and such bodies, which are supposed to exist, do not exist externally; or in universal terms, that there is no such thing as an external world.

Secondly, I profess and declare that, notwithstanding this my assertion, I am persuaded that I see all bodies just as other folks do; that is, the visible world is seen by me, or, which is the same, seems to me, to be as much external or independent, as to its existence, on my mind, self, or visive faculty, as any visible object does, or can be pretended to do or be, to any other person. I have neither, as I know of, another nature, nor another knack of seeing objects, different from other persons, suitable to the hypothesis of their existence which I here contend for. So far from this, that I believe, and am very sure, that this seeming, or (as I shall desire leave to call it) *quasi externity* of visible objects, is not only the effect of the Will of God, (as it is his Will that light and colours should seem to be without the eye, that heat should seem to be in the fire, pain in the hand, &c.) but also that it is a natural and necessary *condition* of their visibility: I would say that though God should be supposed to make a world, or any one visible object, which is granted to be not external, yet, by the condition of its being seen, it would, and must be, *quasi external* to the perceptive faculty; as much so to the full, as is any material object usually seen in this visible world.

Moreover, *thirdly*, When I affirm that all matter exists dependently on mind, I am sure my reader will allow me to say, I do not mean by this—that matter or bodies exist in *bodies*. As for instance, when I affirm or say, that the world, which I see, exists in my mind, I cannot be supposed to mean that one body exists in another, or that all the bodies which I see exist in that which common use has taught me to call *my body*. I must needs desire to have this remembered, because experience has taught me how apt persons are, or will be, to mistake me in this particular.

Fourthly, When I affirm that this or that visible object exists in, or dependently on, my mind, or perceptive faculty, I must desire to be understood to mean no more than I say, by the words *mind* and *perceptive faculty*. In like manner I would be understood, when I affirm in general, that all matter or body exists in, or dependently on, mind. I say this to acquit myself from the imputation of holding that the mind causes its own ideas, or objects of perception; or, lest any one by a mistake should fancy that I affirm—that matter depends for its existence on the will of man, or any creature whatsoever. But now, if any such mistake should arise in another's mind, he has wherewith to rectify it; in as much as I assure him, that by *mind*, I mean that part, or act, or faculty of the soul which is distinguished by the name *intellective* or *perceptive*; as in exclusion of that other part which is distinguished by the term *will*.

Fifthly, When I affirm that all matter exists in mind, or that no matter is external, I do not mean that the world, or any visible object of it, which I (for instance) see, is dependent on the mind of any other person besides myself; or that the world, or matter, which any other person sees, is dependent on mine, or any other person's mind, or faculty of perception. On the contrary, I contend as well as grant, that the world which John sees is external to Peter, and the world which Peter sees is external to John. That is, I hold the thing to be the same in this as in any other case of sensation; for instance, that of sound. Here two or more persons, who are present at a concert of music, may indeed in some sense be said to hear the *same* notes or melody; but yet the truth is, that the sound which one hears, is not the *very same* with the sound which another hears—because the souls or persons are supposed to be different; and therefore, the sound which Peter hears is external to, or independent on, the soul of John, and that which John hears is external to the soul or person of Peter.

Lastly, When I affirm that no matter is altogether external, but necessarily exists in some mind or other, exemplified and distinguished by the proper names of John, Peter, &c., I have no design to affirm that every part or particle of matter, which does or can exist, must needs exist in some *created* mind or other. On the contrary, I believe that infinite worlds might exist, though not one single created, (or rather merely created,) mind were ever in being. And, as in fact there are thousands and ten thousands, I believe, and I even contend, that there is an Universe, or Material World in being, which is, at least, numerically different from every material world perceived by mere creatures. By this, I mean the great Mundane Idea of created (or rather twice created) matter, *by* which all things are produced; or rather, (as my present subject leads me to speak,) *by* which the great God gives sensations to all his thinking creatures, and by which things that are not are preserved and ordered in the same manner as if they were.

And now I presume and hope, that my meaning is sufficiently understood, when I affirm, That all matter which exists, exists in, or dependently on, mind; or, that there is no such thing as an External World.

Nevertheless, after all the simplicity to which this question seems already to be reduced, I find myself necessitated to divide it into two. For, in order to prove that there is no External World, it must needs be one article to shew that the *visible* world is not external; and when this is done, though in this all be indeed done which relates to any opinion yet entertained by men, yet something still is wanting towards a full demonstration of the point at large, and to come up to the universal terms in which the question is expressed.

Accordingly, I shall proceed in this order. *First*, to shew that the visible world is not external. *Secondly*, to demonstrate more at large, or simply, that an external world is a being utterly impossible. Which two shall be the subjects of two distinct Parts or Books.'

Collier in the end resolves the difference between sense-perception and imagination into a difference in degree merely. To imagine an object is to perceive it less vividly than we perceive it in the senses. ' I can no more,' he says, ' understand how we can create the objects we imagine than the objects we are said to see.' What is imagined 'exists as much, to all appearance, without, or external to, the mind which perceives it as any of those objects usually called visible—*but not so vividly;* and this is that whereby I distinguish the act which we call imagination from the act which we call vision: but why is this, but because the common cause of both, viz. God, does not, in the former act, impress or act so strongly upon my mind as in the latter. If He did, both acts would become one, or require the same name; and there would be no difference between seeing and imagining¹.' So Hume afterwards. Berkeley's position in relation to the difference between sense-perception and mere imagination I have elsewhere noted.

The difference is surely more than one of degree. There is a difference in kind between real existence in place, and a subjective imagination, peculiar to an individual mind. Is not this difference consistent with the real things present in sense, and also the space or place in which they exist, being alike dependent for their actual existence on Mind—in short, with their being grounded on Knowing, and not on an abstracted Unknown? May not space be the uncreated or necessary condition of the possibility of all sense-experience like ours, but yet dependent for its actual existence upon the existence of the sense-experience? This is not to make it the *abstract* space against which Berkeley argues, nor need it involve quantitative infinity.

[1] See Benson's *Memoirs of Collier*, pp. 16, 17.

C.

THE THEORY OF VISION VINDICATED.

EXPERIENCE OF PERSONS BORN BLIND.

In the last Section of the *Vindication* (p. 299), Berkeley refers to the now well-known experiment of Chesselden, in which sight was given to a boy born blind. As this case is described imperfectly in the *Vindication*, and as it is often referred to in the controversy as to whether our power of interpreting the tactual, muscular, and locomotive meaning of visual signs is, on the one hand, original and instinctive, or, on the other hand, the acquired result of mental association and habit, I here reprint the entire Communication, given in the *Philos. Trans.*, No. 402 :—

'*An account of some observations made by a young gentleman, who was born blind, or who lost his sight so early, that he had no remembrance of ever having seen, and was couched between 13 and 14 years of age.* By Mr. Will. Chesselden, F.R.S., Surgeon to Her Majesty, and to St. Thomas's Hospital.

Tho' we say of the gentleman that he was blind, as we do of all people who have ripe cataracts, yet they are never so blind from that cause but that they can discern day from night; and for the most part in a strong light distinguish black, white, and scarlet; but they cannot perceive the shape of anything ;—for the light by which these perceptions are made, being let in obliquely through the aqueous humour, or the anterior surface of the chrystalline (by which the rays cannot be brought into a focus upon the retina), they can discern in no other manner, than a sound eye can thro' a glass of broken jelly, where a great variety of surfaces so differently refract the light that the several distinct pencils of rays cannot be collected by the eye into their proper foci; wherefore the shape of an object in such a case, cannot be at all discern'd, tho' the colour may. And thus it was with this young gentleman, who though he knew these colours asunder in a good light, yet when he saw them after he was couch'd, the faint ideas he had of them before were not sufficient for him to know them by afterwards; and therefore he did not think them the same, which he had before known by those names. Now scarlet he thought the most beautiful of all colours, and of others the most gay were the most pleasing, whereas the first time he saw black, it gave him great uneasiness, yet after a little time he was reconcil'd to it; but some months after, seeing by accident a Negroe woman, he was struck with great horror at the sight.

When he first saw, he was so far from making any judgment about distances, that he thought all objects whatever touched his eyes (as he express'd it) as what he felt did his skin; and thought no objects so agreeable as those which were smooth and regular, tho' he could form no judgment of their shape, or guess what it was in any object that was pleasing to him: he knew not the shape of anything, nor any one thing from another, however different in shape or magnitude; but upon being told what things were, whose form he knew before from feeling, he would carefully observe, that he might know them again; but, having too many objects to learn at once, he forgot many of them; and (as he said) at first he learn'd to know, and again forgot a thousand things in a day. One particular only (tho' it may appear trifling) I will relate:—having forgot which was the cat and which the dog, he was asham'd to ask; but catching the cat (which he knew by feeling) he was observ'd to look at her steadfastly, and then setting her down, said, 'So, Puss! I shall know you another time.' He was very much surpris'd that those things which he had lik'd best did not appear most agreeable to his eyes, expecting those persons would appear most beautiful that he lov'd most, and such things to be most agreeable to his sight that were so to his taste. We thought he soon knew what pictures represented which were shew'd to him, but we found afterwards we were mistaken; for about two months after he was couch'd, he discovered at once, they represented solid bodies; when to that time he consider'd them only as party-colour'd planes or surfaces diversified with variety of paint; but even then he was no less surpris'd, expecting the pictures would feel like the things they represented, and was amaz'd when he found those parts, which by their light and shadow appear'd now round and uneven, felt only flat like the rest; and ask'd which was the lying sense,—feeling or seeing?

Being shewn his father's picture in a locket at his mother's watch, and told what it was, he acknowledged a likeness, but was vastly surpris'd; asking how it could be that a large face could be express'd in so little room, saying, it should have seem'd as impossible to him as to put a bushel of anything into a pint.

At first he could bear but very little sight, and the things he saw he thought extreamly large; but upon seeing things larger, those first seen he conceiv'd less, never being able to imagine any lines beyond the bounds he saw; the room he was in, he said, he knew to be but part of the house, yet he could not conceive that the whole house could look bigger. Before he was couch'd he expected little advantage from seeing, worth undergoing an operation for, except reading and writing; for he said he thought he could have no more pleasure in walking abroad than he had in the garden, which he could do safely and readily. And even blindness, he observ'd, had this advantage, that he could go anywhere in the dark much better than those who can see; and after he had seen, he did not soon lose this quality, nor desire a light to go about the house in the night. He said every new object was a new delight, and the pleasure was so great that he wanted ways to express it; but his gratitude to his operator he could not conceal, never seeing him for some time without tears of joy in his eyes, and other marks of affection: and if he did not happen to come at any time when he was expected, he would be so griev'd that he could not forbear crying at his disappointment. A year after first seeing, being carried upon Epsom Downs, and observing a large prospect, he was exceedingly delighted with it, and called it a new kind of seeing. And now being lately couch'd of his other eye, he says that objects at first appeared large to this eye, but not so large as they did at first to the other; and looking upon the same object with both eyes, he thought it look'd about twice as large as with the first couch'd eye only, but not double, that we can anyways discover.'

No very satisfactory inference can be drawn from a narrative so deficient in the refinement of thought and expression which the subject requires. The question is too subtle for experiments conducted in this fashion. Nor can more be said in favour of a succession of somewhat similar experiments recorded in the *Philosophical Transactions*. The most important are the following:—

1. Case described by Mr. Ware, Surgeon, in the *Philos. Trans.* (1801).
2. Two cases described by Mr. Home, in the *Philos. Trans.* (1807).
3. Case of the lady described by Mr. Wardrop, Surgeon, in the *Philos. Trans.* (1826).

To these may be added Stewart's 'Account of James Mitchell, a boy born deaf and blind,' in the seventh volume of the *Transactions of the Royal Society of Edinburgh*. See Hamilton's Edition of Stewart's Works, Vol. III. Appendix, pp. 300—370; also p. 388.

As I have quoted one of the earliest described cases—that of Chesselden, I shall end by giving the following, which is one of the last and most philosophically described of any I have met with. It is contained in Mr. Nunnely's valuable scientific treatise on *The Organs of Vision: their Anatomy and Physiology* (1858):—

'The case was that of a fine and most intelligent boy, nine years of age, who had congenital cataract of both eyes, in whom the retina was more perfect than it commonly is at so advanced an age, as shown by the excellent sight he subsequently acquired. He had always lived in a very large manufacturing village, about sixteen miles from Leeds. He could find his way all about this place. Walking along the middle of the road, when he heard any object approaching, he at once stopped, groped his way to the side of the road, and remained perfectly still until it had passed. Any one whom he knew he was able to recognise by the sound of the voice, and by passing his hands over the face and body of the person. He could perceive the difference between a bright, sunny, and a dark, cloudy day, and could follow the motions of a candle without discerning what it was. He had been sent to school for some time, and by means of models and a raised alphabet, could by touch alone arrange the different letters into short words. I presented to him in succession a great number of different objects, each one of which he took into both hands, felt it most carefully over with both, then with equal minuteness with one, turning the object over and over again, in every direction; the tongue was next applied to it; and lastly, he applied it so near to the eye as to touch the eyelids, when he pronounced his opinion upon it, and generally with correctness, as to the nature and form of the object, when these were distinct. Thus he recognised books, stones, small boxes, pieces of wood and bone of different shapes, a broken piece of hard biscuit. A cube and a sphere he could readily recognise, saying the one was square and the other round, and that both were made of wood; but a sphere which was made of perfectly smooth, hard wood, he was very confident was bone. In an object where the angles were not very distinct, he made constant mistakes in the shape, first saying that it was square, then that it was round. Very bright light colours, when touching the eyelids, he could at once recognise, calling them all white; all dull and dark colours he said were black. Between a thin circle of wood and a sphere or a cube he instantly decided by the hand alone. On putting half-a-crown piece into his hands he immediately said it was money, but for long was undecided whether it was half-a-crown or a penny; however, after carefully turning it over for some time, so as frequently to bring every part into contact with the hand, then putting it to the tongue, and afterwards so close to the eye that it touched the eyeball itself, he said decidedly, "It is half-a-crown."

The lenses were very large, milky, with caseous particles, quite white and opaque, the capsules being clear and transparent. As is well known, in most cases, before this period of life, the lens itself has been absorbed, leaving only a leathery, opaque capsule, and, of course, not nearly so favourable for such observations as this one. After keeping him in a dark room for a few days, until the opaque particles of lenses were nearly absorbed, and the eyes clear, the same objects, which had been kept carefully from him, were again presented to his notice. He could at once perceive a difference in their shapes; though he could not in the least say which was the cube and which the sphere, he saw they were not of the same figure. It was not until they had many times been placed in his hands that he learnt to distinguish by the eye the one which he had just had in his hands, from the other placed beside it. He gradually became more correct in his perception, but it was only after several days that he could or would tell by the eyes alone, which was the sphere and which the cube; when asked, he always, before answering, wished to take both into his hands; even when this was allowed, when immediately afterwards the objects were placed before the eyes, he was not certain of the figure. Of distance he had not the least conception. He said everything touched his eyes, and walked most carefully about, with his hands held out before him, to prevent things hurting his eyes by touching them. Great care was requisite to prevent him falling over objects, or walking against them. Improvement gradually went on, and his subsequent sight was, and now is, comparatively perfect.'

None of these experiments, taken by themselves, unequivocally determine the question—Whether the power of interpreting the visual signs of real or tangible extension is inspired, or is, on the contrary, acquired by association and constructive activity of intellect. But they confirm the conclusion, that visible signs are not less indispensable to an imagination of trinal extension than the artificial signs of language are necessary to abstract thought and reasoning—that one born blind can have only a vague perception of an external world. Moreover, when once we are experimentally acquainted with distances, a mathematical analysis of the perspective lines leading from any object to the eye is possible, with an involved sense of necessity, which seems to presuppose relations common to the visible signs and the felt reality. The difficulty which confronts Berkeley is, that on his theory space and its mathematical relations are relative to sensations which, *per se*, are contingent and phenomenal, and thus wanting in the element which alone gives absolute stability to mathematical science: quantitative infinity disappears, and space and its relations are the real but arbitrary results of creation or the voluntary activity of God.

www.ingramcontent.com/pod-product-compliance
Lightning Source LLC
Chambersburg PA
CBHW032005300426
44117CB00008B/905